Looking into the Future

Looking into the Future

Evangelical Studies in Eschatology

Edited by
David W. Baker

Baker Academic

A Division of Baker Book House Co
Grand Rapids, Michigan 49516

Published by Baker Academic
a division of Baker Book House Company
P.O. Box 6287, Grand Rapids, MI 49516-6287

Printed in the United States of America

Library of Congress Cataloging-in-Publication Data

Looking into the future : evangelical studies in eschatology / edited by David W. Baker.
      p.   cm.
    Papers from the 1999 Annual Meeting of the Evangelical Theological Society.
    Includes bibliographical references and index.
    ISBN 0-8010-2279-7 (paper)
    1. Eschatology. 2. Evangelicalism. I. Baker, David W. (David Weston), 1950–
II. Evangelical Theological Society. Meeting (1999)

BT821.2 .L66   2001
236—dc21   2001037389

For information about Baker Academic, visit our web site:
www.bakerbooks.com/academic

Contents

Editor's Preface

Although they probably do not know the term, eschatology is a perennial hot-button item even for the person on the street. This was evidenced by the recent Y2K pseudocrisis, apocalyptic end-of-the-world scenarios from Oklahoma City and Waco, and (for some of us) memories of Hal Lindsey's *Late Great Planet Earth*, which precipitated speculation as to who might be the Antichrist this week. Even churchgoers who should know better (especially if they have an adequate view of the sovereignty of God) have been caught up in apocalyptic hysteria, stockpiling food and—even more disturbingly—weapons.

This collection of papers, and the annual conference from which they were drawn, is an attempt to address areas of eschatology from a more reasoned perspective. Though passions can run high even in academia, the Christian community is called more to unity in Christ's love for the glory of God than it is to winning points in an argument. Searching for the truth and striving for a clearer understanding of God and his revelation should draw all believers of goodwill together the closer we get to that truth. May these essays serve to increase understanding and dialog in this important area.

While eschatology has a decidedly forward look, it is intriguing how often these authors use different approaches to look toward the future. The first section explores the broad topic of God's kingdom as presented throughout the Bible; and the second section deals with exegesis and eschatology. Eschatology is not just of interest to our contemporaries, as the third section shows. Sections four and five focus on theology, including the currently controversial issue of the openness of God, which will be examined in more detail at the 2001 annual meeting of the Evangelical Theological Society. Academic discussion can too often be of little practical value, so the final section seeks to put landing gear on the topic of eschatology. How does eschatology impinge on worship, on ethical living, and on how we present and defend our faith?

This quick overview should whet the appetite of all readers, for surely some material here will inspire, puzzle, confound, or disturb everyone. As long as we encourage dialog and growth toward understanding ourselves, our brothers and sisters, and, most of all, our God, we have done a good thing.

I would like to thank each contributor to the volume and also the many other presenters at the 1999 annual meeting of the Evangelical Theological

Society. There were so many excellent papers on the topic that my hardest work as editor was to decide, with the guidance of Baker Book House, which could be included and which should be encouraged to find a home elsewhere. We know many such homes have been found.

בָּרוּךְ יהוה הַמְבֹרָךְ

Abbreviations

AB	Anchor Bible
ABD	*Anchor Bible Dictionary*
Ad. Val.	*Adversus Valentinianos*
An.	*Anabasis*
Antiq.	*Antiquities*
Apoc. Abr.	*Apocalypse of Abraham*
Apoc. Bar.	*Apocalypse of Baruch*
As. Mos.	*Assumption of Moses*
ASV	American Standard Version
BAGD	W. Bauer, W. F. Arndt, F. W. Gingrich, F. W. Danker, *Greek-English Lexicon of the New Testament and Other Early Christian Literature,* 2d ed.
Bar.	Baruch
BC	*Book of Concord*
BDF	F. Blass, A. Debrunner, R. W. Funk, *A Greek Grammar of the New Testament and Other Early Christian Literature*
BJRL	*Bulletin of the John Rylands University Library of Manchester*
bk.	book
b. Pesah.	Babylonian Talmud tractate *Pesahim*
BSac	*Bibliotheca Sacra*
b. Sanh.	Babylonian Talmud tractate *Sanhedrin*
b. Shabb.	Babylonian Talmud tractate *Shabbat*
BTB	*Biblical Theology Bulletin*
BZAW	Beihefte zur Zeitschrift für die alttestamentliche Wissenschaft
Catech.	*Catechesis*
CBC	Cambridge Bible Commentary
CBQ	*Catholic Biblical Quarterly*
CEV	Contemporary English Version
Chron.	Chronicles
Col	*Colloquium*
Col.	Colossians
Cor.	Corinthians
D	Western text
Dan.	Daniel
De consum. Mundi	*De consummationis Mundi*

De Praescr. Haer.	*De praescriptione haereticorum*
Deut.	Deuteronomy
diss.	dissertation
DM	T. H. Darlow and H. F. Moule, *Historical Catalogue of Printed Editions of the English Bible, 1525–1961*
EKKNT	Evangelisch-katholischer Kommentar zum Neuen Testament
Eph.	Ephesians
ERK	*The New Schaff-Herzog Encyclopedia of Religious Knowledge*
ET	English translation
EvQ	*Evangelical Quarterly*
EVV.	English versions
Exod.	Exodus
Ezek.	Ezekiel
fol.	folio
GA	Gesamtausgabe
Gal.	Galatians
Gen.	Genesis
Gk	Greek
Hab.	Habakkuk
HB	Hebrew Bible
Heb.	Hebrew(s)
Herm. *Vis.*	Shepherd of Hermas, *Vision*
Hos.	Hosea
HTR	*Harvard Theological Review*
ICB	International Children's Bible
ICC	International Critical Commentary
Isa.	Isaiah
ISBE	*International Standard Bible Encyclopedia*
JB	Jerusalem Bible
Jer.	Jeremiah
JETS	*Journal of the Evangelical Theological Society*
Josh.	Joshua
JSNTSup	Journal for the Study of the New Testament: Supplement Series
JSOTSup	Journal for the Study of the Old Testament: Supplement Series
JTS	*Journal of Theological Studies*
Jub.	*Jubilees*
KJV	King James Version
Lam.	Lamentations
Lev.	Leviticus
LW	*Works of Martin Luther (Philadelphia: Fortress, 1955–86)*
LXX	Septuagint
Macc.	Maccabees

Matt.	Matthew
Mic.	Micah
MS(S)	manuscript(s)
m. Sota	Mishnah tractate *Sota*
NASB	New American Standard Bible
NASBU	New American Standard Bible Update
NCB	New Century Bible
Neh.	Nehemiah
NET	New English Translation
NICNT	New International Commentary on the New Testament
NICOT	New International Commentary on the Old Testament
NIV	New International Version
NKJV	New King James Version
No(s).	number(s)
NRSV	New Revised Standard Version
n.s.	new series
NT	New Testament
NTS	*New Testament Studies*
Num.	Numbers
Obad.	Obadiah
OL	Old Latin
OT	Old Testament
p(p).	page(s)
par.	parallel(s)
PD	Progressive dispensationalism
PE	*Works of Martin Luther* (Grand Rapids: Baker, 1982)
Phil.	Philippians
Prov.	Proverbs
Ps.	Psalms
ref(s).	reference(s)
RelS	*Religious Studies*
rev.	revised
Rev.	Revelation
Rom.	Romans
RSV	Revised Standard Version
Sam.	Samuel
SBL	Society of Biblical Literature
SBLDS	Society of Biblical Literature Dissertation Series
Sib. Or.	*Sibylline Oracles*
S-J	P. Smith and C. M. Jacobs, eds., *Luther's Correspondence*
T. Asher	*Testament of Asher*
T. Benj.	*Testament of Benjamin*
TDNT	*Theological Dictionary of the New Testament*, ed. G. Kittel

TEV	Today's English Version
Thess.	Thessalonians
Tim.	Timothy
T. Jud(ah)	*Testament of Judah*
TNTC	Tyndale New Testament Commentaries
T. Mos(es)	*Testament of Moses*
TPhil	*Theologie und Philosophie*
TR	Textus Receptus
TS	*Theological Studies*
UBS	United Bible Societies
v(v).	verse(s)
Vg	Vulgate
vol.	volume
WA	*Luthers Werke: Kritische Gesamtausgabe*
WA Br	*Luthers Werke: Kritische Gesamtausgabe. Briefwechsel*
WA DB	*Luthers Werke: Kritische Gesamtausgabe. Bibel*
WA Tr	*Luthers Werke: Kritische Gesamtausgabe. Tischreden*
WBC	Word Biblical Commentary
Wis.	Wisdom of Solomon
WTJ	*Westminster Theological Journal*
WUNT	Wissenschaftliche Untersuchungen zum Neuen Testament
Zech.	Zechariah
Zeph.	Zephaniah
ZNW	*Zeitschrift für die neutestamentliche Wissenschaft und die Kunde der älteren Kirche*
ZTK	*Zeitschrift für Theologie und Kirche*

Part 1

God and His Kingdom

The Kingdom of God in Biblical Theology

BRUCE WALTKE

Reformed Theological Seminary (Orlando)
and Regent College

Most agree that the kingdom of God is a central tenet in the teachings of the Lord Jesus Christ and plays an important role in the preaching and teaching of the apostle Paul. The expression "kingdom of God," however, never occurs in the Old Testament, and its equivalents are relatively rare and late terms in the progressive revelation of the Bible. In the Old Testament the phrase "kingdom of the LORD" occurs in various forms in only fifteen isolated texts (Ps. 22, 103, 145; once in Obadiah; four times in Chronicles; and seven times in Daniel).[1] If I restricted myself to the use of the term in these fifteen mostly relatively late texts, the Old Testament has little to say about my assigned topic. Nevertheless, in this paper I aim to defend the thesis that the Primary History, which traces Israel's history from the creation of the world (Genesis 1) to the fall of Israel (2 Kings 25), is all about what the New Testament calls "the kingdom of God."

Though composed of many earlier blocks of writings, the Primary History in its final form consists of two great collections. The Pentateuch (Genesis through Deuteronomy) traces the history of Israel from the creation of the cosmos to Israel's being perched on the threshold of entering the Promised Land. The so-called Deuteronomistic History (Deuteronomy through

---

1. Ps. 22:29 (EVV. 28); 103:19; 145:11–13 [four times]; Obad. 21; Dan. 2:44; 3:33 (EVV. 4:3); 4:31(EVV. 34); 6:27 (EVV. 26); 7:14, 18, 27; 1 Chron. 17:14; 28:5; 29:11; 2 Chron. 13:8.

Kings)[2] continues that history from Israel's entrance into the land to its exile from it. The linchpin of the Primary History, binding together these two great histories, is the Book of Deuteronomy. Paradoxically, Deuteronomy is both the capstone of the Pentateuch and the foundation stone of the Deuteronomistic History. This is so because the core of the original book of Deuteronomy is Moses' three addresses to Israel, his song about Israel's future course of history, and his blessings on the tribes of Israel. During the Babylonian exile the Deuteronomist added fifty-six verses to Deuteronomy in order to incorporate the core within the narrative of his so-called Deuteronomistic History. Through this double authorship it becomes the book that binds together the two great documents of the Primary History.

This history is the backbone of the Old Testament. The superscriptions of the prophetic books, the Psalms, and Proverbs are set within the context of this history. Just as in the case of other heuristic theological schemes, such as the Trinity, it may be possible to identify a theme such as the kingdom of God, even though the term itself is not used in the Old Testament's most important document.

In a paper of this restricted scope it is impossible to present a comprehensive scheme of that term. Martin Selman, after analyzing the various understandings of the expression "kingdom of the LORD" in Chronicles, Daniel, and the Psalms, drew the conclusion that "the nature of the kingdom of God cannot be expressed in a single thought."[3] It seems prudent, then, for the purpose of this paper to restrict the meaning of "kingdom of God" to how Jesus understood that term. Paul Drake draws two obvious conclusions about Jesus' use of the phrase. First, it has a historical dimension: "the kingdom comes at the end of time as the culmination of everything that has happened from the creation until now."[4] Second, this eschatological reality has a legal dimension. God exercises the authority of a sovereign in realm where his subjects obey his commands.

Drake defends from the Lord's Prayer the idea "that the synoptic tradition understands the kingdom of God as the establishment of God's sovereignty over the human race."[5] The Matthean version reads, "Your kingdom come, your will be done on earth as it is in heaven. Give us this day our daily bread" (Matt. 6:10–11). The Lukan version, however, reads, "Your kingdom come.

2. Joshua 1 is a pastiche of Deuteronomy. Judges 2:6 repeats Josh. 24:8, but in a chiastic structure bringing closure. First Samuel 8 brings closure to the period of the Judges. First Kings 1–2 brings the so-called Succession narrative begun in 2 Sam. 9 to closure. We need here only to observe this unity, not debate how it came to be.

3. Martin Selman, "The Kingdom of God in the Old Testament," *Tyndale Bulletin* 40 (1989): 161–84.

4. Paul Drake, "The Kingdom of God in the Old Testament," in *The Kingdom of God in 20th-Century Interpretation*, ed. Wendell Willis (Peabody, Mass.: Hendrickson, 1987), 67–79.

5. Ibid., 71.

Give us each day our daily bread" (Luke 11:2), lacking the petition "your will be done on earth as it is in heaven." Matthew probably added "your will be done" to explicate the petition for the coming of the kingdom.[6] Drake says: "That explication virtually states the definition of sovereignty just offered."[7] Drake, however, fails to differentiate adequately the difference between God's universal kingdom and the particular kingdom in view in the Lord's Prayer. By the former, theologians mean God's activity in exercising his sovereignty over all things, even giving the nations their pagan deities (Deut. 4:19). By the latter, Jesus meant God's activity in establishing a realm in which his subjects obey *ex animo* his law. This paper assumes that sense of the term.

The question facing us, then, is whether the Primary History can be integrated into the idea that God is establishing a kingdom on earth in which nations submit to his moral rule. In the Primary History, God's kingdom mostly took the shape of national Israel, a political state with geospatial boundaries in contradistinction to other nations. The principal concern of the Primary History is the irruption (i.e., the breaking in from without), not eruption (i.e., the breaking out from within), of God's righteous kingdom through the political state of Israel.

The Call of Abraham: The Key to the Primary History

D. J. A. Clines demonstrated that the scene recounting God's call of Abraham (Gen. 12:1–3) expresses tersely and succinctly the theme of the Pentateuch.[8] Here I argue that this scene presents the scheme for understanding the Primary History, not just the Pentateuch, and that this scheme pertains to God's establishing his moral rule over the earth.

God's call of Abraham contains seven (i.e., the symbolic number of completeness) promises: (1) "I will make you into a great nation." (2) "I will bless you." (3) "I will make your name great." (4) "You will be a blessing." (5) "I will bless those who bless you." (6) "Whoever curses you I will curse." And (7) "all peoples on earth will be blessed through you." These seven promises pertain to three expanding horizons.

The scene begins within the narrow confines of God's call to Abraham to disassociate himself from his family (v. 1). This call expands to the LORD's promise to make Abraham into a nation of blessing, and it is within that context that he will experience the first four promised blessings (v. 2). Finally, the last three promises expand the horizon to God's blessing the whole earth for all time through Abraham and the nation he fathers (v. 3). Abraham and his nation bless the earth, however, only to the extent that the nation he fathers

6. R. Hamerton-Kelly, *God the Father* (Philadelphia: Fortress, 1979), 73–74.

7. Drake, "The Kingdom of God," 71.

8. D. J. A. Clines, *The Theme of the Pentateuch*, JSOTSup 10 (Sheffield: JSOT Press, 1978).

submits itself to God's law. Elsewhere God says, "For I have chosen [Abraham] so that he will direct his children and his household after him to keep the way of the LORD by doing what is right and just, so that the LORD will bring about for Abraham what he has promised him" (Gen. 18:19). Moreover, the rest of humanity qualifies itself for this blessing by recognizing that Abraham and his obedient nation are possessed of God's power to mediate abundant and effective living and so prays for God's blessing upon them. By acknowledging Abraham's God as the source of life and of transforming power for good and by praying that his blessing will come upon his chosen mediator, they "bless themselves" or "are blessed."[9]

In sum, the theme of the Pentateuch, and foundational to the Primary History, are the notions that God establishes Abraham as the father of a nation that is subservient to his law and that through this nation he blesses formerly rival nations as they themselves submit to this mediatorial kingdom.

In order to unpack this idea that God is establishing his moral rule over the earth through national Israel, it is helpful to parse that idea into its four constituent themes. A nation consists of a common people, normally sharing a common land, submissive to a common law, and having a common ruler. The Book of Genesis is concerned principally with identifying both the people who submit to God's commands and the land that sustains them. The rest of the Pentateuch focuses mainly on God's law. The Deuteronomistic History (especially Joshua through Kings) develops the theme of the nation's ruler. In the remainder of the paper I will examine these four themes in the Primary History and how they are interpreted in the New Testament.

First Motif: The People of God's Kingdom

Genesis sometimes uses the metaphor of "seed" for human offspring.[10] Fundamental to that metaphor is the notion of reproduction "after its kind." To oversimplify the matter, just as the seed of plants and trees produce according to their kind (Gen. 1:11–12), so human seed grows according to the type of person that produces the seed.

In the beginning God created humanity in his image, that is, as his regents to represent his rule on earth. In the Temple-Garden of Eden his first word to them is a command. They must not eat of the tree of the knowledge of good and evil. That famous tree symbolized the ability to discern good (i.e., what advances life) and evil (i.e., what hinders life). Such knowledge belongs to God alone, for, as Agur inferentially argued in Proverbs 30:1–6, to speak ab-

---

9. So interpreted, it makes little difference whether the *Hithpael* is understood as reflexive or passive.

10. T. D. Alexander (*From Paradise to the Promised Land: An Introduction to the Main Themes of the Pentateuch* [Carlisle, U.K.: Paternoster, 1995/Grand Rapids: Baker, 1998], 8) counts 59 occurrences of *zeraᶜ* out of 172 times in the Old Testament.

solutely about what is good and bad one must know comprehensively. However, finite humanity in Adam and Eve refused to accept their limitation and transgressed the established boundary. Tempted by Satan to doubt God's goodness and the truth of God's word, they ate the forbidden fruit, making themselves their own lawmakers apart from God.

As God had threatened, Adam and Eve became alienated from God and from one another. In response to their rebellion in setting up a rival kingdom, the gracious Sovereign intervened by changing Eve's religious affections so that she would love God and submit to his rule and hate Satan who defied it. Addressing Satan, God said, "*I will* put enmity between you and the woman, and between your offspring and hers" (Gen. 3:15, emphasis added). From then on humanity was divided broadly into two spiritual races, though both physically reproduced Adam and Eve. The seed of the woman as seen in Abel reproduced her love for God, and the seed of the Serpent as seen in Cain reproduced his spiritual enmity against God.

The Book of Genesis is all about this seed of the woman. It is structured by means of linear genealogies to trace this holy seed from Adam and Eve to the twelve tribes of Israel. A decisive development in this theme occurred in God's call of Abraham. God elected Abraham and his offspring who reproduced his faith to represent God's moral rule and to mediate God's blessing to all the tribes and nations of the earth. In a binding covenant God obligated himself to make Abraham and his circumcised seed the unique representatives of his blessed rule. Although most of this seed carried his physical genes, the Abrahamic covenant has in view principally the seed that both reproduces the patriarch's faith and mediates God's law to the nations. Not all who came from Abraham's loins and were marked by circumcision are part of the mediatorial kingdom. Ishmael is one such example; he was a physical seed, born of Abraham and a recipient of the mark of the covenant, but he was not elected by God to share his father's faith that historically preceded circumcision.

God's covenant with faithful Abraham in Genesis 17 explicates in a fresh way God's promise in Genesis 12:3 to bless all nations through Abraham's offspring. Now God says, "I am going to make you a father of many nations . . . and kings will come from you" (Gen. 17:5). God's promise to make Abraham a father of many nations, on the one hand, has a biological sense. Through Hagar, Abraham physically fathered the Ishmaelites (see vv. 20; 21:13; 25:12–18; see 25:23; 36:1–43); through Keturah the Midianites, among others (25:1–4a); and through Isaac and Rebekah, the Edomites (see 25:23; 36:1–43). The genealogies of Keturah (25:1–4), Ishmael (25:12–18) and Edom (36) validate this interpretation.

On the other hand, the promise also pertains to the nations that reproduce Abraham's faith; that cannot be said of the Ishmaelites, the Edomites, and the descendants of Keturah. In its reference to this spiritual seed, "father" should be understood as a "spiritual father." Joseph calls himself a father to Pharaoh

(Gen. 45:8) and the Ephraimite Micah called a Levite his father (Judg. 17:10). Significantly, whereas God says that the kings will come from Abraham's loins, God does not say that of the nations Abraham will father. Further validating this spiritual understanding of "father" is the extension of circumcision, the sign of the covenant, to every male in Abraham's household, "whether born in your household or bought with your money" (Gen. 17:12–13). The psalmist also supports this interpretation. He anticipates the nations becoming part of the people of God by rebirth: "I will record Rahab and Babylon among those who acknowledge me—Philista too, and Tyre, along with Cush—and will say, 'This one was born in Zion.' . . . The LORD will write in the register of the peoples: 'This one was born in Zion'" (Ps. 87:4–6).

Turning to the New Testament, Jesus essentially severs the link between the people of God and Abraham's physical offspring. At the end of Matthew, our Lord asserts his authority over all nations, and commissions his disciples, not old Israel, to "make disciples of all nations, . . . teaching them to obey everything I have commanded you" (Matt. 28:18–20). Mark records the scene where his physical mother and brothers symbolically stand outside the house where he was teaching. To those seated in the circle around him he asked, "'Who are my mother and my brothers?' he asked. Then he looked at those seated in a circle around him and said, 'Here are my mother and my brothers! Whoever does God's will is my brother and sister and mother'" (Mark 3:33–35). In Luke, Jesus forecasts through the parable of the tenants that God will take the vineyard (i.e., the people chosen to mediate his moral rule) away from Israel and give it to the Gentiles (Luke 20:9–19). In John he speaks of having other sheep (i.e., the Gentiles) who are not from this sheep pen (i.e., physical Israel, John 10:16).

Paul and Barnabas fulfill what Jesus predicted. When the Jews, for the most part, rejected the gospel, Paul turned away from them to the Gentiles (Acts 13:46; 18:6). By the second century, the church was composed almost entirely of Gentiles. In Galatians, Paul refers the seed God covenanted to give Abraham as finding fulfillment both uniquely in Jesus Christ and collectively in all, Jew and Gentile alike, baptized into Jesus Christ (Gal. 3:15–29). In Romans, Paul interprets God's promise to make Abraham a father of many nations in the way consistent with the grammatico-historical hermeneutic suggested above. The church at Rome undoubtedly had representatives from many nations at this center of the Roman Empire. To them the apostle writes that "the promise . . . [is] guaranteed to all Abraham's offspring—not only to those who are of the law but also those who are of the faith of Abraham. He is the father of us all. As it is written: 'I have made you the father of many nations'" (Rom. 4:16–17). In Romans 16:20 the apostle probably identifies the promised seed of the woman with the church at Rome, which represented the nations subject to his rule: "The God of peace will soon crush Satan under your feet." However, in that letter Paul also teaches that God is not yet finished with Abraham's physical progeny. God always retains a remnant among them that also reproduces Abraham's faith. Indeed, the apostle implies that they may again become the dominant group among the people of God (Rom. 11).

In sum, under the Old Covenant Abraham's spiritual seed is mostly, but not exclusively, reproduced in Abraham's physical offspring. Under the New Covenant his spiritual seed is reproduced mostly, but not exclusively, among the Gentiles.

Second Motif: The Land

When God created the world he gathered the primeval waters to let dry land appear, and in it he caused all kinds of vegetation to grow. In this way he provided both space for the representatives of his rule to live and food to sustain them. More particularly he placed his earthly rulers in a garden, that is, in an enclosed, protected area where the flora flourishes. This garden represents unique territorial space in the created order where God intended human beings to enjoy bliss and harmony between him and them, with one another, the animals, and the land.

God is uniquely present in this temple-garden. Humanity lost this temple when it set up its rival kingdom. Later, when God called Abraham to become a great nation, he promised to give Abraham's offspring the land of the defiled Canaanites. As God's covenant with Abraham recorded in Genesis 17 explicates the promise in Genesis 12:3 to make Abraham and his seed a blessing to the nations, so his covenant with Abraham to give him the land of Canaan as recorded in Genesis 15 explicates his promise in Genesis 12:2 to make Abraham into a great nation.

God reckoned Abraham's faith in the LORD's promise to give him innumerable offspring as qualifying Abraham to become the recipient of an irrevocable land grant idealized as extending from the river of Egypt to the Euphrates (Gen. 15:6–21). In this land flowing with milk and honey, his people will be protected and sustained. This land promise was fulfilled progressively several times but never consummated. God fulfilled the promise through Joshua (Josh. 21:43–45), but not completely (Josh. 13:1–7); and through David and Solomon (1 Kings 4:20–25; Neh. 9:8), but still not completely (see Ps. 95:11; Heb. 4:6–8; 11:39, 40).

In the New Testament the land theme undergoes a paradigm shift similar to that of the seed theme. As the physical aspect of the seed was mostly dropped in favor of the spiritual, so also the physical aspect of land is dropped in favor of its spiritual significance. The paradigm shift can be inferred from the fact that the term *land*, the fourth most frequent word in the Old Testament, is never used in the New Testament with reference to Canaan. Indeed, the Old Testament's use of the term *land* with reference to Canaan is resignified to encompass the whole earth in Matthew 5:5 and Romans 4:13. Neither

Christ nor his apostles ever taught that dispersed ethnic Israel will again return to Canaan. Rather, for them Canaan seems to function as a type of the Christian's life in Christ, both from a historical or chronological perspective and from a conceptual perspective.

Regarding the historical aspect of this typology, note a number of significant parallels between old Israel and the church in their relationship to the "land." (1) God began Israel's pilgrimage to the land by saving it from slavery and death in Egypt under the tyranny of Pharaoh, and he begins the church's pilgrimage by saving it out of the slavery of sin and death in the world under Satan. (2) Israel is delivered by the blood of the Passover lamb and by the *rûaḥ* (wind or spirit) at the Red Sea, and the church is delivered by Christ, its Passover Lamb, and by the *pneuma* (wind or Spirit; 1 Cor. 5:7; Acts 2). (3) Israel is baptized with Moses in the sea, thereby dying to Egypt and embarking on its pilgrimage, and the church is baptized with water and Spirit into Christ, thereby dying to the old life and being raised to new life. (4) Old Israel in the wilderness fed on manna in its pilgrimage to the holy land; the church feeds upon Christ the Manna from heaven in its pilgrimage (1 Cor. 10:4; John 6). (5) The church's forefathers "drank the same spiritual drink; for they drank from the spiritual rock that accompanied them, and that rock was Christ" (1 Cor. 10:4; cf. John 4). (6) Israel was tested in the wilderness before inheriting the land, and the church suffers in its wilderness on the way to the heavenly city where Christ is the light. (7) Finally, Israel entered the land, but it will not consummate its possession of that land, presumably in the new heaven and the new earth, without the church (Heb. 11:39–40). In the interim, the church has already entered into rest and is seated with Christ in heavenly places (Matt. 11:28; Col. 3:1).

Significant typological parallels also exist on the conceptual level between Israel's life in Canaan and the Christian's life in Christ: (1) Both "lands" are a divine gift (Gen. 15:7; 18; Deut. 1:8; Rom. 6:23). (2) Both are entered by faith alone (Num. 14:26–44; Josh. 7; John 3:16). (3) Both are an inheritance (Deut. 4:20; Eph. 1:14; Acts 20:32). (4) Both uniquely offer blessed rest and security (Exod. 23:20–31; Deut. 11:12; 19:9, 10; 28:1–14; Matt. 11:28; John 1:51; 14:9 Heb. 4:2–3). (5) Both offer God's unique presence (Exod. 40:34; Deut. 12:5; 1 Sam. 4:21; 1 Kings 8:10, 27; John 14:18–20, 23; 15:1–8; 1 Cor. 3:16; 6:17). (6) Both demand persevering faith (Deut. 28:15–19; Heb. 6:4–6; 10:19–39). (7) Both have an already-but-not-yet quality (see Heb. 11:39, 40; Rev. 21:1–22:6). In sum, the theme of "land" is "Christified" in the New Testament.

Third Motif: God's Rule

If Genesis presents God as making an irrevocable covenant with the patriarchs to make of them a nation to be a light to the Gentiles, Exodus–Deuteronomy represent Israel as accepting God's covenant or laws to become that light to the nations. Prior to God's mediating his laws to Old Israel through Moses, God made known his laws through the general revelation of conscience and through special revelations such as theophanies and visions. In connection with the transforming of the twelve tribes of Israel into a nation, he gave the people his covenant, setting forth in detail their religious and ethical obligations. Not surprisingly, in the context of being transformed from twelve tribes into a nation bound together by God's law, Israel for the first time calls God "King" (Deut. 33:3–5; cf. Exod. 15:18; Num. 23:21), and he calls them "a kingdom of priests" (Exod. 19:6). All Israel is a priesthood (i.e, separated as holy to mediate between God and the nations) by virtue of its obedience to God's covenant.

The Book of Exodus presents God's law in three hierarchies of authority.[11]

Pride of place is given to the Ten Commandments (Exod. 20:1–17). The book of the covenant applies these commands to specific situations (Exod. 20:2–23:33), and after the people ratify these two (Exod. 24:3–8), God instructs the people on how to worship him (Exod. 24:1–2, 9–18; 25:1–40:38). The Ten Commandments also have priority in being the only part of the law spoken by God and written down by him. In response to the people's request, he mediated the rest of the law through Moses (Exod. 20:1–17; 31:18; Deut. 5:22–33). According to Numbers 12:6–8, the more immediate form of revelation has priority in authority over the less immediate. Also, the Ten Commandments were the only part of the law deposited in the ark in the most Holy Place, a replica of heaven itself (Exod. 25:9; Deut. 10:1–5; Heb. 8:5). In other words, the transcendent moral will of God as expressed in the Ten Commandments is represented as being at the center of heaven itself. Finally, in Deuteronomy the Ten Commandments alone are called "the covenant" (Deut. 4:13).[12] Jesus drew an even higher abstraction of the most important laws. The greatest commandments, he said, are: "'Love the Lord your God with all your heart and with all your soul and with all your mind.' This is the first and greatest commandment. And the second is like it: 'Love your neigh-

---

11. Bruce Waltke, "Theonomy in Relation to Dispensational and Covenant Theologies," in *A Reformed Critique of Theonomy,* ed. William S. Barker and W. Robert Godfrey (Grand Rapids: Academie, 1990), 59–86.

12. Brevard Childs (*The Book of Exodus* [Philadelphia: Westminster, 1974], 397) agrees: "The evidence that it is assigned a unique place of importance by the Old Testament itself, not just by subsequent Jewish and Christian interpreters, is manifold. The commandments have a special name, the 'ten words' . . . (cf. also Exod. 31:18; Deut. 4:13; 9:9, etc.). Again, they are repeated in Deuteronomy as providing the foundation for the new promulgation of the covenant. The narrative framework of Exodus, but particularly of Deuteronomy, stressed the finality of the commandments: 'These words Yahweh spoke . . . and added no more' (Deut. 5:22). Finally, the reflection of the commandments in the prophets (Hos. 4:1ff., Jer. 7:9ff.), and in the Psalms (50 and 81) testify to their influence upon Israel's faith."

bor as yourself.' All the Law and the Prophets hang on these two commandments" (Matt. 22:37–40). Here in a nutshell is the summary of the Sovereign's laws for his moral kingdom.

With the giving of the law, Israel became divided into national Israel and
individual Israelites. Christopher Wright notes that, on the national level, the
Sovereign brought the nation into being even before the giving of the Sinai
covenant.[13]

The nation of Israel was bound together by God's covenant to Abraham,
including circumcision, and by their deliverance from Egypt. Because of
God's faithfulness to Abraham and the irrevocable promises he made the patriarch, Israel becomes God's son not by its own choice but by God's procre-
ative action (i.e., the LORD brought it into existence). Wright comments that
this indicative existence "remains to be invoked even after the judgment of the
Exile on the nation's disobedience as the basis for a fresh redemption and restored relationship (Hos. 11:1ff; 1:10; Jer. 31:9, 20; Isa. 43:6; 63:16; 64:8)."[14]
However, with the giving of the Law each Israelite household must choose for
itself to accept this rule. Joshua, for example, commands the people: "If serving the LORD seems undesirable to you, then choose for yourselves this day
whom you will serve, whether the gods your forefathers served beyond the
River, or the gods of the Amorites, in whose land you are living. But as for me
and my household, we will serve the LORD" (Josh. 24:15). Whereas on the national level Israel is called "son of God" (singular), on the individual level they
are addressed as the LORD's "sons" (plural). It is on this individual level that
they must obey to enjoy the status and rights as faithful sons. Thus an inherent
tension is set up between the givenness of the filial relationship (the indicative)
and the demands it imposes (the imperative).

The Sinai covenant threatened the nation with exile should they break their
covenant obligations. Eventually the longsuffering God sent the nation into
exile, but in that connection he promised to make a new covenant with them.
Now God says that, unlike the old covenant written on rock and copied in
ink, he will write his law on the hearts of all the Israelites, thereby ending the
distinction between national Israel and the remnant of believing Israel. The
new covenant does not replace the eternal substance of the Mosaic law as expressed in the Ten Commandments and summarized by Jesus as love of God
and love of neighbor. Rather it replaces its mode of administration. Among
many differences between the two styles of administration, suffice it to note
here that the old covenant was effected through the blood of animals, but the
new was brought about through the cleansing blood of Jesus Christ. The old
covenant was written on rock and copied in ink; the new is written on the

13. Christopher J. H. Wright, *God's People in God's Land: Family, Land, and Property in
the Old Testament* (Grand Rapids: Eerdmans/Exeter: Paternoster, 1990), 16–22.
14. Ibid., 21.

heart by the Spirit (2 Cor. 3:3). Israel obligated itself to keep the old covenant; God obligates himself to keep the new (Heb. 8:6).

In sum, God now reckons the church—because it is baptized into Jesus Christ, who is the true Judah and Israel—as the recipient of the new covenant (cf. Heb. 8). Peter says to a church composed of Jews and Gentiles: "But you are a chosen people, a royal priesthood, a holy nation, a people belonging to God, that you may declare the praises of him who called you out of darkness into his wonderful light. Once you were not a people, but now you are the people of God; once you had not received mercy, but now you have received mercy" (1 Peter 2:9–10). Paul calls the church "the Israel of God" (Gal. 6:16). Christ administers this "nation" (i.e., the church) by means of the new covenant.

Fourth Motif: The Human Ruler

Prior to the establishment of the monarchy, the Primary History regarded God as the sole ruler of his kingdom. When the people asked for a king, the LORD regarded it as a rejection of his rule over them as their king (1 Sam. 8:6–8). Now, with the institution of kingship, the LORD hands over the rule of Israel to a human king, which by definition entails dynastic succession.[15] The Chronicler even speaks of the king as sitting on the LORD's throne (1 Chron. 28:5). However, the LORD chose the king through prophetic designation (Deut. 17:15). The LORD also retained the right to transfer the kingship from one house to another, as in the case of taking it away from the house of Saul to give it to the house of David. Throughout the history of the northern kingdom he transferred kingship to different houses, such as the houses of Jeroboam and Omri. Selman comments: "If God has a kingdom to give, then he too must have a kingship of his own, and one that is of a higher order than that which is . . . entrusted to Saul, David, or Abijah. . . . God was directly involved with this one, specific, earthly kingdom, and through it he, as well as the human king, worked out his royal purposes."[16]

After the rejection of Saul, the LORD lays the foundation for the future course of history in his covenant with David to establish David's house forever over his kingdom (2 Sam. 7; 1 Chron. 17; Ps. 89).

The Davidic covenant is intrinsically connected with the Abrahamic and Mosaic covenants. With regard to the Abrahamic covenant, the Davidic covenant fulfills, confirms, and supplements it. With regard to the Mosaic covenant, the tenure of individual kings was dependent upon their obedience to it. Indeed, the king's primary responsibility was to retain Israel in the land and expand the rule of God precisely by obeying the Mosaic covenant. However,

15. Tomoo Ishida, *The Royal Dynasties in Ancient Israel*, BZAW 142 (New York and Berlin: Walter de Gruyter, 1977), 7–25.
16. Selman, "Kingdom of God," 166.

David's sons broke faith with the LORD, and God disciplined them as he had threatened.

Though the enjoyment of David's throne by his successors was conditioned on their obedience to God's law, God's grant to the house of David to rule forever was irrevocable: "If [David's] sons forsake my law . . . I will punish their sin with the rod, their iniquity with flogging; but . . . I will not violate my covenant or alter what my lips have uttered" (Ps. 89:30–34; cf. 2 Sam. 7). The Deuteronomist concludes his work with Jehoiakim, David's last son to rule de facto, in exile but on a seat of honor higher than those of the others kings who were with him in Babylon. The house of David endures even in exile.

The grant that David's house would rule God's kingdom forever lays the foundation for the messianic hope. J. J. M. Roberts says, "The . . . claim that God had chosen David and his dynasty as God's permanent agent for the exercise of the divine rule on earth was the fundamental starting point for the later development of the messianic hope."[17]

Israel's kings were always regarded in a general way as God's messiah, literally "anointed." Their prophetic anointing publicly designated them as God's chosen, consecrated them as God's property, bestowed authority on them, and equipped them for the task. But the term took on a narrower meaning in connection with the exile. This development can be seen in the use of the Psalter. The Psalms augmented in an idealistic way the royal ideology associated with the historical king. The Psalter envisions God's son, as the king was called, as endowed with justice and righteousness, and as such his rule extended from sea to sea and from the river to the ends of the earth (Ps. 2; 72). For the psalmist, the king stood in God's stead: "Your throne, O God, will last for ever and ever" (Ps. 45:6 [7]). These songs celebrating the king were like royal robes with which Israel draped each successive son of David at his coronation, but none had shoulders broad enough to wear them. Shakespeare says of Macbeth when he was exposed as Duncan's traitor, "How does he feel his title hang loose about him, like a giant's robe upon a dwarfish thief."[18]

The Psalter's giant robes hung loosely on David's dwarfish successors, though some, like Hezekiah and Josiah, had broader shoulders than others. After Jehoiakim, the psalmist's hope for an ideal king slipped off the stooped shoulders of David's successors with none to wear them, leaving Israel with a wardrobe of magnificent purple robes waiting for an Anointed One from David's house worthy to wear them. In the exile, the royal Psalms—and that

17. J. J. M. Roberts, "In Defense of the Monarchy: The Contribution of Israelite Kingship to Biblical Theology," in *Ancient Israeite Religions: Essays in Honor of Frank Moore Cross*, ed. Patrick D. Miller Jr., Paul D. Hanson, and S. Dan McBride (Philadelphia: Fortress, 1987), 378.

18. *Macbeth* 5.2.20–22.

is most of the Psalter—were referred to as announcing a coming, hoped-for Son of David. At this point the term *Messiah* acquired its specifically eschatological and strict sense vis-á-vis the expected king and deliverer of Israel.

That hope for this ideal king was also augmented in the prophetic literature and heightened in the apocalyptic literature and in the inter-testamental Jewish literature (200 B.C.–A.D. 100).[19]

In the fullness of time God sent his Son, who became incarnate in Jesus of Nazareth. Here was a Son of David with shoulders broad enough to wear the Psalter's magnificent robes. At his birth an angel of the LORD proclaimed: "Today in the town of David a Savior has been born to you; he is Christ the Lord" (Luke 2:11). John the Baptist identified Jesus as the Messiah (John 1:19–34). The disciples confessed him to be the Messiah (Mark 8:29; Luke 9:20; John 11:27). John wrote his Gospel that his audience might believe that Jesus is the Christ, the Messiah. The words of Jesus and his works bore witness to his deity and were all done in truth, righteousness, and justice. He is the One who is worthy to rule over all humanity forever and ever.

Conclusion

Jesus Christ's offer of the kingdom of God in the Synoptic Gospels brings the expectation of the Primary History that God would establish his moral kingdom over the nations through national Israel to its fulfillment. On the other hand, in the New Testament his kingdom now transcends the geospatial boundaries of national Israel. The people of the kingdom are now no longer primarily Abraham's physical progeny, but the nations themselves. The theme of land has been Christified. God's law is no longer written on rock tablets housed in Jerusalem, but inscribed by the Holy Spirit on the hearts of all the subjects of this kingdom. Finally, the king's throne is no longer in earthly Jerusalem but in heavenly Mount Zion from which the King of Kings and Lord of Lords administers his kingdom through the Holy Spirit.

---

19. See Marinus de Jonge, "Messiah," *ABD* 4:785–86.

The Kingdom of God in New Testament Theology

DARRELL L. BOCK

Dallas Theological Seminary

The kingdom of God has been one of the dominant topics of New Testament study in the twentieth century. The reason is obvious. Many scholars, both conservative and critical, regard the kingdom of God as "the central theme" of Jesus' public proclamation.[1] In fact, a plethora of monographs have poured forth since Johannes Weiss and Albert Schweitzer made the case that Jesus' teaching was profoundly Jewish, drenched in intense eschatological hope.[2] This new view contended against nineteenth-century views, which moralized the kingdom and made it palatable to modern taste by arguing it was merely an expression of ethical sensitivity raised up in the hearts of humans. In contrast, Weiss and Schweitzer argued that Jesus' claim for the kingdom anticipated God's stark intervention in the very near future that would reshape the creation. The view became known as "consistent," "thorough-going," or "imminent" eschatology.

For Weiss, the kingdom was purely religious, not ethical; purely future, not present in any way. The kingdom would be God's final miracle, with Jesus functioning in his current ministry as *Messias designatus*.[3] For Weiss, Jesus be-

---

1. So Joachim Jeremias, *New Testament Theology: The Proclamation of Jesus* (New York: Scribner's, 1971), 96. This was a translation of the 1971 German edition, *Neutestamentliche Theologie I. Teil: Die Verkündigung Jesu* (Gütersloh: Gerd Mohn, 1971).

2. Johannes Weiss, *Die Predigt Jesu vom Reiche Gottes* (Göttingen: Vandenhoeck und Ruprecht, 1892). This edition was translated into English in 1971 under the title *Jesus' Proclamation of the Kingdom of God*. Though this study was short, its impact has extended through the twentieth century. Albert Schweitzer, *Das Messianitäts und Leidensgeheimnis, Eine Skizze des Lebens Jesu* (Tübingen: Mohr, 1901). This was also translated into English in 1956 under the title *The Mystery of the Kingdom of God: The Secret of Jesus' Messiahship and Passion*, trans. Walter Lowrie (New York: Schoken, 1964). This is the version cited in this essay.

3. See the summary of Weiss and Schweitzer in Gösta Lundström, *The Kingdom of God in the Teaching of Jesus* (Richmond, Va.: John Knox, 1963), 35–81. This is a translation of the Swedish edition of 1947.

lieved that he would one day become the Son of Man. At first, Jesus believed that this would occur during his lifetime, but later in his ministry, he anticipated it to come shortly after his death.[4] It is a heritage that Jesus believed he possessed, though he had not yet entered into it.

For Schweitzer, Jesus expected the end before he concluded his public ministry. As he sent out the Twelve in mission (Matt. 10), he believed that before they finished their tour of the cities of Israel, the Son of Man would come and bring the kingdom. Its appearance would mean the end of the present age, and he would be transformed into the Son of Man. When the disciples returned from their mission without this taking place, Jesus' hopes of the end changed. It would take suffering, his own suffering, for the kingdom to come.[5] His death would bring the kingdom.

Though very different than Schweitzer, the oldest dispensationalists also stressed the Jewish roots of kingdom hope and placed its ultimate expression, as originally expressed through the hope of Israel's Scriptures, strictly in the future, what they referred to as the "kingdom of heaven." Whatever relationship Jesus' work in the present had to the kingdom, it was part of a previously unrevealed "mystery" that made its current expression something distinct from what had been promised to Israel and distinct from what was to come one day in fulfillment. This distinction between what would happen for Israel one day and what happens to the church today was a major element in the traditional dispensational distinction between Israel and the church in the plan of God. However, in the middle of this century, that clear dis-

4. Weiss, *Jesus' Proclamation of the Kingdom of God*, 129–31, states Weiss's ten conclusions. Here are some of the highlights of that summary. His first conclusion declared that Jesus believed the messianic time was imminent, but that his vision of Satan's defeat was so strong that he sometimes declared that the kingdom had dawned. No. 4 argues that Jesus understood himself as the one who will receive authority when the kingdom does come. No. 5 argues that Jesus originally expected to see the establishment of the kingdom, but that he eventually became convinced it would only come after his death. He then expected to return within the lifetime of the generation that rejected him. No. 8 is, "The land of Palestine will arise in a new and glorious splendor, forming the center of the new kingdom. Alien peoples will no longer rule over it, but will come to acknowledge God as Lord." No. 9 argues that Jesus and the Twelve will rule over the newborn people of the twelve tribes, which include even the Gentiles.

5. Schweitzer, *The Mystery of the Kingdom of God*, 62–63, describes this pivotal point in his typical flourish of style: "For the realisation of the Kingdom there remained but one way still open to him,—namely, conflict with the power which opposed his work. He resolved to carry this conflict into the Capital itself. There fate should decide. Perhaps the victory would fall to him. But, even if it should turn out that in the course of earthly events the fate of death awaited him inevitably, so long as he trod the path which his office prescribed, this very suffering must signify in God's plan the performance by which his work was to be crowned. It was then God's will that the moral state appropriate to the Kingdom of God should be inaugurated by the highest moral deed of the Messiah. With this thought he set out for Jerusalem—in order to remain Messiah." Elsewhere (114–15) he states that Jesus "no longer conceives of it [the final event] as an intervention of God in history; but rather as a final cosmical catastrophe. His [Jesus'] eschatology is the apocalyptic of the book of Daniel, since the Kingdom is to be brought by the Son of Man where he appears upon the clouds of heaven (Mark 8:38; 9:1)."

tinction was somewhat blurred, though how it worked precisely was never agreed to or clearly set forth. Four separate views were espoused.[6] Unlike Schweitzer, these dispensationalists saw no "error" or "change" in Jesus' understanding, but like him they regarded the promise of the future to be so rooted in Jewish hope and so grand in its scale that nothing Jesus did currently could be seen as the fulfillment of that great promise of old. For both classical and revised dispensationalists, the mystery introduced into the kingdom program, conceived in various ways in this century, represented an "intercalation" in the kingdom program of God, distinct from the hope

6. The notes to Matt. 3:2 and 6:33 in *The Scofield Study Bible*, published in 1909, pp. 996 and 1003, distinguish completely between the kingdom of heaven and the kingdom of God, as was common in the oldest expressions of dispensationalism, but is not as common today among either revised or progressive dispensationalists. In fact, the note on Matthew 6:33 in the *Oxford NIV Scofield Study Bible*, published in 1967 and 1984, p. 979, has been changed to speak only of a distinction "in some instances." The parables of Matthew 13 for this earliest, classical expression of dispensationalism were about the "mystery" form of the kingdom, were for this age and dealt with Christian profession, but had connection to the kingdom promised in the Old Testament, because it was "mystery" (new truth). The "at hand" kingdom was rejected, causing its coming (its "prophetic aspect") to await the return of the King in glory. Though the note on Matthew 3:2 does not explain the "mystery" kingdom connection to the prophetic kingdom, it speaks of a "mysteries" dimension that is fulfilled in the present age with reference to professing (and partially corrupt) Christendom. The kingdom of heaven is defined as "the rule of the heavens over the earth." The phrase, says the Old Scofield note to Matthew 3:2, comes "from Daniel, where it is defined (Dan. 2.34–36, 44; 7.23–27) as the Kingdom which 'the God of heaven' will set up after the destruction by 'the stone cut out without hands' of the Gentile world system. It is the Kingdom covenanted to David's seed (2 Sam. 7.7–10, refs.); described in the prophets (Zech. 12:8, note); and confirmed to Jesus the Christ, the Son of Mary, through the angel Gabriel (Luke 1.32, 33)." The note to Matthew 6:33 in the *Oxford NIV Scofield Study Bible*, p. 979, sees the rule of the kingdom of heaven, like the kingdom of God, realized "in the present age and will also be fulfilled in the future millennial kingdom. It continues forever in the eternal state (cp. Dan. 4:3)." Thus, even in a theological system as futuristic as dispensationalism, there has been a sense of the already–not yet tension about the kingdom among most of its most recent adherents. Even in dispensationalism's original form the tension was there, though obscured by the attempt to distinguish kingdom of God in the present from kingdom of heaven in the future. (What gets confusing for modern readers of the tradition is that what they mean by kingdom of God entails what original dispensationalists meant by both kingdom of God and of heaven, though modern readers tend not to read the kingdom of God as having the negative overtones the earliest dispensationalists gave to it.) What Schweitzer and dispensationalists affirm is that the formulation of the kingdom victorious has deep roots in Old Testament expression and expectation. For a survey of the various ways this "mystery" form of the Kingdom was explained in the mid–twentieth century, see Craig A. Blaising and Darrell L. Bock, *Progressive Dispensationalism* (Grand Rapids: Victor, 1993), 39–46. Blaising notes four distinct approaches to the question among revised dispensationalists. The four approaches represented in this revised period are: (1) Alva McClain and Stan Toussaint (no mediatorial kingdom today, but a limited, interim rule; McClain actually interacts with Schweitzer and Weiss and stands closest to a consistent eschatological view), (2) Charles Ryrie (a spiritual kingdom today [the church] within a mystery form of the kingdom [which entails Christendom]), (3) John Walvoord (spiritual form of the kingdom is the church), and (4) Dwight Pentecost (kingdom today is part of the present theocratic kingdom, a part of God's ongoing theocratic kingdom program). Where the first three approaches stress discontinuity with the past and future kingdoms, the last option is an attempt to articulate a continuity in that program. Dispensationalism has never been as monolithic as its proponents and critics have contended.

given to Israel. So throughout this century, the idea that kingdom hope was richly Jewish and pointed strongly, if not exclusively, to the future has been prominent in New Testament theology, whether conservative or not.[7] As we shall see, this emphasis on the future form of the kingdom is well grounded in biblical hope.

Other views also have emerged in this century. Two approaches were like the nineteenth-century "romanticized" efforts to redefine the kingdom in ways moderns could embrace. So efforts were made to demythologize Jesus' image of the apocalyptic kingdom into either an existential claim for a crisis decision (Bultmann) or to turn kingdom language into a mere metaphorical symbol of hope and transformation (Wilder and the later Perrin).[8] Both of these attempts, representing more liberal readings of Scripture, tried to redeem the kingdom concept by redefining it. However, two other approaches seriously sought to engage the biblical text and assess the model Weiss and Schweitzer introduced. These two other main views of the kingdom in this century have reacted to the "strictly future" model of the kingdom in two very diverse ways. One view, associated with C. H. Dodd, opted for a reading that the kingdom hope was totally realized in Jesus' ministry.[9] This became known as "realized" eschatology. The other, rooted in the work of Werner Kümmel, R. H. Fuller, and Joachim Jeremias, argued that the view of the kingdom had both present and future elements.[10] This became known as the "already/not yet" view of the king-

---

7. Fundamentally Schweitzerian views of the kingdom are still being defended today. See Dale C. Allison, *Jesus of Nazareth: Millenarian Prophet* (Minneapolis: Fortress, 1998) and Scot McKnight, *A New Vision for Israel: The Teachings of Jesus in a National Context* (Grand Rapids: Eerdmans, 1999), esp. 70–155. McKnight emphasizes apocalyptic imminence with a stress on A.D. 70 as the point of realization, a view similar to Tom Wright, *Jesus and the Victory of God* (Minneapolis: Fortress, 1996), although Wright's reading of eschatology appears more exclusively focused on A.D. 70 than McKnight's. For my evaluation of Wright's views, see my essay in *Jesus and the Restoration of Israel: A Critical Assessment of N. T. Wright's Jesus and the Victory of God*, ed. Carey C. Newman (Downers Grove, Ill.: InterVarsity, 1999), 101–25.

8. Norman Perrin, *The Kingdom of God in the Teaching of Jesus* (Philadelphia: Westminster, 1963), 112–19, notes how Bultmann followed Weiss on the historical questions. What Bultmann stressed was the crisis of decision Jesus' challenge raised. The best place to see Bultmann's views summarized is his *Jesus Christ and Mythology* (New York: Scribner's, 1958). For Wilder, see his "Eschatological Imagery and Earthly Circumstance," *New Testament Studies* 5 (1959): 229–45. For the later Perrin, see *Jesus and the Language of the Kingdom: Symbol and Metaphor in New Testament Interpretation* (Philadelphia: Fortress, 1976). Many members of the Jesus Seminar fit into one of these categories.

9. His initial key article was "The Kingdom of God Has Come," *Expository Times* 48 (1936): 138–42. The view in its developed form appears in his *The Parables of the Kingdom* (New York: Scribner's, 1961).

10. Werner Georg Kümmel, *Verheissung und Erfüllung* (Zürich: Zwingli, 1953). The English translation by Dorothea M. Barton is entitled *Promise and Fulfillment: The Eschatological Message of Jesus*, 3d rev. ed., Studies in Biblical Theology 23 (London: SCM, 1957). In his concluding chapter, Kümmel says, "In the course of the previous discussion it has already become clear that the very numerous pronouncements of Jesus about the future of the Kingdom of God and the equally indisputable ones about the presence of the *eschaton* demolish the arguments

dom or "eschatology in the process of realization." In fact, Jeremias in his conclusion to his volume on the parables closes this way, "In attempting to recover the original significance of the parables, one thing above all becomes evident: it is that all the parables of Jesus compel his hearers to come to a decision about his person and mission. For they all are full of 'the secret of the Kingdom of God' (Mark 4.11), that is to say, the recognition of 'an eschatology in the process of realization.' The hour of fulfillment is come, that is the urgent note that sounds through them all."[11] This view was made famous in evangelical circles by George Ladd.[12] It is probably the most prominent view currently in New Testament circles at large, both conservative and critical. It is known as "inaugurated" eschatology.[13] The kingdom was inaugurated or

---

for those descriptions of Jesus' message according to which Jesus announced either only eschatological occurrences in the future or only a present time of eschatological fulfillment. It is therefore completely certain that Jesus' eschatological message cannot be regarded simply as a particular form of Jewish apocalyptic, and also that it does not detach itself completely from the expectations for the future of the contemporary Jewish eschatology by reason of its interpretation concerned only with the present." For a summary of Fuller's work, see R. H. Fuller, *The Mission and Achievement of Jesus: An Examination of the Presuppositions of New Testament Theology*, Studies in Biblical Theology 12 (London, SCM, 1954). On p. 48 Fuller says, "The Kingdom of God is not yet present, it is imminent; but the imminent event is already at work, producing signs of its coming. The Kingdom is dawning, but it has not yet arrived." Jeremias, *New Testament Theology*, closes his section on the kingdom (108) saying, "For Jesus' proclamation of the dawn of the time of salvation is without analogy. With regard to his environment, he is the 'only Jew known to us from ancient times,' who proclaimed 'that the new age of salvation had already begun.'" (Jeremias is citing the remarks of the Jewish scholar David Flusser here.) Earlier on p. 102 he makes the point that kingdom is "always and everywhere understood in eschatological terms; it denotes the time of salvation, the consummation of the world, the restoration of the disrupted communion between God and man." He appeals to Daniel 2:44 and 7:27. Jesus is proclaiming that the eschatological hour is very near. For Jeremias (102), though, the stress is on the future and the kingdom's nearness, the call of Jesus is really that "God is coming, he is standing at the door, indeed (ἔφθασεν), he is already there." One should note a slight difference between Kümmel and Fuller-Jeremias. For Kümmel, Jesus proclaimed an "already–not yet." Fuller-Jeremias hold that Jesus proclaimed the dawning of a kingdom in signs that showed it was very close but had not yet come.

11. Joachim Jeremias, *The Parables of Jesus*, 2d rev. ed. (New York: Scribner's, 1963), 230. This is a translation of *Die Gleichnisse Jesu*, 6th ed. (Göttingen: Vandenhoeck und Ruprecht, 1962).

12. George Eldon Ladd, *The Presence of the Future: The Eschatology of Biblical Realism* (Grand Rapids: Eerdmans, 1974). This was an update of his earlier *Jesus and the Kingdom* (New York: Harper & Row, 1964). Ladd's thesis is stated on p. 149: "The presence of the Kingdom of God was seen as God's dynamic reign invading the present age without transforming it into the age to come." For him, it was this in-breaking without a change of age (a "victory over Satan without being consummation") that was the mystery contained in Jesus' teaching.

13. Other major studies arguing for this view include Rudolf Schnackenburg, *God's Rule and Kingdom* (New York: Herder & Herder, 1968), a translation of *Gottes Herrschaft und Reich*, 4th ed. (Freiburg: Herder, 1965); G. R. Beasley-Murray, *Jesus and the Kingdom of God* (Grand Rapids: Eerdmans, 1986); John P. Meier, *A Marginal Jew: Rethinking the Historical Jesus*, vol. 2: *Mentor, Message and Miracles*, The Anchor Bible Reference Library (New York: Doubleday, 1994), 237–506; as well as many of the essays in *The Kingdom of God*, ed. Bruce Chilton, Issues in Religion and Theology 5 (Philadelphia: Fortress, 1984).

was dawning in Jesus' words and deeds, but its consummation was yet future. As we shall see, there are also good reasons why this view is held.

I lay out this "map" of views at the start, because what the kingdom is, when it begins, and how it proceeds have been the key questions in the past century. But treating the theology of the kingdom involves far more than these questions, as we hope to show and survey. In fact, I hope to consider a series of issues tied to the kingdom. They include: (1) Linguistics and the Kingdom in Jewish Expectation; (2) Kingdom as Apocalyptic; (3) Kingdom: Present, Future, or Both?; (4) Defining the Kingdom; (5) The Kingdom and Ethics; (6) Beyond the Term *Kingdom*; (7) Kingdom outside the Gospels; and (8) So What? So not only is the kingdom theme an important New Testament concept generating a rich history of discussion, it is also one of the most complex topics in Scripture.

Linguistics and the Kingdom in Jewish Expectation

When Jesus used the expression "kingdom of God," how much of its meaning can we assume he and his audience shared? This becomes an important question because the expression itself, surprisingly, is totally absent in the Hebrew Scriptures.[14] Here is a case where the study of an idea has to move past a study of the set phrase to get anywhere. The idea, however, is more frequent.[15] Yahweh is King (1 Sam. 12:12; Ps. 24:10; Isa. 33:22; Zeph. 3:15; Zech. 14:16–17). He rules over Israel (Exod. 15:18; Num. 23:21; Deut. 33:5; Isa. 43:15). He rules over the earth or the creation (2 Kings 19:15; Isa. 6:5; Jer. 46:18; Ps. 29:10; 47:2; 93; 96:10; 145:11, 13). He possesses a royal throne (Ps. 9:4; 45:6; 47:8; Isa. 6:1; 66:1; Ezek. 1:26). His reign is ongoing (Ps. 10:16; 146:10; Isa. 24:23). Rule or kingship is his (Ps. 22:28). It is primarily God's special relationship to Israel that is in view here as the Son of David is said to sit on Yahweh's throne (1 Chron. 17:14; 28:5; 29:23; 2 Chron. 9:8). When Israel was overrun by the nations, a longing existed that one day God would reestablish his rule on behalf of his people and show his comprehensive sovereignty to all humanity. After all, God had committed himself to David concerning a dynasty of duration (2 Sam. 7:13). It is here that the hope of a future kingdom of God, made not with hands, came to be contrasted with the human kingdoms in Daniel 2 and 7. It is in the context of such expectation that Jesus used the term "kingdom of God." What was hoped for was something that had existed in the past, but only as a mere glimpse of what had been promised— a rule to come involving total peace for God's people. In sum, kingdom hope by the time of the Babylonian captivity is driven forward by the vision of the fullness of God's rule showing up one day. It was to this hope that Jesus preached.

---

14. The expression does occur in Wisdom 10:10.
15. Chrys C. Caragounis, "Kingdom of God/Kingdom of Heaven," *Dictionary of Jesus and the Gospels*, ed. Joel Green, Scot McKnight, and I. Howard Marshall (Downers Grove, Ill.: InterVarsity, 1992), 417.

Such a hope had been nurtured in some circles of second temple Judaism.[16] The kingdom became linked (sometimes) to the messianic hope, but (always) to judgment of the nations and vindication of the saints. Some Jewish documents, content with the current religious and political arrangement, do not reflect any such hope. The concept is expressed with some variety, but central to its expression is that God will assert his comprehensive rule (*1 Enoch* 9:4–5; 12:3; 25; 27:3; 81:3). God's powerful presence will involve the removal of Satan's influence (*Assumption of Moses* 7–10). He will destroy his enemies and free his people. These enemies are described in both earthly terms, like the Romans in *Psalms of Solomon* 17–18 and *2 Baruch* 36–40, and in spiritual terms, where Belial stands among the evil forces who will be defeated (1QS 3–4). Often the coming of the kingdom was seen as preceded by a period of intense upheaval and tribulation (*Sib. Or.* 3:796–808; *2 Bar.* 70:2–8; *4 Ezra* 6:24; 9:1–12; 13:29–31; 1QM 12:9; 19:1–2). The cry of the prayer of 2 Maccabees 1:24–29 summarizes well the hope of deliverance. The call was for God to deliver and vindicate his people. The text of *Psalms of Solomon* 17–18 gives the most detailed expression of messianic hope in all the texts, though the idea of kingdom in this period of Judaism did not always entail a messianic hope.[17] In fact, sometimes the Messiah is seen in very earthly terms, as in the *Psalms of Solomon*, while in other texts, he clearly possesses a more transcendent power (*1 Enoch* 37–71) or has a seeming mix of the two (*4 Ezra* 7:28–29; 12:32–34; 13:26). Thus, associated with the consistent idea of God's coming comprehensive and vindicating rule for his people is a complex and varying array of sub-themes tied to the kingdom's coming. In Judaism, there was no unified view of the kingdom beyond the hope of God's powerful coming and vindication. It is important to appreciate that it is into this somewhat confused backdrop that Jesus preached the hope of the coming of the Kingdom.

This complex background raises a question: Could Jesus use the phrase and really be understood? More importantly, in presenting his understanding of the idea represented in the kingdom, could he assume an understanding of the term by his audience? Given the paucity of Old Testament use of the phrase and the variety of details attached to the hope within Judaism, Jesus needed to explain his usage in order to be clear. It is this complexity that raises the issue of whether Jesus' use of the term was "static" (steno) or "tensive."[18] Nor-

16. Michael Lattke, "On the Jewish Background of the Synoptic Concept 'The Kingdom of God,'" in *The Kingdom of God*, ed. Bruce Chilton (Philadelphia: Fortress, 1984), 72–91.

17. Jacob Neusner, William Green, and E. Frerichs, eds., *Judaisms and Their Messiahs* (Cambridge: Cambridge University Press, 1987).

18. This linguistic contrast was introduced by the later work of Norman Perrin, *Jesus and the Language of the Kingdom* (Philadelphia: Fortress, 1976), esp. 16–32, 127–31, 197–99. In discussing this point from Perrin I wish only to highlight the linguistic element of his discussion without embracing his language about "myth" associated with the use of the term "kingdom of God."

man Perrin posed two options. Did Jesus use the term one way all the time with a fixed referent (steno)? Or was his use of the term something that he used with symbolic force but that could not be contained in one referent alone (tensive)? We opt for a third possibility: Did Jesus' use operate within a fixed parameter, which he filled with a variety of detail because of the richness of the basic concept he was defining and detailing (tensive yet with a steno-like base)?[19] How one approaches Jesus' terminology will impact how one reads it.

Four factors favor this third option. First, the number of and variety within the kingdom sayings in the Gospels placed alongside the paucity of older references in the Hebrew Scriptures suggests that Jesus is developing the concept along additional lines from what the Old Testament taught. However, Jesus' respect for that revelation means that he is *not altering* the concept, but *developing* and *complementing* it. We hope to show the variety within his teaching that validates this point. Second, the very consistency of the fundamental image within Judaism means that a basic understanding of kingdom did exist on which Jesus could build. It is *God's* kingdom and rule that is presented as the hope. The sheer number of texts that discuss judgment and vindication under this theme both in Scripture and in later Judaism show that Jesus works with a given understanding at its base. Reflection taking place within Second Temple Judaism represented attempts to put the hope of Scripture together in terms of the details. Jesus both accepts and rejects elements of these reflections. Third, this idea that Jesus works with a rarely used Old Testament term and yet develops it using larger categories of scriptural teaching has precedent elsewhere in his own use. Jesus does the same type of thing with the Son of Man concept. That description of a human invested with eschatological authority appears in Daniel 7 (note the conceptual overlap with the kingdom theme—Dan. 7 is also a key kingdom text). Jesus takes this one image and uses it as a collection point for his Christology. In the same way, Jesus takes the kingdom concept and uses it as a collection point for both soteriology and eschatology.[20] Fourth, the very confusion of detail within Judaism of Jesus' time demanded that he take this type of approach to the concept. Here was a phrase that basically did not exist in the Old Testament. However, by Jesus' time, multiple concepts swirled around it, even though its basic meaning was well established. The phrase clearly sought to summarize a major strand of Jewish hope, yet it

---

19. For an incisive critique of Perrin, see Meier, *A Marginal Jew*, 2:241–43. He accuses the later Perrin of making Jesus sound like a twentieth-century Bultmannian versus a first-century Jew. Interestingly, the earlier Perrin made a similar statement about such a view in his earlier work! See Norman Perrin, *The Kingdom of God in the Teaching of Jesus* (Philadelphia: Westminster, 1963), 86. He states, "A 'timeless' Kingdom is as foreign to first-century Judaism as a transcendent order beyond time and space,' and if Jesus held such views he singularly failed to impress them upon his followers."

20. I suspect the same premise operates with Jesus' use of the law, but with the opposite dimension. Here the term is so used in the Old Testament that Jesus' use in any context must be carefully examined for its point and scope.

needed defining. Its absence in the Old Testament gave Jesus room to make it a helpful synthesizing concept. Its familiarity and importance within Judaism, because of the hope it encapsulated, made it a key term to nail down. The very diversity in its contemporary usage required that Jesus explain and develop the term. Thus, as we turn to Jesus' use, we can expect that on the one hand he was referring to a hope his audience understood in its most basic terms, but something that also needed more detail and development.

Here is the major thesis of this essay: Jesus' use of the term *kingdom* is tensive with a stable base. In each of the categories we shall examine it will be shown that Jesus' use is complex and must be examined one text at a time. Choices of either-or in his usage inevitably err in narrowing the depth of Jesus' usage. To make the kingdom a static technical term for every use is to miss the variety of nuances he uses within the stable base meaning he gives.

Kingdom as Apocalyptic

As a synthetic term for scriptural hope, two issues are tied to the question of the kingdom and apocalyptic hope.[21] First is the question of imminence: Did Jesus expect the end in his lifetime as Weiss and Schweitzer argued? Those who argue for imminence either say that Jesus was wrong (Schweitzer, Weiss) or that the temple's destruction in A.D. 70 is what Jesus meant all along as an event of decisive, eschatological vindication (Wright, McKnight). The second problem associated with the kingdom is whether the term looks to a remade "new age" or to a continuation emerging within this history. We tackle these questions in reverse order. We need to start here, because understanding the scope of Jesus' claim and how it works sets the stage for understanding how the Gospels see the kingdom.

The problem concerning a remade new age or an eschaton within this history has sometimes been highlighted by pointing out the difference in Old Testament hope between prophetic-eschatological expectation and apocalyptic-eschatological hope.[22] Prophetic hope is defined in terms of God's work

21. I leave out of this account a view that argues that Jesus did not teach an apocalyptic or eschatological view of the kingdom, such as has been made popular in the Jesus Seminar. The most eloquent attempt to make this argument appears in the work of Marcus Borg, *Jesus in Contemporary Scholarship* (Valley Forge, Pa.: Trinity, 1994), 74–84. For a critical assessment of this view, see Allison, *Jesus of Nazareth: Millennial Prophet*, 96–129.

22. For a summary of this distinction, see Paul D. Hanson, *The Dawn of Apocalyptic: The Historical and Sociological Roots of Jewish Apocalyptic Eschatology*, rev. ed. (Philadelphia: Fortress, 1979), 10–12, and Ladd, *The Presence of the Future*, 45–101, esp. 79–83, 93–95. Unlike many of the discussions of this distinction, Ladd correctly sees something less than a clean distinction between these categories, noting how the "apocalyptic" Daniel actually has many "prophetic" features. Ladd thus avoids the implicit tendency in many critics to pit the two approaches against each other. Given the "mix" in Daniel, the mix in Jesus' own presentation has precedent in the older Scripture.

within history, usually tied to God's raising up a delivering regal figure for Israel. Apocalyptic hope is defined as God's powerful work manifesting itself in an "in-breaking" from outside into normal history. Apocalyptic hope entails cosmic change, the presence of a transcendent-like figure, and the backdrop of an almost dualistic conflict with the cosmic forces of evil.[23] In sum, the Messiah represents prophetic-eschatological hope, while the "one like the Son of Man" is more apocalyptic.

The interesting feature in Jesus' kingdom teaching is that both strands are present, though it appears that the more eschatological features dominate. The more apocalyptic features include the imagery of the Son of Man coming on the clouds, drawn directly from Daniel 7:13 (Mark 13:26 par.), along with the cosmic disturbances associated with his coming (Mark 13:24–25 par.).[24] Here is divine judgment crashing the earthly party down below, an in-breaking of God's authority. This imagery is significant, for it is this return that brings judgment and allows the vindicated righteous to "inherit the Kingdom" (Matt. 25:34). Here kingdom and returning Son of Man are linked. Here are standard Jewish apocalyptic themes of the kingdom. The images of a gathering up for a comprehensive judgment and a bridegroom coming who shuts some out also have these overtones (Matt. 25:1–13, 31–46). Other imagery having a catastrophic, apocalyptic feel includes the comparisons of the judgment with the flood (Luke 17:26–27; Matt. 24:37–39) and Sodom and Gomorrah (Luke 17:28–29). The Son of Man's sudden coming is compared to lightning, revealing the "shock" of the coming (Luke 17:24; Matt. 24:27).

Other images of the kingdom in the future are harder to classify. The reversal of suffering or oppression, as reflected in the promises of the Beatitudes, could fit either emphasis, as do their hopes of reward (Matt. 5:3–10). The image of the rejoicing and fellowship at the banquet table also could belong in either scheme (Matt. 8:11–12; Luke 14:15–24; 22:16–18). One text seems to indicate that Israel is still very much in view in the plan, as the Twelve will judge the twelve tribes of Israel (Luke 22:30). In addition, the selection of the Twelve has been seen by many New Testament scholars as an indication that

23. Rather than appealing to a genre distinction, John Collins (*The Scepter and the Star: The Messiahs of the Dead Sea Scrolls and Other Ancient Literature*, The Anchor Bible Reference Library [New York: Doubleday, 1995], 11–14) argues for a distinction in the form of the messianic expectation between regal figure and a heavenly messianic figure. These are two of the four categories he notes exist in Judaism. The others are prophet and priest.

24. I make this point against the view of Kümmel, *Promise and Fulfillment*, 104. He splits the eschatological elements from the apocalyptic ones and argues that only the eschatological elements are authentic. Though Jesus' kingdom imagery is primarily eschatological, there is no inherent reason why the key turning point in the program should not be linked to apocalyptic imagery of God's decisive "in-breaking," especially if Jesus saw himself in any sense as sent by God.

what Jesus was working for was a restoration of the nation, preparing them for the era of "regeneration" (Matt. 19:28).[25]

On the other hand, some teaching appears to shy away from the more overt apocalyptic themes of Judaism. Jesus specifically denies that signs accompany the time of the kingdom's appearing (Luke 17:20–21), though he does indicate that that general signs exist in the age that should keep one watching. Such signs indicate that God is at work (Luke 12:54–56; Mark 13:1–37; esp. vv. 28–31). Jesus explicitly refuses to name an exact time for his return, precluding us from excessive calendrical calculating (Mark 13:32 par.).

Other texts are decidedly more eschatological and lack apocalyptic features. The parables of the sower, mustard seed, leaven, and husbandmen appear to place kingdom preaching and presence as having invaded this history with no "apocalyptic" feel at all, operating more like a covert CIA operation, so unnoticed that it is hardly appreciated as the presence of the kingdom program at all. Nevertheless, one day what has been started will reach a point of covering the whole. These parables, explicitly presented as revealing a "mystery," show how Jesus' kingdom teaching spans more than a single catastrophic event or a given moment. It is here that Jesus makes his distinctive contribution, by foreseeing a long-running program that was declared and initiated in his teaching and work, but that will one day culminate in a comprehensive judgment. It is to this goal that the kingdom is always headed. Thus the emphasis in the kingdom teaching of the Gospels is always aimed toward this fully restorative future. In this sense, Jesus' teaching is at one with the traditional Jewish hope. The emphasis explains why the disciples, after spending years with Jesus listening to him teach about the kingdom, could ask after his resurrection if now was the time he was restoring the kingdom to Israel (Acts 1:6). Nothing in what Jesus had taught them had dissuaded them from this aspect of the hope. And in equally characteristic style, Jesus replied not with a time or a date nor a correction, but with an emphasis on our current call in light of that certain future.

It is the juxtaposition of these various strands that shows how eclectic and synthetic, even creative, Jesus' kingdom teaching is. Jesus did preach a hope Jews could recognize, but he also preached a whole lot more. He embraced strands of Jewish apocalyptic hope, but did not merely parrot these themes. The sense of these texts as a whole is that Jesus works both within this history and yet will reshape it one day. But how soon, O Lord?

It is here that three texts have dominated the discussion about how imminent the kingdom was in Jesus' view. Those who wish to credit Jesus with a view of imminence within a generation or so of his coming point to these texts as decisive. On the other hand, one text within the Olivet Discourse warns us

---

25. Allison (*Jesus of Nazareth*, 101–2) notes the parallels in Judaism that point in this direction: 1QM 2:1–3; 4QpIsa[d] frag. 1; *T. Jud.* 25:1–2; *T. Benj.* 10:7; also Rev. 21:12.

not to make a judgment before all the sayings are considered. The three "imminent" texts are Matthew 10:23, which notes that before the disciples finish going through all the cities of Jerusalem, the Son of Man will come; Mark 9:1, which explains that before some of the disciples die, they will see "the Kingdom of God come in power";[26] and Mark 13:30=Matthew 24:34, which argues that "this generation" will not pass away until "all these things" take place.

Mark 9:1 is often explained by appealing to the transfiguration as the event alluded to, a moment when the inner circle saw a sneak preview of Jesus' kingdom glory. Though some complain that Jesus would hardly refer to an event six days or so hence against a time frame of the disciples' death, the fact is only "some" did see this glimpse of glory. That event, and the Gospels' juxtaposition of transfiguration with the saying, seem to commend this reading.

The case for imminence surrounding Matthew 10:23 may be a case of an overly literal reading. The expression "finish going through all the cities of Israel" may mean nothing more than "completing your mission to Israel." In other words, they are to continue pursuing the nation until the Son of Man returns. When he does come, they will still be engaged in that calling. As we shall see in a moment, this will fit with something Jesus says at Olivet.

Mark 13:30=Matthew 24:34 is the most difficult saying. The initial impression many gain from the text is that all these Olivet events are predicted to happen by the end of "this generation," so the Son of Man's return is predicted within the disciples' lifetime. However, as Don Carson has pointed out, to have the remark about this generation and "all these things" include the event of the return would be contradictory to earlier imagery about the coming being obvious like lightning, as well as not fitting the precursor "budding leaf" imagery of the Marcan context.[27] In other words, the remarks about the Son of Man's appearing, given the seemingly obvious cosmic signs that accompany it, mark that event as excluded in the "leaf" remark of the parable that is pointing to that which indicates the approach of the end, not its conclusion. This would mean that "all these things" refer to those events described before we get to the cosmic signs. Those events will happen within a generation, and that was just as it was, given the fall of Jerusalem in A.D. 70 as a sign of the end.

One text in the same context as the Mark 13:30 generation text also points to the fact that Jesus did not teach the kingdom would come within the gen-

---

26. Another possible argument for this distinction is that Jesus speaks of this generation not passing away with regard to "these things," but of "that day" (i.e., a later day) no one knows the time, suggesting a distinction between the two sets of events. Interestingly, the Matthean parallel in 16:28 has "before they see the Son of Man coming in his Kingdom," again showing a link between Son of Man and kingdom.

27. See D. A. Carson, "Matthew," in *The Expositors' Bible Commentary*, ed. Frank C. Gaebelein (Grand Rapids: Zondervan, 1984), 8:506–7.

eration of the disciples. It is Mark 13:10=Matthew 24:14. Here Jesus notes that before the end comes, the "gospel of the Kingdom" (Matthew) will be preached in all the world. Thus, a mission that would take some time seems to be in view in this remark.

So we argue that Jesus did draw on the apocalyptic-eschatological imagery of Judaism for his general portrait of the kingdom, but he also added new imagery to that portrait. Jesus' teaching stressed where the kingdom was headed. It would be a time when God would vindicate his people through the Son of Man and judge the nations. But other texts hint that this is merely the end of the story. Jesus refused to predict the time of the end. Neither did he preach imminence in such a way as to declare it would come within the generation of the disciples. Signs in their lifetime did and would indicate its approach, but the times and seasons for its coming were known only to the Father.

So Jesus' teaching had roots in Judaism, but what was fresh about his teaching? This brings us to the topic of when the kingdom comes.

Kingdom: Present, Future, or Both?

When it comes to the use of the term "kingdom," Chrys Caragounis has numbered its use with "of God," "of the Heavens,"[28] and by itself.[29] "Kingdom of God" appears five times in Matthew, fourteen times in Mark, thirty-two times in Luke, and twice in John. "Kingdom" by itself occurs thirteen times in Matthew, seven times in Luke, and three times in John, while being absent in Mark. When one puts all the uses together, "kingdom" appears fifty times in Matthew, fourteen times in Mark, thirty-nine times in Luke, and five times in John.

C. H. Dodd notwithstanding, the bulk of the uses look to the future consummation of the kingdom, to the final judgment, the coming of the Son of Man, to being seated at the banquet table in an era of joy and fellowship, to a period when the kingdom is received or inherited or prepared.[30] The kingdom Jesus preached was a goal of God's promise and hope that brought deliverance and vindication through the working of God's power. But key to the groundwork for that golden age was the work of one in whom and through whom God was working and would work. It is in this context that the issue of the presence of the kingdom since the time of Jesus' ministry must be raised. The

---

28. This usage is limited to Matthew and occurs thirty-two times. The rendering in the plural reflects the Greek, which itself reflects the Aramaic circumlocution for God.

29. "The Kingdom of God/Heaven," *Dictionary of Jesus and the Gospels*, 426.

30. Jeremias (*New Testament Theology*, 32–34) cites the variety of phrasing that occurs and notes how Jesus' teaching is unique within Judaism in showing such variety of expression. Bruce Chilton (*Pure Kingdom: Jesus' Vision of God: Studying the Historical Jesus* [Grand Rapids: Eerdmans, 1996], 56–101), lays out a summary of this entire teaching along a series of coordinates of themes: eschatology, transcendence, judgment, purity, and radiance. The listing shows the scope of major sub-topics the kingdom theme covers.

kingdom as future is clear in Jesus' teaching, but is there any sense in which it can be said to have begun? If it has begun, then what does that mean for understanding the kingdom in the New Testament and in its potential presence today?

On one point all are agreed: Jesus' message was about the kingdom. He preached the arrival of the messianic age and its activity of deliverance, contrasting the greatness of the kingdom era with the era of the Baptist, which seemingly had now passed (Luke 4:16–30; Luke 7:22–23, 28 par.; 16:16; Matt. 11:12–14).

Some texts highlight the kingdom's approach or proximity (Mark 1:15; Luke 10:9, 11).[31] The parable of the sower makes it clear that it is the word about the kingdom that is presently sowed (Matt. 13:19). The word is compared to seed. The image extends in other parables to include the image of a mustard seed planted. At the start, it is a tiny seed, but it ends up as a tree where birds can rest. This cannot be a reference to the apocalyptic kingdom of the end, for that kingdom is decidedly great and comprehensive from its appearing with the Son of Man. Nor can it be the theocratic kingdom as seen in Old Testament declarations of God's rule, for that cosmic, total rule also has been comprehensive from its inception. What is in view here is the launching of the eschatological kingdom, which surprisingly is "breaking-in" in miniscule form. So this parable is our first clue that a "mystery" of the kingdom involves its seemingly insignificant start in the present with the "planting" of Jesus' Word. The parable of the leaven makes the same point with differing imagery.

Equally suggestive about the significance of Jesus' present activity for the presence of the kingdom are the images of Jesus as a bridegroom (Mark 2:18–22 par.), a shepherd (Matt. 9:36 par.; 10:6; Luke 12:32; see Ezek. 34), and as a harvester sending messengers out to reap the harvest (Matt. 9:37–38; Luke 10:1–2), all eschatological images. All of this suggests that if the kingdom has not come, it is very, very close. It is so close that what the disciples are experiencing is what prophets and kings longed to experience, a clear allusion to the arrival of hoped-for promise (Luke 10:23–24 par.). The offer of forgiveness Jesus declares as present is one of the great hoped-for blessings of the new era (Jer. 31:31–34; Mark 2:5; Luke 7:36–50; 19:1–10).

At the center of all of this activity was Jesus. That Jesus could interpret the Torah and even explain its scope, so that religious practice could change,

31. Texts such as these make it clear that whatever is being raised, it is not the universal kingdom of God that declared God's rule in a generic sense or his rule over creation (e.g., Ps. 47; 96). The approach of the kingdom in Mark 1:15 par. looks to the approach of something that has not been previously in place and that is longed for and anticipated. Thus any attempts to make present kingdom texts in the New Testament fit into this more generic category fail. It is an eschatological kingdom that is drawing near.

pointed to the arrival of a new era (Matt. 5:21–48; Mark 7:1–23). Now it is true that not all the texts I have cited mention the kingdom, but most do. The others are describing the delivering and teaching activity of the One through whom the promise comes.

In Judaism, the kingdom was about the age to come or the messianic era. Remember that in the Hebrew Scriptures the term "kingdom of God" does not appear, though it is a topic of many other related themes. So the work of the Messiah would seemingly qualify as kingdom work, especially given teaching in the parables that the kingdom is being planted in Jesus' teaching. The fact that this teaching is "new" or "mystery" does not alter the fact that it is kingdom teaching connected to the original promise of the kingdom. That the kingdom is not delayed because of Israel's rejection is shown in the parable of the great banquet (Luke 14:15–24). Here the refusal to come to the celebration when it is announced does not lead to the postponing of the banquet, but to the inviting of others to fill it. Though banquet imagery is normally looking to the future in Jesus' teaching, in this case it is his preaching and the invitation to experience blessing starting now that is in view. These texts show that at the heart of the kingdom is the mediating of promised blessing and deliverance, an exercise of divine power and authority through a Chosen One who also acts with unique authority.

In the talk about the presence of the kingdom, however, it is two texts that stand out the most in the discussion. They are Matthew 12:28=Luke 11:20 and Luke 17:21. It is in these texts that two key elements of the kingdom surface, one already made obvious by our survey, the other focusing on a key element that makes deliverance possible.

In Luke 17:20–21, Jesus declares that one need not go on a search for signs to find the kingdom. This reinforces a point he has already raised in his teaching in the rebuke about being able to read the weather but not the signs of the times (Luke 12:54–56 par.). It also parallels the warning about the sign of his preaching being the only sign this wicked generation must respond to (Luke 11:29–32 par.). The kingdom does not come, in this phase, with such heavenly portents. Rather it is "in your midst." With all due respect to the NIV, the rendering is surely not "within you."[32] Though linguistically ἐντός can have such a meaning and most often does, Jesus is not speaking of some potential within each person's heart to establish the kingdom. This reading sounds like the romantic notions of nineteenth-century scholars on the kingdom. This personalized reading is highly unlikely because Jesus' audience is made up of Pharisees. Such heart potential for them does not exist without a powerful work of God and the effect of his transforming presence. Rather, the point is that the kingdom, in a sense, is right in front of their face in Jesus. It is "in

32. I raise this also against the reading of Caragounis in his "Kingdom of God/Heaven," *Dictionary of Jesus and the Gospels*, 423.

their midst" or "in their reach" in that the hunt for that which represents the kingdom's presence and authority stands before them.[33]

That Jesus is speaking of the present and not the future becomes clear when the present tense of Luke 17:21 is contrasted to the future perspective of verses 22–37. Such a reading highlights how Jesus is placed at the center of kingdom activity and fits with all the themes pointing in this direction just noted above.

The second text is a famous passage where Jesus is defending himself against the charge that he casts out demons by the power of Beelzebul. He replies, "If I cast out demons by the Spirit of God [Matthew]/finger of God [Luke], then the kingdom of God approaches or has come upon (ἔφθασεν) you." Is Jesus noting that the kingdom has come close to overtaking them or that it has come? The key here is the aorist form of the verb φθάνω. It appears in the Gospels only in this passage. In 1 Thessalonians 4:15 it means "to anticipate." However, in all its other aorist uses it has the meaning of "has arrived" or "has reached" (Rom. 9:31; 2 Cor. 10:14; 1 Thess. 2:16; Phil. 3:16). It is not synonymous with the earlier declaration that the kingdom of God has drawn near, using ἤγγικεν.[34]

It is a stronger saying than that the kingdom is near. Contextually a real exercise of divine power is being defended as visibly present. The image is reinforced immediately in both contexts by the parable of a man overcoming a strong man and plundering his possessions. Jesus is describing what *is* taking place, *not what has approached*. The point is that the miracles are a picture of God's authority and rule working through Jesus to defeat Satan. In other words, the Jewish claim that Jesus does miracles by satanic authority could not be more incorrect.

This saying is significant for a series of reasons. First, it shows that the kingdom is about divine deliverance through Jesus in the releasing of authority and power that overcomes the presence and influence of Satan. It is an "invasion" of a realm this evil one seemingly controls. Jesus is able to exercise such authority now. Jesus' ministry means Satan's defeat and the arriving of the kingdom. Though the kingdom means ultimately a much more comprehensive exercise of power, as the future kingdom sayings show, it is operative now in the work of deliverance that Jesus' miracles portray. A second point is also im-

---

33. On the question of whether Greek papyri and other texts ever evidence a meaning of "amongst," see Kümmel, *Promise and Fulfillment*, 33–36, esp. n. 50. This evidence, texts from Xenophon [*An.* 1.10.3], Herodotus [7.100.3] and Symmachus' translation of Ps. 87:6, challenge Caragounis' claim of the absence of such attestation. Kümmel argues that an objection based on the audience being the Pharisees is not persuasive in arguing against "within you," because we cannot be sure they are the original audience for this saying. We do not share his skepticism about the setting. Such a challenge to his opponents fits in nicely with numerous such challenges pointing to Jesus' centrality in God's work. See also Meier, *Marginal Jew*, 412–23, who defends the authenticity of the saying and discusses its likely Aramaic form.

34. Again, for details, see Kümmel, *Promise and Fulfillment*, 105–7.

portant. The miracles themselves are *not* the point, but what they portray is. A study of Jesus' ministry shows how he worked hard to deflect excessive attention being drawn to the miracles. The miracles were "signs," as the Johannine perspective argues. They painted in audiovisual terms the presence of Jesus' authority and victory over Satan. Such power had to be exercised and established if deliverance were to take place. So here lies the third point. This passage shows the injection again of an apocalyptic-type theme into Jesus' kingdom teaching. The kingdom manifests itself as part of a cosmic battle, expressed in dualistic terms, in which God through Jesus is defeating Satan, who himself is doing all he can to keep humanity opposed to God. With the coming of Jesus and the kingdom inaugurated, eschatology has entered into the present. Future hope dawns as present reality, but with much more reality to come.

The importance of this text can be highlighted by making an observation about its form as a miracle story–pronouncement account. Unlike most miracle accounts, which spend most of their time on the details of the miracle and little time on the reaction, this account gives one verse to the healing and then spends all its time on the reaction, which itself is a commentary on the significance of Jesus' miracles as a unit. What emerges is that the kingdom is ultimately about God's work to redeem humanity according to his promise. The kingdom is God's ultimate response to the grip Satan has on that needy humanity. The kingdom's coming in Jesus' ministry is the *inaugurating* of that reversal and a manifesting of delivering power. The miracles are not the point, but serve as evidence for and an illustration of a far more comprehensive deliverance that one day will extend across the entire creation. That is in part why the preaching of the kingdom was also called "good news." Jesus' ministry preached and presented a kingdom hope. That hope had made an appearance through Jesus in the exercise of divine power that served as a kind of cosmic email and invitation to share in what God was doing through this chosen one.

So the kingdom teaching of Jesus involved declarations about both his present ministry and the future tied to it. A kingdom long viewed as strictly future and greatly anticipated was being pulled into the present and made initially available in an exercise of redemptive power that showed that the struggle was not merely with flesh and blood, but with principalities and powers. His kingdom, again to use the language of John's Gospel, was not of this world, though it was breaking into that world. Though it would come in comprehensive power one day, it was invading now in Jesus. Humanity could experience that victory over Satan, both now and in the age to come.

All of this explains a remark that John the Baptist made about "the stronger one to come." Though the remark does not invoke kingdom imagery directly, it does invoke messianic imagery and is a part of a ministry where John was preparing people for the coming of the Lord and the kingdom's approach. How would one know that Messiah had come (and thus that this kingdom promise was arriving)? Luke 3:15–17 answers the question. John explains that he was not the Christ, but that the Christ's coming would be marked out by a baptism different from his own, one not with water but with Spirit and fire. So the new era would be marked by a dispensing of the Spirit, a dispersal of enablement and a mark of incorporation into the redeemed community of God. The kingdom is ultimately future, but its formation began with the powerful preaching and work of Jesus drawing citizens to the new rule he was in the process of establishing.

Defining the Kingdom

The remaining issues I shall cover more quickly as the basic foundation is now laid to address them. The texts already covered on the presence of the kingdom make it clear that the kingdom can be defined in terms of the dynamic or active presence of God's power and authority. God's rule is expressed in terms of the exercise of his authority. Thus, Jesus' miracles evidence the inbreaking of God's authority, the presence of his power. Jesus' presence means the kingdom's presence. We would also suggest that the mediation of the Spirit through Jesus is evidence of the presence of this rule, as the giving of the Spirit is a key messianic work. This idea is not explicit in the Gospel material, but it will show up in Acts and the Epistles. Most New Testament scholars accept this "dynamic" element as central to Jesus' teaching.[35] More discussed is the issue of realm.[36]

This problem is exceedingly complex, for once again Jesus' use shows a variety of contexts. First, several texts indicate that Israel or activity associated with Israel are an element in kingdom teaching. I already have noted the choosing of the Twelve (Matt. 10:2–4 par.), and Jesus' remark about the disciples sitting on the twelve thrones over Israel (Luke 22:28–30 par.). Other texts indicate that the disciples, after hearing all of Jesus' teaching, still expected a role for the nation of Israel. Acts 1:6 has the disciples ask if Jesus would now be restoring the kingdom to Israel. Jesus, though he does not directly answer the question of when, does not reject the premise of the question. In fact, two chapters later in Acts 3:21, Peter makes the point that the "times of refreshing" that Jesus will bring on his return, a kingdom theme, are

---

35. A key work arguing this emphasis is Bruce Chilton, *God in Strength: Jesus' Announcement of the Kingdom*, Studien zum Neuen Testament und seiner Umwelt B/1 (Freistadt: Plöchl, 1979).

36. It is often said by older dispensational writers that George Ladd denied the presence of an idea of realm in Jesus' teaching because Ladd highlighted the dynamic force. But this characterization is wrong. Ladd simply argued that the dynamic sense was the more prevalent idea in the sayings. See *The Presence of the Future*, 195–205.

already described in the Scripture.[37] Thus, the eschatological dimensions of the kingdom hope emerging from the Old Testament seem affirmed in this Spirit-inspired speech. One final text is associated with the celebratory banquet imagery. When Jesus refuses the wine at the Last Supper and notes that he will not partake of the Passover again until he does so in the context of fulfillment in the kingdom (Luke 22:16–18), he suggests a day when the celebration will commemorate the completion of promise with a celebration rooted in Old Testament expression. Whatever additional elements there are to the kingdom realm—and there are additional elements as we shall see—they do not preclude an element involving the old Israelite expression of hope.

Other texts suggest the language of gathering to a specific place. Luke 13:28–29 looks to people coming from "east and west" to sit at the table with the patriarchs. My only point here is that this is standard Jewish imagery.[38] Matthew 8:11 is the parallel. It suggests that the surprising inclusion of Gentiles is in view, but not the entire exclusion of Israel. After all, the disciples represented a remnant of the nation.

Another key set of texts is Matthew 11:12 and Luke 16:16. Many treat these as parallels and point to the Matthean conflict imagery of men seeking to take the kingdom by violence as key to both texts.[39] My own suspicion is that Luke does not parallel Matthew's conflict imagery here, but points to the persuasion of preaching in his version of the image. However this exegetical debate does not alter the key point for us here, namely, that the kingdom is a "thing" contended over (or preached about), even in the present. The image is of a realm introduced into the world and as an object of contention (and discussion) within it.

Another unusual use is in Luke 23:42–43. Here the thief on the cross asks to be remembered when Jesus comes into his kingdom. The request, understood in normal Jewish terms, looks to the future. Jesus' reply brings the future into the present yet again. For he tells the thief that this very day he will

---

37. It is texts like these that preclude any appeal to a "sociology of knowledge" as a way of saying the prophets were limited in what language they could use to express what later developed in their expression of hope. Not only does this seem to affirm that the Old Testament does not mean what it appeared to mean at the time it was given, but the question could be raised, why limit such a hermeneutical category to the Old Testament? A denial of such an appeal means that Israel is a reference to national Israel in such texts and God's commitment is affirmed for them in such texts.

38. See Allison, *Jesus of Nazareth*, 141–43, though he dismisses the significance of the Matthean context too easily to deny a Gentile dimension to this image.

39. In Matthew 11 I have in mind the second half of the verse where men are contending over the kingdom, part of the battle motif. In the first half of the verse, the reference to βιάζεται is disputed. It either refers to the kingdom suffering violence, a reading that matches the latter half of the verse, or to the kingdom advancing. Even if the idea of advance is present, it probably still refers to the in-breaking of the kingdom moving into the world, as opposed to the idea of a continuously ascending advance.

be with Jesus in paradise. Though the reply does not use the term kingdom, the idea of paradise is a part of that hope in Judaism. There is a sense where Jesus reveals a current, cosmic claim and dimension to the kingdom when it comes to the issue of death. This appears to be another fresh dimension to Jesus' teaching.

Finally stand the host of texts looking to the judgment of the end, where the Son of Man carries out the eschatological assessment of humanity. I highlight one dimension of one text, the Matthean version of the wheat and darnel (Matt. 13:24–30, 36–43). Here Jesus notes the field is "the world." In that world, good seed has been sown, but the evil one has also sown what has come up as "weeds." Jesus will not sort them out until the "end of the age." Now my point here is that the kingdom, though present in the activity and presence of those sown by the Son of Man (Jesus!), makes a claim on all humanity for which each one is one day accountable in the judgment at the end. Thus, there is an aspect of the realm of the kingdom that extends beyond the believing people of God and makes a claim on all humanity in the world, even from the present "sowing" (i.e., preaching) of the kingdom.[40]

Thus, the kingdom in terms of realm operates at several levels at once, depending on the context. The realm in terms of its comprehensive presence looks to the future and the comprehensive establishment of peace and fellowship, after a purging judgment. This realm appears to include hopes of old from Israel, and yet it also looks to far more—a comprehensive exercise of authority over the whole of creation, including the blessing of many from outside of Israel.

However, there is also a sense in which we can talk about a realm in the present. First, an operative but invisible realm is at work in the community Jesus is forming, as the power and presence of God is at work among those "sown by the Son of Man." I call it an "invisible" realm because, as the rest of the New Testament indicates, it is a power of God working in the midst of Jesus' absence and in anticipation of his visible return and rule. It is the community that recognizes and responds to Jesus as Lord, Son of Man, Christ. It is the place where he is Head. Second, there is a "claimed, potential" realm, in that the kingdom makes a claim on the entirety of humanity in anticipation of its eventual scope.[41] That claim is the foundation for the judgment to come. It is a basis for taking the gospel into the world. It justifies the preaching of the gospel of the authoritative Jesus to every tribe and nation. In my own view,

40. In other words, this text is not about some professing Christendom within what became the church, but is about the Word's work in the world and Christ's claim upon it through his preached Word.

41. Note how my reading does not limit the authority here to "Christendom." The claim is far more comprehensive in scope than this. The weeds in the world are not a reference to professing Christians, but to humanity at large in the world, including those outside of the sown Word Jesus brings.

it establishes an accountability for every person before the one true God and his chosen One, so that there is only one way to God. In both the invisible presence of God's authority in the reformed community and the claimed, potential presence of divine authority in the challenge to all to respond to God, the future is pulled into the present by the preaching, presence, and challenge of the Son of Man. Responding to him brings one into this new realm, though in other contexts one can speak of entering or inheriting this kingdom later, when it is ultimately fully realized. The exceptional text with the thief on the cross shows that ultimately what is at stake is eternal presence and fellowship with God in unending and renewed life. This final text represents another foretaste of the ultimate, comprehensive victory to come that will be the kingdom "fully and coercively" present, the hope that the majority of kingdom texts in the Gospels affirm.

Thus, the kingdom is about the powerful, even transforming presence of God's rule through Christ. That rule is expressed today in the community of those whom he "planted," what became the church. But the kingdom is bigger than the church. Its presence now is but a precursor to a more substantial presence in the future. Jesus will redeem and judge what is being claimed now, when the authority of the Son of Man will judge humanity and bless those who sit with him at the table. Then the kingdom will fully show itself with traits the Scripture of Israel had long promised, along with features of rule Jesus himself revealed. The kingdom "invisible," "claiming and potential," and "fully and coercively" present in the future summarizes the way the issue of realm is treated in kingdom texts. In other words, kingdom texts treat Israel, the church, the world, and the cosmos as a whole, depending on which passage we are considering. Here the "tensive" character of the term *kingdom* becomes obvious. The later New Testament did much to fill in the details of what is outlined here in Jesus' teaching. For Jesus' teaching set certain trajectories in kingdom teaching that the rest of New Testament revelation develops.

In the Gospels, one final issue remains, namely the connection between righteousness and the kingdom, or what has been called the kingdom and ethics. It is to this topic we now turn.

The Kingdom and Ethics

In the end, the transformation associated with the inbreaking of the kingdom is not merely an abstract exercise in theology or definition. It is designed to impact life. Thus, the connection between kingdom and living or kingdom and ethics needs attention.[42] In this era, the kingdom involves the inaugural

---

42. This section is indebted to three studies: Perrin, *The Kingdom of God in the Teaching of Jesus*, 201–6; Ladd, *The Presence of the Future*, 278–304; and McKnight, *A New Vision for Israel*, 156–237.

inbreaking of God's power, presence, and rule among a people he has claimed as his own, forming them into a community that looks forward one day to the total inbreaking of his authority expressed throughout the world. Those who are his have acknowledged their need for God and his provision by faith alone. As a result, they have entered into an enduring relationship with God. That relationship entails a call from God on the life of the disciple. Thus, in a sense, all aspects of Jesus' teaching about discipleship involve teaching about the kingdom and ethics. In sum, what Jesus presents is the idea that the inbreaking of God's rule into one's life demands a total response to that rule. However, by means of God's grace, the disciple is enabled to move into that demand and grow in one's experience of it. Relationship to that rule is to be more important than family, possessions, vocation, even life itself. Whether Jesus alludes to the fact that his family is made up of those who do God's will, mentions that one must hate the family for his sake, teaches that possessions are to be given to the poor, or mentions the need to bear one's cross, he is pointing out that no demand on a person's soul is greater than the one made by God in the context of his kingdom program. It is the greatness of the kingdom that creates the totality of its call for faithfulness.

To develop this area, I wish to examine four themes: faith/repentance; following at all costs from within; imitation in the context of reconciliation, love, and service; and reward. I would wish to argue that any treatment of kingdom that does move into this area of practical application has failed to appreciate a major goal of the kingdom program as seen in the New Testament.

(1) The theme of faith/repentance is seen in two key elements.[43]

First, there is the preparation that John the Baptist brought in declaring that the kingdom draws near. This preparation highlighted the preaching of a baptism of repentance, a baptism that included a concrete call for turning expressed in practice toward others (Luke 3:10–14). This idea will be taken up more fully when we get to the theme of imitation, but its groundwork was laid in John's initial, preparatory declaration as an Elijah-like figure. His work involved a call to reconciliation where people were implored to turn back to God. Included within this turning was a bringing of sons back to their fathers

---

43. I group these terms together because they work as equally adequate summary terms for the appropriate response to the message. However, they are not exact synonyms. Repentance looks at that response from the angle of where one starts (there is a change of direction), while faith highlights where one ends up (trusting God). Such terms overlap without being exact overlays, much like a Venn diagram in math. Thus they can serve as equivalents for each other, while focusing on distinct aspects of the fundamental response. Baptism and indwelling are similar. Baptism points to washing, while indwelling points to what results from the washing, the entering in of the Spirit. In Old Testament conceptual terms, forgiveness yields cleansing (or washing) so the Spirit may come in and indwell (Ezek. 36:24–27). God cleanses so he can enter into a clean space. Careful attention to such lexical relationships adds depth to the text's message.

and the disobedient back to the wise (Luke 1:16–17). Reconciliation with God shows itself in reconciliation with others.

The second element is Jesus' teaching that to enter the kingdom one must be like a child (Matt. 18:2–4). Here there is a humility and dependence that is invoked. In fact, it is humility that defines "greatness" in the kingdom.[44] In this context, it is clear that it is not the kingdom in the future that is addressed, because the whole of the chapter is looking at relationships in the newly formed community (see Matt. 18:17). Such faith in God extends to a recognition that even daily needs are in his hands and that he will care for his own (Matt. 6:11, 25–34; Luke 11:3; 12:22–31). Faith ultimately is a humble recognition that one needs God and so moves to trust him, relying on his rule and provision. It is in the context of relying on God's provision that the gospel moves in a direction we are most familiar with: the Pauline emphasis on the work of the cross in relationship to sin. However, one should not forget that alongside that fundamental provision of God comes an enablement of provision and power through the Spirit that changes one's identity and allows the disciple to live in a way that honors God and reflects sonship with him. In fact, Paul's burden in Romans 1–8 is to make this very point about the gospel.

(2) Following at all costs from within raises the issue of how "demanding" Jesus' call to discipleship was. It was a cost to be fully counted and not entered into lightly or unadvisedly, to steal a phrase from the initiation of another important relationship (Luke 14:25–35). Thus, the call of many disciples notes how they left their nets or tax collection booths to follow him (Mark 1:16–20 par.; Luke 5:27–28). Jesus expresses it as hating or leaving mother and father for his or the kingdom's sake (Luke 18:29; Matt. 10:37; 19:29). It means hating worldly gain (Matt. 6:24; Luke 12:13–21; 16:13). It involves a carrying of the cross, even daily, even at the risk of life (Matt. 10:38–39; Luke 9:23). The assumption in all of this is that the way will not be easy, nor is the road one of powerful triumph. Victory comes through suffering and rejection like that Jesus himself would experience. Jesus sought to reveal the whole program to the multitudes. He desired that they understand what the relationship with God they were entering into involved. God's rule was not selective; it makes claims on the whole of life. So Jesus defines the members of his family as those who do God's will (Mark 3:31–35 par.; 10:29–30 par.). Sons and daughters respond to the Father. They "seek his kingdom" and rest by faith in his care (Luke 12:31), what Matthew's version calls seeking "first his kingdom and his righteousness" (Matt. 6:33).

44. It is probably this note of humility that explains Jesus' focus on reaching out to those on the "fringe" of society—the poor and the tax collectors. Here are people who more easily understand their need for God as seeming "outsiders." It is clear that Jesus focused his message toward such people (Luke 4:16–18).

This following also entails a response from within. Mark 7:1–23 shows this clearly when Jesus defines defiling in terms that look at "what is inside" the person. The list highlights those acts that defile as primarily associated with relational categories. The six antitheses of the Sermon on the Mount press the law in this inward direction. It is not only murder but anger, nor is it only adultery but lust, that violates God's righteous standard (Matt. 5:21–48). This internal feature stands at the heart of kingdom spirituality.[45]

This internal feature is central to what goes into spiritual formation. That formation is spiritual because God calls and goes to work on the inner person, on our spirit, through His Spirit. This also is not a mere triumphalism, as Paul makes clear, since we groan for the completion of redemption in the salvation to come (Rom. 8). In the meantime, the call is to be faithful and walk by the Spirit.

(3) The following leads naturally to the theme of imitation. The child is to be like the Father. One dimension of this concept is the theme of reconciliation. We noted reconciliation as a defining quality of a "prepared" people for God. In responding to the Baptist, people were accepting the call of God to be a reflection of him and his holiness. What God would provide through the Messiah, as John noted, would be a grater baptism of the Spirit, one of the great provisions of the new era. That Spirit, by his grace, enables the transformation God's kingdom calls for from those who trust God to provide for their spiritual well being and deliverance. Jesus makes the same point in the upper room (John 14–16). So Jesus issues a call to love and serve that is an imitation of God's own character (Luke 6:27–36). This extends even to loving one's enemies. Jesus holds up his own life as the example to be imitated (Mark 10:41–45; John 13:1–17). Such a character is revealed in the Beatitudes (Matt. 5:3–12; Luke 6:20–23). In fact, it is character like this that is salt and light in the world, reflecting the call of what the kingdom citizen is to be (Matt. 5:14–16). So the disciple is to show mercy (Luke 10:29–37). This is why Jesus responded to the Jew who quoted the two great commandments of loving God and loving one's neighbor as "not far from the kingdom" (Mark 12:28–34). It is also why the commandment to "love one another" was the sign that would show them to be Jesus' disciples (John 13:34–35). A major goal of the kingdom was to produce children in kind, which is why the standard for character is so high and the demand of the kingdom is so great (Luke 6:36; Matt. 5:48).

(4) The kingdom is not without its rewards. Primary is vindication in judgment and unending relationship with God as represented in the image of the banquet table. The Father sees the sacrifice and honors it. Such is

45. For a fine discussion of this theme in light of the Sermon on the Mount, see Dallas Willard, *The Divine Conspiracy: Rediscovering Our Hidden Life in God* (San Francisco: Harper, 1998).

the promise of Jesus to an uncertain Peter who desperately asks who can be saved in the midst of a discussion about how hard it is for the rich to enter the kingdom (Luke 18:23–30). Jesus' reply reassures Peter and those he represents. Jesus summarizes the reward that accompanies participation in the kingdom, saying, "I tell you the truth, no one who has left home or wife or brothers or parents, or children for the sake of the Kingdom of God will fail to receive many times as much in this age and, in the age to come, eternal life." The Marcan parallel, which speaks of the gospel and not the kingdom—showing the inherent relationship between the two—adds the note that what is received in the present age is "homes, brothers, sisters, mothers, children and fields—and with them persecutions." Matthew 25:31–46 shows that the Son of Man's return in his glory brings with him the vindication of those who have reached out to him. The reward noted in the Beatitudes also underscores that though there is suffering and sacrifice now, there will be great reward. Here again an appreciation for what the future brings impacts how we see ourselves in the present and calls us to live in light of what the future will be. The future calls on us in the present to reflect as light what we are becoming and will be. The meek inherit the earth, but they also are to illuminate it. With our security resting in God's power, presence, and hope, the rule of God can bring us to be what God made us to be and redeemed us to become. This is precisely why one of the more important parables about the kingdom pictures God's Word about the kingdom as a seed that is planted and takes root in good soil and whose goal is to produce fruitfulness (Matt. 13:1–9, 18–23 par.). Viewed from the human perspective, it is the goal of the kingdom to produce sons and daughters of God who are fruitful for him.[46]

One other dimension of reward is less clearly developed and is of lesser significance in Jesus' preaching than the theme of vindication and eternal reception. It is the idea of the future exercise of responsibility for a faithful stewardship. Only a few passages hint at this idea. It is suggested by the note of expanded responsibility in the parable of the talents (Matt. 25:14–30) and the idea of having responsibility over cities in Luke 19:17–19. The rewarded servants are "set over much" for their faithfulness. The images do appear within the construct of the parable, but they seem to indicate something in relationship to reward for stewardship. The reward for the blessed servant in Luke 12:43–44 looks to go in a similar direction. It may also be indicated in the note whether to entrust more to a steward who is irresponsible in Luke 16:11–12. The sum of this teaching suggests a period when the kingdom will still be at work in the exercise of its rule, themes that may relate to the idea of an intermediate kingdom.

---

46. In Pauline terms, this is expressed in terms of the work of God's grace in the key mission passage of Titus 2:11–14.

It is time to pull together much of what has been said. So I will now review the description of the kingdom, noting especially what other terms intimately connect to it. This section is important, for it will provide the bridge to the rest of the New Testament teaching on the kingdom.

Beyond the Term *Kingdom*

One of the difficult things about pointing to a concept being at work in association with a biblical term is being sure that the association is legitimate. In this section, I want to suggest other issues that connect to the kingdom of God theme. The effect of this is to expand the texts that relate to the kingdom theme, but the justification for doing so needs attention, as some argue that tying the kingdom to Messiah or to the present era reads into the text rather than reading from it.

The inclusion of the work of Messiah within the scope of kingdom teaching is challenged by some who wish to make reign language tied to the Christ exclusively future.[47] However, it is Luke that makes the connection by associating the explicit teaching of John the Baptist as he proclaims the nearness of the kingdom to remarks he makes about recognizing when the Christ comes and on what basis (Luke 3:15–17). To his Jewish audience, this association of messianic work with kingdom work and presence would be entirely natural. One of the signs of the kingdom, or the eschaton, would be the superior baptism that would indicate that the Messiah had come. The allusion here for John, given that he speaks as one picking up the prophetic hope, would be the promise of the new covenant. Here forgiveness and a work of God from within are promised. The imagery reflects the images of purity from Judaism. Only a washed and clean vessel can be a place that God inhabits. So the provision of forgiveness and the washing that is pictured in it cleanse the vessel so God may enter in. It is in this sense John "prepares" the people for the Lord's coming.

---

47. This is especially the case if one defines the presence of the kingdom and ruling as meaning coercive rule. For this view, see Mark Saucy, *The Kingdom of God in the Teaching of Jesus in 20th Century Theology* (Dallas: Word, 1997), 342–47. I shall argue that rule includes things other than coercive rule, such as delivering and providing pardon and establishing grounds for citizenship. Saucy rejects this claim on the grounds of three arguments. (1) The concept of reign is not unknown to the Bible, so one cannot load the terminology with our own ideas as he argues I am doing. But this is not what is being done. The kingdom terminology does appear with reference to Jesus' current activity/position in Rev. 1:5–6 and 1 Cor. 15:25. The image of Jesus as Shepherd is a ruling image (Ezek. 34; John 10). (2) Christ's present exalted function is not one of rule but intercession. However, this is not an either/or. Hebrews 1 notes the rule of Jesus and appeals to Ps. 110:1 in setting up the declaration of Jesus as an interceding figure on the basis of a Melchizedekian priesthood, a priesthood that is *both* regal and priestly. (3) The New Testament associates the reign of Christ with the reign of the saints with him. This is true ultimately, but it begs the question of whether Christ initially rules before he shares that rule with the saints.

It is precisely this promise with this conclusion that Peter preaches in the great sermon at Pentecost (Acts 2:14–41). Peter also refers back to this base event to determine that Gentiles are rightly included in the community by God (Acts 10:34–43; 11:13–18).[48] This baptism marks a definitive sign of Messiah's work and the presence of eschatological hope. In the Spirit is the down payment of the further kingdom work of God, representing his presence and rule, what Paul simply calls "our inheritance" (Eph. 1:13–14). In this cluster of concepts, one can find the themes not only of Messiah and eschaton but also of salvation and even gospel.

Paul's preaching of the work of the Spirit as a part of new covenant realization and Hebrews' emphasis on the forgiveness of sons coming through the promised Messiah fit in here (2 Cor. 3–4; Heb. 1; 8–10). Here is the inaugural era of promise, which Jesus described as kingdom. Here is why Paul could describe the gospel as that promised to come through the Son of David in Scripture and as the "power of God for salvation" in Romans 1:16–17 (RSV) as an introduction to Romans 1–8. That book presents the work through the exalted Son both in terms of forgiveness, sonship, and Spirit enablement as the essence of the gospel, a reversal of the penalty and power of sin. It is what Paul calls elsewhere a rescue "out of the authority of darkness" and a transfer "to the kingdom of His beloved Son" (Col. 1:13 NASB). Here the work of Jesus as the Christ brings pardon, deliverance, and sonship-citizenship—all regal works of messianic authority.

The kingdom, both in its inception where rescue takes place and at its culmination when victory becomes complete, is part of a great cosmic battle and reversal against sin and Satan. That this kingdom program over which Christ is currently ruling (1 Cor. 15:25; Rev. 1:5–6) is tied to and related to the ultimate realization of the kingdom is seen in 1 Corinthians 15:26–28, where Paul describes the ultimate giving over of this same kingdom to the Father at the end. Seen in a larger theological context, this victory represents the reversal of the fall's effects and evidence of a cosmic battle introduced in Genesis 3. It is why the imagery of Revelation 21–22 and the new heaven and new earth looks back to the Garden of Eden and forward to the New Jerusalem. The Book of Revelation is about the completion of the kingdom program. In the return, the kingdom of the world has become the kingdom of "our Lord and of his Christ" (Rev. 11:15).

In my view, this return includes setting up an intermediate kingdom before the new heaven and earth, because of the way I read Revelation 20. It is here where the things said about Israel and her future role in a kingdom existing in the midst of the nations and within this history fit within the promise of God from both the Old Testament and the New.

---

48. Note the allusion back to Luke 3:15–17 in Acts 11:16, as the indication of promise realized.

For two reasons, much less of this national role is made in the New Testament. First, it is assumed as a given, having already been revealed and treated in detail. Acts 3:19–23 points us back to Moses and the prophets for the "rest of the story." Second, the more comprehensive New Testament concern is the eventual total victory Jesus brings to the whole of humanity and the creation. This relativizes to a degree the importance of national Israel's role in the plan.

Still it makes more hermeneutical sense for the theological unity of Scripture that the New Testament complements what God has committed himself to in promise in the Old. Maintaining a role for national Israel within the kingdom program seems to make the most coherent sense of Paul's argument in Romans 11, where Israel is not a reference to the church, but is treated in distinction from the current structure through which blessing is preached. Seeing a hope for national Israel (as well as for the nations), with Christ functioning as her Messiah in the future kingdom program, and at the same time affirming the fundamental unity of Jew and Gentile in Christ, is a comprehensive approach to the difficult unity-diversity question that plagues our eschatological debates. There is soteriological unity (all are one in Christ and share in one unified plan), while there is structural distinction in the different dispensations of God's administration (period of Israel, period of the Church, period of the consummated kingdom moving to the new heaven and earth). This approach to the kingdom plan is better than separating it into totally distinct programs as traditional dispensationalism does. It is also better than merging it, as covenant theology does, so that the promises made to national and ethnic Israel cease to operate for these original recipients of God's covenental promise of grace. Such a covenantal merger conflicts with God's faithfulness that Paul wishes to defend in Romans 9–11. The apostle maintains hope that one day all Israel will be saved, in contrast to her current rejection of Jesus.[49] What God has started in bringing Jew and Gentile together he will complete one day for both groups.

49. This paragraph outlines my view on a major debate in eschatology that has been a part of the evangelical scene for a long time. Joyfully, we may be coming to a time when evangelicals can discuss these differences calmly as is evidenced in the discussion between Craig Blaising (premillennialism), Robert Strimple (amillennialism), and Ken Gentry (postmillennialism) in a Counterpoints volume I edited, *Three Views on the Millennium and Beyond* (Grand Rapids: Zondervan, 1999). Two points distinguish progressive dispensationalism from covenant theology, including historical premillennialism, though many erroneously wish to connect the two. They are the hermeneutical points made about the significant, *complementary* role of the New Testament and the belief in a continuation of hope for *national* Israel, not just for ethnic Israel. It is the maintenance of a hope for national Israel that makes progressive dispensationalism dispensational. Also dispensational is the desire to read the Old Testament texts about national Israel as not excluding her by whatever is said about promise in the New Testament. Ironically, in light of the debate between covenental theology and dispensationalists, it is in order to defend God's *covenant* faithfulness and program that dispensationalism holds out for a future for national Israel. For more on this question, see my "Why I Am a Dispensationalist with a Small 'd,'" *JETS* 41 (1998): 383–96.

So on the other end of the kingdom calendar is the work of the returning Son of Man to be the vindicating "judge of the living and the dead" (Acts 10:42; Matt. 25:31–46). He is the one who welcomes his own into the "prepared for you Kingdom." In this kingdom is found not only fellowship but "eternal life" (25:46). It is to this great vindicating moment that the kingdom is always aimed, so that the concept is always looking to that bright future that is the kingdom come in full.

It is this cluster of concepts around the kingdom on which the Epistles draw as they make the point that the era of our rule with Christ has not yet come (1 Cor. 4:8). It is why the author of Hebrews, while noting that all things are not yet submitted to the feet of humans as God had promised in Psalm 8:5–7, extols that we do see Jesus through the suffering of his death crowned with glory and honor, looking for the completion of what God has begun (Heb. 2:5–9). It is also why Peter, using the language of Psalm 110:1, argues that Jesus, as a result of that exaltation, is already "at the right hand of God, with angels, authorities, and powers subject to him" (1 Peter 3:22 RSV). Who is right: the incompleteness of what Jesus has done, as Hebrews presents it, or an already extant cosmic subjection, as Peter claims? As with the other tensions noted in the discussion of the kingdom, this is not an either-or, but a both-and. The victory is obtained already, but the full manifestation of that victory awaits and is yet to come.

What Jesus has brought is only a foretaste of what is to come. In that realization is the explanation of why the term *kingdom* becomes less prominent in the rest of the New Testament. It is to that question that I now turn.

Kingdom outside the Gospels

It has always been a point for discussion that the term *kingdom* is not so prevalent in the epistolary materials. For example, the term *basileia* appears 121 times in the synoptics, but only 5 times in John, 8 times in Acts, 14 times in Paul, 5 times in the General Epistles and 9 times in Revelation. Some, including myself, have argued in the past that the reason for this involved hesitation about kingdom language in a Roman context, but this really does not work as an explanation when Jesus is being confessed as Lord or Christ by the church.[50] A better solution is found in three observations.

First, kingdom is present in many other concepts that show up in this material, so that the concept is much more prevalent than mere lexical counting shows. Analogies for this exist. In the Hebrew Scriptures, kingdom is not that prominent a lexical term, but it is a central concept. Jesus' use of the Son of

---

50. So George Ladd, *Theology of the New Testament*, rev. ed. (Grand Rapids: Eerdmans, 1993), 450. Though there is some merit in noting that the predominantly Gentile audience in the Epistles may be a factor, this cannot be a complete explanation for a movement that confesses Jesus as possessing divine authority.

Man is also analogous. By the time of the Epistles, other christological terms covering the same ground became more common (for reasons that still are not clear to us). However, the authority affirmed in the title was still prevalent in the early church, possibly because the alternatives had less ambiguity. So in the epistolary material, themes tied to deliverance operate as equivalents for the current realization of promise. For Paul, this involves themes tied to salvation and Jesus' Lordship. For John, it involves his presentation of eternal life.[51] The shift was a natural one. Rather than proclaiming what had begun to come, the early church highlighted who brought it, personalizing the claim and making it more intimate.[52]

Second, it should also be noted that dividing the Epistles from the Gospels to make this observation is a somewhat artificial exercise. The Gospels are early church documents, presenting the case for Jesus' salvific claims. Though they treat earlier events in a pre-cross setting, they express theology as it was seen in the earliest communities. If there is a place where kingdom declaration should be prominent, it is here. The Epistles, as occasional documents treating internal issues in the community, are less likely to make a point of something its readers have already embraced.

Third, where kingdom does appear explicitly, it fits the future-present emphases already noted above. The kingdom points to an entity coming in the future when the righteous shall be vindicated and unrighteousness judged by a returning, authoritative Jesus, winner of the cosmic battle so painfully evident in the presence of sin. Yet elements of inauguration show up in this usage. So Paul can speak on the one hand of "inheriting the kingdom," looking to its future coming (1 Cor. 6:9–10; 15:50; Gal. 5:21), while also noting that the kingdom today is "not a matter of talk but of power" (1 Cor. 4:20). Nor does it consist of "eating and drinking, but of righteousness, peace and joy in the Holy Spirit" (Rom. 14:17). It is God who "calls you into his kingdom and glory" (1 Thess. 2:12). His laborers work in the service of God's kingdom (Col. 4:11). Acts notes how Philip and Paul preach the kingdom (Acts 8:12; 28:23, 31). On the other hand, Paul can speak in Acts of "entering the kingdom" through many trials, which is a future reference (Acts

51. George Caird, *New Testament Theology*, ed. Larry Hurst (Oxford: Clarendon, 1994), 131–32, says, "To see the Kingdom of God, to enter it, to be born of the Spirit, and to have eternal life are interchangeable descriptions of the one experience of salvation which is to become available to inquirers like Nicodemus only when Jesus has been 'lifted up' ([Jn.] 3:15). Jesus is indeed already King of Israel (1:50; 12:13, 15; cf. 20:31), but not in the only sense his enemies could understand. His sovereignty (18:36) is not derived from military strength and popular acclaim on which political power depends; it is derived from God who has entrusted to His Son the exercise of His own kingly authority."

52. Leonhard Goppelt, *Theology of the New Testament*, vol. 2., trans. John Alsup (Grand Rapids: Eerdmans, 1982), 17–18. Donald Guthrie, *New Testament Theology* (Downers Grove, Ill.: InterVarsity, 1981), 427, says in discussing Paul's use of kingdom that it is "rather assumed than specifically stated."

14:22; cf. 2 Peter 1:11). Yet Hebrews speaks of our "receiving" an unshakable kingdom in a context where we have already come to Mount Zion, the heavenly Jerusalem (Heb. 12:22–28). We already noted above the citation in Colossians 1:13 and 1 Corinthians 15:24–28, where rescue brings one into the kingdom and Jesus' rule proceeds until its completion. Revelation 1:6 makes the same "already" point, as Christ "has made us a Kingdom, priests to his God and Father." We are part, even now, of a kingdom program that one day will be manifested for all the world to see. The kingdom of God is ultimately about God's rule, power, and presence reasserted in a fallen world. The kingdom reflects God's victory over sin on behalf of a needy humanity. We are his trophy case (Eph. 2:7; 3:10). To recast another saying from another context, "All the world is his stage, and we are merely players in it." Only in this case, what God has formed in the church and what he will do in the ultimate expression of the kingdom shows the transforming power that comes through Christ. We have a significant, lead role as witnesses of his way and presence. This brings me to the significance of kingdom for the church, for the hope and essence of the kingdom lead us into its ethical implications and call.

So What?

From what has been said, the kingdom is both distinct from and intimately associated with the church. The kingdom is more than the church, but the church is contained within the kingdom program.[53]

53. For another, more dichotomous, dispensational approach also articulating a relationship between kingdom and church, see Charles Ryrie, *Dispensationalism* (Chicago: Moody, 1995), 135. On p. 142, his more traditional dispensational view is contrasted with a progressive view this way: "Though emphasizing the distinctiveness of the church, the dispensationalist also recognizes certain relationships that the church sustains. He does not say there is no kingdom today but insists that it is not the fulfillment of Old Testament kingdom promises nor is it the Davidic kingdom inaugurated (as revisionists [i.e., progressives] say)." Ryrie's summary fails to note the diversity within the traditional view, as Stan Toussaint argues that the kingdom is not present in any sense today (see n. 6 above). Ryrie's summary does show, however, the traditional dispensational view that the kingdom today is unattached to the promises of old. It is a distinct kingdom program. Progressive dispensationalism rejects this basic premise of dichotomy in the kingdom promise. The dispensational distinctive between Israel and the church, progressives argue, does not involve the kingdom program or soteriological categories. Gal. 3:16–29 and the Rom. 11 olive tree prevent making such a distinction, as do the various already-noted texts connecting kingdom, Messiah, and the promise from the Hebrew Scriptures. For progressives, the dispensational distinction between Israel and the church applies to the structures through which God administers that salvation. Israel is not the church, nor will the kingdom to come be the church. Israel is not the kingdom to come, as that kingdom will entail far more than Israel, though national Israel will have a central role in that kingdom. This will fulfill all the promises a faithful God made to her in the Old Testament. The church glorified will share in the administration of the kingdom to come, but the kingdom itself is also larger than the church. In my view, a value of dispensationalism is highlighting these distinctions between Israel, the church, and the kingdom to come within God's plan in such a way that the role for national Israel is not lost. It is in this sense—articulating a future role for national Israel and keeping her existence structurally distinct from the church—that progressive dispensationalism differs from covenant premillennialism.

There is an ongoing progression to the movement of God's unified kingdom program as it moves through the dispensations or eras of its administration. The program both propels us toward the realization of full hope and pulls that future into the present as a glimpse of what is to come. So how do we as community fit into that dialectic between present and future kingdom?

God has invested in the church. His investment is the indwelling Spirit, mediated through Christ and given in the context of forgiveness and promise, an eschatological down payment on the rest of the hope. The church, then, is the beneficiary of God's power and presence. Satan and sin stand defeated, as the confident language of Romans 8 declares. Sonship means we are able to walk responsively to the presence of God's rule, reflecting his character. In the age to come, the returning Son of Man will make all of this authority clear to the entire cosmos. Those who confess Jesus to be their Savior and Lord are recognizing this authority that God has invested in his mediator. If being prepared for the kingdom community in the time of John the Baptist meant turning to God in the context of reconciliation and being reconciled with others, then the call of the indwelt community is to display the presence of such transformed relationships before a needy world. This fundamental exhortation appears in a text like Ephesians 2:11–22.

A major responsibility we have in witnessing to the world is that the quality of our own relationships, especially to one another, should show itself to be decidedly different from the world. Jesus' "new commandment" to love one another "as I have loved you" is really a kingdom command. Sacrifice and service stand at the heart of relational dynamics. If the world is to understand community in a context of loving God and relating to others, the place it should be most visible in this cosmos is in how those in his community relate to God, each other, and the world. If we walk by the Spirit and manifest the fruit of the Spirit, then the world should be witness to a sneak preview of the way things will be in the end, an audiovisual incarnation of what God transforming lives means. A glimpse of the future will be pulled into the present to the glory of God. Thus, the quality of our own communities, and their integrity, should be priorities for the church.[54] Then not only will our proclamation point to the kingdom and its hope to come, it will be painted as a living

---

54. This is an important priority in light of the tensions of trying to reach out to a fallen world. We are called to witness to the world and the quality of that witness is impacted by our own integrity and the strength of our own illustration of our claims to know the way to God. We are to serve and love the world, even as we challenge it with the claims of Christ and the hopes of transformation that are only realized through him, not through some other political structure. But those kingdom claims are best witnessed to when they are visibly operative within his community rather than imposed on unredeemed unbelievers. This means that our moral and political battles must be undertaken with an appreciation that God calls us to challenge people through inviting them to share in his changing of them, not by the mere passing of laws. The latter without the former risks being an empty, symbolic, even futile, exercise.

portrait for all to see. As 1 Peter 2:9–12 so aptly puts it, "But you are a chosen race, a royal priesthood, a holy nation, God's own people, that you may declare the wonderful deeds of him who called you out of darkness into his marvelous light. Once you were no people but now you are God's people; once you had not received mercy, but now you have received mercy. Beloved, I beseech you as aliens and exiles to abstain from the passions of the flesh that wage war against your soul. Maintain good conduct among the Gentiles, so that in case they speak against you as wrongdoers, they may see your good deeds and glorify God on the day of visitation" (RSV).

So the kingdom has come through the Son invading the world. Because he is the Messiah, we confess that he rules. The kingdom's coming now means the defeat of Satan, the forgiveness of God, and the indwelling enablement of the Spirit. And yet, the kingdom comes one day through the returning Son of Man to vindicate the saints and render God just and his promises true. Then Satan and evil will be removed. Even so, come Lord Jesus.

Part 2

Exegetical Studies on Eschatology

3

The Meaning and Identification of God's Eschatological Trumpets

JAMES A. BORLAND

Liberty University

God's eschatological trumpets[1] have probably sparked disproportionately more interest than their scant mention in Scripture might warrant. These trumpets frequently play a role in establishing one's chronology of the endtimes, especially in the debate between pre- and posttribulation rapture proponents.[2] To elucidate this issue more fully we will examine the broad biblical usage of trumpets to ascertain their nature and function. In this way one can better approach the question of the meaning and identification of God's eschatological trumpets.

Trumpets, both human and divine, appear over 140 times in the Bible. The Old Testament contains slightly over 90 percent of these references,[3]

---

1. Matt. 24:31; 1 Cor. 15:52; and 1 Thess. 4:16.

2. Typical of the debate over these trumpets would be Thomas Ice and Kenneth L. Gentry Jr., *The Great Tribulation: Past or Future? Two Evangelicals Debate the Question* (Grand Rapids: Kregel, 1999), 61–65, 157–58; Marvin Rosenthal's *The Pre-Wrath Rapture of the Church* (Nashville: Thomas Nelson, 1990), 187–94, answered by Paul S. Karleen's *The Pre-Wrath Rapture of the Church: Is It Biblical?* (Langhorne, Pa.: BF Press, 1991), 60–62; and earlier as expressed in Gleason L. Archer et al., *Three Views on the Rapture: Pre-, Mid-, or Post-Tribulational?* (Grand Rapids: Academie, 1984), 148–49, 179–81, 230–31; and even earlier by Robert H. Gundry's *The Church and the Tribulation* (Grand Rapids: Zondervan, 1973), 148–51, with a rebuttal by John F. Walvoord's *The Blessed Hope and the Tribulation: A Biblical and Historical Study of Posttribulationism* (Grand Rapids: Zondervan, 1976), 130–32.

3. These are: 30 in Law; 29 in Joshua and Judges; 37 in the rest of the historical books; 7 in poetic, and 27 in prophetic books; totaling 130.

while 11 are in the New Testament.[4] This paper will show how God used and will use trumpets concomitant with some of his divine undertakings. This varied usage argues against being able to couple certain trumpet blasts in the New Testament that might identify whether the rapture will be before, during, or after the great tribulation.

An Old Testament Biblical Theology of Trumpets

Old Testament Words for Trumpet

Four words are used to indicate trumpet in the Hebrew text: (1) *šôpār;* (2) *yôbēl;* (3) *qeren;* and (4) *ḥăṣōṣĕrâ. Šôpār,* the most common term, may be derived from the Akkadian *sapparu,* a wild sheep or ibex, and refers to the use of the horn of such animals.[5] In the Septuagint it is rendered primarily by *salpinx,* and translated in the KJV as either trumpet or, on occasion, cornet.[6]

Yôbēl may be related to the Phoenician *ybl,* a ram. *Yôbēl* is a rare word,[7] and only appears by itself in Exodus 19:13 ("when the trumpet sounds long," NKJV). *Šôpār* and *yôbēl* are used in close proximity in the account of the giving of the law (Exod. 19:13, *yôbēl;* and 19:16 and 19, *šôpār*), and in the same verses of the conquest of Jericho account (Josh. 6:4, 5, 6, 8, and 13). The two words seem to carry about the same meaning.

Qeren is simply an animal horn.[8] The only times *qeren* is used in the context of a sounding instrument are in Joshua 6:5 ("a long blast with the ram's horn," NKJV) and four times in the instrument list of Daniel 3.[9]

Ḥăṣōṣĕrâ is the term applied to the trumpet made by the Levitical priests. It first appears in Numbers 10:2, 8, 9, and 10, but is also seen largely in the temple ceremonies of the Chronicles.[10] The word may be onomatopoetic, where the word's sound

---

4. These are: 1 in the Gospels; 4 in the Epistles; and 6 in the Apocalypse, totaling 11 uses of *salpinx.* There are, however, 12 additional uses of the verb *salpizō,* to sound a trumpet.

5. Gerhard Friedrich, "σάλπιγξ et al.," *TDNT,* ed. G. Kittel, trans. G. W. Bromiley (Grand Rapids: Eerdmans, 1971), 7:76.

6. Trumpet in 68 places, and cornet only in 1 Chron. 15:28; 2 Chron. 15:14; Ps. 98:6 and Hos. 5:8. Regarding cornet, for example, Ps. 98:6 (97:6 in LXX) has *salpinxin* (trumpet) followed by *salpingos keratinēs* (trumpets of a smaller horn).

7. *Yôbēl* occurs twenty-six times in the OT, but is only translated as *trumpet* in Exod. 19:13 and Josh. 6:4, 5, 6, 8 and 13. In Lev. 25 *yôbēl* appears thirteen times, translated as "jubilee," as also six times in Lev. 27 and once in Num. 36:4, because on the day of atonement in the fiftieth year the *trumpet* was to sound throughout the land, indicating a time of release.

8. *Qeren* occurs seventy-four times in the OT Hebrew text, and fourteen times in the OT Aramaic text in Dan. 3–7.

9. In Dan. 3:5, 7, 10 and 15, *qeren* is translated simply as "horn" in the RSV, NRSV, NIV, NKJV, NASB, Moffatt, and the Jewish Publication Society translation of 1917; as "cornet" in KJV, ASV, and Young's; and as "trumpets" in TEV and CEV, although the TEV also has "oboes" in the list!

10. Besides in the initial Numbers references, *ḥăṣōṣĕrâ* appears in Num. 31:6; 2 Kings 11:14 (twice as trumpeter); 12:13; 1 Chron. 13:8; 15:24, 28; 16:6, 42; 2 Chron. 5:12–13; 13:12, 14; 15:14; 20:28; 23:13 (twice); 29:26, 27, 28; Ezra 3:10; Neh. 12:35, 41; Ps. 98:6; and Hos. 5:8.

hints at its meaning, and Josephus describes it as "from the quivering reverberation of its sound—the straight trumpet."[11] Far from being a ram's horn, this instrument was generally made of metal.[12] Josephus's description is of a narrow tube, somewhat greater in diameter than a flute, with a bell on the end.[13] The *ḥăṣōṣěrâ* is pictured on both some Hasmonean coins and on the Arch of Titus in Rome, where mouthpieces were part of the instrument to aid in the act of blowing into the narrow end.[14]

None of these "instruments" would qualify under the modern connotation of trumpet. Very little variation in pitch could be achieved.[15] They emitted a clear though high-pitched, shrill sound, and were also able to produce one or two harmonic sounds. Murray Harris frankly notes that "the instrument was ill-adapted for music."[16] For example, none of these "trumpets" could play even such simple tunes as "Twinkle, Twinkle Little Star" or "Mary Had a Little Lamb." Instead, Werner categorically states that "all the various usages of the *šôpār* can be viewed under one category: that of a signaling instrument."[17] Werner concludes that "the function of the *šôpār* was to make noise—be it of earthly or of eschatological character—but not to make music."[18]

The First Old Testament Usage of Trumpet

Since these ancient Hebrew horns were used to signal, what kinds of events or occasions did these instruments signal? Instructively, the very first *šôpār* we read of in Holy Writ was God's trumpet, sounded at the inauguration of his covenant with Israel. Moses had received instruction on Sinai, and the people had been prepared for the occasion that was to take place on "the third day" (Exod. 19:11). God had told Moses, "And let them be ready for the third day. For on the third day the LORD will come down upon Mount Sinai in the sight of all the people" (Exod. 19:11 NKJV). Boundary marks were set up so the people would touch the mountain only on the pain of death (vv. 12–15). The people were to wash their clothes and remain celibate for those three days. They were told that a trumpet would sound to indicate the time when they were to "come near the mountain" (v. 13).

11. Josephus *Antiq.* 3.12.6.

12. Num. 10:2 calls for silver, although Eric Werner, professor of liturgical music at Hebrew Union College–Jewish Institute of Religion, notes that bronze, copper, gold, and even bones and shells were sometimes used ("Musical Instruments," *The Interpreter's Dictionary of the Bible* [Nashville: Abingdon, 1962], 3:472).

13. Josephus *Antiq.* 3.12.6.

14. Werner, "Instruments," 3:472.

15. Harold M. Best and David K. Huttar note that "for either instrument [*šôpār* or *ḥăṣōṣěrâ*] only a limited number of pitches (two or three) could be produced, so that they are far removed from the modern trumpet" ("Music; Musical Instruments," *The Zondervan Pictorial Encyclopedia of the Bible*, ed. Merrill Tenney [Grand Rapids: Zondervan, 1975], 4:320).

16. Murray J. Harris, "Trumpet," *The New International Dictionary of New Testament Theology*, ed. C. Brown (Grand Rapids: Zondervan, 1978), 3:873.

17. Werner, "Instruments," 3:473. Speaking of the *yôbēl*, Werner similarly states that it "was strictly a signaling instrument" (3:472).

18. Werner, "Instruments," 3:472.

The occasion was rather spectacular. The eyewitness, Moses, records, "Then it came to pass on the third day, in the morning, that there were thunderings and lightnings, and a thick cloud on the mountain; and the sound of the trumpet was very loud, so that all the people who were in the camp trembled" (Exod. 19:16 NKJV). Upon that signal, obviously God's *šôpār* blast, not a human's, Moses "brought the people out of the camp to meet with God, and they stood at the foot of the mountain" (Exod. 19:17 NKJV). Sinai was engulfed in flame and smoke, accompanied by an enormous earthquake. Thus the first biblical reference to trumpet is God's terrifying blast to signal his approach to meet his people at Sinai.

Old Testament Categories of Trumpet Usage

Nearly all other Old Testament uses of the trumpet were also for the purpose of signaling, namely, to give notice of something. (1) Some signaled the beginning of something, such as Israel's days of gladness, solemn feast days, and the new moon, when they were to sacrifice peace offerings (Num. 10:10).[19] The feast of trumpets (Lev. 23:24)[20] and the year of jubilee were begun with trumpet blasts throughout the land (Lev. 25:9).

(2) Trumpets also signified announcements of a military victory, as when Jonathan had defeated the Philistine garrison at Geba (1 Sam. 13:3–4); Sheba's bitter renunciation of David's kingship (2 Sam. 20:1); or the coronation of a new king such as Absalom intended in Hebron (2 Sam. 15:10); or of Solomon at Jerusalem's Gihon spring (1 Kings 1:33–41).

(3) Many trumpet blasts were actually a summons of one sort or another. Moses was to use the trumpet to call Israel to gather at the tabernacle in the wilderness (Num. 10:2–3, 7), to summon Israel's princes and leaders of thousands (Num. 10:4), and even to summon God's aid against their enemies (Num. 10:9). In Joel's day a fast of repentance, a solemn assembly, was to be convened by sounding the *šôpār* in Zion (Joel 2:15). It might be argued that the purpose of Joshua's trumpet blasts at Jericho was to summon God's mighty power in Israel's behalf, for that was the result (Josh. 6:5, 20). During the Judges era, Ehud summoned Ephraim with trumpets to battle against Moab (Judg. 3:27–28), and that is how Gideon called his father's house into action in his defense (Judg. 6:34). Later, Nehemiah used a trumpet to call for his wall builders to switch swords for trowels (Neh. 4:16–20).

(4) Because of their value as signaling instruments, trumpets were also natural concomitants of war. Troops could be advanced, halted, and retreated by the signal of the *šôpār*. King David's general, Joab, stopped his army's advances on three separate occasions by the trumpet's signal (2 Sam. 2:28; 18:16; 20:22). Gideon and his brave three hundred used *šôpār*s to frighten the Midianites and start a rout of those greedy foes (Judg. 7:16, 18). God himself points out the

19. The use of a trumpet in connection with the new moon festivities is also seen in Ps. 81:3 (v. 4 in the Heb. text).

20. Literally "of blowing," where *těrû'â* is used. This word appears thirty-eight times in the OT mostly in connection with trumpets, signaling, alarms, and joyful shouting.

bravery of the horse, one of his most spectacular creations, in his speech in Job 39:24–25, saying the horse disregards the enemies' trumpets during the battle.

(5) Old Testament trumpets also accompanied the joyful festivities of Israel, as when David returned the ark of the covenant to Jerusalem (2 Sam. 6:15), and in some of the worship denoted in the Psalms.[21] Many of the historical references to temple ceremonies incorporate this worship usage as well.[22]

(6) There is also a figurative use of the trumpet. God told Isaiah, "lift up thy voice like a trumpet" (Isa. 58:1 KJV). Similarly, in the New Testament Christ's voice is likened to a trumpet in Revelation 1:10, and John likewise hears a voice designated by trumpet sounds in Revelation 4:1. Jesus' reference to those who "sound a trumpet" before their almsgiving (Matt. 6:2) is most likely figurative as well.

(7) Much as the air-raid siren is used today, the *šôpār* was used in Bible times to signal an alarm. Trumpets alerted people to the danger of an enemy attack as from Israel's perennial northern rivals (Joel 2:1),[23] and as seen in Ezekiel's watchman (Ezek. 33:3–6). Several of Israel's prophets used *šôpār* in this way (Jer. 4:5, 19, 21; 6:1, 17; 42:14; Hos. 5:8; 8:1; Amos 2:2; 3:6; Zeph. 1:16).[24]

(8) Finally, there are several Old Testament uses of trumpet that are clearly eschatological in meaning. God will lift up the banner, the ensign, and blow the trumpet in Isaiah 18:3 in recovering Israel. Again, Isaiah prophesies the regathering and return of Israel to its land after the apocalyptic destruction pictured in Isaiah 24–27. The final two verses of that section, Isaiah 27:12–13, conclude, "And it shall come to pass in that day, that the LORD shall beat off[25] . . . and ye shall be gathered one by one, O ye children of Israel. And it shall come to pass in that day, that the great trumpet shall be blown, and [Israel] shall come . . . and shall worship the LORD in the holy mount at Jerusalem."

It is interesting, and likely significant, that God will signal the regathering of his people Israel by the use of a great trumpet.[26] Whether it will be heard by everyone on earth or not, the image used in this eschatological setting is the trumpet.

Jeremiah's notable prophecy of the future doom of Babylon says, "Set up a standard in the land, blow the trumpet [*šôpār*] among the nations, prepare the

---

21. For example, Ps. 47:5 (v. 6 in Heb. text); 81:3 (v. 4 in Heb. text); 98:6; and 150:3. The horns blown in Dan. 3:5, 7, 10, and 15 might be similarly classified because of their grouping with other instruments, but this could also be seen as a rousing call or announcement to commence worship of Nebuchadnezzar's golden image.

22. See for instance, 1 Chron. 13:8; 15:24, 28; 16:6, 42; 2 Chron. 5:12, 13; 13:12; 15:14; 20:28; 23:13; 29:26, 27, 28. In all these cases the *ḥăṣōṣĕrâ* was used and the priests were the "musicians."

23. This alert may have been for an expected temporal attack, but with eschatological import as picturing "the day of the LORD."

24. The day of the Lord often signifies both that which is near at hand as a temporal judgment, and what is always approaching in the eschatological sense.

25. NIV, NKJV, and NRSV have "thresh"; ASV has "beat out his grain," and RSV has "thresh out the grain."

26. HB *šôpār gādôl*; LXX, *tē salpingi tē megalē*. Of the nearly six hundred uses of this adjective in the OT this is the only time *great* modifies trumpet. The NT likewise has but a single reference to a *great* trumpet, Matt. 24:31, where Jesus uses the phrase to indicate the signal that will accompany the regathering of God's elect after the great tribulation—*salpingos megalēs*.

nations against her, call together against her the kingdoms . . ." (Jer. 51:27). The eschatological trumpet will be God's signal to the nations to attack, destroy, and plunder Babylon.

The Final Old Testament Usage of Trumpet

Perhaps instructively, both the first and the last Old Testament references to a trumpet are to one that belongs to the Lord himself. God's final recovery of and defense of Israel is pictured in conjunction with another divine blast. Zechariah says, "And the LORD shall be seen over them, and his arrow shall go forth like the lightning: and the Lord GOD shall blow the trumpet . . . and the LORD of hosts shall defend them . . . And the LORD their God shall save them in that day as the flock of his people . . ." (Zech. 9:14–16 KJV). It could not be more clear that another of God's šôpār blasts is again in view. God uses the trumpet again to signal his divine presence in behalf of Israel.

In summary, the Old Testament šôpār was used as a signaling instrument in various aspects of the civilian, military, and religious life of the people. God used the trumpet too, initially at Sinai to gather Israel to his covenant ceremony. God promises to use the trumpet again eschatologically in his recovery and defense of his covenant people Israel.

A New Testament Theology of Trumpets

Of the twenty-three possible New Testament references to trumpet (see note 4), all but five are eschatological.[27] However, of these eighteen eschatological occurrences, all except three verses are speaking of the seven angels who sound the trumpet judgments in Revelation 8–11. Because of the significance of these three verses, we will direct our attention to them. One is from the lips of Jesus, and two are in Paul's writings.

Matthew 24:31

Jesus began his Olivet Discourse (Matt. 24–25) by asserting the future complete destruction of Israel's temple after he walked by it with his disciples (24:1–2). The disciples in turn asked him when this would occur and for a sign of his coming and of the end of the age (24:3). Jesus then prophesied a future landscape of religious deception, betrayal and persecution, wars and natural disasters, yet a spreading of the gospel "in all the world as a witness to all nations, and then the end will come" (24:14 NKJV).

In the very next verse, Matthew 24:15, Christ predicted the coming of the abomination of desolation[28] coupled with "great tribulation, such as was not since the beginning of the world to this time, no, nor ever shall be"

---

27. Matt. 6:2 is probably figurative; 1 Cor. 14:8 is temporal; Heb. 12:19 references the Sinai experience; and Rev. 1:10 and 4:1 speak of voices that were like trumpets.

28. Many believe this one is called "the prince that shall come . . . [who] shall confirm the covenant with many for one week" (Dan. 9:26–27 KJV); "the man of sin . . . the son of perdition, who . . . exalteth himself above all that is called God" (2 Thess. 2:3–4 KJV); the beast that rises out of the sea (Rev. 13:1); and the little horn of Daniel's fourth beast (Dan. 7:8, 20–21).

(Matt. 24:21). Because in Matthew 24:29–30 Christ states that his return in "power and great glory" will be "immediately after the tribulation of those days" (NKJV), this becomes a key chronological reference. Then in 24:31 Jesus says he will "send His angels with a great sound of a trumpet, and they shall gather together His elect from the four winds, from one end of heaven to the other" (NKJV).

We should notice several things about Matthew 24:31. It is clearly eschatological, occurring immediately after the great tribulation. There is the use of a great trumpet sound,[29] and Christ's angels effect the gathering of his elect from all over the world.

Notice also what is missing in Matthew 24:31 that may be crucial to arguments seeking to equate this verse with rapture verses that also mention a trumpet. First, there is no mention of resurrection.[30] There is also no mention of transformation of living believers. Indeed, an instantaneous transformation and a split second meeting with Christ in the air would counter the stated gathering work of Christ's angels.

1 Thessalonians 4:16

Writing some twenty years after Jesus expressed the prophecy recorded in Matthew, Paul tells the Thessalonians that Jesus' return from heaven would coincide with a shout,[31] the voice of an archangel, and "with the trump of God." Coupled with this return would be the resurrection of "the dead in Christ," followed almost instantaneously by the

---

29. The UBS has *salpingos megalēs*, supported by Aleph, five other uncials, a few cursives, most of the Syriac versions, and a handful of church fathers. It is given a "B" reading, indicating some doubt as to the choice. The TR has *phōnēs* between "trumpet" and "great," indicating "sound of a great trumpet." This reading is supported by Vaticanus and three other uncials, by a host of cursive MSS and lectionaries, but no fathers or versions. Henry Alford favors a third reading, that of D, the OL, Vg, Hilary, Jerome and Augustine, which has a *kai* ("and") between "trumpet" and "sound." That would separate the trumpet and the great voice, possibly making the "great sound" an explanation of the trumpet even as 1 Thess. 4:16 does. But none of these readings is crucial to one's understanding of this passage. Henry Alford, *The Greek Testament*, ed. E. F. Harrison (reprint, Chicago: Moody, 1958), 1:243–44.

30. However, Daniel explicitly teaches that "at the time of the end" (Dan. 11:40), when Israel is being overrun by the Antichrist in the final stage of the great tribulation period, "at that time shall Michael stand up" (Dan. 12:1) to defend Israel. This is immediately coupled with resurrection language in Dan. 12:2. I believe this indicates the resurrection of OT saints at the conclusion of the tribulation. The context is entirely Jewish and contains no hint of a rapture.

31. *En keleusmati* indicates a loud command, a command shout, a battle shout, or any voice signal, even that of a captian to his rowers—essentially the command of one who has authority. That shout may be explained epexegetically by the two phrases that follow it (Alford, *Greek Testament*, 3:275). Thomas Constable ("1 Thessalonians," in *The Bible Knowledge Commentary*, ed. J. F. Walvoord and R. B. Zuck [Wheaton, Ill.: Victor, 1983–85], 2:704), however says, "These three phenomena may all refer to the same thing, but probably they are three separate almost simultaneous announcements heralding Christ's return." C. F. Hogg and W. E. Vine (*The Epistles to the Thessalonians* [Fincastle, Va.: Scripture Truth, n.d.], 143) paraphrase an epexegetical understanding of the three phrases as "with a shout in the archangel's voice, even with the voice of the trump of God."

"rapture"[32] of those believers who would still be living on earth at that point.[33] Paul hoped to include himself in that latter grouping ("then *we* [emphasis Paul's] who are living and remaining"), although in other passages he indicated he could die before Christ would return (Phil. 1:23; 2 Cor. 5:1, 8).

Two key ideas to understand about this text are that (1) it definitely and without question speaks of the rapture[34] of believers who are termed "in Christ,"[35] and (2) a trumpet is used to signal this event.[36]

1 Corinthians 15:52

Paul founded both the church at Thessalonica and the church at Corinth on his second missionary journey about A.D. 50–51. In fact, 1 Thessalonians was penned on that journey. About three years later, Paul wrote 1 Corinthians from Ephesus. In 1 Corinthians 15:52, Paul obviously had in mind the same event of which he spoke in 1 Thessalonians 4:16.[37] Several ideas are constant: (1) dead believers will be raised;[38] (2) living saints will be transformed; and (3) a trumpet will sound. However, several new concepts emerge as well: (1) There is more elucidation on the rapid nature of the en-

---

32. Rapture comes from the Latin *raptus*, derived from *rapere*, the verb used to translate the Greek *harpagēsometha*, which means to snatch away, whether violently or otherwise. It is used of Philip being caught away from the eunuch by the Holy Spirit (Acts 8:39), of one being caught up to the third heaven (2 Cor. 12:2, 4), and of the woman's child (Jesus), being snatched away to heaven (Rev. 12:5) and in nine other NT texts.

33. The best treatment of this passage I have seen is Robert L. Thomas, "1 Thessalonians," in *The Expositor's Bible Commentary*, ed. F. E. Gaebelein (Grand Rapids: Zondervan, 1978), 11:278–80.

34. There are only a few NT verses that with any certainty can be said to indicate the rapture. This is one of them. Others are probably John 14:3; 1 Cor. 15:51–52; Phil. 3:20–21; Col. 3:4; and 1 John 3:2. Only those that indicate an instantaneous transformation from mortal to immortal or a sudden appearance in the air with Christ qualify. Just as OT texts must be distinguished between the first and second comings of Christ because they often predict "the sufferings of Christ, and the glory that would follow" (1 Peter 1:11), even so, not all verses about Christ's second coming can be declared dogmatically to refer to the rapture.

35. I will spare the reader an extended discussion of the distinctions that could be listed between Israel and the church, only to note that the term "Israel" always refers to either Jacob or his descendants in the seventy-three times it occurs in the NT, and that the phrase "in Christ" is a significant Pauline expression to refer to those who have uniquely been placed into the spiritual body of Christ during the church age.

36. Some discussion of the purpose of God using a trumpet in conjunction with this event will conclude this paper.

37. The Bishop of Derry (*The Bible Commentary*, ed. F. C. Cook [New York: Scribner's, 1881], 9:724), notes that this verse points to 1 Cor. 15:52, but that it "is perhaps not exactly parallel" with Matt. 24:31.

38. Those who are raised must be believers because Paul uses the phrase, "*we* shall not all sleep" (emphasis mine).

tire transaction—"in the twinkling of an eye."[39] (2) The trumpet is called "the last trump."

This latter phrase has been the occasion of much discussion. Charles Hodge held that this trumpet will be "the last that is ever to sound."[40] Many identify the last trump with the seventh angelic trumpet sounding in Revelation 11:15.[41] However, *eschatē* need not mean (as Hodge insisted) the very last trumpet that is ever to sound, though it could mean that. With regard to time, *eschatos* often indicates last in relation to something preceding it.[42] Thus, the vineyard workers hired at the eleventh hour were last that day (Matt. 20:8, 12, 14), but obviously other workers would be hired the next day. Likewise, the vineyard owner in Mark 12 who rented out his land sent servants to collect the rent, then sent his own son last (v. 6). The son was the last of that series of sent ones, but the parable indicates that the owner would next visit the tenants himself. Jesus also said of a man whom a demon had repossessed that "the last state of that man is worse than the first" (Matt. 12:45 KJV), but this does not imply that such had to be his final state.

Henry Alford interprets *eschatos* in this way also, warning that the word must not be "pressed too closely as if there were necessarily no trump after it,—but is *the trump* at the *time of the end*, the last trump, in a wide and popular sense."[43] In this view, the last trump could be the last of *this* age, with other possible trumpet sounds to follow, such as any that might be scheduled during the tribulation as seen in Revelation 8–11.[44]

---

39. In an effort to express this rapid change, the NLT translates *rhipē* as "blinking"; the NIV has "twinkling," but translates *atomō* as "in a flash"; the TEV, "in an instant" and "blinking"; the JB, "it will be instantaneous"; the CEV, "suddenly, quicker than the blink of an eye"; while the ASV, NASB, RSV, NRSV, KJV, NKJV, Moffatt, Weymouth, Williams, and Young all use the standard "in a moment, in the twinkling of an eye." It is literally "in an atom," and as William Biederwolf nicely puts it, "a little indivisible point of time" (*The Millennium Bible* [1924; reprint, Grand Rapids: Baker, 1964], 442). Charles Hodge explains it as "a portion of time so short as to be incapable of further division" (*An Exposition of the First Epistle to the Corinthians* [reprint, Grand Rapids: Eerdmans, 1965], 356).

40. Hodge, *1 Corinthians*, 356.

41. This would include midtribs, posttribs, and pre-wrath rapture proponents. Their identification is the same; their timing is what distinguishes them. Midtribs place the seventh and final trump near the middle of the tribulation; posttribs place it at the end; and pre-wrath rapturists argue it is near the end, but before God's wrath is poured out. See, for example, Marvin J. Rosenthal, *The Pre-Wrath Rapture of the Church* (Nashville: Nelson, 1990), 193.

42. BAGD 314.

43. Alford, *Greek New Testament*, 2:620, emphasis his. Hans Conzelmann (*1 Corinthians*, trans. J. W. Leitch [Philadelphia: Fortress, 1975]), 291, agrees: "The 'last' trumpet means not the last in a series of trumpet blasts, but 'the eschatological one.'" So does Gordon D. Fee (*First Epistle to the Corinthians* [Grand Rapids: Eerdmans, 1987], 802), who says it simply "signals the End." Gerhard Friedrich says it "is not the last in a series of trumpets" (*TDNT* 7:87).

44. Gordon H. Clark (*First Corinthians: A Contemporary Commentary* [Nutley, N.J.: Presbyterian and Reformed, 1975], 312) says, "The 1st trumpet of I Corinthians is the last trumpet of *this age*," and that it is not to be identified with the seventh trumpet of Rev. but with Paul's in 1 Thess. 4:16.

Conclusion

Trumpets have been used as signals for many purposes: to signify the commencement of something; to announce something; to summon people; for military purposes; in festivals of worship; to alarm people of danger; and in eschatological settings.

God's own trumpet blast sounded at Sinai (Exod. 19:16; Heb. 12:19) and will do so again in connection with regathering Israel (Isa. 18:3; 27:12–13) and also in conjunction with a future defending and saving of Israel (Zech. 9:14–16). God's trumpet will sound at the rapture of the church (1 Thess. 4:16; 1 Cor. 15:52), and also when Christ returns with his angels whom he then sends out to regather his elect from the ends of the earth (Matt. 24:31).

God loves trumpets and likes to use them as significant sound signals denoting his presence and marking certain of his divine workings. The use of God's divine trumpet blasts is rare, but extensive and varied enough to discourage speculation that couples different trumpet events together.

In no case should this be more clear than with an attempt to link Matthew 24:31 with 1 Thessalonians 4:16 and 1 Corinthians 15:52. The former has no resurrection, no change from mortal to immortal, and no instantaneous divine transfer to meet Christ in the air. It pictures a coming of Christ and has a trumpet, but that is the extent of the similarities.[45] On the other hand, 1 Thessalonians 4:16 and 1 Corinthians 15:52 are clearly rapture verses that speak of the immediate resurrection of New Testament believers who are in Christ. The Matthew 24:31 passage talks of Christ sending out angels to gather God's elect, and resembles Isaiah 18:3 and 27:12–13, where Israel is in view. Perhaps significant is the fact that Isaiah 27:13 and Matthew 24:31 are the only two texts in the entire Bible that call the trumpet a "great trumpet."

A second connection is sometimes sought between 1 Corinthians 15:52 and the seventh or "last" trumpet to sound in Revelation 11:15. Such an identification, however, is superficial and imaginary. It lacks any scriptural confirmation.[46] It could be the last trump of this age, meaning the church age, with more trumpets to follow in the next stage of human history, such as would be posited under a futuristic interpretation of the Book of Revelation.

A final suggested possibility for the meaning of the "last" trump is to take it as last in a series, but not in a series of eschatological trumpets. One can recall the series of *šôpārs* that had to be sounded in the wilderness to move Israel from one place to another. Numbers 10:5–6 mentions this procedure. An initial blast would signal, for example, to *pack up* their belongings. Later, there

---

45. These omissions could well be intentional on Jesus' part, so as *not* to cause confusion with the two incontrovertible rapture passages revealed through Paul.

46. James O. Buswell (*A Systematic Theology of the Christian Religion* [Grand Rapids: Zondervan, 1963], 2:459) says, "Frankly, I Corinthians 15:52 does not tell us of what series this particular trumpet is the 'last.' Paul does not say, 'the last trumpet which ever will sound in the history of the universe.' Nor does he explain 'last' of what series." Still, Buswell thinks Paul refers to the seventh trumpet in Revelation.

would be a *šôpār* to signal it was time for the twelve tribes to *line up*. The last trump of that series would signal that it was time to *move on out*. Paul's unique titling of this rapture trumpet as the "last" trump would match the process just described. It would also perhaps be familiar to Paul's readers in Corinth, since Paul had earlier detailed a number of events in Israel's wilderness journeying in 1 Corinthians 10:1–11.[47] Paul's conclusion in that section was that these things happened to Israel as examples for us and were written for our admonition (1 Cor. 10:11). Thus, the last trump could be a reference, as in Israel's wilderness wanderings, to the "move on out" *šôpār*. Not unlike Paul, this would be a unique literary way to refer to the divine *šôpār* blast at the rapture when millions of livings saints will suddenly and miraculously be called to "move on out."

Just as a divine trumpet blast signaled God's presence at Sinai, so also God's trumpet will declare Christ's coming at the rapture. Even as human trumpets sounded in Leviticus 25 on the jubilee, so God's trumpet call will proclaim liberty for his saints as they are delivered from the restraints of death and sin in this world by being caught up "in the clouds to meet the Lord in the air" (1 Thess. 4:17 NKJV).

---

47. These include drinking water from the smitten rock (v. 4), lusting after Egyptian food (v. 6), the golden calf idolatry (v. 7), fornication with the Midianites (v. 8), and murmuring over the manna (v. 9).

4

The Eschatological Prospect in the Context of Mark

Hans F. Bayer

Covenant Theological Seminary

Any student of the Synoptic Gospels quickly isolates their central twin themes of the "kingdom of God" and "Jesus as the Messiah of God." However, one of the most curious aspects is the fact that there is little explanation of the relationship between Jesus' teaching concerning the kingdom of God and his own identity and function. Thus the question concerning Jesus' function in the economy of the imminent and ultimate rule of God remains largely unanswered in the first three canonical Gospels. Nevertheless, toward the end of their testimony concerning Jesus' public ministry, we can glean some hints, which hold clues to the above-stated enigma.

Unique among these hints is Mark 14:25 and parallels. Here, at last, Jesus appears to relate his own, personal circumstances to the unfolding kingdom of God. Scholars have, however, strongly debated what Jesus really meant by exclaiming the so-called eschatological prospect. In order to understand the meaning of the eschatological prospect, it is crucial to explore it in its literary context.

The Literary Context

The Function of Mark 14:25 in the Gospel of Mark

Taking a simple thematic/geographical outline of Mark as a starting point, it becomes readily apparent that Mark 14:25 occupies an important place in the unfolding narrative: commencing at 14:1, the testing of Christ's *exousia* ("authority") reaches its culmination. This culmination begins with the betrayal narrative (14:1–52), in which Mark 14:25 lies at the center.

> Introduction (1:1–15)
> Part I: Demonstration of Jesus' "authority" (1:16–8:26)
>   1. Section: Work in Galilee (1:16–3:12)
>   2. Section: Climax in Galilee (3:13–6:6)
>   3. Section: Work beyond Galilee (6:7–8:26)
> Part II: Testing Jesus' "authority" in suffering (8:27–16:8 [9–20])
>   4. Section: Caesarea Philippi—Journey to Jerusalem (8:27–10:52)
>   5. Section: Work in Jerusalem (11:1–13:37)
>   6. Section: Passion and resurrection in Jerusalem (14:1–16:8 [9–20])

Given this fact alone, a certain focus lies on this culmination section (14:1–52), including Mark 14:25.

We must now analyze phrases and words found in Mark 14:25 that occur elsewhere in Mark. This analysis permits deeper insights into the contextual significance and meaning of Mark 14:25, ostensibly corroborating the culminating emphasis outlined above.

The general structure of the sentence (οὐ μὴ ἕως [ἄν]) features parallels in Mark 9:1 (promise; see also 9:41), 10:15 (a mild conditional declaration concerning entry into the kingdom like a child), and 13:30 (promise/declaration).[1] The structure represents a solemn declaration and does not support the notion that we are dealing with a formal oath.[2]

The solemn introduction ("Amen, I say to you") occurs in the following significant places in Mark: (a) 3:28 (blasphemy against the Holy Spirit); (b) 8:12 (no sign will be given to this evil generation); (c) 9:1 (coming of kingdom in power); (d) 9:41 (blessing for those who bless the disciples of Jesus); (e) 10:15 (receive kingdom as child); (f) 10:29 (promise of discipleship); (g) 11:23 (promise of faith); (h) 12:43 (declaring a poor widow to be generous); (i) 13:30 (fulfillment of eschatological judgment); (j) 14:9 (preaching the particulars of gospel in the world); (k) 14:18 (announcing the betrayer of Jesus); (l) 14:25 (fruit of the vine/kingdom); and (m) 14:30 (denial of Peter).

Of these thirteen "solemn declarations" in Mark, three refer explicitly to the coming and receiving of the kingdom of God (9:1; 10:15; 14:25), two address judgment, three contain warnings, four hold out promises, and one features a declaration. The formula thus adds a certain emphasis to Mark 14:25.

---

1. See below for our discussion on the meaning of this phrase. See Matt. 5:18, 26 par.; Luke 12:59; Matt. 10:23; Matt. 23:39 par.; Luke 13:35. See K. E. Dewey, "Peter's Curse and Cursed Peter," in *The Passion in Mark: Studies on Mark 14–16*, ed. W. H. Kelber (Philadelphia: Fortress, 1976), 103, who refers to W. H. Kelber, *Kingdom and Parousia in the Gospel of Mark* (Ph.D. diss., University of Chicago, 1970), 89–92.

2. See below for further discussion of this declaration.

The references to "drinking" may be significant in Mark, since the only other use of the term is found in Mark 10:38–39, where Jesus teaches figuratively about "drinking of the cup of judgment and discipline." In contrast to this, Jesus anticipates in Mark 14:25 a literal drinking of wine in the consummating celebration of the kingdom of God.

The metonymy τοῦ γενήματος "the fruit" (see par. Matt. 26:29/Luke 22:18/Mark 14:25; 2 Cor. 9:10) . . . τῆς ἀμπέλου "of the vine" (Mark 12:1, 2, 8, 9; 14:25) occurs, taken as a phrase, only here in Mark (par. Matt. 26:29/Luke 22:18).

References to "day" in Mark feature various time frames: an undelimited period following Jesus' suffering (Mark 2:20); near future (13:17); near/far future (13:19); and near/far future (13:20).[3] The mention of "that" in conjunction with "until the day" clearly implies in 14:25 an undelimited, forward-looking perspective similar to that in Mark 2:20.

The expression "new" is rare (Mark 2:21, 22 [wineskin]; 14:25)[4] and adds here to the notion of future hope.

Finally we turn to the expression "kingdom of God."[5] As is true in the other Synoptic Gospels, the phrase can refer either to present (or near present; Mark 1:15; 9:1(?); 10:14, 15, 23, 24, 25; 12:34) or future events (Mark 9:47–48 [entry after judgment]; 14:25 [celebration]). At times both present and future dimension may be alluded to (Mark 4:11, 26, 30). Finally, Mark 15:43 features a very generic and gnomic reference to the kingdom of God.[6]

Results: the most significant terminological echoes for Mark 14:25 in the macro-text of Mark are thus found in three expressions: (a) the solemn "Amen, I say to you" (see especially 9:1; 10:15; 13:30); (b) the coming "days" (see especially 2:20) and (c) the "kingdom of God" (see especially 10:15). This means that the reader (or hearer) of Mark 14:25 will have been especially alerted to (1) expect an important statement following the solemn "Amen, I say to you"; (2) anticipate in the reference to "those days" a significant judgment/blessing event; and (3) hear a clarifying statement concerning the culmination of the presently inaugurated messianic kingdom of God.

Of these three references, it is the recurrence of "kingdom of God" that further places Mark 14:25 in a most prominent place in Mark's account. Prior to Mark 14:25 we hear Jesus teach about the rule of God, both in terms of present (time, conditions of entry, characteristics) and future (relationship to judgment, celebration) dimensions. From Jesus' parabolic teaching we learn further that

---

3. See also Matt. 10:15; 11:22, 24, 36 (Day of Judgment).

4. See 2 Peter 3:13 and Rev. 21:1.

5. M. de Jonge's contribution was not accessible to me: "Mark 14:25 among Jesus' Words about the Kingdom of God," in *Sayings of Jesus: Canonical and Non-canonical Essays in Honour of Tjitze Baarda*, ed. W. Peterson and W. M. Lawrence (Leiden: Brill, 1997), 123–35.

6. Note in Mark 15:43 the durative imperfect ἦν as part of the periphrastic conjugation with present durative προσδεχόμενος, emphasizing the enduring patience of waiting for the coming kingdom of God.

there is an inconspicuous beginning to the kingdom and a glorious culmination of the same. Except for the gnomic reference to the kingdom in Mark 15:43, Mark 14:25 constitutes the last reference in Mark to the future kingdom.

The Gospel never explicitly reports that the present authoritative teacher of the kingdom is its designated King (see, however, the oblique teaching about the ruling Messiah in terms of the suffering, vindicated, and glorified Son of Man).[7] However, Mark 14:25 comes closer than any other statement in Mark to bringing exactly these two separate and crucial strands in Mark's narrative together. The reader/hearer of the Gospel has gradually learned in chapters 1–14:17 how to think about the rule of God, as well as who the (suffering) Messiah of God is. It is with this perspective in mind that Mark 14:25 holds, in the context of the last meal, a significant interpretive key to the Gospel by connecting these two strands (kingdom of God/the identity and work of the Messiah). While the strands are developed, they are, in our view, not "mixed" on account of their historically explosive nature (see John 6:15). Only when the "point of no return" has been reached, does Jesus carefully disclose the connection between the two strands.

Subsequent to Mark 14:25, the strand of references concerning Jesus, especially in terms of "Son of Man" and "Lord," does receive one further interpretive accent in Mark 14:62. While Mark 12:35–37 (Jesus as "Lord" of David; cf. Ps. 110:1, 5) and 13:26 (Jesus as exalted Son of Man; cf. Dan. 7:13–14) anticipate Mark 14:62, the two christological strands are finally combined in Mark 14:62.[8] While Mark 14:62 combines christological strands ("Lord" and exalted "Son of Man"), which both contain allusions to kingdom rule (cf. Ps. 110:2, 6; Dan. 7:14), it is Mark 14:25 that features culminating combinations of the two significant thematic strands developed throughout the Marcan narrative! We may say that Mark 14:62 corroborates the key connection of the strands as stated in 14:25.

The Immediate Literary Context[9]

The section leading up to the preparation and celebration of the Last Supper (Mark 14:12–26) is marked by the following: (a) a final mention of the intention of Jesus' opponents to execute him (Mark 14:1–2; aided by their collaborator Judas, Mark 14:10–11), and (b) the pericope of the proleptic anointing of Jesus in Bethany (Mark 14:3–9).

Mark 14:25–26 concludes the narrative of the Passover meal, which is followed by the pericope predicting the betrayal of Jesus by Peter (14:27–31, cf.

---

7. See also Jesus as "King of the Jews" being featured prominently and only in Mark 15:2, 9, 12, 18, 26, 32, following Jesus' teaching on the kingdom.

8. Mark 16:19, 20 does mention Jesus as "Lord." First, the question remains whether Mark 16:9–20 belongs to the original text of Mark. Second, Mark 16:19, 20 does not add any new interpretation to Jesus as "Lord."

9. See also the discussion below.

14:66–72) and Jesus' prayer in the garden of Gethsemane (14:32–42). Mark 14:42 thus concludes Jesus' fellowship with his disciples prior to his death.

Mark 14:3–9, 12–42 is thus surrounded by death threats of opponents (imprisonment, trial, and conviction). Conversely, Mark 14:3–9, 12–42 is characterized by Jesus' own death references: (a) Jesus' acceptance of his proleptic anointing in Bethany (Mark 14:3–9); (b) Jesus' prediction of the betrayal by Judas (Mark 14:18–20); (c) the lot of the Son of Man (Mark 14:21); and (d) the breaking of bread (Christ's body) and sharing of the cup (Christ's blood) (Mark 14:22–24).

Taking thus the macro-context and the immediate context of Mark 14:25[10] together, we note the theme of the final testing of the ἐξουσία of Jesus in the divinely appointed and humanly devised death as a necessary passage toward his kingdom participation.

Having isolated the key significance of Mark 14:25 in the literary context of Mark, we now turn to explore the origin and particular meaning of the eschatological prospect.

The Origin of the Eschatological Prospect[11]

Synoptic Parallels

Many scholars have argued that the Matthean version of the eschatological prospect (Matt. 26:29) builds on Mark's version.[12] Whether this can actually be demonstrated remains open to question.[13] What concerns us at this point, however, is the conspicuous phenomenon that Luke's (longer: Luke 22:15–20)[14] version clearly deviates from Mark. Furthermore, Luke 22:19b, 20 displays

10. Attempts at separating Mark 14:25 from the literary context and the historical setting of the Passover meal are not convincing. See H. Bayer, *Jesus' Predictions of Vindication and Resurrection* (Tübingen: Mohr-Siebeck, 1986), 29–42. Contra, e.g., J. Becker, *Jesus of Nazareth* (Berlin: de Gruyter, 1998), 340ff.

11. We are here not engaging in the complex and far-reaching historical-critical quest for determining authenticity. Suffice it to say in this context that the skeptical presuppositional and exegetical bias against the Gospel accounts is neither warranted by the accounts nor their setting. In this essay, we are thus merely asking the question of when Jesus pronounced the eschatological prospect in the course of the Passover meal without engaging historical-critical questions. For the latter, see Bayer, *Predictions*, passim.

12. See, e.g., R. Pesch, *Das Abendmahl und Jesu Todesverständnis* (Freiburg: Herder, 1978), 25.

13. The minority views of Matthean priority (Farmer) and literary independence among the Synoptic Gospels (some proponents of the Scandinavian School) have experienced in recent years somewhat minor revivals.

14. See I. H. Marshall, *The Gospel of Luke* (Grand Rapids: Eerdmans, 1978), 800, and B. Metzger, *A Textual Commentary on the Greek New Testament* (London: UBS, 1971), 191–93, for an informative discussion of the longer and shorter Lukan text. More recently, see K. Petzer, "Style and Text in the Lucan Narrative of the Institution of the Lord's Supper (Luke 22.19b–20)," *NTS* 37 (1991): 113–29. Petzer notes that the non-typical stylistic elements in Luke 22:19b–20 are not sufficient evidence for excluding the section text-critically as non-Lukan.

striking similarities to 1 Corinthians 11:24b–25a and thus raises the question whether Luke presents independent tradition from Mark, regardless of their literary relationship.[15] Schürmann and Joachim Jeremias have further noted that Luke's version has an older ring to it than that of 1 Corinthians 11:24b–25a.[16] We have argued elsewhere[17] that these and other particular pieces of evidence point even to the likelihood of literary independence between Luke and Mark.[18]

What has caused considerable discussion is the fact that the longer text of Luke features a "cup—bread—cup" sequence, while Mark, Matthew, and 1 Corinthians 11:24b–25a feature the familiar "bread—cup" sequence. What is interesting is the fact that the eschatological prospect saying in Luke is connected with the first cup he mentions (thus preceding the bread and cup of the covenant sayings), while Mark links the eschatological prospect with the cup of the covenant saying:

Luke 22:15–20:	Cup (eschatological prospect)
	Bread (body broken)
	Cup (of new covenant; the blood of Jesus is poured out [Matt. 26:28/Luke 22:20/Mark 14:24] "for many" [Mark 14:24/Matt. 26:28] / "for you" [plural; Luke 22:20])
Mark 14:22–25:	Bread (body broken)
	Cup (of new covenant *followed by* eschatological prospect)

This poses the question whether the eschatological prospect was originally pronounced prior (Luke), or subsequent (Mark) to Jesus' words of covenantal interpretation of the cup. Given the probability that Jesus indeed celebrated a Passover meal[19] with his disciples (Joachim Jeremias and Schürmann)[20], it is

---

15. See J. Jeremias, *The Eucharistic Words of Jesus* (London: SCM, 1966), 156, and H. Schürmann, "Jesu Abendmahlsworte im Lichte seiner Abendmahlshandlung," in *Ursprung und Gestalt* (Düsseldorf: Patmos, 1970), 100.

16. Jeremias, *Eucharistic Words*, 185, 188, and H. Schürmann, *Der Einsetzungsbericht Lk 22, 19–20* (Münster: Aschendorff, 1953), 18–41.

17. Bayer, *Predictions*, 32–34.

18. See Jeremias, *Eucharistic Words*, 161.

19. The debate has a long history; see R. C. Jones, "The Lord's Supper and the Concept of Anamnēsis," *Word and World* 6:4 (1986): 434–45, for some proponents of diverging views and his own mediating view.

20. Contra Becker, *Jesus*, 340, where Becker presents apodictic pronouncements borrowed from Bultmann, identifying Mark 14:22–25 as an "independent cult etiology." We ask: how does a mere reference to 1 Cor. 11:23–26 "reveal" this? The chronological priority of 1 Cor. 11:23–26 over Mark 14:22–25 cannot be assumed any more. Note the proximity of the Passover meal in Luke 22:15–20 to 1 Cor. 11:23–26. It is plausible that 1 Cor. 11:23–26 was lifted from an original passion narrative context.

very likely that the Lukan sequence reflects the full historical sequence, while Mark presents the eschatological prospect as having been given generally during the Passover meal.

A plausible reconstruction of a first-century Passover celebration as a festival of remembrance (see Exod. 12:14 and Deut. 16:3)[21] points to the following: the house father declares over the first of four cups (Kiddush cup) the eulogy concerning "the fruit of the vine." He says: "Blessed art thou, Yahweh our God, King of the universe, who has made the fruit of the vine."[22] This parallel is conspicuous. It is probable that Luke presents the historical sequence of the meal and features the eschatological prospect in its original place within the four cup meal, while Mark transmits a very old (e.g., "Amen, I say to you") version of the saying.[23]

The conclusion we draw from these observations is that Jesus,[24] as *pater familias*, commenced the Last Supper with his disciples by pronouncing the eschatological prospect (Luke 22:17–18; Mark 14:25) over the first (Kiddush) cup.

Jesus thus opens the celebration of the last Passover meal with the conscious anticipation of imminent death and simultaneously trusts in God's vindication. He thus shifts the emphasis from commemoration (Passover feast) to anticipation (of his death and the culmination of the kingdom of God).[25]

The Eschatological Prospect of Eating

Luke alone features an eschatological prospect concerning the fulfillment of eating the Passover lamb (Luke 22:16). The parallelism with the eschatological prospect of the Kiddush cup is clear. The chief difference between the "cup"—and "lamb"—prospects is the fact that Luke 22:16 does not refer to a personal activity of Jesus in the future but rather the expectation of "fulfillment of the Passover meal" in the kingdom of God (I will not eat it . . . until *it* is fulfilled). We may therefore conclude that Luke 22:16 adds little concern-

---

21. See Jones, "Lord's Supper," 434–45.

22. See H. L. Strack and P. Billerbeck, *Kommentar zum Neuen Testament aus Talmud und Midrasch*, 7th ed. (Munich: Beck, 1978), 4:62 (61–72), 613.

23. L. Goppelt, *Theology of the New Testament* (Grand Rapids: Eerdmans, 1981), 216, and Jeremias, *Eucharistic Words*, 164. Cf. also Bayer, *Predictions*, 41 and n. 96.

24. Among the few exegetes questioning the authenticity of this saying as coming from Jesus we note H. Patsch, *Abendmahl und historischer Jesus* (Stuttgart: Calwer, 1972), 142; and L. Schenke, *Studien zur Passionsgeschichte des Markus* (Würzburg: Echter/Katholisches Bibelwerk, 1971), 293–305. Becker (*Jesus*, 341) concludes that Mark 14:25 is probably "in its essence . . . an authentic saying of Jesus" (albeit attributing to it a very different meaning than is being argued in this essay).

25. I am not implying here that Jewish *anamnēsis* is abolished in the celebration of the Lord's Supper. Jones ("Lord's Supper," 445) suggests that the reference to wine "points forward in time."

ing the personal circumstances of Jesus following his impending death and their connection to the culmination of the kingdom of God.[26]

Brown[27] draws attention to the fact that Jesus did indeed eat, for example, with the Emmaus disciples (Luke 24:30–31)[28] subsequent to the last Passover meal. Since there is no reference to the culmination (or coming) of the kingdom there, the best interpretation is that these post-Easter meals proleptically anticipate the coming of the kingdom.

The Meaning of Mark 14:25[29]

The late R. E. Brown's recent *New Testament Introduction* continues the notion that the eschatological prospect remains enigmatic in its meaning. Says Brown concerning the Lukan parallel to Mark 14:25: "The clauses about Jesus not eating or drinking again 'until it is fulfilled in the kingdom of God' or 'until the kingdom of God comes' (Luke 22:16, 18) enhance the eschatological symbolism of the Supper but are obscure in their precise reference."[30] However, we believe that there is hope for a plausible explanation of the saying.

A Vow of Abstinence or a Prophecy of Death?

If Mark 14:25 were to emphasize the first part of the phrase (affirmation), the first part itself could convey a vow of abstinence. If Mark 14:25 emphasized the second part of the phrase (consequence), the first part would convey a prophecy of death (and hope beyond death expressed in the second part). The following reasons support the latter of these options:

(1) Jesus pronounces the eschatological prospect at the beginning of the Last Supper with his disciples, thus providing an introductory outlook.

(2) More importantly, the phrase is technically neither a vow nor an oath (such as the oath formula in Mark 8:12; 1 Sam. 3:17; Ps. 130:2; LXX 2 Kings 11:11; see also Acts 23:12, 14, 21). A technical vow or oath includes the following: (a) the protasis, which often contains a curse or similar statement (which may be omitted)[31] and (b) an apodosis, which states or implies a demand or posits an ultimatum. The pattern is thus: "God may do this or that /

---

26. We are bracketing the question of whether Luke 22:16 anticipates an imminent or future culmination of the kingdom of God. Note, however, the difference in formulation between Luke 22:16 (until it is fulfilled in the kingdom of God) and Luke 22:17–18 (until the kingdom of God comes).

27. R. E. Brown, *An Introduction to the New Testament* (New York: Doubleday, 1997), 256.

28. See also post-Easter meals mentioned in John.

29. For more detail, see Bayer, *Predictions*, 29–53.

30. Brown, *Introduction*, 256. See Brown for a widespread redactional explanation (two traditions: one Mark/Matt., the other Paul/Luke) of the two cups in Luke 22:17–18 and 22:20.

31. See Blass, Debrunner, Rehkopf, *Grammatik des neutestamentlichen Griechisch*, 15th ed. (Göttingen: Vandenhoeck & Ruprecht, 1979), 384, 385 n. 6, §454.5.

I will not do . . . unless/if this or that happens/does not happen. . . ." Both the curse and especially the ultimatum are missing in Mark 14:25.[32] Mark 14:25a is thus structurally a preamble to the second part (thus "until," "whenever," and "new" function as emphases of the second part of the phrase).

It is therefore correct to conclude that Mark 14:25a constitutes a prophecy of death. Note herein the emphatic negation οὐκέτι οὐ μή and the future tense of "drink." This conclusion is further confirmed by the above-mentioned immediate literary context of Mark 14:25, where Jesus and his opponents refer to his imminent death. Zeller has thus properly paraphrased the meaning of the first part of the statement: "as surely as I am not any more drinking of the fruit of the vine (I shall drink it again in the kingdom of God)."[33] There is no indication whatsoever in this statement that Jesus is presenting God with an ultimatum for the coming of the kingdom by refraining from food.

An Interim Period?

Implied in the eschatological prospect, then, is an non-delimited cessation of physical table fellowship between Jesus and his disciples due to death. That a certain time must elapse between cessation and resumption of table fellowship becomes evident by the language of the verse (as well as in Luke 22:18).

While Mark 14:25 anticipates Jesus drinking the cup again in the kingdom of God, Luke 22:18 anticipates Jesus drinking the cup when the kingdom of God comes (see Luke 22:16, the eating of the Passover lamb when it is fulfilled in the kingdom of God). Probably all three references anticipate the same future culmination of the kingdom of God,[34] and not the inauguration of it through the death and vindication of Jesus.

In conclusion, we thus concur with Kümmel, who states concerning a parallel to Mark 14:25 in Luke 13:35: "This prediction [Luke 13:35] corresponds exactly with the eucharistic saying in Mark 14:25; on both occasions Jesus counts on an absence which begins with his death and then ends with the parousia. . . ."[35]

The Culminating Goal of the Eschatological Prospect of the Cup

Regarding the meaning of Mark 14:25 in the literary and historical context of Mark 14:22–24, we reach the following conclusion from the preceding

32. See J. A. Ziesler, "The Vow of Abstinence: A Note on Mark 14:25 and Parallels," *Col* 5 (1972): 13, and "The Vow of Abstinence Again," *Col* 6:1 (1973): 49; Jeremias, *Eucharistic Words*, 212.

33. D. Zeller, "Prophetisches Wissen um die Zukunft in synoptischen Jesusworten," *TPhil* 52 (1977): 266.

34. The question of the concurrence between the Parousia of Jesus and the ultimate coming of the kingdom still has to be established (see, e.g., Acts 3:18–23).

35. W. G. Kümmel, *Promise and Fulfillment*, 3d ed. (London: SCM, 1966), 81–82.

study: Jesus expects to be physically ("drinking again") vindicated from his covenant ("blood of the covenant"; see Exod. 24:8) inaugurating, substitutionary ("for many/for you") death in order to preside at the anticipated messianic kingdom feast as the *pater familias*. Given this fact, Jesus is specific in his anticipation. He does not merely express a general hope of future celebration, as did the deceased patriarchs of old (see, e.g., Matt. 8:11).[36]

The following observations have led to this conclusion:

In Mark, there are two thematic and seemingly independent strands: Jesus' own person (note the mystery of the Son of Man) and Jesus' unique teaching on the kingdom of God.

The import from the context of Mark is the fact that toward the end of Mark there is a degree of explicit and solemn teaching (once it is assured that Jesus will go the foreordained path [necessity of death]) concerning the relationship of the two strands.[37] Jesus consciously keeps the two strands apart during most of his ministry. He does this in order to (a) avoid a purely political approach to the rule of God (cf. John 6:15) and (b) develop the two multifaceted or relatively undefined concepts of "kingdom of God" (see, e.g., the kingdom parables) and the "Messiah of God" (see, e.g., "Son of Man" and "Messiah as Lord of David"), before joining the corrected concepts toward the end of his public ministry.

Mark 14:25 constitutes the most significant key in linking the kingdom of God strand with the Jesus strand.[38] Even here, there is initially a stark contrast: the Jesus-line leads to crisis and death; the kingdom line leads to future hope. But the notion of (a) continuity (Jesus "drinking again") and (b) of the substitutionary death in a covenantal context (Mark 10:45; 14:24; "for many" / "covenant") lends a significant teleological and soteriological dimension to his death.[39] In sum, Jesus' death is to be seen as a necessary passage before the "kingdom strand" and the "Jesus strand" really converge explicitly and meaningfully.

36. Contrast this conclusion with Becker's (*Jesus*, 342) unconvincing conclusions regarding Mark 14:25. In Becker's view, Jesus merely surrenders himself ("releases" his life by death) to the sure fulfillment of the kingdom of God. Given Becker's view, one is left with the question why Jesus even came to teach about the kingdom, if it was to come regardless of his own teaching, life, and death. Did Jesus teach, live, and die merely to teach "his confidence in the kingdom of God that was being realized" (342)? There is no inner logic to this notion, given the fact that other prophetic teachers (John the Baptist) and communities (Qumran) accomplished that in less dramatic ways.

37. See also Becker, *Jesus*, 341. He cannot "eliminate the connection between Jesus' fate and the Kingdom of God. . . ."

38. Even Becker (*Jesus*), who denies that Jesus understood himself as Davidic Messiah or Son of Man (212), concedes on the basis of Mark 14:25: "Jesus knows that his death will not keep the Kingdom of God from being realized and that he will be able to share in it in spite of his death (Mark 14:25)" (217).

39. It is here that Becker (*Jesus*, 341) follows his historical-critical predecessors most fully in denying Jesus any allusion to "covenant" or "substitution." By separating (against Luke

We must hold the tension: Jesus speaks of the severity of suffering and of the assurance of vindication (including his bodily resurrection to immortality; see the three major passion predictions).

What we are left with is the fact that Jesus is the authoritative teacher and miraculous demonstrator of the dawning messianic kingdom of God (*exousia*). The fact of his bodily resurrection, his death "on behalf of many" (Mark 14:24), and his presiding in the future over the messianic banquet[40] means he is someone to reckon with today. In fact, taking Mark 14:25 and 14:62 together, there is no doubt that the vindicated Son of Man, the Lord of David, is the enthroned King of the eternal kingdom (Dan. 7:14).

Conclusion

The enigma outlined at the beginning of this paper promises to be resolved as we encounter the true, historically plausible Messianic Secret in Mark: The herald of the imminently dawning messianic rule of God has become its appointed, eternal ruler. While many questions concerning the character of the kingdom remain, we know that our salvific relationship to the enthroned Son of Man and Lord is foundational to our involvement in future kingdom life.[41] A central mark of this present relationship is the corporate celebration of the Lord's Supper as a proleptic messianic banquet.

Based on the eschatological prospect in its context, the future kingdom of God is inextricably connected with its inaugurated and presently ruling Messiah Jesus.

22:15–20) "substitution" and "covenant" from the eschatological prospect (Luke 22:17–18), he boldly states (341): "Jesus' view of the Kingdom nowhere shows the influence of the covenant idea." This statement displays no sensitivity to the fact that the rule of God in the Old Testament is always perceived in the context of covenant. In self-contradiction Becker (*Jesus*, 341) states: "The Kingdom of God is God's graciousness toward those lost persons who have abandoned the covenant." With regard to "substitution" (Becker, *Jesus*, 341–42), Mark 10:45 and Mark 14:22–24 are disregarded despite extensive work published to the contrary (see, e.g., S. H. T. Page, "The Authenticity of the Ransom Logion [Mark 10:45b]," in *Gospel Perspectives I*, ed. R. T. France and D. Wenham [Sheffield: Sheffield University Press, 1980], 137–61).

40. See D. E. Smith, "Messianic Banquet," *Anchor Bible Dictionary*, ed. D. N. Freedman (New York: Doubleday, 1997), 4:788–91. Smith notes the recurrent thematic cluster of "victory," "celebration," "abundant food," "the presence of the Messiah," "judgment," and the "pilgrimage of the nations" associated with the messianic banquet motif. He refers especially to 1 Chron. 12:38–40; Isa. 25:6–8; 34:5–7; 54:5–55:5; Joel 2:24–26; Zech. 9:15; 3 Macc. 6:30–41; see especially *1 Enoch* 62:12–14; Matt. 22:1–10; Mark 2:18–20; Rev. 19:7–9; et al.

41. Despite his extensive historical criticism, even Becker (*Jesus*, 217) concedes that "his [Jesus'] activity is relevant not only for the present . . . situation; it has consequences for a person's salvation beyond the final judgment . . . the standard by which a person will be judged . . . will be that person's relationship to the person of Jesus (Luke 12:8–9 . . .)."

5

First Peter and the "Sufferings of the Messiah"

MARK DUBIS

Truett Seminary

While other studies regarding the eschatology of 1 Peter are available,[1] this paper focuses upon one particular question regarding the eschatology of 1 Peter, namely, whether 1 Peter has been influenced by the concept of "messianic woes," a concept that appears elsewhere in Jewish and Christian apocalyptic literature. The question is a matter of disagreement among commentators. In an article dating to 1905, C. A. Scott suggested that this concept was present in 1 Peter, but such a view did not appear to gain much ground until Selwyn argued in its favor.[2] Since Selwyn, numerous scholars have found a messianic woes pattern in 1 Peter, although two of the most important modern commentators (Goppelt and Achtemeier) deny such a pattern.[3] This

---

1. For example, E. G. Selwyn, "Eschatology in 1 Peter," in *The Background of the New Testament and Its Eschatology*, ed. W. D. Davies and D. Daube (Cambridge: Cambridge University Press, 1956), 394–401; R. Russell, "Eschatology and Ethics in 1 Peter," *EvQ* 47 (1975): 78–84; D. C. Parker, "The Eschatology of 1 Peter," *BTB* 24 (1994): 27–32; M. Reiser, "Die Eschatologie des 1. Petrusbriefs," in *Weltgericht und Weltvollendung: Zukunftsbilder im Neuen Testament,* ed. H.-J. Klauck (Freiburg: Herder, 1994), 164–81.

2. C. A. Scott, "The Sufferings of Christ: A Note on 1 Peter 1:11," *Expositor,* 6th ser., 12 (1905): 234–40; and E. G. Selwyn, *The First Epistle of St. Peter* (London: MacMillan, 1946), 263–64, 299–303.

3. Scholars who find messianic woes in 1 Peter include A. R. C. Leaney, *The Letters of Peter and Jude,* CBC (Cambridge: Cambridge University Press, 1967), 64; E. Best, *1 Peter,* NCB (Grand Rapids: Eerdmans, 1971), 175; J. R. Michaels, *1 Peter,* WBC (Waco: Word, 1988), 270; W. L. Schutter, *Hermeneutic and Composition in 1 Peter,* WUNT 2/30 (Tübingen: Mohr, 1989), 106–8; T. W. Martin, *Metaphor and Composition in 1 Peter,* SBLDS 131 (Atlanta: Scholars, 1992), 65–68, 242–52. For opposing views, see L. Goppelt, *A Commentary on 1 Peter* (Grand Rapids: Eerdmans, 1993), 330, and P. J. Achtemeier, *1 Peter,* Hermeneia (Minneapolis: Fortress, 1996), 110, 315 n. 143.

paper attempts to offer a fresh investigation of this matter. My own position is that this concept does indeed shape the eschatology of 1 Peter.

At the outset, it is appropriate to describe briefly the concept of messianic woes as it appears in early Jewish and Christian literature.[4] Early Jews and Christians anticipated a horrific period of suffering and tribulation that would precede the coming of the Messiah and the denouement of history. Stereotypical features of these woes include famine, earthquakes, war, apostasy, disease, family betrayal, rampant wickedness, cosmic signs, and (in some texts) the persecution of the righteous. These woes in early Judaism are "messianic" not because the Messiah suffers them, but because they are a prelude to the Messiah's arrival. The crucifixion of Jesus, however, forced early Christians to adapt this Jewish scheme. In light of the cross, early Christians affirmed that, rather than bringing an end to the woes, the Messiah himself had inaugurated these woes in his first advent. Moreover, the church would continue to suffer these woes as it awaited the second advent of Jesus.[5]

First Peter as Apocalyptic

This essay compares the eschatology of 1 Peter to that of numerous other Jewish and Christian apocalyptic texts. Since the definition of "apocalypse" and related terms has been the subject of much discussion in recent years, I choose my terms carefully here. As a starting point, I turn to the definition of "apocalypse" developed by the Apocalypse Group of the Society of Biblical Literature Genres Project:

> "Apocalypse" is a genre of revelatory literature with a narrative framework, in which a revelation is mediated by an otherworldly being to a human recipient, disclosing a transcendent reality which is both temporal, insofar as it envisages

---

4. Other labels besides "messianic woes" appear for this period including "the great tribulation" (Matt. 24:21; Rev. 2:22; 7:14), "the footprints of the Messiah" (*m. Sota* 9:15), "the time of the crucible" (4QFlor 1–3 i 19-ii 2, 4QCat[a] 5+ i 3, 4QpPs[a] 1+ ii 19), "the time of distress" (Dan. 12:1), "the hour of trial" (Rev. 3:10), and "the birthpangs of the Messiah" (*b. Shabb.* 118a; *b. Sanh.* 98b; *b. Pesah.* 118a). It is the latter rabbinic phrase, traveling to English via its German rendering *die Wehen des Mesias*, that is the origin of the contemporary phrase "messianic woes," and I have adopted this label because this appears to be the term that scholars most widely use and understand. I use the term somewhat loosely, however, since some of the Jewish apocalyptic texts that I cite above do not make mention of a messianic figure, and in these instances it may be best to speak of "eschatological woes." To do so, however, would introduce an added layer of complication, and I have thus refrained from such distinctions in this essay.

5. Scholars have given little attention to the study of messianic woes in early Jewish and Christian thought. The most notable exception is D. C. Allison Jr., *The End of the Ages Has Come: An Early Interpretation of the Passion and Resurrection of Jesus* (Philadelphia: Fortress, 1985). This book in its entirety revolves around the topic of messianic woes, although its title gives little indication of this.

eschatological salvation, and spatial insofar as it involves another, supernatural world.[6]

While 1 Peter is most certainly not an "apocalypse" (e.g., it has no narrative framework), it does share important features with the worldview of this genre of literature. With an eye to the definition above, 1 Peter manifests (a) an eschatologically-oriented temporal axis—1 Peter speaks of both eschatological judgment (1:17; 2:23; 4:5–6, 17–18) and eschatological salvation (1:3–4; 5:1, 4, 10); (b) an otherworldly-oriented spatial axis—1 Peter speaks of otherworldly regions (1:4, 12; 3:19, 22) and otherworldly beings (1:12; 3:19, 22; 5:8); and (c) a concern for supernatural revelation (1:11–12; see also 1:5, 7, 12–13; 4:13; 5:1 in which the term ἀποκαλύπτω or ἀποκάλυψις appears).[7] Observing 1 Peter's apocalyptic character, then, we have additional justification to compare 1 Peter to other Jewish and Christian apocalyptic texts, and we should not be surprised if 1 Peter manifests the messianic woes pattern, since this pattern is so prevalent in other apocalyptic literature.

The Messianic Woes Pattern in 1 Peter

Since 1 Peter 4:12–19 is the most highly eschatological pericope in all of 1 Peter, it is an appropriate focal text for our investigation. In what follows I have enumerated ways in which 4:12–19 and other texts within 1 Peter manifest the messianic woes pattern. For the most part, I follow the textual flow of 4:12–19 in order to organize the following discussion.

Messianic Woes Are a Πύρωσις

First Peter 4:12 urges its readers not to be surprised regarding the πύρωσις ("fiery ordeal," RSV) that has come upon them. Πύρωσις appears only rarely in biblical literature. In the New Testament, apart from 1 Peter 4:12, it only appears in Revelation 18:9, 18 with reference to the "burning" of Babylon. In the Septuagint, it only appears twice: in Amos 4:9 it refers to a crop-destroying heat, while in Proverbs 27:21 it refers to a gold-refining fire. It is this latter metallurgical connotation of πύρωσις that is most relevant to 1 Peter 4:12.[8] In that 1 Peter employs a metallurgical metaphor at the outset of the book

6. J. J. Collins, "Introduction: Towards the Morphology of a Genre," in *Apocalypse: The Morphology of a Genre*, ed. J. J. Collins, *Semeia* 14 (Missoula, Mont.: Scholars Press, 1979), 9.

7. For similar views and argumentation regarding the apocalyptic character of 1 Peter, see Achtemeier, *1 Peter*, 105–7; P. H. Davids, *The First Epistle of Peter*, NICOT (Grand Rapids: Eerdmans, 1990), 15–17. See also J. Holdsworth, "The Sufferings in 1 Peter and 'Missionary Apocalyptic,'" in *Studia Biblica 1978: III. Papers on Paul and Other New Testament Authors: Sixth International Congress on Biblical Studies, Oxford 3–7 April 1978*, ed. E. A. Livingstone, JSNTSup 3 (Sheffield: JSOT Press, 1980), 225–32.

8. The majority of appearances of the cognate verb, πυρόω, also relate to metallurgical refinement (Prov. 10:20; Isa. 1:25; Zech. 13:9, etc.).

(1:6–7), the use of πύρωσις in 4:12 appears to be a return to this same metaphor. The persecution that the readers experience is a refining test—as a metalworker subjects precious metals to a refining fire, so God is subjecting the readers to refining trials.

Drawing upon Proverbs 27:21, E. T. Sander argued that πύρωσις was the closest Greek equivalent to the Hebrew מצרף ("crucible"), a term that had technical significance at Qumran.[9] Sander argued that the use of מצרף at Qumran held significance for the interpretation of πύρωσις in 1 Peter 4:12. A technical phrase, עת המצרף ("the time of the crucible"), appears repeatedly in the Qumran literature (4QFlor 1–3 i 19–ii 2; 4QCat[a] 5+ i 3; 4QpPs[a] 1+ ii 19). This phrase refers to a time of suffering and trial that falls upon the world, and is the equivalent of what is elsewhere designated as "messianic woes." Apart from its appearance in this phrase, מצרף also appears alone with connotations of eschatological trial and tribulation (1QM 16:15, 17:1, 9; CD 20:25–27; 1QS 1:17–18, 8:4; 1QH[a] 6:4, 13:16; 4QFlor 1–3 ii 4; 4QM[a] 8–10 ii 11, 11 ii 12). Sander concluded that by the first century πύρωσις (as well as מצרף) had become a technical term for the climactic period of eschatological tribulation. Sander further supported her claim by noting that *Didache* 16 uses πύρωσις in a messianic woes context:

> In the last days the false prophets and the corrupters shall be multiplied, and the sheep shall be turned into wolves, and love shall change to hate; for as lawlessness increaseth they shall hate one another and persecute and betray, and then shall appear the deceiver of the world as a Son of God, and shall do signs and wonders and the earth shall be given over into his hands and he shall commit iniquities which have never been since the world began. Then shall the creation of mankind come to the fiery trial (τὴν πύρωσιν τῆς δοκιμασίας) and "many shall be offended" and be lost, but "they who endure" in their faith "shall be saved." . . .[10]

Sander's fundamental argument is strong.[11] In light of the above evidence, it is clear that πύρωσις appears early in the Christian period with reference to messianic woes (*Didache* 16:5) and may well have possessed a technical significance as a term for the climactic period of eschatological trial. Such a signifi-

---

9. E. T. Sander, "Πύρωσις and the First Epistle of Peter 4:12" (Th.D. diss., Harvard University, 1966). Sander somewhat misreads the evidence, since πύρωσις appears to translate כור rather than מצרף. But in any case, Prov. 27:21 does indicate that πύρωσις was *a* Greek equivalent, if not *the* Greek equivalent, of מצרף.

10. Loeb Classical Library, 1:332–33.

11. I would, however, disagree with Sander's theory regarding the compositional history of 1 Peter, a theory that is coupled with Sander's view that the technical eschatological character of πύρωσις in earlier Petrine-Palestinian traditions was lost to the second-century redactor who drew these traditions together to form 1 Peter.

cance well fits πύρωσις in 1 Peter 4:12, especially since the entire context addresses the issue of eschatological suffering.[12]

Messianic Woes as a Necessity

First Peter views suffering as a "necessity." This theme emerges in 1 Peter 1:6, 4:12, and 5:9, and is yet another indication that 1 Peter is influenced by the messianic woes concept. The use of the verb δεῖ ("it is necessary") in 1 Peter 1:6 points to the inevitability of the readers' suffering. Here this verb is part of a first-class conditional clause, "if it [i.e., the readers' suffering] is necessary." First-class conditions assume the truth of a statement either for the sake of argument or in reality. Since the rest of the letter indicates that suffering is already a reality among the readers, the first-class condition here is not for the sake of argument but rather indicates that the readers' suffering is indeed necessary. For this reason, Michaels is justified to translate "*since* it is necessary."[13]

But what is the background of this view that understands Christian suffering to be "necessary"? Partly it stems from a conviction that the Old Testament Scriptures must be fulfilled, Scriptures that speak of the suffering of God's people (e.g., Zech. 13:7–9; Dan. 12:1). But part of the answer also derives from a conviction that God's purposes regarding the end are fixed and must follow a certain plan (e.g., the man of lawlessness and associated apostasy must precede the day of the Lord in 2 Thessalonians 2:3; the worldwide proclamation of the gospel must precede the end in Matthew 24:14; see also the use of δεῖ with reference to apocalyptic events in Revelation 1:1; 17:10; 20:3; 22:6). A similar apocalyptic necessity appears with regard to the woes—they must occur before the end; indeed, they are signs of the end (Mark 13; Matt. 24; Luke 21). Similarly, 1 Peter views the suffering of Christians as an unavoidable component in the outworking of God's eschatological plan. This eschatological necessity explains the admonition in 4:12: "don't be surprised."[14] A more common line of interpretation, however, is as follows: since Christ suffered, the readers should not be surprised that they too must suffer in the same way as their Lord. Without denying this, a fuller explanation lies in the catechesis of early Christians that taught them about the inevitable character of Christian suffering as the eschaton approached (Acts 14:22; 1 Thess. 3:3–4). The readers of 1 Peter should not be surprised at the πύρωσις that is now upon them because their catechesis taught

12. The expectation of a period of eschatological refinement has origins in OT texts such as Dan. 12:10 and Zech. 13:9.

13. Michaels, *1 Peter*, 29. BDF §372 notes that the first-class condition is "often closely bordering on causal 'since.'" Some question the unity of 1 Peter, bifurcating the book on the grounds that 1:3–4:11 reflects a situation of potential suffering, while 4:12–5:11 reflects a situation of actual suffering. See, for example, C. F. D. Moule, "The Nature and Purpose of 1 Peter," *NTS* 3 (1956): 1–11. Such scholars, however, have overblown the evidence (cf. Achtemeier, *1 Peter*, 58–62).

14. Michaels, *1 Peter*, 29.

them to expect such eschatological suffering. First Peter simply reminds them of this truth once more: in the same way that Jesus had to pass through the eschatological woes in order to experience eschatological glory, so must they.

This same theme appears again in 1 Peter 5:9, although once more obscured by most English translations. In the midst of suffering, 1 Peter reminds the readers of the sufferings of the Christian community elsewhere. The NRSV translates "your brothers and sisters in all the world are undergoing (ἐπιτελέω) the same kinds of sufferings." The NRSV's rendering of ἐπιτελέω as "undergoing," however, does not convey the sense of completion or fulfillment that this verb bears elsewhere; 5:9 does not simply speak of sufferings that Christians are "undergoing," but of sufferings that fellow Christians are bringing to completion. The comfort in this seems to be that God has fixed a certain measure of endtime suffering and this measure will not be exceeded. Compare *4 Ezra* 4:36, where the righteous dead ask "How long?" and are told "when the number of those like yourselves is completed" (cf. also Rev. 6:11; *1 Enoch* 47:4; *2 Apoc. Bar.* 30:2). First Peter 5:9, then, represents a reemergence of the same theme we saw earlier in 1 Peter 1:6; thus, this theme of the necessity of suffering forms an *inclusio* across the entire book. If Peter does indeed have the messianic woes pattern in mind, this explains why Peter believes the readers must suffer—the readers must pass through the woes before they can enter the consummated messianic age.[15]

Messianic Woes as "the Sufferings of the Messiah"

The phrase τὰ τοῦ Χριστοῦ παθήματα ("the sufferings of Christ") appears in both 1 Peter 4:13 and 5:1.[16] Interpreters usually read both occurrences of this genitival phrase as subjective genitives, that is, to refer to that which Christ suffered. I argue, however, that we should read these as descriptive genitives, and we should also understand χριστός as the title "Messiah" rather than a personal name.[17] The resulting translation would be "messianic sufferings" or, in more common parlance, "messianic woes." This phrase, "the sufferings of the Messiah," is thus similar in form and connotation to the rabbinic phrase חבלו של משיח ("the birthpangs of the Messiah").[18]

---

15. Best (*1 Peter*, 175) and Martin (*Metaphor and Composition*, 243 n. 371) adopt such an interpretation of 5:9.

16. Although τὰ εἰς Χριστὸν παθήματα in 1:11 is somewhat different, employing a prepositional phrase rather than a genitival construction, English translations usually also render this phrase as "the sufferings of Christ." For a messianic woes interpretation of 1:11, see especially Schutter, *Hermeneutic and Composition*, 106–8.

17. So also Best, *1 Peter*, 162–63; Leaney, *Letters of Peter*, 64.

18. Although the rabbinic uses of this phrase are late, the use of "birthpangs" for eschatological tribulation in Matt. 24:8 and Mark 13:8 suggests that the full phrase may have been in use in the NT period (cf. Allison, *End of the Ages*, 6 n. 6). A phrase in Col. 1:24 ("the tribulations of the Messiah") has also been understood to parallel the rabbinic phrase. See P. T. O'Brien, *Colossians, Philemon* (Waco: Word, 1982), 78–80.

To read this phrase as a descriptive genitive is not to deny that these sufferings include those that Jesus suffered, but rather to affirm that they are broader than this, including the sufferings of all Christians as well.[19] The eschatological tribulation, the period of the woes, began at the cross, and all Jesus' followers continue to participate in these woes until the end of the age.[20]

Messianic Woes as the Climax of Exilic Suffering

One theme that runs throughout 1 Peter is the application to the church of Old Testament imagery that originally pertained to Israel. The readers, primarily Gentiles, are described, for example, as "a chosen race, a royal priesthood, a holy nation, a people for God's own possession" (2:9 NASB). That these Gentiles are now grafted into Israel, so that Israel's story has become the story of these Gentile readers, is perhaps nowhere better seen than in 1 Peter's description of his readers as awaiting the restoration from exile (and this is despite the return from Babylon centuries before). This restoration predicted by the Old Testament prophets, then, is only ultimately realized at the parousia. Although the readers are currently "exiles" (1 Peter 1:1, 17; 2:11–12; 5:10, 13), one day they will come into the glorious redemption from exile. This restoration theme appears yet again in 1 Peter 4:14 with its reference to God's Spirit of glory resting upon the readers. The gift of the Spirit is one of the hallmark features of prophetic descriptions of the restoration from exile (Isa. 44:3; Ezek. 36:27; 37:14; Joel 2:28–29). But the restoration theme in 1 Peter 4:14 is even more likely given that this verse alludes to Isaiah 11:2, a text that appears in a context that describes the anticipated restoration from exile.

Of interest is that Jewish apocalyptic literature at times represents the messianic woes as the climax of exilic suffering (*T. Mos.* 8; *Jub.* 23). Such an understanding fits well into the framework of 1 Peter's theology. The readers are suffering in exile, and their transition from exile to restoration involves a time

---

19. Schutter (*Hermeneutic and Composition*, 108 n. 76) well states: "That the unthinkable had happened to God's Anointed might have compelled many to interpret it in terms of the 'Woes,' which was surely the category closest at hand from an eschatological perspective. . . . And if such a fate could befall the Messiah, then, or so the reasoning might have gone, where would that leave his followers? Hence it is reasonable to suppose that there was a basis to move directly from a personal frame of reference in early Christian thinking about the Messianic 'Woes' to a corporate one. On this view, the Crucifixion would quickly come to represent an unprecedented, concrete definition of the nature and scale of the 'Woes' attending the End that would necessarily imply a collective frame of reference wherever one was not explicit."

20. A strong argument that early Christians understood the messianic woes to have begun at the cross appears in the parallels between Jesus' eschatological discourse and the passion narratives. Since Jesus' passion experience mirrors various elements of the woes that appear in the eschatological discourse (e.g., betrayal, defense before authorities, darkening of the sun), the Synoptic Gospels imply that the woes are inaugurated with Jesus himself. For such parallels in Mark, see Allison, *End of the Ages*, 36–39.

of particularly terrible suffering. Such is the period in which the readers find themselves, as Jesus at the cross also found himself at the turning point of the eschatological ages.

Messianic Woes, Eschatological Lawlessness, and Apostasy

First Peter 4:15–16 reminds the readers that they must not be murderers, thieves, evildoers, or slanderers, but rather they must remain true to their Christian identity. In the interpretation of these verses, scholars have generally been occupied with questions of vocabulary (especially ἀλλοτριεπίσκοπος), whether the offenses are real or rhetorical, whether the context is a legal setting or not, etc. As a result of these preoccupations, scholars have neglected the fact that these verses appear in the midst of the most eschatologically-charged pericope of the entire book. If one takes account of this eschatological context, a new interpretive option opens up. One of the most common descriptions of the period of the woes is that this period will be characterized by unbridled wickedness (see *1 Enoch* 91:4–7; *4 Ezra* 5:1–3, 9–11; 5:24; 14:16–18; *2 Apoc. Bar.* 27:3–12; 48:37; 70:1–6; *T. Mos.* 7; 2 Tim. 3:1–4). Mindful that his readers live in the last days, Peter warns his readers not to capitulate to the temptation to sin, especially as society becomes increasingly depraved with the approach of the eschaton. If the readers suffer, it must not be because they themselves have joined in the lawlessness that marks the eschatological climax. Rather, they must hold fast to their Christian confession, as verse 16 urges.

Indeed, verse 16 highlights a corollary to the eschatological lawlessness during the woes, namely that apostasy will also mark this period (*1 Enoch* 93:9; *4 Ezra* 5:1; Matt. 24:5–12 par.; 1 Tim. 4:1; 2 Tim. 3:5; 2 Thess. 2:9–12). The concern that Christians not be "ashamed" (αἰσχύνομαι) when they suffer as Christians is much more than a concern for the readers' subjective disposition. Rather, αἰσχύνομαι connotes the possibility of a concrete denial of one's faith (cf. Mark 8:38; Phil. 1:20; 2 Tim. 1:8, 12). Thus, Peter reminds his readers of the pressure to apostatize in the midst of the woes, a pressure to which they must not give in (cf. the "stand fast" of 5:12).

Messianic Woes and the Beginning of the Final Judgment

First Peter 4:17 interprets the sufferings of the readers as the beginning of the final judgment. This theme is consistent with the presentation of messianic woes in various Jewish and Christian apocalyptic texts where the woes are a prelude to, or even an inauguration of, eschatological judgment. As an example, the *Apocalypse of Abraham* 30:2–8 describes the last days as characterized by the following woes: fiery conflagrations, pestilence, famine, earthquakes, war, hail and snow, mauling by wild animals, flight from war and violence, thunder, etc. Immediately following this description, 31:1–3 describes the appearance of a messianic figure ("my chosen one") who consigns the wicked to the underworld regions and the fire of Hades. Thus, here we find the messianic woes immediately followed by the final eschatological judgment.

The Testament of Levi 4:1 provides another example:

> Know, then, that the Lord will effect judgment on the sons of men. For even when stones are split, when the sun is extinguished, the waters are dried up, fire is cowed down, all creation is distraught, invisible spirits are vanishing, and hell is snatching spoils by sufferance of the Most High, men—unbelieving still—will persist in their wrongdoing. Therefore they shall be condemned with punishment.[21]

Here again the eschatological woes appear in stereotypical terms: earthquakes (stones splitting), the darkening of the sun, drought, fire, etc. In light of the opening phrase ("the Lord will effect judgment on the sons of men"), these woes are part and parcel of God's judgment in the last days. But these woes are not yet the *consummation* of judgment, since in the midst of these woes the wicked continue to rebel against God. The consummation of judgment only appears in the final sentence of the above paragraph ("they shall be condemned with punishment"). Once again, then, the final judgment chronologically follows the woes and stands in close association with them since the woes, too, are God's "judgment."

Yet another Jewish apocalyptic text which exhibits this close association between the messianic woes and the consummation of eschatological judgment is *2 Apoc. Bar.* 48:30–41. This passage describes the last days as characterized by a lack of wisdom, reversals of the status quo, rumors, violence, strife, and war. People do not realize that this period of chaos itself is the beginning of judgment (48:32: "they are unaware that my judgement has come upon them").[22] Nevertheless, eventually it becomes painfully apparent that the end has come (48:38) and final judgment falls. The Judge comes and the wicked come to a fiery end (48:39–40). Here again, then, the woes are a foretaste of eschatological judgment, or perhaps better stated, the inauguration or first installment of eschatological judgment.

In the above texts, the messianic woes are the beginning of the eschatological judgment, a judgment that falls upon the *wicked*. What makes 1 Peter distinct from these texts is that in 1 Peter the woes fall upon the people of God. While this is a rarer perspective of the woes in Jewish literature, it is not altogether ab-

---

21. James H. Charlesworth, ed., *Old Testament Pseudepigrapha* (Garden City, N.J.: Doubleday, 1983), 1:789.

22. Translation from *The Apocryphal Old Testament*, ed. H. F. D. Sparks (Oxford: Clarendon, 1984), 867.

sent (especially at Qumran).[23] Consider also *T. Moses* 8–9, where the woes fall upon Israel. The woes here largely take the form of persecution. Although their persecutors are godless and the persecution vis-à-vis their persecutors is unjust, this persecution is simultaneously the just judgment of God upon Israel. Only after a description of the woes upon Israel does the *Testament of Moses* go on to describe the woes that fall upon the wicked. The parallels with 1 Peter at this point are striking: (a) The woes fall upon the people of God; (b) the woes come in the form of persecution; (c) the woes constitute the judgment of God; and (d) judgment falls first upon the people of God, then upon the wicked.

Turning to a New Testament text, Revelation 6–16 exhibits this same connection between the messianic woes and final judgment. While the seals, trumpets, and bowls are not the climax of eschatological judgment, they are nevertheless a preliminary realization of that judgment.[24]

In summary, 1 Peter 4:17's reference to the sufferings of the readers as the beginning of the final judgment bears marked similarities to the representation in apocalyptic literature of the messianic woes as the prelude to or inauguration of final judgment.

Messianic Woes as Barely Escapable

First Peter 4:18's citation of Proverbs 11:31 expands upon 4:17's assertion that judgment will begin with God's own people. Since the righteous are only barely saved, where then will the wicked appear after the judgment? Both halves of this quotation are best illuminated against the backdrop of messianic woes. Drawing upon the Old Testament's remnant theology (Amos 9:8–15; Mic. 4:6–8; Isa. 4:2–3), early Judaism conceived of the remnant as those who survive the messianic woes, emerge on the other side of God's eschatological judgment, and thus experience eschatological salvation.[25] Early Jews often viewed these final days with trepidation, since they believed that even the righteous could only with difficulty be numbered among the eschatological survivors. In *2 Apoc. Bar.* 28:3, Baruch concludes that while it would be wonderful to see God's mighty acts in the endtimes, it is better that one *not* live until that time because of the pressure to apostatize during the messianic woes. Similarly in *4 Ezra* 13:16–20, Ezra debates whether the experience of living in the last days is worth the risks and dangers that

---

23. So Allison, *End of the Ages*, 19–22. Contrast R. J. Bauckham, "The Great Tribulation in the Shepherd of Hermas," *JTS*, n.s., 25 (1974): 35–36: "Contrary to common assertion the final period of suffering and persecution for the people of God is scarcely to be found in Jewish apocalyptic literature: descriptions of the 'Messianic woes' are concerned with natural and social disintegration and with judgement on sinners, not with the sufferings of the righteous."

24. I. T. Beckwith, *The Apocalypse of John* (1919; reprinted, Grand Rapids: Baker, 1979), 38–39.

25. M. E. Stone (*Fourth Ezra: A Commentary on the Book of Fourth Ezra* [Minneapolis: Fortress, 1990], 148), rightly notes that *4 Ezra* uses "the survivors" as a technical term for those who survive the messianic woes (*4 Ezra* 5:41; 6:21–25; 7:27; 9:7–8, 21; 12:34; 13:16, 26, 48).

the woes will pose. Turning to Christian literature, the eschatological discourse in the Synoptic Gospels also describes the difficulty of surviving the messianic woes. The trials and temptations of those days will be so intense that many will apostatize (Matt. 24:10–12). Indeed, were it not for a divine shortening of those days, a sign of God's protective intervention, none of the elect would be saved (Matt. 24:22; Mark 13:20). This need for God's protection in the midst of the woes is also a prominent theme in other messianic woes texts (*4 Ezra* 13:23; 7:27; *Apoc. Abr.* 29:17; *2 Apoc. Bar.* 29:3; 32:1; 71:1; Rev. 3:10; 7:3–8; Herm. *Vis.* 4.1.7; 4.2.3–4). I would argue that this stream within Jewish and Christian apocalyptic illumines 1 Peter 4:18's reference to the righteous only scarcely being saved. It is only with difficulty that anyone—even the righteous person—emerges through the days of eschatological tribulation. And if one does emerge, it is only due to God's enabling power and protection (cf. this theme in 1:5, which describes the readers as those whom God is protecting as the eschaton approaches).

We might further ask, Does this conceptual framework within Jewish apocalyptic shed any light on the second half of 1 Peter 4:18's question regarding the destiny of the wicked? The phrase ποῦ φανεῖται is quite often understood to mean what will *become of* the sinner (so NIV, NASB). But the more literal rendering of the RSV ("where will the impious and sinner *appear*") is preferable. This latter rendering better points to the image of the eschatological judgment sweeping away the wicked so that they are not among the eschatological survivors and thus can be found nowhere in the new creation.[26]

Messianic Woes and the Trust of the Righteous

The readers of 1 Peter, according to 4:19, are ones "who suffer according to the will of God" (NASB), that is, their suffering comes to them as a part of God's sovereign plan for them. While they could become embittered against God, the proper response is to entrust themselves to God in the midst of the eschatological ordeal. Such trust is especially vital if even the righteous require God's protection in order to emerge from the messianic woes. Such trust manifests itself in a humble submission to God's purposes, even though his purposes involve trials and tribulation. This theme of humble submission in the midst of trial appears in 1 Peter 5:6 ("humble yourselves, therefore, under God's mighty hand" NIV), and is a theme that appears in other messianic woes texts. Consider, for example, 4QpPs^a ii 9–11, a text that interprets Psalm 37:11 to refer to "the congregation of the poor who will accept the appointed time of affliction and will be saved from all the traps of Belial."[27] Note that those who are saved from the eschatological ordeal are those

---

26. The description of God as a "faithful Creator" in 4:19 does not, as most commentators argue, look backward to God's initial act of creation, but rather looks forward to the new creation that the righteous will inherit.

27. Translation from M. A. Knibb, *The Qumran Community* (Cambridge: Cambridge University Press, 1987), 250.

who "accept" this time of affliction, rather than chafing at it (cf. Zeph. 3:11–12; *b. Sanh.* 98a; *2 Apoc. Bar.* 48:17–19). In contrast to those who humbly accept eschatological affliction are the wicked in the Book of Revelation who curse God when the woes fall upon them, refusing to repent (Rev. 9:20–21; 16:9, 11). The readers of 1 Peter must not respond as the wicked to the woes. Rather, they must find their example in Jesus, who humbly entrusted himself to God in the midst of eschatological suffering and judgment (2:23).[28]

Conclusion

In conclusion, 1 Peter reflects the concept of messianic woes that appears so frequently in other apocalyptic literature. To be sure, the woes in 1 Peter do not appear in the same form as in other apocalyptic texts. First Peter has nothing to say of earthquakes, famines, or cosmic signs. The woes in 1 Peter primarily take the shape of persecution, although the book also has an eye to the moral decay of society and the concomitant threat of apostasy and betrayal. So the form of the woes in 1 Peter is rather abbreviated. Nevertheless, 1 Peter's language and fundamental conceptualization of the eschatological ordeal finds strong resonance with the pattern of messianic woes in other apocalyptic literature. This pattern is especially manifest in 4:12–19, but this concept also stands behind other texts within 1 Peter and, indeed, the theology of the book as a whole.

So what are the implications of this analysis of 1 Peter's eschatology for contemporary believers? Believers today live, as did first-century readers of 1 Peter, in a period of tension between the already and the not yet. On the one hand, believers have come to the long-awaited era of redemption (1:10–12), have been born again (1:3, 23), experience the presence and gifts of the Spirit (4:10–11), and have an unquenchable hope for the future (1:3–5, 8, 13, 21; 3:15; 5:1, 4, 10). On the other hand, the consummation of salvation is yet to come, or, in 1 Peter's terms, the restoration from exile is not yet fully realized. While Jesus' glory marks the experience of believers, so does his suffering. The eschatological tribulation that began in Jesus' own suffering continues to characterize the experience of believers in the present age. So believers must commit themselves to a life of faithful endurance, trusting God to bring them through eschatological trial into the fulness of their inheritance.[29]

---

28. This theme emerges elsewhere in 1 Peter in 5:7's citation of LXX Ps. 54:23 (ET 55:22), a text which Hermas (*Vis.* 4.2.4) also cites as an appropriate response in the midst of the messianic woes. Since this psalm text is cited both in 1 Peter and in Hermas within the context of eschatological trial, Bauckham ("Great Tribulation in the Shepherd of Hermas," 37) argues that this OT text developed into an early Christian tradition as to how one should respond in the ultimate eschatological crisis.

29. For a fuller treatment of the theme of this paper, see M. Dubis, *Messianic Woes in First Peter: Suffering and Eschatology in 1 Peter 4:12–19* (New York: Lang, forthcoming).

6

The Eschatology of 1 John

DONALD W. MILLS

Central Baptist Theological Seminary

In contrast to the Fourth Gospel, the eschatology of 1 John has largely been overlooked.[1] If it is examined, its treatment is usually one-sided so that realized eschatology, i.e., the idea that future expectations such as eternal life are at least to some extent integral to the believer's present experience, receives little or no attention.[2] In other cases it is treated as a foil for issues pertaining to its relationship to the Fourth Gospel in such matters as authorship, date, priority of composition, the "Johannine Community," and redactional hypoth-

---

1. For example, in G. E. Ladd's work (*A Theology of the New Testament* [Grand Rapids: Eerdmans, 1974]), the eschatology of 1 John is merely touched upon (613), whereas the eschatology of the Fourth Gospel has several pages devoted to it (298–308). Although the treatment by W. Dumbrell (*The Search for Order: Biblical Eschatology in Focus* [Grand Rapids: Baker, 1994], 235–58) devotes a valuable chapter to "Johannine Eschatology," only *one passing reference* is made to 1 John. When the author turns to the eschatology of the General Epistles (317–29), 1 John is not mentioned at all. L. Morris touches upon the eschatology of the Fourth Gospel, but not the Epistles (*New Testament Theology* [Grand Rapids: Zondervan, 1986], 255).

2. Examples include D. Guthrie, *New Testament Theology* (Leicester: Inter-Varsity, 1981), 801, 855; R. Kysar, "Epistles of John," in *The Anchor Bible Dictionary*, ed. D. N. Freedman (New York: Doubleday, 1992), 3.911; R. Bowman, "John, 1, 2 & 3, Eschatology of," *Dictionary of Premillennial Theology*, ed. Mal Couch (Grand Rapids: Kregel, 1996), 219–20. J. Lieu swings the pendulum the other direction and essentially denies future eschatology (*Theology of the Johannine Epistles* [Cambridge: Cambridge, 1991], 73, 87–90, 107).

eses, among other things.[3] Accordingly, the eschatology of 1 John is usually considered, at best, to be of secondary importance to Johannine theology, even to 1 John itself. Other theological themes emphasized in the commentaries and other literature (i.e., the nature of God, Christology, and ethics) generally overshadow eschatology.

In view of this, the argument of this study is to show that the overall framework of 1 John is shaped by the author's eschatological worldview as part of that larger redemptive-historical outlook characteristic of New Testament theology.[4] It is maintained that 1 John abounds both in realized and future eschatological themes and shares the same general eschatological outlook as the Fourth Gospel.

Gospel and Epistle

A Common Eschatological Outlook?

During the last several years, mainstream Johannine scholarship has directed much of its attention to the existence of a group of early Christians in Asia Minor known as the "Johannine community."[5] According to this hypothesis, multiple authors and/or redactors holding to differing views of eschatology were involved in the composition of the Johannine corpus over a period of the community's history.[6] As a result, the two writings are said to reflect disparate eschatological viewpoints. The writer (or writers) of the Fourth Gospel modifies the traditional eschatology of Christ's imminent and bodily return in order to address acute needs in the community. Community members had recently been expelled from the syn-

---

3. See, for example, R. Bultmann, *Theology of the New Testament* (New York: Scribners, 1951, 1955), 2.39; idem, *The Gospel of John: A Commentary* (Oxford: Basil Blackwell, 1971), 11; idem, *The Johannine Epistles*, ed. R. W. Funk (Philadelphia: Fortress, 1973), 2; A. Mattill, "Johannine Communities behind the Fourth Gospel: George Richter's Analysis," *TS* 38 (1977): 294–315. Since 1 John places more emphasis upon traditional eschatology than realized, Dodd argues that it was written before the Fourth Gospel by a different author ("The First Epistle of John and the Fourth Gospel," *BJRL* 21 [1937]: 143).

4. For a helpful treatment of our topic, see Wai Yee Ng, "Johannine Eschatology as Demonstrated in 1 John" (Th.M. thesis, Westminster Theological Seminary, 1988).

5. Out of the vast literature devoted to this subject we mention J. L. Martyn, *History and Theology of the Fourth Gospel* (Nashville: Abingdon, 1968); O. Cullmann, *The Johannine Circle* (Philadelphia: Westminster, 1975); A. R. Culpepper, *The Johannine School* (Missoula, Mont.: Scholars, 1975); J. Bogart, *Orthodox and Heretical Perfectionism in the Johannine Community as Evident in the First Epistle of John*, SBLDS 33 (Missoula, Mont.: Scholars, 1977); Mattill, "Johannine Communities"; R. Whitacre, *Johannine Polemic: The Role of Tradition and Theology*, SBLDS 67 (Chico, Calif.: Scholars, 1982).

6. M. E. Boismard, "L'évolution du thème eschatologique dans les traditions Johanniques," *RB* 68 (1961): 507–24; G. Klein, "'Das Wahre Licht Scheint Schon.' Beobachtungen zur Zeit- und Geschichtserfahrung einer urchristlichen Schule," *ZTK* 68 (1971): 261–326; G. Richter, "Präsentische und futurische Eschatologie im 4. Evangelium," in *Gegenwart and Kommendes Reich*, ed. P. Fiedler and D. Zeller (Stuttgart: Katholisches Bibelwerk, 1975), 117–52. Cf. Mattill, "Johannine Communities," 294–315.

agogue (John 9) and were enduring intense persecution from the outside.[7] In order to comfort them and help them compensate for what they had lost from their previous associations with Judaism, the author of the Gospel shows them that the eschatological promises of Jesus have already been realized.[8] The parousia becomes redefined in terms of the Spirit's coming and indwelling after Christ's ascension into heaven.[9] It is as if Jesus himself were present among them, since the "other Paraclete" so closely resembles the person of Jesus.

By the time of 1 John traditional eschatology reappears, largely as the result of the community's interaction with other streams of early Christianity and as a polemic against the extremes of the "secessionists" whose realized eschatology finds support in the Fourth Gospel.[10] This marks a return to an earlier or more traditional concept.

However, apart from speculating about sources, redaction, or elaborate sociohistorical reconstructions of a "community," we maintain from a synchronic point of view that both writings in fact share a common eschatological outlook.[11] It is certainly true that the Gospel places emphasis upon such present eschatological aspects as judgment (3:18), eternal life (5:24), and resurrection (5:21; 11:25), and that the expression "children of God" refers to a present status (1:12).[12] On the other hand, there *are* elements of future eschatology in the Fourth Gospel, such as resurrection on the "last day" (6:39–40), final judgment (5:28–29; 12:48), and the second coming (14:1–3; 21:22).[13] It is also true that 1 John describes the second coming (1 John 2:28; 3:2) and

---

7. R. E. Brown, *The Community of the Beloved Disciple: The Life, Loves, and Hates of an Individual Church in New Testament Times* (New York: Paulist, 1979), 51.

8. Ibid., 166.

9. C. H. Dodd, *The Interpretation of the Fourth Gospel* (Cambridge: Cambridge University Press, 1953), 395, 403–5. Although Dodd's interpretation of John 14:2–3 predates the Johannine community hypothesis, one dovetails with the other. However, not all advocates of a Johannine community interpret John 14:2–3 this way (Brown, *The Gospel according to St. John*, AB 29A (New York: Doubleday, 1970], 626–27).

10. Brown, *Community*, 136; idem, *The Epistles of John*, AB 30 (New York: Doubleday, 1982), 99; R. Kysar, *John: The Maverick Gospel* (Louisville: Westminster, 1993), 144.

11. The idea of a "Johannine community" is not entirely without merit, if we are careful to avoid the tendency of reading "behind" the Johannine corpus to reconstruct it. There can be no question that the author considered himself part of a community of believers in his local area. For this reason we still employ the term "community" when referring to John's readers.

12. Dodd, "The First Epistle of John," 143.

13. In addition to Dodd (*Interpretation* 395, 403–5), R. Schnackenburg (*The Gospel according to St. John* [New York, Crossroad, 1987], 3:62), P. W. Comfort (*I Am the Way: A Spiritual Journey through the Gospel of John* [Grand Rapids: Baker, 1994], 122–27), and Dumbrell (*Eschatology*, 254) do not see the parousia here. On the other hand, R. H. Gundry ("'In My Father's House Are Many Monai' (John 14.2)," *ZNW* 58 [1967]: 68–72) argues that 14:2–3 refers both to the fellowship the disciples of Jesus will enjoy with him through the Spirit *and* to the parousia (and is another example of Johannine double meaning). Despite arguments to the contrary, it is difficult to understand the language of John 14:3 as *strictly present* in orientation (see G. Burge, *The Anointed Community: The Holy Spirit in the Johannine Tradition* [Grand Rapids: Eerdmans, 1987], 145). Moreover, after his resurrection Jesus could still speak of his "coming" (John 21:22).

judgment (4:17; cf. 5:16–17) as exclusively future and employs other eschatological terms not found in the Gospel, including "antichrist" (2:18; 4:3), "lawlessness" (3:4), and "parousia" (2:28). The expression "children of God" is to be connected, at least in part, with future hope (1 John 3:2). On the other hand, there *are* elements of realized eschatology in 1 John, such as eternal life (which is seen as a present possession in 5:13), the dawning of the light (2:8), the defeat of the evil one (2:13–14), and the possession of the Spirit (3:24; 4:13), among others. The disparities between them, accordingly, do not necessarily result from a neglect of one aspect of eschatology in favor of another.[14] These should be seen more as complementary rather than contradictory, reflecting different purposes and emphases.[15]

Correcting an Overrealized Eschatology?

In connection with this, one must consider whether the author of 1 John was combating an "overrealized" eschatology held by the opponents of the Johannine community.[16] This is based upon the premise that the "secessionists" (2:19) developed a faulty theology, and, to be specific, a faulty eschatology, at least in part, from a misreading of the Fourth Gospel.[17] Certain statements in the Gospel could potentially be misconstrued to suggest that disciples of Christ "have it all now": (1) they already have eternal life (e.g., John 3:36; 5:24; 6:54); (2) they will never die (6:50; 8:51; 11:25–26); (3) they are already declared free from condemnation (3:18; 5:24); (4) they have seen God (12:45; 14:7–9); (5) they are in the light (John 8:12); (6) Jesus has already come (especially if John 14:1–3 is understood in light of 14:18–23);[18] and (7) they already have knowledge (of God, 17:3; of the Shepherd, 10:14; of the truth, 8:32; of the

---

14. A. E. Brooke, *The Johannine Epistles*, ICC (Edinburgh: T & T Clark, 1912), 37; W. F. Howard, "The Common Authorship of the Johannine Gospel and Epistles," *JTS* 48 (1947): 22; W. G. Kümmel, *Introduction to the New Testament* (Nashville: Abingdon, 1973), 443.

15. Ng, "Johannine Eschatology," 3; M. Hengel, *The Johannine Question* (London: SCM/Philadelphia: Trinity Press International, 1989), 32–33; D. A. Carson, "The Three Witnesses and the Eschatology of 1 John," in *To Tell the Mystery: Essays on New Testament Eschatology in Honor of Robert H. Gundry*, ed. T. E. Schmidt and M. Silva, JSNTSup 100 (Sheffield, England: JSOT Press, 1994), 218.

16. All things considered, when addressing the difficult matter of the opponents in 1 John, a judicious use of both external and internal evidence is the wisest course. This suggests that the author of 1 John was combating some form of incipient Gnosticism (D. Guthrie, *New Testament Introduction* [Downers Grove, Ill.: InterVarsity, 1970], 869–72; D. A. Carson, D. J. Moo, and L. Morris, *An Introduction to the New Testament* [Grand Rapids: Zondervan, 1992], 455).

17. Bogart, *Perfectionism*, 2–3, 51–122; Brown, *Community*, 135–38. Contra D. Rensberger, who sees no conflict between author and opponents in this area (*1 John, 2 John, 3 John* [Nashville: Abingdon, 1997], 42).

18. Dodd, *Interpretation*, 395, 403–5.

Spirit, 14:17).[19] From these could be inferred that all the blessings of the eschaton are available right now, and so (1) believers are already "perfect"—there are no further ethical obligations incumbent upon them—and (2) there is nothing forthcoming that they do not already possess—hence, no future eschatology.[20]

Therefore, in all likelihood the author of 1 John was refuting these false inferences. He does so by (1) connecting realized eschatology to ethical obligation (i.e., contrasting 2:8 with 2:9–11 and 3:14a with 3:14b–15), and (2) reemphasizing future eschatology and the incentives attendant with it (2:28–3:3).[21]

Present Eschatological Reality

The Appearing of the Eternal Life

From a careful reading of 1 John this vital principle emerges: the advent of Christ commenced a new era that carried with it implications of unprecedented proportions for the history of redemption. An integral element of Johannine theology is this fundamental tenet: eternity has invaded time.[22] The prologue (1 John 1:1–4) gives eloquent testimony to this pinnacle of redemptive history. It is the first, most significant, and most dramatic reference to the incarnation. Standing at the very beginning of the Epistle, its theme and message are programmatic.

Some words and phrases in the prologue carry significant eschatological overtones. First, "from the beginning," a very elastic concept, refers in this context to Christ's preexistence, or "the absolute beginning."[23] The One who was "from the beginning" appears in time (1:2).[24] The term "life" is rich in

19. For an extensive summary of the present eschatological realities enjoyed by the believer in the Gospel of John, see Bogart, *Perfectionism*, 62–82.

20. Bogart, *Perfectionism*, 73–74; Brown, *Community*, 136. S. Pétrement believes that the Gnostics received their concept of realized eschatology from the Fourth Gospel (*A Separate God: The Christian Origins of Gnosticism* [San Francisco: Harper & Row, 1984], 160).

21. Brown, *Community*, 137–38; idem, *Epistles*, 99–100.

22. S. Smalley, *1, 2, 3 John*, WBC (Waco: Word, 1984), 96; G. Beale, "Eschatology," *Dictionary of the Later New Testament and Its Developments*, ed. R. P. Martin and P. H. Davids (Downers Grove, Ill.: InterVarsity, 1997), 335.

23. H. Conzelmann, "Was von Anfang war," in *Neutestamentliche Studien für Rudolf Bultmann zu seinem siebzigsten Geburtstag am 20. August 1954* (Berlin: Töpelmann, 1957), 195–96. Cf. I. H. Marshall, *The Epistles of John*, NICNT (Grand Rapids: Eerdmans, 1978), 100 and note. It is a multipurpose expression in 1 John, referring to eternity past (1 John 2:13–14; cf. John 1:1), the beginning of redemptive history in Genesis (3:8; cf. John 8:44), and the beginning of the readers' Christian experience (2:7; 2:24; 3:11).

24. The person of Christ is primarily in view in v. 2, which is, of course integrally related to the message about him, since the main verb in 1:3 ("proclaim") is picking up the "which we have heard . . ." of 1:1. Likewise, the "Word" refers primarily to Christ himself (R. Law, *The Tests of Life: A Study of the First Epistle of St. John* [Grand Rapids: Baker, 1968], 44; R. Schnackenburg, *The Johannine Epistles* [New York: Crossroad, 1992], 59; contra J. R. W. Stott, *The Epistles of John*, TNTC [Leicester: Inter-Varsity, 1960], 58).

connotation, referring to Jesus himself, who embodies life (1:1–2; 5:20), or to the salvation he offers (2:25; 3:14–15; 5:11–13).[25] "Eternal life" occurs in 1:2; 2:25; 3:15; 5:11, 13; 5:20 with 1:2 and 5:20 forming an *inclusio*. Although the *word* "fellowship" is confined to chapter one (1:3, 6–7), the *idea* is developed extensively. This idea is an integral element of the purpose of the proclamation (1:3a), refers ultimately to union with God (1:3b) and participation in divine life, reverberates throughout the remainder of the Epistle as an underlying theme, and is grounded in the incarnation.[26] Because "fellowship" carries eschatological connotations, "joy" is to be understood the same way.[27]

The significance of the prologue is, therefore, to lay out the eschatological plan of God from eternity past: the appearing of the (Eternal) Life leads to the proclamation of the message of that Life, which, in turn, leads to fellowship (with God and the author), resulting in joy.[28] In light of this, the primary focus of 1 John goes beyond combating secessionists, or preventing and/or correcting the ideas of errant Christians. It also transcends the historical occasion of the Epistle.[29] The picture is a more comprehensive one, with its implications worked out in 2:8–17. The coming of Christ signifies that the darkness of the old age under the rule of sin and the evil one is gradually giving way to the light of the new (2:8). Authentic believers (those whose lives are characterized by love) already abide in the light, in contrast to the other group that remains in darkness (2:9–11; or death, 3:14b). In a real sense, the blessings of this new age are already part of the community's present experience (2:12–14), for in this section the writer affirms the forgiveness of sins, the knowledge of God, and victory over the evil one, ideas that echo throughout the epistle. On this basis John exhorts his readers not to love the world (2:15), for it is passing away (2:17, cf. v. 8). This grand theme reaches its highest point in the threefold affirmation of "the Great Christian Certainties" (5:18–20).[30]

---

25. Smalley *1,2,3 John*, 10. In 1 John, eternal life is always in view whether or not the term "life" is accompanied by the adjective "eternal" (cf. Brown, *Epistles*, 168). "Life" occurs three times in two verses (1:1–2): the Word of life, the life, and the eternal life.

26. The concept of fellowship is expressed most frequently by two very important "interiority" phrases: "to remain, abide, live, or reside in" (2:6, 24, 27–28; 3:6, 9) and "to be in" (2:5). See E. Malatesta, *Interiority and Covenant: A Study of "Einai en" and "Menein en" in the First Letter of Saint John* (Rome: Biblical Institute, 1978), 24–36, for a survey of the way these expressions are used in 1 John.

27. Stott, *Epistles*, 66; Bultmann, *Epistles*, 14; Bogart, *Perfectionism*, 69; Brown, *Epistles*, 173–74; Smalley, *1, 2, 3 John*, 15; Ng, "Eschatology," 25; G. Strecker, *The Johannine Letters*, ed. H. Attridge (Minneapolis: Fortress, 1996), 20–21.

28. Ng, "Eschatology," 25.

29. Contra Klein ("Das wahre Licht," 261–326), who argues that the realized eschatology of the Fourth Gospel is modified in 1 John in order to address the specific occasion of the Epistle. Specifically, he maintains that it is the application of a predetermined theological principle to a concrete historical situation. Because there is already a measure of historicization in the Fourth Gospel, this "modification" is overstated (Brown, *Epistles*, 287).

30. C. H. Dodd, *The Johannine Epistles* (London: Hodder and Stoughton/New York: Harper, 1946), 138.

The Assurance of Eternal Life

The eschatological notion of "eternal life" in 1 John is very prominent, such that it "constitutes the basic framework of the letter. . . ."[31] Indeed, the primary purpose of 1 John, set forth in 5:13, is to offer assurance to community members that they can know with confidence they already have eternal life, that life of the age to come.[32] The clause "so that you may know that you have eternal life" underscores the place of realized eschatology as integral to the controlling purpose of the Epistle. In the original text, the adjective translated "eternal" appears at the end of the clause, separated by the verb "to have," in order "to make the eternal quality of life prominent."[33] This verse (5:13) introduces the final section (5:13–21), one permeated with a confidence that echoes throughout the whole Epistle.[34] The fundamental theme of the pericope is the *present experience of eternal life* (5:13; cf. 5:20), which reaches its high point in 5:18–20 and the three successive occurrences of "we know." Because eternal life is a present gift, one does not need to wait for the age to come to receive it. At the same time, however, the author realizes that believers do not experience it in a vacuum, for he connects it with various ethical obligations, such as love in 3:14–15.

The Gift of the Holy Spirit

The viewpoint of the Fourth Gospel and 1 John generally coincides with that larger redemptive-historical outlook whereby the outpouring of the Holy Spirit signifies the dawning of the new era, encompasses new covenant blessings, and inaugurates the period known as "the last days."[35] Indeed, the place of the Spirit occupies center stage for Johannine eschatology.[36] However, both

31. Lieu, *Theology*, 22.

32. There are many references to writing (1:4; 2:1; 2:12–14; 2:21; 2:26; 5:13), but the controlling purpose of the Epistle is summed up in 5:13: (1) it appears near the end of the work, summarizing all that has been said, (2) it parallels the purpose statement in John 20:31, which is believed by most to control the message of the Gospel (Brown, *John*, 2:1055–61), (3) its major idea—life—is a recurring theme in the Epistle (1:1–2; 2:25; 3:14–15; 5:11–13, 16, 20), and (4) it echoes the initial statement in 1:3b–4 regarding fellowship with God and joy. See, for example, B. F. Westcott, *The Epistles of St. John* (London: MacMillan, 1883), 188; Marshall, *Epistles*, 243; Smalley, *1, 2, 3 John*, 289–90.

33. J. L. Anderson, *An Exegetical Summary of 1, 2 and 3 John* (Dallas: Summer Institute of Linguistics, 1992), 208; cf. Marshall, *Epistles*, 243 n. 3; Smalley, *1, 2, 3 John*, 290. The Greek in 5:13b reads: ὅτι ζωὴν ἔχετε αἰώνιον (that you have eternal life).

34. Lieu, *Theology*, 27.

35. D. Holwerda, *The Holy Spirit and Eschatology in the Gospel of John* (Kampen: J. H. Kok N.V., 1959), 1–2; G. Vos, *The Pauline Eschatology* (Phillipsburg, N.J.: Presbyterian and Reformed, 1991), 58–60, 159–71; H. Ridderbos, *Paul: An Outline of His Theology* (Grand Rapids: Eerdmans, 1975), 64–65, 86–87, 215–23.

36. R. Schnackenburg, "Die johannische Gemeinde und ihre Geisterfahrung," in *Die Kirche des Anfangs: für Heinz Schürmann*, ed. R. Schnackenburg, J. Ernst, and J. Wanke (Freiburg: Herder, 1978), 277–306; Carson, "Three Witnesses," 219. Conversely, Lieu deemphasizes the significance of the Spirit for 1 John (*Theology*, 49).

the Fourth Gospel and 1 John share a distinctive perspective of the interface between eschatology and pneumatology. Although the Fourth Gospel still retains traditional futuristic eschatology of a final consummation, "John's chief concern is not the past or the future but the present. His is an eschatology shaped by the presence of Christ in the believer's present existence. His emphasis on the Spirit is the means by which this presence is realized."[37]

In 1 John a crisis of major proportions has rocked the community over the issue of pneumatology (first seen in 2:18–20).[38] The debate rages over the following issues: (1) who possesses the truth (1 John 2:20, 27); (2) what constitutes orthodox faith (4:1–6; 5:6, 8); (3) who makes up the true community (3:24; 4:13); and (4) why only those truly born of God (4:7; 5:1, 4) are righteous (3:9). The Epistle carefully preserves the Johannine tradition of the Spirit set forth in the Fourth Gospel, namely, the realized-eschatological presence of Christ in the life of the believer mediated through the Spirit.

"You Have an Anointing" (1 John 2:20, 27)

It is virtually certain that the Spirit is to be identified with the "anointing."[39] Johannine Christians would have recognized this, for the Fourth Gospel associates the Spirit's sending with Jesus (John 14:16, 26; 15:26). Jesus as the "Holy One" (John 6:69) gives the Spirit to believers (John 14:16). The "anointing" occurs in the context of an eschatological crisis, as seen in the way the secessionists (1 John 2:19) who are disseminating christological errors (1 John 2:22–23, 26) are linked with the coming apocalyptic Antichrist (1 John 2:18).[40] From the standpoint of Johannine theology, the "anointing" is eschatologically significant. The community would have seen in the person of Jesus and his relationship to the Spirit, which is a sign of the Messianic Age (Isa. 11:1–2; 42:1; 48:16; 61:1), a paradigm for their own Christian experience.[41] This image (1 John 2:20, 27) also reflects new covenant thought, which is applied to the crisis facing the community.[42] Their possession of the Spirit enables them to discern the "big lie" (2:22) of the antichrists (2:18), whose apostasy from the community already foreshadows the Lawless One of the end times. These seductive teachers attempt to deceive (2:26) the commu-

---

37. Burge, *Community*, 116, 137–49.

38. Burge observes that "the final crisis of the Johannine community was essentially pneumatic" (*Community*, 224).

39. This view is espoused by the great majority of interpreters, including W. Nauck (*Die Tradition und der Charakter des ersten Johannesbriefes* [Tübingen: Mohr, 1957], 94–95) and Schnackenburg (*Epistles*, 141).

40. Brown, *Epistles*, 365; G. Burge, *The Letters of John* (Grand Rapids: Zondervan, 1996), 127.

41. Burge, *Community*, 85.

42. Malatesta, *Interiority*, 220, citing P. Couture, *The Teaching Function in the Church of 1 John* (Rome: Gregorian University, 1968), 44–49; M. Boismard, "Je ferai avec vous une alliance nouvelle," *Lumière et vie* 8 (1953): 104; A. Edanad, *Christian Existence and the New Covenant* (Bangalore: Dharmaram Publications, 1987), 174–76.

nity into believing that their experience of the Spirit is somehow deficient and that a "pneumatic" instructor is a necessary mediator (2:27) for gaining true knowledge about Christ (2:22–23) and eternal life (2:25). The author of 1 John affirms that his readers are indwelt and taught by the Spirit, whose realized-eschatological presence is portrayed under this image. Thus they are kept from that eschatological apostasy characteristic of the last days, for he tells them in 2:27b, "you are abiding in Him."[43]

"The Spirit He Has Given Us" (1 John 3:24; 4:13)

These two passages demonstrate that the Spirit mediates fellowship with God, a concept to be equated with eternal life.[44] Both verses indicate that the indwelling Holy Spirit is the possession of true believers and stands out as "the hallmark of fellowship with God."[45] The gift of the Spirit effects union with God and grants a twofold assurance: (1) present possession of the life of God, and (2) confidence of belonging to Christ. In addition, both passages indicate that the Spirit provides the believer with confidence in view of judgment day (3:19–21; 4:17–18). Malatesta writes: "just as in 3,24 the Spirit is the ultimate source of peace of heart (3,19–24) and the answering of our petitions (3,22), so in 4,13 the same Spirit is the source of our confidence on the day of judgment (4,17) and of the absence of fear (18)."[46] This is closely associated with the idea of "perfect love," which is presently actuated in the life of the believer.[47] In this particular context (including 4:13 and the work of the Spirit), love is associated with God's very nature (4:7) and is reflected in his true children. Perfect love stands as the very antithesis of fear (4:18). Therefore, a person already perfected in love does not need to fear judgment day.

Eschatological Separation

Certain New Testament passages indicate that the righteous and wicked are allowed to coexist in this present age but will be distinguished and separated at the end (Matt. 13:24–30, 36–43; 25:31–46, etc.), at which time character is eternally fixed (Rev. 21:8; 22:11, 14–15). In Johannine thought, however, these activities of identifying and separating righteous from wicked as well as the cementing of their character have in some sense *already taken place*.[48]

---

43. In contrast to the NIV ("remain in him"), it is probably better contextually to understand this verb as indicative, with the imperative introduced in 2:28a.

44. Strecker, *Letters*, 158.

45. Schnackenburg, *Epistles*, 191. The language is reminiscent of such Paraclete passages as John 14:26; 15:26; 16:7.

46. Malatesta, *Interiority*, 303.

47. Elsewhere in 1 John love is associated with the "true light already shining" (2:7–8) and with eternal life (3:14–15).

48. Strecker (*Letters*, 33) points out that the dualism of 1 John "represents an ontological and eschatological opposition."

Three passages especially emphasize this: 1 John 2:18–27; 3:4–12; 4:1–6. In the first passage, the antichrists display their true colors by secession from the community of the faithful, which is the antithesis of those who show the genuineness of their commitment by their remaining in what they had heard "from the beginning" (2:24). This exodus from the community is an incontestable sign of the "last hour" (2:18–19) and is part of the divine purpose that "those who have already chosen a way of life in contradiction with the faith of the community [might] be revealed and finally recognized for what they are, namely, antichrists."[49]

A dialectic runs through the second pericope (2:28–3:12). Here, two diametrically opposite groups of people—the children of God and the children of the devil—are identified and clearly distinguished (3:10) and are either under God's influence or the devil's. On the one side, believers are called children of God (3:1–2, 10) and doers of righteousness (2:29; 3:7). They live in him (3:6) and are born of God (3:9; cf. 2:29b).[50] Because they are born of God (2:29b), they are righteous (3:7b) and do not (even cannot) sin (3:6b; 3:9bc).[51] They are also implied models of Abel whose works were righteous (3:12). Those on the devil's side are called doers of sin (3:4, 8) or sinners (3:6), children of the devil (3:10), and a group utterly devoid of righteousness and love (3:10). Certain things are predicated of them: they commit sin (characterized as lawlessness, 3:4), have neither seen nor known Christ (3:6b), are of the devil (3:8b), and are not of God (3:10bc). They are imitators of Cain (3:12), who belonged to the evil one and performed evil works (i.e., murder, cf. 3:14–15).

In the third passage, the content of the message (4:2–3) and the response of the listeners (4:5–6) serve as two inextricably related tests that distinguish true claims to possess the Spirit from false. These tests set apart those who are "of God" from those who are "of the world." Two opposing spirits operate beyond the human realm, the Spirit of truth and the spirit of error, and exert their influence on either the children of God or those who are "of the world."[52]

The writer of 1 John could not have portrayed the radical character of this eschatological antithesis more dramatically. It is one that has its antecedents in the coming of Christ (1:1–4) who as the light (2:7–8; cf. John 3:19–21) precipitates a crisis that ultimately results in the departure of the secessionists

49. Malatesta, *Interiority*, 202. The idea of "apostasy" is not confined to 1 John (see John 6:66–70; 13:10–11, 18, 27–30). Ἵνα φανερωθῶσιν ("their going showed that") in 2:19b is a purpose clause.

50. More technically, "begotten of God."

51. For further study on 3:6, 9 see D. Mills, "The Concept of Sinlessness in 1 John in Relation to Johannine Eschatology," (Ph.D. diss., Westminster Theological Seminary, 1998).

52. The kind of dualism in 1 John is always set against the monotheistic context of God's sovereign rule (1 John 4:4).

(2:19), their exposure as the children of the devil (3:10), and their antithetical relationship to the true children of God.

Future Eschatological Prospect

Despite 1 John's emphasis upon realized eschatology, future eschatology is by no means marginalized. Various concepts in the Epistle demonstrate that the author espoused the traditional notion that the eschaton was at hand.

Apocalyptic Eschatology

The eschatology of 1 John was, to a certain extent, shaped by an apocalyptic worldview. This approach incorporates such traits as eschatological dualism, which contrasts this present evil age with the age to come (*4 Ezra* 4:26; 7:50, 113). It also includes ethical dualism, which sharply contrasts the wicked and the righteous (*T. Judah* 20:1; *T. Asher* 1:3–9; 3:1–2; 6; 1QS 3–4) and their destinies.[53] It is noted for its pessimistic outlook regarding this present age, which is evil and under the reign of the evil one and Antichrist (*T. Judah* 25:3; *As. Mos.* 8:1–5). Other characteristics include the nearness of the end (*2 Bar.* 85:10), the glorious future (*4 Ezra* 6:1–6; 7:30), and apocalyptic possession of wisdom and knowledge (*4 Ezra* 4:21; 8:62), where knowledge is available only for the initiated. Apocalyptic eschatology is distinctive in this sense, that "the transition from this age will not be achieved by historical processes, but only by an unmediated cosmic act of God."[54]

The Epistle has all of these traits of apocalyptic eschatology (of course molded into its own distinctive framework).[55] Many interpreters recognize this fact.[56]

Eschatological dualism is seen in the distinction between this age and the age to come (1 John 2:15–17). This age is under the complete domination of the evil one (5:19), is hostile to the children of God (3:13), and does not recognize

---

53. The *T. Judah* 20:1 passage is especially arresting: "two spirits await an opportunity with humanity: the spirit of truth and the spirit of error" (H. C. Kee, trans., "Testaments of the Twelve Patriarchs," in *The Old Testament Pseudepigrapha*, ed. J. Charlesworth, 2 vols. (New York: Doubleday, 1983), 1:800. Cf. 1 John 4:6.

54. G. E. Ladd, "Apocalyptic Literature," *The International Standard Bible Encyclopedia*, ed. G. Bromiley, 4 vols. (Grand Rapids: Eerdmans, 1979): 1:153.

55. There are, of course, many things about apocalyptic not characteristic of 1 John, including the bizzare symbolism, pseudonymous character, and use of angels as mediators. Because of the epistle's realized eschatology, its eschatological dualism, while present, is not as sharply drawn as in apocalyptic. Also, the Epistle does not share the *utter pessimism* of apocalyptic regarding this present age (2:8). Therefore, the author announces victory (5:4–5), for the devil's works have already been destroyed by Christ (3:8).

56. Dodd, *Epistles*, 80; J. C. O'Neill, *The Puzzle of 1 John* (London: SPCK, 1966), 15, 33–36; Bogart, *Perfectionism*, 104; Brown, *Epistles*, 415; Schnackenburg, *Epistles*, 27ff.

them for who they are (3:1). People who belong to this age are "from the world" (4:5).[57] On the other hand, that believers will be "like him" (3:2) at the parousia (2:28) reflects the hope (3:3) of the age to come.

Ethical dualism is described in various ways: darkness and light (1:5–10; 2:9–11), the dichotomy of "we" (or you) and "they" (2:18–27), children of God and children of the devil (3:4–12), Spirit of truth and spirit of error (4:1–6), etc. Both groups have contrasting destinies: those who do the will of God "live forever" while the world "passes away" (2:17). Believers will have confidence when the Lord returns (2:28) as well as on the day of judgment (4:17). However, the "outsiders" will be judged at the parousia (2:28).[58] Even the cryptic "sin unto death" (5:16 KJV) is probably a pronouncement of judgment upon those who apostatized from the Johannine community (2:19).[59]

The Epistle also echoes some of the *pessimism of apocalyptic eschatology* toward this present age. As noted above, the author writes that the "whole world is under the control of the evil one" (5:19). It is not getting any better but is "passing away" (2:17). Not only is "Antichrist" a significant theme (2:18, 22; 4:3), but the fact that many "little antichrists" are already overrunning the world is a sign of the end (2:18; cf. 4:1 where "false prophets" are mentioned). The Epistle implies that both the author and his readers constitute a very small minority in the world, which is indicative of the righteous remnant common to the thought of apocalyptic eschatology. This mindset is evidenced in 4:5, where the author characterizes secessionists as those who have gained a hearing with the world.[60]

The "last hour" (2:18) echoes the sentiment of apocalyptic eschatology that *the end is imminent,* that the community is standing at the threshold of the eschaton. Found only in the letters of John, "last hour" refers to the final time immediately before Christ's return and the end of the world.[61] Because of this,

---

57. P. Achtemeier ("An Apocalyptic Shift in Early Christian Tradition: Reflections on Some Canonical Evidence," *CBQ* 45 [1983]: 246) rightly points out that the Johannine notion of *world* is "almost surely the Johannine equivalent of the apocalyptic 'this world' or 'this age.'"

58. The phrase "not be put to shame by him" does not refer to psychological shame but objective condemnation (Marshall, *Epistles,* 166; Schnackenburg, *Epistles,* 153) and thus does not apply to true believers.

59. A short list of scholars holding a similar view include Stott, *Epistles,* 190–91; D. Scholer, "Sins within and Sins Without," in *Current Issues in Biblical and Patristic Interpretation,* ed. G. Hawthorne (Grand Rapids: Eerdmans, 1975), 240–42; Brown, *Epistles,* 617–19, 636; Smalley, *1, 2, 3 John,* 299.

60. In light of this verse, Brown (*Community,* 103) rightly speculates that those who seceded from the Johannine Community (1 John 2:19) constituted the larger group.

61. The author of 1 John reflects the general mood among NT writers that he, like they, were already living in the last days (Acts 2:16–17; Heb. 1:2; 9:26; 1 Peter 1:20; 2 Tim. 3:1; 1 Cor. 10:11c). The fact that nearly 2000 years have elapsed since John wrote his epistle does not prove he was wrong in his perspective. For a helpful explanation of the concept "last hour" in light of the 2000-year delay, see Marshall, *Epistles,* 149–50.

the author exhorts the community (2:28) to be prepared for his coming (*parousia*),[62] which includes self-purification (3:3).

Hints or brief glimpses of *the glorious future* frequently mentioned in apocalyptic literature can also be found. Perhaps the clearest example of this is 3:2 where likeness to Christ and seeing him are set forth as glorious prospects. It is also found in the recurring expression "life" or "eternal life" (1:2 and passim), which, while having present ramifications, also carries on into eternity (cf. 2:17—"lives forever").

Finally, despite secessionists claims to the contrary, John affirms that his readers are the ones *who possess wisdom and knowledge* (2:20, 27), as seen especially (1) in the frequency of the expression "to know" (οἶδα or γινώσκω), which occurs dozens of times and (2) in the climactic affirmations of Christian *knowledge* (5:18–20).

The Purifying Hope (2:28–3:3)

No discussion of the eschatology of 1 John would be complete without some reference to our Lord's parousia (2:28–3:3). In this passage, the return of Christ is mentioned as an incentive for "remaining in Him" (2:28) and for self-purification (3:3). The unit (2:28–3:3) is imbedded in a larger one (2:28–3:12) that distinguishes the children of God from the children of the devil based upon the litmus test of doing righteousness (an idea introduced in 2:29, reiterated repeatedly, and climaxed in 3:12).[63] The overrealized eschatological viewpoint of the secessionists would have downplayed or denied the need for righteous living (3:7–8). The prospect of the Lord's return serves as that vital corrective to this false idea.[64]

The purpose of John's directive to "continue in Him" is set forth by wordplay, to the effect that one who has confidence (παρρησία) will avoid eschatological judgment at his coming (παρουσία).[65] This is followed by the above-mentioned "litmus test" of those who have truly been begotten of God. The remainder of the unit (vv. 1–3) is probably best understood as parenthetical, extolling the extraordinary wonders of divine filiation (3:1).[66]

---

62. H. J. Klauck (*Der Erste Johannesbrief*, EKKNT [Zürich: Benziger, 1991], 173) reminds us that the "last hour" of 2:18 is still in view when we come to 2:28.

63. Interpreters are divided over the boundaries of this pericope (see Anderson, *Exegetical Summary*, 97, 100). The approach of R. Longacre is based upon various discourse markers, especially the distribution of the vocative, as a means of identifying its parameters ("Towards an Exegesis of 1 John Based on the Discourse Analysis of the Greek Text," in *Linguistics and New Testament Interpretation: Essays on Discourse Analysis*, ed. D. A. Black [Nashville: Broadman, 1992], 271–86). When this is combined with the structural pattern of the passage (the use of ten substantival participles), 2:28–3:12 emerges as a discrete section.

64. Brown, *Community*, 136–37.

65. Smalley, *1, 2, 3 John*, 132.

66. Brown, *Epistles*, 419; Burge, *Letters*, 144; *The Net Bible: New English Translation* (n.p.: Biblical Studies, 1996–1999). Online: http://www.bible.org.

Of particular interest is the dialectical tension between the *present and fu-ture status* of the children of God, explicitly set forth in 3:2a. On the one hand, the insight that true believers *are* presently children of God accounts for the exclamatory response from the writer (emphasized by "and that is what we are!" of 3:1). On the other hand, the full manifestation of this reality "has not yet been made known," but will take place at the parousia when "we shall be like Him." Indeed "the author is remarkably subtle in combining Johannine realized eschatology with a future eschatology that he wants to hold out to his adherents as an incentive."[67]

An important question regarding 3:2 has to do with its emphasis. The "al-ready/not yet" dialectic is evident, but the basic issue concerns "how much separates the future expected state from the present situation of believing Christians."[68] Those who give greater weight to the realized-eschatological side might paraphrase the verse as follows: "At his coming our present status of likeness to Christ (or God) will become clearly evident for what it truly is."[69] At the parousia, then, the true identity of the children of God will be vindicated before a world that presently knows neither them nor God.[70] Thus, "a strong emphasis on realized eschatology would imply little change from one [state] to the other."[71]

Those who prefer the future-eschatological side understand the verse this way: "When we see Him as He is we shall be transformed into His likeness." Thus, likeness to Christ is caused by seeing him, implying some change from our present status.[72] This latter viewpoint is slightly preferred, since John speaks of a future "becoming" vis-à-vis a present status.[73] Although there is continuity between the present and future states, this verse indicates that there will be some change at Christ's coming (2:28).[74] Thus, despite the obviously present aspects of divine filiation in this unit, the future transformation is em-

---

67. Brown, *Epistles*, 423.

68. Ibid., 396.

69. This idea is supported by 3:14, where the "we know" is explained by the clause intro-duced by "because" (ὅτι). Those who support the "already" side include M. De Jonge, *Jesus: Stranger from Heaven and Son of God: Jesus Christ and the Christians in Johannine Perspective* (Missoula, Mont.: Scholars, 1977), 182; Ng, "Johannine Eschatology," 82–85; Schnacken-burg, *Epistles*, 159–60.

70. As Ng ("Eschatology," 84) writes: "the hope of Parousia causes us to know for sure that we have a future status."

71. Brown, *Epistles*, 396.

72. Those who support the "not yet" side include the NET Bible and Smalley, *1, 2, 3 John*, 147.

73. The "for" (ὅτι) in 3:2b is to be understood as causal, because it states the reason why believers will ultimately be like Christ. John writes "what we will be (τί ἐσόμεθα) has not yet been made known," not "what we are (τί ἐσμέν)."

74. Brown, *Epistles*, 396. This would square with other NT passages, including 1 Cor. 15:51; Phil. 3:21.

phasized here. As mentioned above, this would have corrected the overrealized eschatology of the secessionists, who placed all the emphasis upon present status.

Finally, as already mentioned, the certain prospect of the Lord's return becomes the driving force behind personal sanctification (3:3). This in turn bolsters confidence in light of that future day (an idea also echoed in 3:18–21 and 4:16–18).[75]

Concluding Implications

As we have seen, the eschatology of 1 John is indispensable for understanding the Epistle and its other themes. For example, the phrase "God is light" (1:5) is more than an ontological description of God but also refers to the irruption of the new age, an idea unpacked in 1:6–2:17. The metaphors "walk[ing] in the light" (1:7) and "walk[ing] in the darkness" (1:6; 2:11) are best understood as redemptive-historical in character and are more than just portrayals of individual lifestyle. Thus, one who is walking in the darkness belongs to the old age that is "passing away" (2:8, 17 NASB), an age characterized by self-deception (1:6), lying (1:8, 10; 2:4), hatred (2:9, 11), and various kinds of lusts (2:15–16). On the other hand, the person who is walking in the light has begun to enjoy the blessings of the new era that has dawned in Christ's coming, an age characterized by truth (2:5, 8; cf. 1:6; 2:4), fellowship with true believers (1:7), a true perspective on sin (1:9), the forgiveness of sin (1:7, 9; 2:1–2, 12), the knowledge of God (2:3, 13–14), perfected love (2:5), love for fellow believers (2:10), and victory over the evil one (2:13–14).

Some of the difficult passages in the Epistle can also be clarified in light of its eschatology, including two major problems: (1) the puzzling verses affirming the present perfection of the believer (3:6, 9; 5:18) and (2) the cryptic "sin unto death" passage (5:16–17 KJV). In both contexts two pairs—people and epochs—are contrasted and the language carries significant eschatological overtones. Whatever else can be said for these difficulties, the eschatology of 1 John can help solve them. But these await further study.

75. As J. Walters writes: "In 1 John ethics flows from eschatology" (*Perfection in New Testament Theology: Ethics and Eschatology in Relational Dynamic* [Lewiston, N.Y.: Mellen, 1995], 168).

Part 3

Eschatology in Historical Theology

7

The Epistle to Rheginos: Christian-Gnostic Teaching on the Resurrection

J. ROBERT DOUGLASS

Ashland (Ohio) Brethren in Christ Church

The following is essentially an apologetic for the relevancy of quality historical research to the church at large. This is accomplished first by examining the *Epistle to Rheginos* and briefly summarizing the research on the text. Afterward, issues of relevancy are explored. I am convinced and hope to demonstrate that texts such as the *Epistle to Rheginos* are not only interesting for their novelty but may be beneficial for the church in the twenty-first century.

Although the primary concern of this paper is with the relevancy of texts like the *Epistle to Rheginos*, the text itself is alluring. This is undoubtedly true for several reasons, but one of the more basic reasons must be the Gnostic aspect of the text. Not only is the substance of Gnostic teaching intriguing, but Gnosticism, like the Dead Sea Scrolls, is a relatively new field of research. While describing a second-century heretical movement as a new field of research might seem odd, the numerous archeological discoveries that have occurred in the last fifty years have completely redefined what is known about Gnosticism.

Until recently, the primary source for Gnostic material was the accounts of the early heresiologists. This was problematic because in attempting to refute Gnosticism, the heresiologists were engaged in polemics. As a result, it was not their intent to provide an objective view of Gnosticism. Instead, they were striving to protect the church from its poison. Thus, it was their intent, if not their duty, to portray the Gnostics as unfavorably as possible. As Giovanni Filoramo states, "One could not expect the ancient heresiologists to offer what he could not offer; scientific objectivity and exactness."[1]

---

1. Giovanni Filoramo, *A History of Gnosticism*, trans. Anthony Alcock (Cambridge: Basil Blackwell, 1990), 3.

The understandably biased account of Gnosticism by the early church fathers is basically all that was known until the unexpected discovery at Nag Hammadi in December of 1945. The story of the discovery shares some similarities with the tales from Qumran. It includes murders, smuggling, and the unfortunate burning of several manuscripts for fuel. While the story is quite dramatic, further elaboration on the account would take us far beyond my purposes here.

The Nag Hammadi text with which this paper is concerned is codex I tractate 4, the *Epistle to Rheginos*, also known as the *Treatise on the Resurrection*. When analyzing texts, establishing the genre is crucial. This is due in large part to the inextricable link between a text's genre and its intended purpose. In this regard, one of the most interesting characteristics of the *Treatise on the Resurrection* is that it is a Christian-Gnostic document. Any attempt to understand the *Treatise* must recognize the tension between the Christian and Gnostic elements.

The Gnostic aspect of the text is self-evident. In the introduction to his translation, Malcolm Peel offers a helpful summary of the evidence indicating the influence of Valentinian Gnosticism.[2] According to Peel, the evidence includes parallels between "the spiritual resurrection that [had] already occurred and the charges of Valentinian 'realized eschatology'" as reported by Tertullian and Irenaeus.[3] Also noted by Peel are the references to the Valentinian cosmogony in the *Letter to Rheginos*, such as the primordial pleroma and human preexistence.

In terms of the Christian aspect of the *Treatise*, the evidence is equally as strong but slightly less obvious. Craig Evans, Robert Webb, and Richard Wiebe dedicate four pages of their book, *Nag Hammadi Texts and the Bible*, to cataloging the numerous biblical allusions in the *Treatise on the Resurrection*.[4] In light of the text's dual nature, an important question is, What does the combination of Christian and Gnostic aspects within the *Treatise* imply about the text? Could this be an indication of an early date of composition, perhaps before Gnosticism experienced a complete break with orthodox Christianity?

Author and Date

The author of the *Treatise on the Resurrection* is anonymous. What is fairly certain is that the author was from the Valentinian school or at least highly influenced by the Valentinian school.

2. Malcolm L. Peel, "The Treatise on the Resurrection," in *The Nag Hammadi Library*, ed. James M. Robinson, (San Francisco: Harper & Row, 1988), 53.
3. Ibid.
4. Craig Evans, Robert L. Webb, and Richard A. Wiebe, eds., *Nag Hammadi Texts and the Bible: A Synopsis and Index* (Leiden: Brill, 1993), 42–47.

A few scholars have suggested that the *Treatise on the Resurrection* may be attributable to Valentinus himself. This could account for the dual nature of the document, since it is possible that the Gnostic Valentinus was closer to orthodox Christianity than any other Gnostic.[5] In fact, Quispel claims that "on the whole there can be no doubt that Valentinus and his Gnostics remained more faithful than Origen and his followers to the essence of primitive Christianity."[6] Undoubtedly, other scholars would take issue with this notion, and I do not wish to be distracted by the issue, but it is entertaining to note that Valentinus's orthodoxy has some defenders.

The dates for Valentinus's life are uncertain. He was born between A.D. 100 and 110 in northern Egypt. He received a Hellenistic education in Alexandria and eventually traveled to Rome around 136. He remained in Rome and was a member of the church in Rome. According to Tertullian, while in Rome, Valentinus aspired to become bishop of Rome. In addressing Valentinus's episcopal hopes, Tertullian stated that "he was an able man both in genius and eloquence."[7] Tertullian further described how Valentinus's challenger succeeded over Valentinus for bishop, because the challenger was a confessor.[8]

While recalling the previous caveat about the fact that the early heresiologists were involved in polemics, it is somewhat surprising to notice that Tertullian does not cite Valentinus's heterodoxy as a reason for his failing to make bishop. He is simply beaten by a more popular confessor. Eventually, Valentinus is cast out of the church.

The questions that emerge but cannot be adequately addressed here are: If what Tertullian offers is an accurate account of Valentinus, how and at what point did Valentinus cease being a Christian and become the despised heretic? How does one go from almost being elected pope, whose orthodoxy was apparently not an issue, to the person who according to Tertullian has done violence to Scripture "with a more cunning mind and skill than Marcion"?[9] Perhaps, if the *Treatise* was written by Valentinus, it may offer a glimpse of the transformation that Valentinus must have experienced, a missing link so to speak.

Despite the fact that Valentinus's authorship of the *Epistle to Rheginos* could explain the Christian-Gnostic quality of the text, the notion of his authorship has been largely rejected today. Among those who doubt Valentinus's authorship is Malcolm Peel. Yet even Peel acknowledges that on several important points the author of the *Epistle to Rheginos* is closer to Paul than to

5. G. C. Stead, "In Search of Valentinus," in *The Rediscovery of Gnosticism*, vol. 1, ed. Bentley Layton (Leiden: Brill, 1980), 75.

6. Gilles Quispel, "Gnosis and the Apocryphon of John," in *The Rediscovery of Gnosticism*, 127.

7. Tertullian *Ad. Val.* 4.

8. Ibid.

9. Tertullian *De Praescr. Haer.* 38.

Valentinian Gnosticism.[10] Thus, the primary reason for discounting the possibility of Valentinus having authored the text is a matter of timing.

One of the central issues in determining whether or not Valentinus may have authored this document is its date. While this is a less than precise task, there are some clues in the text. For example, the author's considerable appeal to Saint Paul necessarily places him or her after Paul.[11] Moreover, it is generally conceded that the approximate date for the existing manuscript is A.D. 350. Scholars also agree that the existing manuscript is a Coptic translation of a Greek text, thus making the date of composition sometime before 350.[12] More precisely, the fact that the letter is about the subject of resurrection strongly suggests a date within the second century, when resurrection was an extremely important theological issue.

Despite my conviction that none of these factors (the author's use of Paul, the late date of the Coptic MS, or the subject of the letter) necessarily precludes Valentinus as the author, it is the author's reliance on Paul that scholars find problematic. This is almost entirely because they are operating with particular presuppositions about the development of the New Testament canon and an early date for Gnosticism. It is argued that due to the canon's late development, the *Treatise* must have been written in the late, not the middle, of the second century. This excludes Valentinus as a possible author because he is believed to have died around 165.

Why are these important issues? They are not important because subscribing to the idea of Valentinus's authorship relieves the Christian-Gnostic tension. In fact, there is little argument that the Gnostic sect that developed from Valentinus strayed considerably from orthodox Christianity. The Valentinian cosmogony with its multiple emanations and aeons is virtually impossible to reconcile with the Christian faith.

In order to be careful, it is important to note that this cosmogony is more accurately attributable to Ptolemy, a student of Valentinus. Irenaeus received the cosmogony that he discusses in his *Adversus Haereses* from an anonymous student of Ptolemy.[13] Yet, despite the possibility that the cosmogony did not originate with Valentinus, it is difficult to imagine how a system this elaborate could be propagated by the Valentinian school and not have its origin with Valentinus, but this is an argument from silence because there is no specific extant Valentinus corpus, only questionable fragments. Corruption of the

10. Peel, "Treatise," 53.

11. W. C. Van Unnik, "The Newly Discovered Gnostic 'Epistle to Rheginos' on the Resurrection," *Journal of Ecclesiastical History* 15 (1964): 156.

12. Bentley Layton, "Treatise on Resurrection," in *The Gnostic Scriptures* (New York: Doubleday, 1987), 317.

13. Rowan Greer, "The Dog and the Mushroom: Irenaeus' view of the Valentinians Assessed," in *The Rediscovery of Gnosticism*, vol. 1, ed. Bentley Layton (Leiden: Brill, 1980), 168.

material could have occurred at many points during the transmission process. In fact, Tertullian seems to indicate that such a process occurred:

> Ptolemaeus afterwards entered on the same path, by distinguishing the names and the numbers of the Aeons into personal substances, which, however, he kept apart from God. Valentinus had included these in the very essence of the Deity, as senses and affections of motion.[14]

If the issues of authorship and date do not resolve the Christian-Gnostic tension of the text, why are they important? They are important because they have implications for the genre of this document. As previously mentioned, the *Treatise on the Resurrection* is a Christian-Gnostic text. The manner in which the document is interpreted is due, in large part, to whether one emphasizes the Christian or the Gnostic aspect.

The major proponent of the first approach is W. C. van Unnik, who presented his position in two lectures at King's College in London. Van Unnik's view is that the letter was intended to be hortatory, with the intention of bolstering Rheginos's confidence in the reality of the resurrection. This view emphasizes the Christian aspect of the Christian-Gnostic text and understands the tension as a sign of an early composition date when the distinctions between Christian and Gnostic may have been blurred.[15]

The second view is best articulated by Bentley Layton. Layton believes that the author is attempting to proselytize the Christian, Rheginos, into Valentinian Christianity. In substantiating his position, Layton naturally emphasizes the Gnostic aspect of this document and minimizes the Christian dimension.

Parenthetically, there is at least one other theory regarding the genre of the *Treatise*. Luther Martin argues that the *Letter to Rheginos* is a polemic against philosophy and philosophers.[16] My impression is that he presented some strong evidence for a weak argument. While convincing of various anti-philosophical elements in the text, he fails to convince that the notion of a polemic against philosophy is related to any of the essential elements of the text: Christianity, Gnosticism, and resurrection.

Contents and Theology

The opening section of the letter begins by identifying the recipient, by offering an argument against so-called learned people, and by informing us about the subject of the letter, resurrection (43–44). In wanting to minimize the Gnostic aspect and emphasize the Christian aspect of the text, Van Unnik

---

14. Tertullian *Ad. Val.* 4.
15. Van Unnik, "Newly Discovered," 151.
16. Luther Martin, "The Anti-Philosophical Polemic and Gnostic Soteriology in the 'Treatise on the Resurrection,'" *Numen* 20 (1973): 20.

writes that the *Letter to Rheginos* "does not in any way take the form of a mystery book or a secret revelation."[17] He is also careful to observe the occurrences of the title "Lord" in the opening sections. This is significant for his position as he recalls Irenaeus's claim that the Gnostics used the terms "Savior" and "Christ" but avoided the term "Lord."[18]

The next section of the document discusses the two natures of the Savior, the Savior's resurrection, and the resurrection of the Christian. With a couple of exceptions, the majority of the material is quite orthodox. Lest anyone think that our author is completely orthodox, in the midst of the discussion of Christ's dual natures, the incarnation is declared to be the means of restoring the pleroma (44.30–32). Furthermore, in addressing the resurrection of believers, we learn that what is meant by resurrection is spiritual resurrection (45.40).

In this section Layton appears to tip his hand in choosing to translate a particular phrase, "the son of god was a human son" instead of "the Son of God was a Son of Man," thereby indicating his emphasis on the Gnostic part of this Christian-Gnostic text.[19]

Next, the author turns the discussion to the issue of faith (46.3–18). The author states that a person who is not a believer cannot be convinced or persuaded to believe in the resurrection (46.3–5). Van Unnik happily notes that this text, unlike most other Christian texts on the resurrection from the second century, does not appeal to nature or to God's omnipotence.[20] Instead, it appeals to faith. It could almost be inferred that this text is more Christian, in some respects, than others by more orthodox authors.

Layton, on the other hand, is clearly unimpressed with the discussion of faith. He argues that the author's use of faith should be understood to be equal to γνῶσις. He states that "the author takes pains to use ordinary Christian language."[21] He also believes that the author understood Christ's resurrection allegorically. Most surprising in Layton's analysis of this section is his translation of the second occurrence of the phrase υἱὸς ἀνθρώπου. What would appear to be an obvious reference to Christ in the expression "Son of Man" becomes anesthetized by Layton's rendering, "the child of the human being."[22]

In the next section, the author continues on the subject of resurrection. This appears to be the most intensely Gnostic part of the work. It contains comments about the "fact" that Rheginos existed prior to taking on flesh (47.4–5), that the soul or intellect is superior to the flesh (47.9ff.), and that it is the soul that en-

17. Van Unnik, "Newly Discovered," 147.
18. Ibid., 148.
19. Layton, "Treatise on Resurrection," 320–21.
20. Van Unnik, "Newly Discovered," 147.
21. Layton, "Treatise on Resurrection," 321 n. 46.d, e, j.
22. Ibid., 321.

livens the body. The author proceeds to detail the implications of these ideas for understanding resurrection.

It is argued that since there is no resurrection of the flesh, salvation is immediate (47.30–36). If preexistence is true, such that the real person existed before assuming flesh, then resurrection is, by definition, an uncovering. The body is not needed, since it is the soul that enlivens the body and not the body providing life to the soul (47.38–48.5). Citing the transfiguration as an example, the resurrection is said to be real, but spiritual (48.13). In fact, in comparison to the realm of the spiritually resurrected, the material world is unreal (48.22–32). Finally, those with this perspective already have resurrection (49.16, 25).

Van Unnik acknowledges the "ontological and metaphysical twist" that the author gives to redemption and election in this section.[23] Except for the issue of preexistence, on which van Unnik makes no comment, he understands the author to be quite orthodox in his understanding of the resurrection. He understands that the flesh is taken up in the total resurrection so that it is not purely spiritual. He also cites the example of the transfiguration as evidence for a corporeal aspect of the spiritual resurrection.[24]

Layton notes in his examination of this passage that "the author now begins an open attack on the ordinary, literal understanding of the resurrection of the Christian believer."[25] In support of this idea, Layton later observes that while traditional orthodoxy believed in a period of time between death and resurrection, this author rejects the notion.[26]

The document ends on a positive note. First, there is encouragement to practice what has been written (49.26–36), which includes another reference to Rheginos's preexistence (47.36). Then, there is an invitation for further explanation (49.37–50.7), which includes an obvious allusion to 1 Corinthians 15 (49.37ff.). Last, there is a salutation (50.8–15), which includes permission to share the letter with others.

So who's right? I find myself most attracted to van Unnik's view. I appreciate the fact that he attempted to take seriously the genuinely Christian element of this text. Unfortunately, I am also convinced that he was too generous at times in his interpretation of the text. An example of this occurred when he noted the "metaphysical and ontological twist" that redemption and election were given by the author. It would have been equally, or perhaps more, accurate to call this a "Gnostic" twist. A second issue for van Unnik was raised by Layton. If van Unnik is willing to acknowledge a redefinition of redemption

23. Van Unnik, "Newly Discovered," 150.
24. Ibid.
25. Layton, "Treatise on Resurrection," 322 n. 47.a.
26. Ibid., 323 n. 47.q.

and election, then perhaps Layton was correct in noting a non-traditional use of the term *faith*, which Layton believed should be synonymous with *gnōsis*.

Ultimately, I believe that Layton's view is most believable, although I am confident that he overstated his case. There are too many elements in the text that are difficult, if not impossible, to reconcile with traditional Christianity. I am also convinced that Layton was too pessimistic, almost cynical. For example, I do not think that it is necessary to understand spiritual resurrection as being allegorical. Moreover, as has already been demonstrated, Layton's tendency to ignore or neglect several Christian elements in the text resulted in what appeared to be a strained translation.

I know that this look at the *Treatise on the Resurrection* raised more questions than it answered. Unfortunately, this seems to be the nature of the text. Addressing this same ambiguity, van Unnik states:

> Why was this different turn given to that central doctrine? Not to please outsiders, but to fit the Gnostic conception of the Pleroma and the world. Here lies the real difference. It is the great question, to which I see no answer, at present, why this Valentinian with this idea of the deity was so deeply attached to Christianity.[27]

I am a scholar in training and a pastor by vocation. While I personally enjoy this type of inquiry, as a pastor I have learned the importance of the question: So what? Does any of this really matter outside the walls of academia? I am convinced that both the doctrine of the resurrection of the body and Christianity's struggle with Gnosticism are significant issues for the church today.

In his book *Omens of Millennium: The Gnosis of Angels, Dreams, and Resurrection*, renowned literary critic and Yale professor Harold Bloom offers what he calls his spiritual autobiography. In explaining why he considers himself a Gnostic, Bloom writes that "our American Religion . . . is more of a gnostic amalgam than a European kind of historical and doctrinal Christianity, though very few are able to see this, or perhaps most don't wish to see it."[28] To those who would reject his notion, Bloom cites America's fixation with angels, near-death experiences, and astrology as evidence of a prevalent Gnosticism.[29]

Unfortunately, this does not seem to be limited to nonbelievers. It has been my experience that many Christians subscribe, at least subconsciously, to an idea of the immortality of the soul rather than the historic belief in the resurrection of the body. Even within evangelicalism we talk about saving souls.

27. Van Unnik, "Newly Discovered," 165.
28. Harold Bloom, *Omens of Millennium: The Gnosis of Angels, Dreams, and Resurrection* (New York: Riverhead, 1996), 31.
29. Ibid.

Seldom do our sermons elucidate it, few of our people contemplate it; and almost none of our songs celebrate the doctrine of the resurrection of the body.

One need only to browse the writings of Irenaeus and Tertullian to conclude that the early church fathers understood the doctrine of the resurrection of the body as central to Christianity and Gnosticism as a serious threat to it. The question for us is, has the danger to Christianity from Gnosticism been expunged over the centuries, or is it that we have simply forgotten the seriousness and subtlety of its challenge?

If Harold Bloom is correct, Gnosticism is not merely a second-century heresy that may pique the interest of the occasional scholar. Rather, it remains a challenge to historic Christian orthodoxy. Perhaps by attending to what has been argued in the past and how it has been refuted, we can gain some insight into how to confront the present challenge of Gnosticism and how to accomplish the ever-present task of accurately rearticulating the historic Christian faith.

8

Martin Luther's Theology of Last Things

Fred P. Hall

American Lutheran Theological Seminary

Martin Luther's theology of last things flows from the concept of reality that characterizes his overall theology. In justification by faith, God in Jesus Christ rescues sinners from the condemnation and punishment of sin in the eternal fires of hell. When a baby is immersed in the waters of baptism, Christ is present in the Word and the water, and the child arises to a new life into which he is truly born of God and rescued from the power of the devil. When the bread and wine are distributed in the Holy Supper, Jesus Christ's body and blood are truly physically present and received in and under the elements as Christ acts to forgive sins. The Holy Spirit comes through the preaching of the Word of God and his sacraments to be truly present with those who receive them in faith. Therefore, to understand Luther's eschatology one must grasp the reality of his total theological view.[1] Jane Strohl relates Luther's theology, view of history, and eschatology:

1. Cf. Jane E. Strohl, *Luther's Eschatology: The Last Times and the Last Things* (Ph.D. diss., University of Chicago Divinity School, 1989), 4: "For Luther, the eschatological reality of the Gospel makes itself known in and through the vicissitudes of history." Strohl (4–6) notes that Ulrich Asendorf, *Eschatologie bei Luther* (Göttingen: Vandenhoeck & Ruprecht, 1967), attempts to integrate the totality of Luther's theology into an overarching eschatological framework. Asendorf tends to spread out the last day from being a specific future point in time to being a new reality already filling the life of the believer and the church in this world.

Luther's eschatology intertwines with his understanding of the dynamics of history. The ultimate truth, the *Christus solus* of the Gospel, as enshrined in the article of justification by faith, stands at history's beginning and at its end, driving it forward and drawing it to its goal. The continuity of the Word produces constant, repeated patterns. It enters the human realm at particular points in space and time. Both for those who hear and those who reject its promise, it generates turmoil and causes change. Then the Word fades, without ever entirely disappearing, only to emerge once again with fierce intensity among another in another era. The days of its manifest presence are the last times for the subjects of its visitation. . . .

The article of justification was not for Luther one doctrine among others. Its insistence on the sole sufficiency of Christ in the accomplishment of salvation became the point of orientation for his reformulation of the whole of Christian theology, including eschatology. . . . [His] expectation of the imminent end was distinguished by its genesis out of the article of justification . . . [and] forms an essential part of his proclamation of the Gospel.[2]

In this paper we recap the essence of Luther's theological views and consider several aspects of his eschatology. In addition to material from Luther, much of the treatment depends upon reliable summaries of Luther's theology found in Althaus, Elert, Köstlin, Plass, Rupp, Watson, et al.

Eschatology Related to Luther's Basic Theology

Paul Althaus notes Luther's emphasis on the relationship of forgiveness of sins to the present reality of salvation and life for Christians.[3] In this life, however, Luther maintained that faith is continually under attack in its experience of the apparent contradiction of the hiddenness of God. Luther's theology of the cross looks to the future: "We do not wait for forgiveness and all graces as though we would not receive them until the life to come; rather, they are now present for us in faith, even though they are hidden and will be revealed only in the life to come."[4] For Luther the present life is one of faith and expectation waiting for the final revelation, and is therefore an eschatological reality. It is a life of having and being and yet not having and not being in completeness. Christ is Lord of his church, yet the church still suffers under its weakness, the world, and the attacks of Satan until Christ's lordship is finally and fully revealed. Philip Watson points to Luther's understanding of Christ as the Redeemer who wins the cosmic conflict over sin, death, the devil, the law, and the wrath of God. Though this battle continues until

2. Strohl, *Luther's Eschatology*, 9–10.
3. Paul Althaus, *The Theology of Martin Luther*, trans. Robert C. Schultz (Philadelphia: Fortress, 1966), 404.
4. *WA* 17[II], 229.

the last day, the victory for believers is assured.[5] Watson notes that this is a consistent theme of Luther's theology, which gives an eschatological cast to Luther's emphasis on justification in the setting of the theology of the cross.[6]

Gordon Rupp characterizes Luther's theology in his understanding of *Anfechtung:*

> The whole meaning of "*Anfechtung*" for Luther lies in the thought that man has his existence "*Coram Deo*," and that he is less the active intelligence imposing itself on the stuff of the universe around him, than the subject of an initiative and action from God who employs the whole of man's existence as a means of bringing men to awareness of their need and peril.[7]

Luther saw this position of being before God, *Coram Deo*, under the wrath of God for his human failings as the worst of struggles, *Anfechtung*. It is "what it means to feel guilty and condemned under the wrath of God."[8] Werner Elert calls this Luther's understanding of the primal experience, *das Urerlebnis*, humans under the wrath of God. This is a situation that does not end with death but continues for eternity.[9]

Strohl maintains that Luther suffered under a tension of despair at the present evil and its danger for the faithful and exultant expectation for the dawning future of salvation for the righteous and judgment for the wicked. In Strohl's view, Luther accommodated this tension with an apocalyptic framework of present trial and impending salvation and judgment.[10] This view, however, seems to miss the dynamic of faith at work in Luther's theology of the cross in which God is hidden from the natural eye but revealed to faith in suffering and the cross.

With this potentially terrifying understanding of humanity's state before God, Luther, the theologian of reality, had a view of last things as the culmination of all of his theology, which featured God's having dealt with humanity's sin and guilt for all time in Jesus Christ. At the end unrepentant sinners will be judged and the faithful justified. Before God, humans are either forgiven or condemned. They are either ushered into eternal

---

5. Philip S. Watson, *Let God Be God! An Interpretation of the Theology of Martin Luther* (London: Epworth, 1947), 116–17, citing Martin Luther, *A Commentary on St. Paul's Epistle to the Galatians*, ed. Erasmus Middleton (London, 1807) 185–95 and 255ff. on Gal. 3:13 and 4:4.

6. Watson, *Let God Be God!*, 117ff.

7. Gordon Rupp, *Righteousness of God* (London: Hodder and Stoughton, 1947), 106.

8. Ibid., 107.

9. Werner Elert, *The Structure of Lutheranism*, trans. Walter A. Hansen (St. Louis: Concordia, 1962), 17ff.

10. Strohl, *Luther's Eschatology*, 23.

blessedness in the love of God, or into eternal punishment under the wrath of God.

Elements of the Last Things

Death

Death—The Instrument of Law and Gospel

Luther's understanding of the last things is based on how he related death to baptism.[11] This he explained in his interpretation of Psalm 90.[12] "Man is a being created for this purpose: to live forever in obedience to the Word and to be like God. He was not created for death."[13] It is a great tragedy that because of sin humankind is punished with death by God's wrath. In this it is prevented from realizing the seriousness of death and so plans to live life with its pleasures until its end and that is all. Luther notes that this is not only wrong, but also, as the fruit of sin, it perverts one's understanding from the necessary way that sin and death must be approached.[14]

In Psalm 90, Luther said Moses used death as an instrument of law and gospel. Moses spoke of death as the confrontation between the sinner and God, the righteous judge. As the law, death is the eternal wrath of God, overcoming sinful humans with all sorts of miseries that last forever. Death is not only a physical death but is also the eschatological judgment at the last day. As a lawgiver, Moses called sinners to be fearful of death and to pray for repentance and consolation.[15] Through repentance this latter hope is the veiled gospel of Moses, which finds a fuller revelation in Christ. However, Luther noted that since Psalm 90 is a prayer of Moses,

> Moses indirectly suggests that there is still hope for life. For what does it mean to pray? Does it not mean to seek help? Again, what does it mean to pray to God when one is encompassed by sin and death? Is it not to believe that with God there is the possibility of forgiveness and sure help against deadly ills? . . .
>
> And so the principle is correct: wherever a Commandment of the First Table or works of the First Table are involved (prayer is a work of the First Table), there, of necessity, faith is included and the hope of the resurrection of the dead.[16]

Thus the Lord has reminded us that he is the God of the living, not the dead (Matt. 22:32).

11. Watson, *Let God Be God!* 165–66, citing *Works of Martin Luther* (Philadelphia: Holman, 1915–32), II, 230.
12. *WA* 40[III], 485ff, *LW* 13, 75–141, cf. Althaus, *Theology*, 405.
13. *WA* 40[III], 513, *LW* 13, 94
14. *WA* 40[III], 485, *LW* 13, 76.
15. *LW* 13, 77–78.
16. *LW* 13, 82.

All people, therefore, who worship this God, who believe in him and pray to Him, will be alive even in death . . . because they manifestly do not worship, adore, and believe in the God of the dead but of the living. Therefore the worship of God, faith, and prayer truly include the article of the resurrection and of life everlasting.[17]

Thus Moses combined the doctrine of the horror of death and the remedy so that smug, hardened sinners are terrified and trembling sinners are encouraged as he called them to believe and pray.

Luther said that death is the final leap into the abyss, leaving the "so-called certainty" of this life and trusting God for eternity. In it, all humans experience the fear of God's wrath; but as they stand under the wrath of God, which they understand as God's "no" in light of the law, Christians flee to the mercy of God and receive God's "yes" to them in Christ. "Death then fulfills God's promise to Christians in their baptism, that is, their sin is put to death."[18] Death for the faithful becomes the remedy for sin as the Christian "hears the voice of the Gospel only as a man who still stands under the law as a sinner and also hears the voice of the law."[19] Christians in life and in death experience the ambiguity of the terror of the law and the hope of the gospel. Thus they are clearly aware of their great guilt and great salvation.

Strohl maintains that Luther was ambiguous concerning Christians at death, vacillating between the confidence that good works are evidence that God has been at work in their lives and the medieval terror and temptations of the devil at death. While this seems to fly in the face of Luther maintaining the confidence of faith in his theology of the cross, Strohl continues to cite this ambiguity of the dying Christian as *simul iustus et peccator* ("at once justified and a sinner") who has confidence in the victory of Christ.[20] Thus death becomes a bittersweet occasion for expectation, release,[21] and even joy mixed with sorrow, as when Luther reported on the death of his daughter Magdelena, aged thirteen:

I believe the report has reached you that Magdelena, my dearest daughter, has been reborn into the everlasting kingdom of Christ, and although I and my wife ought to do nothing but joyfully give thanks for such a felicitous passage and blessed end, by which she has escaped the power of the flesh, the world, the Turk and the devil, nevertheless, so great is the force of our love that we are unable to go on without sobs and groaning of heart, indeed without bear-

---

17. *LW* 13, 82–83.
18. Althaus, *Theology*, 407, cf. *WA* 31[1], 160; *LW* 14, 90; *WA* 2, 727–737, *LW* 35, 29–43 (Luther's 1519 Treatise, *The Holy and Blessed Sacrament of Baptism*).
19. Althaus, *Theology*, 408–9.
20. Ibid., 121–30.
21. Ibid., 138, citing Luther's letter to von Amsdorf (1538), *WA Br* 8, No. 3277 (11–29).

ing in ourselves a mortal wound. The countenance, the words, the gestures of our daughter, so very obedient and respectful both while she lived and as she died, remain firmly fixed in the old heart so that the death of Christ (in comparison to which what are all other deaths?) is unable to drive out sorrow from our inmost depths as it ought to do. You therefore give thanks to God in our stead.[22]

As time passed, Luther was able to rejoice in her sleep in the bosom of Christ with her heavenly Father, which is a demonstration of the divine love of God to Luther.[23] In the end Luther saw a separation of body and soul in death awaiting the last day of resurrection and judgment.[24]

The Resurrection—the Hope of all Christians

As we see above, Luther did not see death as defeat for Christians, but the experience of entry into eternal victory, which is derived from his understanding of being baptized into the death and resurrection of Jesus Christ. Althaus summarizes the bases for Luther's hope:

> Luther's certainty that there will be a new life arising out of death is based on the totality of God's redeeming work in Christ. . . . The heart and center of this whole position is the resurrection of Jesus Christ and the victory over death which he won in it. This is the only true comfort for all of us who must die.[25]

This is comforting because believers will join in with Christ's "first fruit" bodily resurrection through their own baptism and faith. In Christ the greater part of the resurrection has already taken place.[26] Therefore the only hope for life beyond the grave is based on the resurrection of Christ. If God speaks to humankind as their God, then they are involved in an immortal relationship, and he is the God of those living in that eternal domain, since he speaks only to those who are alive. This is true for all people, whether God speaks to them in his wrath, or in blessing, they are immortal. For the unbeliever, God's Word condemns for all eternity. For believers, when they hold fast to God's Word, when they die, God's dependable Word gives them a certainty that they will be awakened out of death and that God's Word will preserve them for all eternity.[27] Luther based this hope on his understanding of 2 Corin-

22. Strohl, *Luther's Eschatology*, 151f., citing *WA Br* 10, No. 3794 (20–29).

23. Strohl, *Luther's Eschatology*, 152ff., citing *WA Br* 10, Nos. 3805 (4–14), 3829 (43); *WA Br* 11, No. 4122 (9–10, 19–23).

24. Althaus, *Theology*, 414; *WA* 36, 241; *LW* 51, 234; *WA* 39^{II}, 386; *WA* 39^{II}, 354.

25. Althaus, *Theology*, 410.

26. Ibid., 410–11; *WA* 36, 543, commenting on 1 Cor. 15; explanation to the second article in the *Small Catechism*; *WA* 30^{I}, 297; *BC*, 345; *WA* 36, 547; *WA* 37, 68.

27. Althaus, *Theology*, 411–11; *WA* 31^{I}, 155; *LW* 14, 87; *WA* 43, 479, 481.

thians 12:9 ("My grace is sufficient for you") and continued to present God's promise from that text:

> Be grateful that you have My word and Myself in My Word. How can distress, hunger, and pestilence hurt you? What damage can be done to you by the feuding of the bigwigs, the malice of the peasants, the rage of the papists, the censure of the whole world, or the anger of all devils? You have God's Word; they don't! You are in My grace; they are not! You are My child; they are My enemies. Beloved, let My Word as Myself be a treasure, a kingdom, even a heavenly kingdom, to you in your poverty, misery, and woe. My Word is eternal, and in this Word you are eternal.[28]

Sleep of Death

Luther believed that after death, believers who hold on to the Word of God when they die "rest in the bosom of Christ."[29] As Christ said, "Whoever believes in me will never die" (John 11:26ff.), so in Christ they find a place to rest until the last day. Based on the death of Abraham (Gen. 25:7–10), Luther observed that the gentle gathering of the old man to his people

> declares that the death of the saints is peaceful and precious in the sight of God (Ps. 116:15) and that the saints do not taste death but most pleasantly fall asleep (cf. Isa. 57:1–2, 26:20). . . .
>
> In the eyes of the world the righteous are despised, spurned, and thrust aside. Their death seems exceedingly sad. But they are sleeping a most pleasant sleep. When they lie down on their beds and breathe their last, they die just as if sleep were gradually falling upon their limbs and senses.[30]

Therefore, as Abraham (and later Ishmael, Isaac, and Jacob) went to his waiting people, the Holy Spirit reveals that after this life there is a land of the living. So Christians go to the waiting Christ, the Guardian of their souls, at the right hand of the Father.

> Accordingly this serves to comfort us, lest we, like others, who have no hope, be frightened by or shudder at death. For in Christ death is not bitter, as it is for the ungodly, but it is a change of this wretched and unhappy life into a life that is quiet and blessed. This statement should convince us fully that we do not pass from a pleasant life into a life that is unhappy, but that we pass from afflictions into tranquility. For since the fathers had this comfort from these few passages long before Christ, how much more reasonable it is for us to guard and preserve the same comfort![31]

28. *LW* 14, 134f.; *WA* 31[1], 456 (commenting on Ps. 147:20).
29. Althaus, *Theology*, 412; *LW* 4, 314; *WA* 43, 361.
30. *LW* 4, 309; *WA* 43, 357–58.
31. *LW* 4, 311; *WA* 43, 358.

Using Jesus' story of the rich man and Lazarus (Luke 16:22), Luther declared that the Old Testament "bosom of Abraham" for all the saints who died before Christ is replaced with the "promise of Christ," who in his death and resurrection provides a "better bosom." Christians who die believing "are gathered into the bosom of Christ, the Savior who was born, suffered, was crucified, and rose again for us."[32] This assures us that after we die, our souls are living and sleeping in peace in Christ, waiting for the call of the God of the living (Matt. 22:32). Luther saw the soul in a state of sleep as in a safe chamber, yet living before God—sleeping yet awake, cradled in the bosom of Christ.[33] This is heaven or paradise, as Jesus said to thief (Luke 23:43), where the blessed rest and Christ is busy ruling his church. In contrast, the wicked go ultimately to their damnation.[34]

The Last Day, the Second Coming of Christ

Luther saw the great last day, judgment day, and the day of Christ's second coming, as that to which Christians look forward with great expectation. He held throughout his life that the end was near, and that the pope's rule would not be overcome by the laity, but by the soon coming Christ.[35] It will come while people are eating and drinking and conducting the normal matters of life, never expecting it; and it will come soon. The last day must be soon since the gospel has spread over most of the earth;[36] yet the world is unaware of the imminence of the Lord's coming and wickedness continues to increase. After the revelation of Antichrist the world will continue to do what it pleases.[37]

The Creation anticipates the end of this present epoch:

> All creation shall be astir; heaven and earth shall creak as an old house that is on the very verge of falling and crashing down. In every respect creation shall act as though it sensed that the world will soon end . . . and that the day of its dissolution is standing at the door.[38]

32. *LW* 4, 312; *WA* 43, 359.
33. *LW* 4, 313; *WA* 43, 361.
34. *LW* 4, 316; *WA* 43, 362–63.
35. Julius Köstlin, *Life of Luther* (reprint; London: Longman, Green, and Co., 1900), 178f., citing *Why the Books of the Pope and His Disciples Were Burnt by Dr. Martin Luther.* In 1520, in response to the bull of excommunication, he published several important tracts to the nobleman, the clergy, the emperor, and the pope. In them he indicated that he felt the last day was at hand since the Antichrist was ruling in Rome. This is the abomination of desolation. This signaled his final rupture with Rome (p. 181).
36. Ewald Plass, *What Luther Says* (St. Louis: Concordia, 1959), 696, citing *WA* 45, 336–37; 47, 621; *WA Tr* 5, No. 5488.
37. Plass, *What Luther Says*, 696–97; *WA Tr* 5, No. 5488; *WA Tr* 6, No. 6985; *WA Tr* 2, No. 1477.
38. Plass, *What Luther Says*, 697; *WA* 34[II], 461 (Luke 21:25–36).

Yet, though many signs will come to fulfill the predictions of Scripture, the world will generally ignore them and ridicule those who take them seriously.[39]

Christ will awaken the Christian's body and soul to enter into life, not just a sleep, with him forever.[40] On the day of their death believers experience this last day immediately, since the measurements of time no longer constrain things and everything is one eternal moment.[41] Althaus describes Luther's understanding of this intersection of time and eternity:

> It comes no sooner to the departed than to us and to all generations after us until the temporal end of the world. Because our periods of time are no longer valid in God's eternity, the Last Day surrounds our life as an ocean surrounds an island. Wherever we reach the boundaries of this life—whether in dying yesterday or today or at some other time or whether at the end of the world—everywhere the Last Day dawns in the great contemporaneity of eternity.[42]

This coming last day of Jesus Christ is the goal or end of the present form of this world. Luther saw that while Christ rules in the church, it is not the church of the papacy but a hidden church. Luther held that Satan was active in the papistic Roman Catholic Church of his day. When Christ finally comes, his victory over Satan will completely overcome Satan's influence in the church.[43] He found the Antichrist in the bitter daily reality of the doctrine of the papacy of his day:

> For the papacy places itself above God's word and thereby God and Christ by abandoning the comfort of the Gospel and placing the human doctrines of work righteousness in the place of the Gospel. And, according to Daniel 11:36 and Paul's prophecy in II Thessalonians 2:4, these are the decisive characteristics of the antichrist.[44]

Therefore, eschatological events were manifest in Luther's time in the theological differences between medieval Catholicism and the Reformation. An-

---

39. Plass, *What Luther Says*, 697f.; *WA* 10^I, 2, 93f, 101.

40. Althaus, *Theology*, 415; *WA* 37, 151.

41. Althaus, *Theology*, 416; *WA* 14, 70–71.

42. Althaus, *Theology*, 416; *WA* 12, 496; *WA* 13, 349; *WA* 40^{III}, 525; *LW* 13, 101.

43. Althaus, *Theology*, 418–19. Cf. Paul Althaus, *Die Letzten Dinge* (Gütersloh: Bertelsmann, 1933), 299–300.

44. Althaus, *Theology*, 420; *WA* 39^{III}, 381; *WA* 7, 741–42. Cf. Rupp, *Righteousness of God*, 10, where he notes that Luther pored over data of church history in preparation for the Leipzig Disputation in March 1519. He wrote to Spalatin, "I do not know whether the Pope is anti-Christ himself, or only his apostle, so greviously is Christ, i.e. Truth, manhandled and crucified by him in these decretals." *WA Br* I.359.29. Later in 1520, he had no doubt that the pope was Antichrist, so clearly he fit the description (*WA Br* 2.48.26).

tichrist is not in external forces but in the pope who, through the church, diverts Christians from the true gospel. He notes this in the Smalcald Articles (1537):

> The pope is the real antichrist who has raised himself over and set himself against Christ, for the pope will not permit Christians to be saved except by his own power, which amounts to nothing since it is neither established nor demanded by God. This is actually what St. Paul calls exalting oneself over and against God.[45]

He didn't think that Mohammed was the Antichrist, since he was so obvious, like all pagans who have attacked the church externally. But,

> The papacy is assuredly the true realm of Antichrist, the real anti-Christian tyrant, who sits in the temple of God and rules with human commandments as Christ in Matthew 24 [:24] and Paul in II Thessalonians 2 [:3f.] declare.[46]

Since Luther believed that he was living on the very edge of the end of time, the papacy was manifesting the perversion of spiritual power, which could only fit the biblical category of Antichrist.[47] Strohl notes Luther's understanding that a specific pontiff was not the Antichrist, but the Antichrist was manifest by the false doctrine and usurped authority, as claimed by the Hussite and Wycliffite movements from the previous centuries.[48] She summarizes Luther's idea that the pope is the mighty tyrant spoken of in Daniel 11: "The pope dares to put himself on a par with God by giving laws and thus creating sin where there formerly there was none."[49] Though terrible persecutions come upon the church from worldly governments and powers, the worst is that within the church, which pretends to represent Christ, but which really distorts and falsifies Christ and forgets the gospel of his cross.[50] Strohl notes that since he thought of the papacy as the Antichrist, Luther rejected armed opposition to Charles V, since, as a minion of the Antichrist, he and his allies would all be defeated by the victorious Lord in the imminent last eschatological battle.[51] Therefore, rather than fear the coming of Christ in the last day, as did medieval Catholicism, Luther, like the New Testament Christians and

---

45. Althaus, *Theology*, 421. *WA* 50, 217; *BC*, 300.
46. *WA* 26, 507; *LW* 37, 367. Cf. Althaus, *Theology*, 421.
47. Rupp, *Righteous of God*, 11ff.
48. Strohl, *Luther's Eschatology*, 28.
49. Ibid., 42–43, citing *WA Br* 11^{II}, 53 (comments on Dan. 11:37).
50. Althaus, *Theology*, 421–22. *WA* 51, 217; *LW* 13, 167–68; *WA DB* 7, 413ff., *LW* 13, 405ff.
51. Strohl, *Luther's Eschatology*, 172–73.

early church, looked forward to it since it meant the end of the Antichrist and the coming of redemption.[52] He would soon be with the Lord.

Resurrection

Althaus summarizes Luther on human resurrection:

> Luther teaches the resurrection of all the dead and not only believers. All enter into judgment. The believers enter into eternal life with Christ; evil men enter into eternal death with the devil and his angels. Luther expressly rejects the idea that the devil will finally also be saved.[53]

Judgment

Luther correlated humanity and the rest of creation in the process of judgment. As Althaus notes,

> As all men must pass through the judgment of death and through the corruption of their bodies and can only enter into the glory of eternal life in this way, so the present form of this world must be destroyed through fire before a new and final world can be created.[54]

This is a glorious real hope, which flows out of his theology of the cross and characterizes Luther's total view. Therefore, the coming of judgment day should be encouraging to Christians. As wickedness increases, the end comes closer:

> The more we preach, the less attention people pay . . . bent on increasing wickedness and wantonness at an overwhelming speed. We cry out and preach against this . . . . But what good does it do? It does, however, do *us* good in that we may expect the Last Day sooner. Then the godless will be hurled into hell, but we shall obtain eternal salvation on that Day. . . . So we may confidently expect that the Last Day is not far away.[55]

Christians should look forward to and pray for the hastening of the last day, the day of judgment, when they will finally be redeemed from the punishment of evil and be relieved of their misery in this life, since the Savior Jesus Christ carries the day and stands at their side.[56] Judgment day will be a wonderful

---

52. Althaus, *Theology*, 420ff.; *WA* 53, 401; *WA Br* 2, 567; S-J 2, 130; *WA Br* 9, 175.

53. Althaus, *Theology*, 417. Althaus cites the explanation to the Third Article in the *Small Catechism*, "He will raise me and all the dead and grant eternal life to me and to all who believe in Christ," *WA* 30¹, 250, *BC* 345, *WA* 26, 509; *LW* 37, 372.

54. Althaus, *Theology*, 424; *WA* 39¹, 95, *LW* 34, 164. Luther depended upon Rom. 8:20ff.; 2 Peter 3:10, 13; and Isa. 65:17.

55. Plass, *What Luther Says*, 698; *WA* 47, 623.

56. Plass, *What Luther Says*, 698; *WA* 34¹¹, 466 (Luke 21:25–33).

event and is a motivator for Christians to continue to preach to and encourage one another:

> Who will harm the man when the great God and Savior, Jesus Christ, to whom the Day of Judgment belongs, is on his side and stands before him in all His glory, greatness, majesty, and might? None other will hold court on the Day of Judgment than He who gave Himself for us. He will . . . declare that He gave Himself for your sins, as you believe. . . . Who will accuse you? Who will judge the judge? . . . Now since He has given Himself for you, what can terrify you? . . .
>
> Oh here is great, sure security. It only depends on the strength and firmness of our faith. Christ will certainly not waiver. He is firm enough. Therefore we should diligently exercise it with preaching, working, and suffering.[57]

All will stand before the Judge on that day. The Judge has power to call up the devils and the dead, and is the friend of believers. It will be a universal event, with no middle ground:

> He will call us His friends and brethren and will look at His gift and Holy Spirit in us; and the dead will again be full of joy. Although human nature is bound to be appalled at such divine majesty, the spirit will look at it with joy. He who will not have this comfort will be tormented by the devil. . . . No one will be able to hide . . . even though he were a thousand fathoms under the sea . . . or in the abyss of hell.[58]

Therefore, the great day of the last judgment is doom for the wicked and deliverance for Christians, whom God will help out of this wretched world to go, without any judgment, to a place among the angels to live in eternal glory.[59] Luther eagerly looked for the revealing of the Lord on this great day of judgment.

Heaven

After the judgment, the creation will be destroyed and returned to its original chaos, after which there will be a new heaven and earth and believers will be changed.[60]

The Christians' hope for the day of judgment is a better life beyond it:

> I desire *this* with far greater intensity than any physical liberation . . . . It would be better if everything were at once overturned and done away with, together

57. Plass, *What Luther Says*, 699; WA 10[I], 1, 49.
58. Plass, *What Luther Says*, 700; WA 17[I], 221.
59. Plass, *What Luther Says*, 699; WA 52, 20; WA 42, 102–3.
60. Plass, *What Luther Says*, 700; WA Tr 3, No. 3861.

with all the evils and troubles of this life, than if some temporary change for the better took place. For we know that an unspeakable joy and an imperishable crown, which we do not see now, are prepared and laid up for us forever.[61]

Luther understood that heaven is more blessed than the paradise lost:

The future glory will be far greater than was the glory of Adam in Paradise before the Fall. Had Adam remained in innocence . . . he . . . would not have forever remained in this state in Paradise. . . . He would have been received into yonder glory, not by death—for he would have remained immortal—but by translation.[62]

Plass notes, "Though Luther's hand was very busy here below, his heart was in heaven."[63] The Christians' priority should be their hope in heaven,[64] which they receive the day they first believe,[65] and which is continually held open in Christ until the last day.[66]

Because of their hope in heaven, Christians should hope for an early death so they can appropriate that which they already have in heaven as children of God.[67] This hope of glory is different for different believers,

such as that now existing here on earth, where one is stronger, more beautiful, and more eloquent than another yet all enjoy the same physical existence. So there will also be many degrees of splendor and glory in yonder life, as St. Paul teaches in 1 Cor.15:40; and yet all will be alike in the enjoyment of the same eternal blessedness and delight, and there will be but *one* glory for all, because we shall all be the children of God.[68]

This is Luther's understanding of the rewards that are in store in heaven for Christians. Though all will be equally granted the gift of eternal life, there will be different degrees of glory according to the works each one has done, "In that life it will all be revealed, for the whole world to see what each one has done from the degree of glory he has."[69]

The action of heaven will be neither eating or drinking but gazing at God and transporting from heaven to earth in the spark of a moment. Everything

---

61. Plass, *What Luther Says*, 698; WA 44, 613.
62. Plass, *What Luther Says*, 621; WA Tr 1, No. 1155.
63. Plass, *What Luther Says*, 618.
64. Plass, *What Luther Says*, 619; WA 34[II], 111.
65. Plass, *What Luther Says*, 620; WA 44, 718, WA 40[II], 517.
66. Plass, *What Luther Says*, 619; WA 46, 711–12.
67. Plass, *What Luther Says*, 621; WA 40[I], 598.
68. Plass, *What Luther Says*, 622; WA 41, 306.
69. Plass, *What Luther Says*, 623; WA 32, 543f.; cf. WA 41, 305.

of creation will be perfectly new in the new creation. God will transform, impart, and sustain the life of all who gaze upon him.[70]

In heaven the law will finally be perfectly fulfilled through faith and love. After that, the law will cease to exist as the angels rejoice over the new and pure creation.[71]

Hell

Luther wasn't sure if hell exists before the last day, since it is where the devil and his angels are active in the world today. But he was sure of its existence after the last day, as the place where the devil, his angels, and all the condemned wicked will be cast forever[72] and from which it will be impossible to escape.[73]

In a poignant glimpse of Luther's concept of the experience of hell on earth, Rupp describes a man suffering the anguish of conscience wherein he felt the horrifying anger of God, from which there is no possible escape.

> God appears horrifyingly angry with him. . . . In this moment, marvelous to relate, the soul cannot believe it can ever be redeemed . . . . This is the soul stretched out with Christ, so that all his bones can be numbered, nor is there any corner not filled with the most bitter bitterness, horror, fear, dolour, and all these things seem eternal.[74]

For Luther the beginning of hell is the constant contradiction between the reality of guilt and shame, and the promise of God's hidden deliverance. He experiences hell when he doubts and despairs of God' grace.[75]

> We are constantly tempted to believe that God would abandon us and not keep His word; and in our hearts He begins to become a liar. In short, God cannot be God unless He first becomes a devil. We cannot go to heaven unless we first go to hell. We cannot become God's children until we first become children of the devil. All that God speaks and does the devil has to speak and do first. And our flesh agrees. Therefore it is actually the Spirit who enlightens us and teaches us in the Word to believe differently.[76]

Therefore God uses the law to terrify the conscience, which is the real punishment of hell. In this way man begins to experience hell on earth. This is

---

70. Plass, *What Luther Says*, 623f.; *WA* 36, 594f. (1 Cor. 15:27–28), 660 (1 Cor. 15:42–44).

71. Plass, *What Luther Says*, 624; *WA* 39^I, 203 (Rom. 3:28).

72. Plass, *What Luther Says*, 625; *WA* 19, 225–26 (Jon. 2:3).

73. Plass, *What Luther Says*, 626; *WA* 40^{III}, 512 (Ps. 90:2).

74. Rupp, *Righteous of God*, 110, citing *WA* I, 558.7.33.

75. Althaus, *Theology*, 33; *WA* 31^I, 249; *LW* 14, 31–32.

76. *LW* 14, 31; cf. *WA* 44, 617 (Prov. 15:15).

Luther's understanding of the theology of the cross. Althaus, with very generous reference to Luther's works, describes the dynamic of Luther's theology of the cross:

> The real torture of hell, as it already begins to be felt in this life, comes when a man feels in his conscience that God is against him and he cannot endure to be close to God. He tries to run away from God and cannot get away. For the omnipresent God meets him everywhere in his conscience and is close to him in his wrath. The omnipotent God holds man in his hands. . . . This is the terrible condition of the man whose conscience is awakened and now experiences the wrath of God. He burns with hatred against this God who so painfully holds him prisoner in his wrath. . . . He, being under the wrath of God, should turn to this same God and call on him in prayer. If he would only turn to *this* God, fleeing from the wrathful God to the gracious God, he would be helped. . . . But sinful man is not able to do that. . . . In his terrible bondage to himself which makes him hate God, he can neither see nor believe God's mercy, nor can he produce trust in it. . . . [He] remains hopelessly lost under the wrath of God. Only God can open this prison by confronting man with the Gospel and opening his heart to faith through his Spirit.[77]

Thus Luther's theology of the cross bridges the gap from the present to eternity through the present experience of the wrath of God as a foretaste of the potential life under the wrath of God to come. This present terror of the future wrath of God in hell is overcome by Christ, who experienced the wrath of God on the cross and through the descent into hell. Through his resurrection he has emerged triumphant over death and the devil to remove the cause for anxiety from all who have faith in him. God did not intend the fires of hell for humankind, but his Son the Savior has willed to suffer our hell to the fullest extent to gain a present and future redemption for all who believe.[78]

Therefore, Luther believed that before the last day, hell is not a particular place but an inner condition of man. After the last day, hell is a particular place under the wrath of God to which wicked men will go with body and soul.[79] He described this in his comments on Psalm 21:9, with reference to Hebrews 12:29 ("God is a consuming fire"):

> The Day of Judgment will last for a moment only but will stand throughout eternity and will thereafter never come to an end. Constantly the damned will be judged, constantly they will suffer pain, and constantly they will be a fiery oven, that is, they will be tortured within by supreme distress and tribulation. Not as though the ungodly see God and His appearance as the godly see Him;

---

77. Althaus, *Theology*, 178, citing several locations in Luther's works.
78. Althaus, *Theology*, 424; Plass, *What Luther Says* 623f.; *WA* 52, 726–27.
79. Althaus, *Theology*, 177; *WA* 19, 225.

but they will feel the power of His presence, which they will not be able to bear and yet will be forced to bear.[80]

This is linked to Luther's understanding of the wrath of God, which for false Christians will be even more severe.[81] These are those whom Jesus would have taken in but they would not be his (Matt. 23:37), "Because they do not want to hear God, they must do without Him. . . eternally be the devil's own in hell . . . bereft of all they once had on earth."[82]

Hell, "The Infernal Blessing, or the Blessing beneath Us," reveals the majestic sovereignty of God.

> We must love and laud His justice and thus rejoice in God even when He miserably destroys the wicked in body and soul; for in all this His high and inexpressible justice shines forth. And even so in hell, no less than in heaven, is full of God and the highest Good. For the justice of God is God Himself; and God is the highest Good. Therefore even as His mercy, so His justice or judgment must be loved, praised, and glorified above all things.[83]

According to Luther's understanding, hell begins as the existential agony of one who knows his rebellion against God warrants an eternity under his wrath, and ends as the real place of God's eternal wrath prepared for the devil, his angels, and the wicked who unrepentantly continue to oppose God.

Chiliasm

Luther rejected the literal thousand-year reign as the end of history and agreed with the church's teaching since Augustine. The thousand years of Revelation 20 describes the church from the time of the writing of the Revelation to the coming of the Turks or with the papacy becoming the Antichrist. However, rather than glorifying the earthly institutional church, he said the true church is hidden and will be revealed at the coming of Christ at the last day.[84] Preaching on Psalm 110:1, Luther rejected the Anabaptist "dream" of his day,

> that before the Last Day all the enemies of the Church will be physically exterminated and a Church assembled which shall consist of pious Christians only; they will govern in peace, without any opposition or attack. But this text [Psalm

---

80. Plass, *What Luther Says*, 627; *WA* 5, 590 (Ps. 21:9).
81. Plass, *What Luther Says*, 627; *WA* 52, 513 (Matt. 22:1–14).
82. Plass, *What Luther Says*, 627; *WA* 36, 596–97 (preaching on 1 Cor. 15:25–30).
83. Plass, *What Luther Says*, 628; *WA* 6, 127; *PE* I 157–58 (*The Fourteenth of Consolation*, 1520).
84. Althaus, *Theology*, 418–19; *WA DB* 7, 409; *LW* 35, 409 (Rev. 20).

110:1] clearly and powerfully says that there are to be enemies continuously as long as this Christ reigns on earth. And certain it is, too, that death will not be abolished until the Last Day, when all His enemies will be exterminated with one blow.[85]

Luther's and Lutheranism's understanding is—for the most part—that the Scriptures teach that Christ's kingdom exists now as he rules over his church and defeats his wicked enemies in the present world order.[86]

Purgatory

As justification by faith alone became clearer in Luther's understanding, the concept of purgatory became to him more and more inconsistent with the teaching of Scripture. Since the merits of the saints have nothing to do with their standing before God, the idea of cleansing, and being endowed with the merits of the saints before being received into heaven didn't fit at all.[87] This is the repeated message of his 95 Theses. By 1521 he wrote that if one said there was no purgatory, they should not be considered a heretic, and by 1530 he answered arguments in favor of purgatory.[88]

The Kingdom of God

Luther doesn't distinguish between the church and Israel. In the earthly kingdom, in which Christ rules, the church includes all—Jew and Gentile alike—who, by repentance and faith in him, are forgiven and hope for a home in heaven. Those without faith in Christ are the wicked who are rejected and

---

85. *LW* 13, 263–64 (preaching on Ps. 110:1, May 10, 1535).

86. Elert, *Structure*, 511–12; *WA* 47, 561, 12ff. It should be noted that there are confessional Lutherans holding premillennial views, e.g., J. W. Montgomery. In his article "Millennium," in *The International Standard Bible Encyclopedia*, ed. G. Bromiley (Grand Rapids: Eerdmans, 1986), 3:359, he notes that the condemnation of Article XVII of *The Augsburg Confession,* Tappert, *BC* 38–39, "expressly rejected such 'Jewish opinions' (but, let it be noted, did not reject millennianism *per se*)." F. Monseth ("Millennialism and the Augsburg Confession," paper presented at the 51st annual meeting of the Evangelical Theological Society [Danvers, Mass., 17 November 1999]) presents the thesis that confessional Lutherans must observe cautious freedom to allow for amillennial and premillennial views of a spiritual kingdom to coexist against an earthly temporal pre-resurrection kingdom. Neither Montgomery nor Monseth address only Luther's view, and their provisions for the latitude of the statement of Article XVII seem to be excluded by Luther's limited statements on chiliasm. Cf. John R. Stephenson, *Eschatology*, vol. 13 of Confessional Lutheran Dogmatics, ed. Robert Preus (Fort Wayne, Ind.: Luther Academy, 1993), 83ff. He rejects all forms of literal millennialism and holds that "Revelation 20 is not concerned with describing a single episode just prior to the last judgment, but rather with encouraging the beleaguered people of God in the setting of a description of the whole New Testament age from the incarnation to the parousia. . . . The chaining of Satan achieved in the work of Christ (Matt. 12:29, and parallels) renders possible the 'thousand years' in which the Gospel makes its triumphal march through history" (93).

87. Althaus, *Theology*, 300.

88. *LW* 35, 98 n. 33 (*Treatise on the New Testament* [1520]); cf. *WA* 30[II], 367–90 (1530).

defeated by the ruling Christ and who will spend eternity in hell with the devil and his angels.

Althaus explains that Luther related the human resurrection to the renewed creation, which is the heavenly kingdom:

> Luther, as does the New Testament, expects not only that the individual will continue to exist in the future beyond death and that history will come to an end and be completed in the ultimate kingdom of God, but he also expects the future renewal of the entire world and its perfection as God's creation. Christ's resurrection guarantees not only the bodily resurrection of Christians but also the redemption and perfection "of all creation with us" according to Romans 8:21.[89]

In this God conjoins his work with his entire creation though the life, death, and resurrection of the incarnated Word of God—Jesus Christ—to transform and glorify all that is created.[90]

Summary and Conclusions

Luther's eschatology is a logical continuity and completion of his overall view of the way things are. The key is justification by faith in Christ. As many suffer the *Anfechtungen* of this life and contemplate the horror of eternity under the wrath and condemnation of God, the Holy Spirit through the gospel of Jesus Christ links the faithful to the hidden reality of God's victory in Christ's cross and resurrection. For the believer, as *simul iustus et peccator*, Christ's victory today is the manifestation of his ultimate victory over wickedness for all time.

Luther emphasized that baptism is being joined with Christ in his death and resurrection. At physical death—the end of this life—all enter into a sleep-like state until the great last day. The last day is a moment of determinative action when Christ's rule to defeat sin and the devil finds decisive expression in his role as the Judge of the righteous and the wicked. Luther rejected the idea of a thousand-year reign at the end of history. Rather, he maintained that Christ reigns now through the church, defeating the devil and his angels through the good news of the gospel. His reign obtains the victory for believers to gain access to eternal life in heaven. On the other hand, Christ's judgment convicts and condemns all the wicked—the devil, his angels, and those who resist God's grace in Christ—and they are cast into eternal condemnation and punishment.

Althaus closes his discussion of Luther's eschatology with a quote from *Table Talk:* "We know no more about eternal life than children in the womb

---

89. Althaus, *Theology*, 424; WA 37, 68.
90. Cf. WA 39[1], 177; LW 34, 39; and Althaus, *Die Letzten Dinge*, 351ff.

of their mother know about the world they are about to enter."[91] However, Luther knew that it is a living reality fulfilling justification by faith and to which we should look with joyful expectation.

Bibliography

Primary Sources

Luther, Martin. *A Commentary on St. Paul's Epistle to the Galatians*. Ed. Erasmus Middleton. London, 1807.

———. *Luthers Werke: Kritische Gesamtausgabe [Schriften]*. Weimar, 1883–. [*WA*]

———. *Luthers Werke: Kritische Gesamtausgabe. Tischreden*. Weimar, 1912–1921. [*WA Tr*]

———. *Works of Martin Luther, American Edition*, 55 vols. Philadelphia: Fortress, 1955–86. [*LW*]

———. *Works of Martin Luther*, 6 vols. Philadelphia, 1915–1943; Grand Rapids: Baker, 1982. [*PE*]

Secondary Sources

Althaus, Paul. *Die Letzten Dinge*. Gütersloh: Bertelsmann, 1933.

———. *A Synopsis of Dr. Paul Althaus'—The Last Things*. Saint Paul: Luther Seminary, 1963.

———. *The Theology of Martin Luther*. Trans. by Robert C. Schultz. Philadelphia: Fortress, 1966.

Asendorf, Ulrich. *Eschatologie bei Luther*. Göttingen: Vandenhoeck & Ruprecht, 1967.

Bakker, J. T. *Eschatologische Prediking bij Luther*. Uitgeversmij: J. H. Kok N. V. Kampen, 1964.

Book of Concord. Trans. and ed. by Theodore Tappert et al. Philadelphia: Fortress, 1959. [*BC*]

Elert, Werner. *The Structure of Lutheranism: The Theology and Philosophy of Life of Lutheranism Especially in the Sixteenth and Seventeenth Centuries*. Trans. by Walter A. Hanson. St. Louis: Concordia, 1962.

Kerr, Hugh T. *A Compend of Luther's Theology*. Philadelphia: Westminster, 1966.

Köstlin, Julius. *Life of Luther*. Reprint. London: Longmans, Green, and Co., 1900.

———. "Martin Luther." *ERK*, 1950.

———. *The Theology of Luther in Its Historical Development and Inner Harmony*, 2 vols. Trans. by C. E. Hay. 2d ed. Philadelphia: Lutheran Publication Society, 1897.

---

91. Althaus, *Theology*, 425; *WA Tr* 3, No. 3339.

Lehmann, Martin E. *Luther and Prayer*. Milwaukee: Northwestern, 1985.

Loewenich, Walter von. *Luther's Theology of the Cross*. Trans. Herbert J. A. Bouman. Minneapolis: Augsburg, 1976.

Lohse, Bernard. *Martin Luther: An Introduction to His Life and Work*. Trans. Robert C. Schultz. Philadelphia: Fortress, 1986.

Monseth, Francis Wesley. "Millennialism and the Augsburg Confession." Paper presented at the 51st annual meeting of the Evangelical Theological Society, Danvers, Mass., 17 November 1999.

Montgomery, John Warwick. "Millennium," *The International Standard Bible Encyclopedia*. Ed. G. Bromiley (Grand Rapids: Eerdmans, 1986), 3:359.

Oberman, Heiko. *Luther: Man between God and the Devil*. Trans. Eileen Walliser-Schwarzbart. New Haven: Yale, 1989.

Plass, Ewald. *What Luther Says: A Practical In-Home Anthology for the Active Christian*. Saint Louis: Concordia, 1959.

Prenter, Regin. *Luther's Theology of the Cross*. Philadelphia: Fortress, 1971.

———. *Spiritus Creator*. Trans. John M. Jensen. Philadelphia: Muhlenberg, 1953.

Rupp, Gordon. *The Righteousness of God*. Luther Studies. London: Hodder and Stoughton, 1953.

Schlinck, Edmund. *The Theology of the Lutheran Confessions*. Trans. Paul F. Koehneke and Herbert J. A. Bouman. Philadelphia: Fortress, 1961.

Stephenson, John R. *Eschatology*. Volume 13 of Confessional Lutheran Dogmatics. Ed. Robert Preus. Fort Wayne: Luther Academy, 1993.

Strohl, Jane E. *Luther's Eschatology: The Last Times and the Last Things*. Ph.D. diss., University of Chicago Divinity School, 1989.

Watson, Philip S. *Let God Be God! An Interpretation of the Theology of Martin Luther*. London: Epworth, 1947.

9

The Coming of the Kingdom and Sixteenth-Century English Bibles

CAMERON A. MACKENZIE

Concordia Theological Seminary

The sixteenth century was remarkable for its production of vernacular Bibles. In England alone, from the publication of William Tyndale's first New Testament in 1525–26 to that of the King James version in 1611, there were over three hundred distinct editions of the Bible or parts thereof printed in the English language. Although most of them are different editions of a few basic types like the Great Bible or the Geneva Bible, nonetheless they presented God's Word to the English-reading population in this period in a wide variety of formats and with different kinds of helps designed to direct the reader in the study of the Scriptures.[1]

In the English text and its accompanying materials, these versions reveal the theological proclivities of those who produced them. Not surprisingly, as with most things religious in the sixteenth century, the major difference between versions is that between Catholic and Protestant Bibles. Even though

---

1. T. H. Darlow and H. F. Moule, *Historical Catalogue of Printed Editions of the English Bible, 1525–1961*, ed. A. S. Herbert (London: British and Foreign Bible Society, 1968). In this paper, references to items in this catalogue are designated by DM and an Arabic numeral. The first edition of the King James version is DM 309. Good introductions to the history of the English Bible in this period are F. F. Bruce, *History of the English Bible* (New York: Oxford, 1978), 24–126; and S. L. Greenslade, "English Versions of the Bible, 1525–1611," in *The Cambridge History of the Bible: The West from the Reformation to the Present Day*, ed. S. L. Greenslade (Cambridge: Cambridge University Press, 1963), 141–74.

Protestants were first in the production of English Bibles, English-speaking Roman Catholics produced a New Testament of their own in 1582 (DM 177) and an accompanying Old Testament in two volumes in 1609–10 (DM 300). These Catholic editions are distinct in the text they chose to translate (the Latin Vulgate and not the Hebrew and Greek), in the kind of English style they employ for the biblical text, and in the annotations that accompany the text.

To a much smaller but still significant degree, the Protestant versions also manifest differences between versions regarding text, English style, and accompanying matter. Although virtually all of them depend upon Tyndale's pioneering work in the 1520s and 1530s, they depart from it on account of different judgments about how the text should be translated and about what the reader should have available to him or her in addition to the sacred text itself. In this last respect especially—the nature and scope of prefaces, annotations, indexes, and the like—the Protestant versions, like the Catholic version, reveal the underlying convictions of those who translated and published them about which doctrines and beliefs they thought were most important for their readers to know and understand.

In short, the English Bibles of the sixteenth century were an important vehicle for the various religious parties to popularize their ideas and ideals. Since all of them affirmed the authority of the Scriptures, what better way to persuade English readers of their position on the vexed issues of the day than to present that position in immediate proximity to the biblical text? It is one thing to present a theological argument that is bolstered by Bible passages and still another to print a Bible that is glossed by theological observations. Both methods may have the same objective of persuading the reader to adopt a particular position, but an argument in the margins of a Bible attaches it directly to the church's sacred book.

Therefore, the marginalia and other accompanying matter of sixteenth-century English Bibles provide opportunities for assessing the significance of eschatology and the coming of the kingdom in the religious views and attitudes of Catholics and Protestants who produced them. Since an exhaustive study of all extant versions is beyond the scope of a paper, we propose to sample the opinions offered on the topic in just three of the more important versions from the period: Tyndale's New Testament (1534); the Catholic version, the Rheims New Testament (1582); and the Geneva Bible of 1560. Tyndale and Rheims are obvious choices because they represent the earliest Protestant and Catholic versions respectively. The Geneva version is also important, however, as a principal vehicle by which Elizabethan Protestants assimilated Reformed theology during the long reign of Queen Elizabeth (1558–1603).

In addition to limiting ourselves to these particular versions, it also seems reasonable to restrict our attention to particular portions of the Bible dealing with eschatological themes. In this respect, I propose looking especially at that most eschatological of books, the Revelation of St. John, as well as 2 Thessalonians.

William Tyndale

The Tyndale version is dealt with most speedily.[2] Although one can hardly exaggerate the significance of William Tyndale for the history of the English Bible, his notes and notices regarding eschatology are neither extensive nor especially pointed in the portions of Scripture we are considering. With respect to 2 Thessalonians, Tyndale summarizes the second chapter in these words:

> He showeth them that the last daye shuld not come, tyll there were fyrst a departinge (as some men thynke) from under the obedyence of the Emperour of Rome, and that Anti christ shuld set up him selfe in the same place, as God: and deceave the unthankfull worlde with false doctrine, and with false and lyenge myracles wrought by the workinge of Satan, untill Christ shuld come and slee him with his glorious commynge and spirituall preachinge of the worde of God.

Clearly, one can read this description as a testimony against the papacy, but in point of fact, Tyndale does not make the identification explicit. He does, however, strike a characteristically Protestant note by defining Antichrist's deception as "false doctrine" and describing our Lord's victory over him by "spirituall preaching of the worde of God." Likewise, in a note on the second chapter, Tyndale comments, "Where no love is to the truthe [,] on them dothe god let slype false prophetes to deceave them."[3] Certainly, it would not take too much imagination for a Protestant believer to interpret this note in terms of his or her own times, but it would demand some imagination, since Tyndale does not say definitively that his times are the last times or that the pope is the Antichrist.

Tyndale's remarks on the Book of Revelation are even less pointed than those of 2 Thessalonians. For one thing, contrary to his usual practice, Tyndale does not introduce the book with a preface. Instead, he simply writes at the end of Jude, "Her after foloweth the Apocalyps." Second, his annotations are remarkably slight for such a difficult book, and the only annotation that reveals any theological predilections occurs in chapter 7, when in defining the term "angel" in the text, Tyndale notes:

2. Although Tyndale's first complete New Testament was the edition of 1526 (DM 2), it did not contain any marginal notes. The 1534 edition (DM 13) contains notes and prefaces, the latter based chiefly on the corresponding prefaces in Luther's German Bible. See Bruce, *History*, 36, 42–48.

3. *The New Testament Translated by William Tyndale 1534*, reprint of the 1534 ed., ed. N. Hardy Wallis (Cambridge: Cambridge University Press, 1938), 433, 436.

Prophetes, preachers and the prelates of the churche are called angelles: that is to saye messengers, be cause their offyce is to bringe the message of god unto the people. The good angelles here in this booke are the true bysshopes and preachers, and the evell angelles are the heretyckes and false preachers which ever falsifye gods worde, with which the churche of Christ shal be thus miserablye plaged unto the ende of the worlde as is paynted in these fygures.[4]

By implication, once again, Tyndale places his own times into an eschatological context, but there is hardly a sense of urgency nor even a sense of uniqueness, for the church of Christ is to be "miserablye plaged" by false preachers until the end of the world—obviously including the sixteenth century but not necessarily restricted to it.

Of course, Tyndale's work represents an early stage in the story of English Bibles. Although his 1534 edition contains a response to the translation efforts of his erstwhile associate, George Joye,[5] Tyndale did not otherwise feel compelled to use his Bible to answer alternative versions and interpretations. The situation was quite different when at length English Catholics produced a New Testament in 1582. By that time, well over one hundred different editions of the Protestant version had been published and, apparently, even Catholics found them appealing.

Catholic Reaction

For more than a generation following the publication of Tyndale's New Testament, Catholic polemicists had been saying no to the English Bible; but in the 1560s they began to reassess their opposition due to the situation of their coreligionists in the Protestant England of Elizabeth I. In 1567, two leaders of the exiled English Catholic community, Thomas Harding and Nicholas Sanders, wrote to the cardinal-protector of England, Giovanni Morone, regarding the English Bible. When the whole country is "boiling over in heresy," they argue, ". . . those who are compelled to drink poison everywhere ought not be compelled to defer a remedy until a doctor arrives when there isn't one or else he is far away and always lies hidden." The poison they are referring to is Protestant versions of the English Bible: "When heretics abuse the word of God for the sake of deceiving the rude and ignorant, they do this as much as possible by a perverse interpretation of the Bible."

Furthermore, Harding and Sanders contend that the people found it so hard to put the Bible aside, even when Catholics were in control, that the more it was prohibited, the more persistently the people retained it. Once they

---

4. Ibid., 530, 539–40.
5. Joye had published his own revision of Tyndale's New Testament (DM 12) in which he had substituted phrases like "life after this life" for "resurrection"—an editorial freedom that Tyndale did not appreciate. See Bruce, *History*, 42–44.

had gotten a taste for the vernacular Scriptures, they refused to give them up. Accordingly, as a remedy for bad Bibles, these controversialists request a good one or at least parts of a good one:

> To this evil [the Protestant vernacular Bibles] it seems to some a remedy can be offered if at least the historical and moral books of the Old Testament and the gospels and epistles would be published in vernacular speech by Catholics. For thus, at last it might be possible to persuade the people to discard their former books, corruptly interpreted, if new ones, accurately translated according to the Vulgate edition, were given to them.[6]

Not until fifteen years later would the English Catholic community be in a position actually to accomplish what Harding and Sanders had requested; but when at last the Rheims New Testament appeared, it was clearly aimed at answering Protestant criticisms of the old religion that had appeared in English Bibles and elsewhere. In fact, the title page of the Catholic version informs the reader that all kinds of helps have been provided "for the better understanding of the text" and "specially for the discoverie of the Corruptions of divers late translations, and for cleering the Controversies in religion, of these daies." Accordingly, using the preface, summaries of books, indexes, and annotations, the reader of this version finds the Catholic position on justification, the sacraments, sacred tradition, papal primacy, purgatory, and the cult of the saints affirmed and the corresponding Protestant positions repudiated.[7]

But what about eschatology?

By 1582, it was virtually a commonplace among Protestants that the church was in the last times and that the pope was the Antichrist.[8] That conviction made it not only into Protestant confessions like the Schmalkald Articles of the Lutheran Reformation and the Scottish Confession of 1580 but, as we shall see, also into the marginalia of English Bibles. Given its apologetic purposes, therefore, the Rheims New Testament addresses this charge directly in its annotations on both 2 Thessalonians and Revelation and in so doing, tempers Protestant apocalyptic expectations.

Regarding 2 Thessalonians 2, for example, the Catholic annotators insist upon a literal reading of "the man of sin" and a partly political understanding of the great falling away. In both interpretations they also claim to be relying upon

---

6. Thomas Harding and Nicholas Sanders, Louvain, to Giovanni Morone, June 11, 1567, printed in Arnold O. Meyer, *England and the Catholic Church under Queen Elizabeth* (New York: Barnes & Noble, 1967), 475–78. Translation from the Latin is my own.

7. Rheims New Testament, DM 177, title page. For the Catholic character of this work, see my dissertation, "The Battle for the Bible, 1557–1582" (Ph.D. diss., University of Notre Dame, 1991), 371–449.

8. *Oxford Encyclopedia of the Reformation*, 4 vols. (New York: Oxford University Press, 1996), s.v. "Antichrist."

the church fathers. Interestingly, although they are translating the Latin text, they are perfectly capable of referring to the Greek as here when they write:

> The Heathen Emperours were many, Turkes be many, Heretikes have been and now are many, therefore they can not be that one great Antichrist which here is spoken of, and which by the article alwaies added in the Greeke, is signified to be one special and singular man.[9]

According to Richard Bauckham, this notion of the Antichrist being one single person had roots deep in the Middle Ages, going back at least to a tenth-century French abbot by the name of Adso, whose work *Libellus de Antichristo* was popular throughout the Middle Ages and was current in English translation among English Catholics of the sixteenth century. In this work, Adso describes the Antichrist as a Jew, born of the tribe of Dan and under the control of Satan, who will appear only after the Holy Roman Empire comes to an end and will rule the world for three and a half years, after which Christ will return.[10]

At least some of these details are present in the Rheims notes on 2 Thessalonians 2:

> The particular stocke and tribe whereof he should be borne . . . [is] of the Jewes . . . and of the tribe of Dan . . . the time of his appearing so neere the worldes end: his short reigne . . . all these & many other arguments prove him to be but one special notorious Adversarie in the highest degree, unto whom al other persecutors, Heretikes, Atheistes, and wicked enemies of Christ and His Church, are but members and servants.[11]

The point of these notes is to refute the Protestants who identified *the* Antichrist with the succession of persons who occupied the office of pope. In commenting on the biblical text at hand, they emphasize its literal meaning. Not only does it refer to a single individual, it also says that he will "sit in the temple of God." "Most auncient writers," they maintain, "expound this of the Temple in Hierusalem, which they thinke Antichrist shal build up againe . . . he shal be adored there by sacrifice and divine honour, the name and worship of the true God wholy defaced."[12] The Rheims editors acknowledge that Au-

9. Rheims New Testament, DM 177, 557. In the margin, they cite the Greek, "*ho antichristos*," "*ho huios apoleias*," and "*ho antikeimenos*."

10. Richard Bauckham, *Tudor Apocalypse* ([Oxford]: Sutton Courtenay, 1978), 91–93. See also *Dictionary of the Middle Ages*, 13 vols. (New York: Scribner's, 1982–89), s.v. "Antichrist."

11. Rheims New Testament, DM 177, 557. The proof here is Gen. 49:17 and citations from Irenaeus, Jerome, and Augustine.

12. Ibid., 557. Their citations include Irenaeus (bk. 5 in fine); Hippolytus (*De consum. Mundi*); Cyril of Jerusalem (*Catech.* 15); Jerome on Dan. 11; and Gregory (bk. 31. *Moralia*, c. 11).

gustine and Jerome both understood "sitting in the Temple of God" as a reference to the Church of Christ and not the temple of Jerusalem; but even in this interpretation, Antichrist must still replace Christ literally so that he, Antichrist, "shal be adored in all the Churches of the world which he list to leave standing for his [own] honour."[13]

By taking a strictly literal approach to this text in 2 Thessalonians, these Catholic apologists are seeking to refute any Protestant identification of Antichrist with the pope whom, of course, they present as a paragon of Christian piety, "How then can the Pope be Antichrist, as the Heretikes fondly blaspheme, who is so far from being exalted above God, that he praieth most humbly not onely to christ, but also to his B. mother and al his Sainctes."[14] It is not immediately evident that Protestants would find this last bit of evidence particularly persuasive, but followers of the old religion would certainly find it so, as well as the literal reading of the biblical text offered in the annotations. Second Thessalonians could not apply to the pope.

Besides protecting the papacy from Protestant attacks, an additional consequence of the approach to this text in the Rheims New Testament is a tempering of apocalyptic expectations. Although the annotators suggest that the increase of heretics and accompanying defections from Rome in the sixteenth century may presage the appearance of Antichrist, such opponents are not *the* Antichrist even if they are all "antichrists."[15] Heretics pave the way for the Antichrist but they do so surreptitiously, deviously, under a cloak of piety, so to speak, but the great Antichrist shall reveal his opposition to Christ and his church openly. Commenting on the phrase "mysterie of iniquitie," the Rheims annotators say:

> The mysterie of iniquitie is commonly referred to Heretikes, who worke to the same, and do that that Antichrist shal do, but yet not openly, but in covert and under the cloke of Christes name, the Scriptures, the word of the Lord, shew of holines, etc. Whereas Antichrist him self shal openly attempt and atchieve the foresaid desolation, and Satan now serving his turne by Heretikes *underhand* shal toward the last end utter, reveale, & bring him forth *openly*.[16]

13. Ibid., 558.
14. Ibid., 554.
15. Ibid., 556. "If the Adversaries had said that this revolt which the Apostle foretelleth shal come before the worldes end, is meant of great numbers of Heretikes & Apostates revolting from the Church, they had said truth of them selves and such others, whom S. John calleth Antichristes. And it is very like . . . that this great defection or revolt shal not be onely from the Romane empire but specially from the Romane Church, and withal from most points of Christian religion. . . . Which revolt having been begunne and continued by Heretikes of divers ages . . . and being now wonderfully increased by these of our daies the next precursors of Antichrist as it may seeme, shal be fully atchieved a litle before the end of the world by Antichrist him self."
16. Ibid., 558.

Clearly, much had to happen before the end would come. Translating *discessio* in verse 3 as "revolt" (Gk, *apostasia*; NIV, "rebellion"), the Rheims annotations refer to "the general forsaking & fall of the Romane empire." Although the ancient empire had fallen as also Byzantium, the Holy Roman Empire existed still, so that one might conclude that the great falling away had not yet taken place. Furthermore, Antichrist would

> abolish the publike exercise of *al other religions true and false*, and pull downe both the B. Sacrament of the altar, wherein consisteth specially the worship of the true God, and also al Idols of the Gentils, and sacrifices of the Jewes, generally al kind of religious worship, saving that which must be done to him self alone.[17]

This too had not yet taken place.

As far as the end times are concerned, therefore, the reader of the annotations on 2 Thessalonians in the Rheims New Testament might very well conclude that the last day was as yet some way off.

Regarding the Book of Revelation, the evidence is similar. Although the Rheims New Testament maintains that the purpose of the Apocalypse is to rehearse the "storie" of the church "to the end . . . by way of prophecie," there is little sense in the annotations that the end is imminent. The editors attempt to make the book relevant by applying its content to their own times and situation, but do not conclude that the Antichrist is present in the sixteenth century. So for example, regarding the blasphemies spoken by the beast in Revelation 13:6, the notes say, "No heretike ever liker Antichrist, then these in our daies, specially in blasphemies against Gods Church, Sacraments, Sancts, ministers, al sacred thinges";[18] but being "like" Antichrist is not the same as "being" Antichrist.

As in 2 Thessalonians, the notes on Revelation maintain that this apocalyptic figure is a unique human being and not the papacy. He will rule for three and a half years and Jerusalem will be his capitol. He will persecute the church and will put to death many, including Enoch and Elijah, who will literally return from heaven to preach against him. He will perform "wonders" to deceive many and will set up his own name, sign, and image in place of our Lord's. Hence, Protestant efforts in the sixteenth century to eliminate Christian images and altars from the churches can be said to prepare the way for Antichrist, but he has not arrived yet.

Of course, the pope is not the Antichrist. Nor should "Babylon" in Revelation 17 be identified as the church of Rome. Although the annotators of the

---

17. Ibid., 555, 557, emphasis mine. Tyndale too had referred to "adepartinge (as some men thynke) from under the obedyence of the Emperour of Rome" (*1534 New Testament*, 433).

18. Rheims New Testament, DM 177, 696, 722.

Rheims New Testament admit that the text could refer to ancient Rome, the seat of those who persecuted the church in its early days, they are adamant that what the term really represents is the "general societie of the impious, & of those that preferre the terrene kingdom and commoditie of the world, before God & eternal felicitie." Nor do the "seven hills" of verse 9 persuade them, since John uses "seven" symbolically throughout the book to represent "universally al of that sort whereof he speaketh." In this case, therefore, "seven hills" represents "al the kingdoms of the world that persecute the Christians," one of which has not yet even appeared, the seventh and last, that is, "Antichrists state, which shal not come so long as the Empire of Rome standeth."[19]

Although certainly a far different book from Tyndale's 1534 New Testament, the Rheims New Testament agrees with its Protestant counterpart in playing down eschatological expectations. However much these Catholic translators may have been suffering from exile and the loss of their homeland to a Protestant regime, they were compelled in their annotations to read passages dealing with the Antichrist literally so as to refute Protestant efforts to discredit the papacy by portraying it as the great foe of Christ in the last days. But a literal reading of Antichrist passages meant also a diminished sense of an imminent judgment day. It was far otherwise in the Geneva versions of the Bible, to which we now turn our attention.

Geneva Bible

Originally produced by Protestant exiles during the reign of Queen Mary and so designated "Geneva" after their place of refuge, the Geneva Bible in its various editions became the most popular of all the Protestant Bibles printed during the reign of Mary's successor, Elizabeth. These versions were heavily annotated and so they conveyed large doses of Protestant theology to their readers along with the biblical text.[20] The first complete Geneva Bible was printed in 1560, and its annotations provide a clear indication that as far as the Antichrist was concerned, they were definitely living in the last times because the pope was the Antichrist.

This is especially evident in the Genevan annotations on the book of Revelation; but it is not so evident in those attached to 2 Thessalonians. The latter do make the point that "that man of sinne" of verse 3 is not a single person. They write, "This wicked Antichrist comprehendeth the whole succession of the persecuters of the Church"; but there is no identification of this "succession" with the papacy, and there is no note at all on verse 4 regarding Antichrist's exalting himself and sitting in the temple of God.[21]

---

19. Ibid., 718, 721, 719, 722–24, 730, 731–33.
20. MacKenzie, "Battle for the Bible," 20–54.
21. Geneva Bible 1560, DM 107, New Testament, fol. 96 (verso).

The reticence of the notes on 2 Thessalonians is more than made up for by those on Revelation since over and over they maintain that the pope is the Antichrist. The "Argument" or preface to the book indicates that "Antichrist" is one of the great themes of the Apocalypse, "The livelie description of Antichrist is set forthe"; and regarding the "Angel of the bottomles pit" (9:11), a note remarks, "Which is Antichrist the Pope, king of hypocrites & Satans ambassadour." Likewise, the "great whore" of Babylon (ch. 17) is identified as "the Antichrist, that is, the Pope."[22]

In many contexts, the terms "pope" and "Antichrist" are used synonymously. For example, an annotation on 13:16 says, "this *Antichrist* wil accept none but such as wil approve *his doctrine*: so that it is not ynough to confesse Christ, & to believe the Scriptures, but a man must subscribe to the *Popes doctrine.*" Similarly, one note on 11:13 refers the reader to "the power of *Antichrist*" but the next note on the same verse talks about those who "fall from the *Pope.*" Notes on Revelation 10:8; 13:18; 16:13; 16:19; and 19:4 exhibit the same sort of easy identification between the two.[23]

Unlike the Rheims New Testament, the Geneva Bible readily identifies Babylon in the text with Rome, and not just the Rome of the Caesars (as even Rheims might acknowledge) but the Rome of the pope, as for example in a note on Revelation 14:8: "Babylon the great citie," the editors write, "signifying Rome, for asmuche as the vices which were in Babylon, are founde in Rome in greater abundance . . . as Babylon the first Monarchie was destroyed, so shal this wicked kingdome of Antichrist have a miserable ruine."[24]

Routinely, references to the pope, Rome, and the "Romish" church dot the margins of the Geneva text in chapters 8 through 19. Sometimes they draw correlations between the symbolic details in the text and the Roman papacy, as for example, in the note that explains the angel with the "keye of the bottomles pit" (Rev. 9:1), "This autoritie cheifly is committed to the Pope in signe whereto he beareth the keyes in his [coat of] armes." Even 666 (Rev. 13:18) receives a papal interpretation: "this nomber is gathered of the smale nomber, λατεινος, which in the whole make 666: & signifieth Lateinus, or Latin, which noteth the Pope or Antichrist who useth in all things the Latin tongue."[25]

Frequently, the notes exhibit a certain historical understanding to make sense of the text. For example, the editors interpret chapter 17 as the record of papal Rome succeeding ancient Rome in its hostility to the church. When the

22. Ibid., 114 (verso), 117 (verso), 120 (recto).

23. Ibid., 119 (recto), 118 (recto), 119 (recto), 120 (recto), 121 (recto).

24. Ibid., 119 (recto). Also 119 (verso). See also Rheims New Testament, DM 177, 730–31.

25. Geneva Bible 1560, DM 107, New Testament, 117 (recto), 119 (recto). Actually, this interpretation of 666 can be found in Irenaeus *Against Heresies* 5.30, although he does not regard it as conclusive.

text describes the "whore of Babylon" sitting upon a "skarlat coloured beast" (Rev. 17:3), the notes explain, "The beast signifieth the ancient Rome: the woman that sitteth thereon, the newe Rome which is the Papistrie, whose crueltie and blood sheding is declared by skarlat." Later, the "seven mountaines" and "seven kings" (17:9) are explained in terms of ancient Rome and seven emperors from Nero to Nerva. Likewise, regarding the two beasts of chapter 13, the first that rises from the sea (v. 1) represents "the Romaine empire" and the second "out of the earth" (v. 11) the "Popes kingdome." According to the notes, this chapter also teaches that the "first empire Romaine was as the paterne, & this seconde empire is but an image & shadowe thereof."[26]

But in what specifically does papal Rome resemble ancient Rome? The notes tell us, "The Pope in ambition, crueltie, idolatrie, and blaspheme did folow & imitate the ancient Romaines." The last two items refer, of course, to the teaching and practices of the Roman Church, described by another note as "devilish doctrine . . . mans traditions . . . things contrairie to God and his worde." Besides false doctrine, however, the notes strongly indict the papacy for its cruelty to the elect, "Antichrist sonne of perdicion destroieth mens soules with false doctrine, & the whole worlde *with fyre & sworde* [emphasis mine]."[27]

On account of their situation as exiles from a monarch called "bloody" for her treatment of Protestants in the name of Rome, it is understandable that the Geneva annotators might emphasize religious persecution as a principal characteristic of the Antichrist, and they do.[28]

The pope overcomes the two witnesses of chapter 11 by "cruel warre"; chapter 12 is described as a vision of how the "Church . . . is persecuted of Antichrist" and in verse 6 the devil is depicted as "red with the blood of the faithful"; and in chapter 14, Rome is said to surpass ancient Babylon in "persecution of the Church of God, oppression & sclaverie with destruction of the people of God," as well as "confusion, superstition, idolatrie, and impietie."[29]

As one reads the Geneva notes, it is difficult to avoid the conclusion that the translators believed themselves to be in the last days, since virtually all the signs of the end in connection with Antichrist were being fulfilled in their very own times. Satan had already been bound for a thousand years (Rev. 20:1)— explained as the period of pure doctrine "after a sorte" between the birth of Christ and the reign of Pope Sylvester II (999–1003)[30] but now he was loose

26. Ibid., 120 (recto), 118 (verso)–119 (recto).

27. Ibid., 119 (recto), 117 (verso).

28. For the Genevan exiles, their story and their theology, see Dan G. Danner, *Pilgrimage to Puritanism* (New York: Peter Lang, 1999).

29. Geneva Bible 1560, DM 107, New Testament, 118 (recto), 118 (verso), 119 (recto).

30. According to Bauckham (*Tudor Apocalypse*, 218, 49, 230), this dating reflects the interpretation of John Bale. Otherwise the Genevan notes on Revelation demonstrate dependence on Heinrich Bullinger.

for a little while, during which the "true preaching of Gods worde is corrupt" and Gog and Magog were appearing, explained as "divers and strange enemies of the Church of God as the Turke, the Sarazins, and others . . . by whome the Church of God shulde be grievously tormented." Since "the Pope and the worldlie princes shal fight against Christ, even until this last day," the church can only look forward to that moment of the "seconde coming of Christ." Indeed, the second last note of the entire book, while counseling against using "our owne imagination" in contemplating how long until our Lord returns, nevertheless reminds the faithful that "*seing the Lord is at hand*, we oght to be constant and rejoice [emphasis mine]."[31]

Comparisons between Translations

Given the strong sense of imminent eschatology in these Geneva notes, it is interesting to compare them with both Tyndale and Rheims. In spite of the fact that the Geneva and Tyndale versions originated on the same side of the sixteenth-century religious divide, their differences in tone—if not in content—regarding eschatology in notes on 2 Thessalonians and Revelation are striking. Of course, this may be due in part to the fact that Tyndale's annotations are far fewer. However, it is also clear that the Geneva translators had a greater appreciation for the relevance of such texts to their own situation than did Tyndale. Tyndale's notes could characterize any era in the history of the church, but Geneva's notes especially in their identification and description of the pope as Antichrist, persecutor of the church as well as false teacher, demand a conclusion that the last days have come.

According to Richard Bauckham, apocalyptic fervor was strong in Elizabethan England (and elsewhere as well, for that matter);[32] and certainly, there were many reasons for this, not the least of them the continuing hostility between Catholics and Protestants that sometimes resulted in conspiracies and attempted overthrows of the queen.[33]

Nevertheless, when people tried to make sense of their circumstances by referring to the Geneva Bible, the notes on Revelation directed them to understand the antagonism of Rome as the enmity of Antichrist, and the presence of Antichrist as a sign of the last times. Thus, situation and text would combine to heighten apocalyptic expectations.

On the other hand, for some English readers, after 1582 the Rheims New Testament offered an alternative vision. In spite of the fact that English Catholics were in a much more precarious position politically and legally than English Protestants during the reign of Elizabeth, their Bible did not encourage

31. Ibid., 121 (recto–verso), 122 (recto).
32. Bauckham, *Tudor Apocalypse*, 11.
33. See, for example, Penry Williams, *The Later Tudors: England, 1547–1603* (Oxford: Oxford University Press, 1998), 255–61, 299–324.

end time expectations nearly so much as Geneva, since a strictly literal reading of the biblical texts led them to look for Antichrist in a single individual who would suppress all outward forms of religion except his own and who would set up his temple in Jerusalem.

Of course, more people read Geneva than Rheims since there was only one reprint of the Rheims New Testament before 1611 and more than 120 of the Geneva version.[34]

However, the purpose of this essay is not to argue that one version had more influence than any other, but simply to show how religious communities already divided from each other by fundamental issues of soteriology and authority also differed in their understanding of eschatology as it pertained to the figure of Antichrist. In spite of certain outward similarities between the two communities of religious exiles that produced the Geneva and Rheims versions, they understood their circumstances much differently, at least as this is evident in their annotations on 2 Thessalonians and Revelation. For the one, it was a matter of living in the end times and surviving the oppression of Antichrist; for the other it meant remaining faithful to the old and true church under the vicar of Christ. For them, the end times were still a long way off.

---

34. Lloyd E. Barry, introduction to *The Geneva Bible: A Facsimile of the 1560 Edition* (Madison: University of Wisconsin Press, 1969), 14. The Rheims second edition came out in 1600. See Darlow and Moule, *Historical Catalogue*, 118.

10

From Ecclesiology to Eschatology: The Changing Puritan Understanding of the Reign of Christ

HARRY L. POE

Union University

During the period from 1558 to 1642, the group within the Church of England known as the Puritans placed great emphasis on Christ the King and his reign. Their understanding of the reign of Christ changed in its emphasis, however, during the different phases or periods of Puritanism. During the reign of Elizabeth I the emphasis lay on the reign of Christ in his church and the need for all ceremonies and church government to be "according to" rather than "not contrary to" the rule Christ laid down in Scripture. During the second phase, largely during the reign of James I, the Puritans backed away from their demands for presbyterian government and the abandonment of ceremonies that seemed to perpetuate the symbolism of Roman theology as they placed emphasis on the reign of Christ in the heart. The hallmarks of this phase are represented by preaching and casuistry as introduced by William Perkins. In the final phase, the reign of Christ took on apocalyptic dimensions under the reign of Charles I and his archbishop of Canterbury, William Laud. While the earlier dimensions of the reign of Christ continued to be expressed by different "parties" among the Puritans, the expectation of the return of Christ in the near future lead to a radicalism that saw full flower in the Civil War.

The Reign of Christ in the Church

The empasis on the reign of Christ in the church grew out of the Puritan understanding of Scripture.[1] The Puritans disagreed with the authorities in one fundamental matter. While the authorities took the general Lutheran position that things might be allowed in the church that Scripture does not specifically prohibit, the Puritans took the Calvinistic position that only those things commanded by Scripture may be allowed in the church. For those who saw the gospel as the proclamation of the kingdom, letting Christ be king in the church as well as priest meant adherence to all the commands of God. This stream of thought tended to level all Scripture as of equal import. As well as differing on the authority of Scripture, the Puritans lacked an accepted hermeneutic for interpreting Scripture even among themselves. The disintegration of Puritanism came when the Puritans could not agree among themselves what government and ceremonies God had commanded in his word. The failure of an agreed principle for interpreting the Scripture continued to give rise to controversies that diverted the Puritans from their concern for conversion.

Attitude toward Scripture

The sixth article of the Thirty-nine Articles expressed the official position of the Church of England on the authority of Scripture:

> Holy Scripture conteyneth all things necessarie to saluation; so that whatsoever is not read therein, nor may be proved thereby, is not to be required of any man, that it should be believed as an article of faith, or be thought requisite as necessary to saluation.[2]

The Puritans willingly agreed to at least this much, but they believed more needed to be said. In devoting themselves to the pragmatic problem of evangelizing England, they realized that the practice of religion influenced the spread and content of the gospel as much as official doctrine.

The Puritans viewed the Scriptures as a divine blueprint and rule for all time. Walter Travers, an advocate of presbyterian government associated

---

1. Cf. John S. Coolidge, *The Pauline Renaissance in England: Puritanism and the Bible* (Oxford: Clarendon, 1970). Coolidge argues that the Puritans interpreted Scripture through the eyes of Paul. Stanley P. Fienberg ("Thomas Goodwin's Scriptural Hermeneutics and the Dissolution of Puritan Unity," *The Journal of Religious History* 10 (1978): 32–49) argues that presbyterian Puritans interpreted Scripture through the Old Testament with an emphasis on reason while independents interpreted Scripture through Christ. John R. Knott Jr. (*The Sword of the Spirit: Puritan Responses to the Bible* [Chicago: University of Chicago Press, 1971], 4) stresses the Puritan belief in "the dynamism of the Holy Spirit acting through the Word."

2. Horton Davies, *The Worship of the English Puritans* (Glasgow: Glasgow University Press, 1948), 3.

with Thomas Cartwright, presented the reasoning that characterized the Puritan attitude toward the Scriptures in *A Full and Plain Declaration of Ecclesiastical Discipline* (1574). Travers's arguments rest heavily on the Old Testament and the example of Moses and the law of Israel.[3] The structure of Jewish worship in the law of Moses was rigidly and absolutely laid down. Nothing could be added or taken away. God, the King of Israel, gave the law fully and completely, and Moses, the faithful prophet, delivered the commandments to Israel whereby she was disciplined. Even kings David and Solomon, when they altered the fashion of singers, the offices of Levites and when they built the temple, did nothing by their own authority, but "by the will of God Himself, who appointed it so by His prophet, as appeareth in the Second chronicles."[4]

Travers then turned to Christ who embodied the offices of king and prophet in his establishment of the church. He reasoned that Christ must have done at least as much as Moses in giving a rule of government for the church.[5] Travers considered it unreasonable to think that God would take less care with the church than he took with Israel. Furthermore, if Christ is a prophet like Moses, then he must have done at least as much as Moses or prove to be an inferior prophet. Unwilling to let Christ be inferior in any way to Moses, Travers argued that Christ "fully and perfectly declared unto us whatsoever was needful for the government of the Church."[6] To reason otherwise would put the servant before the Son as having omitted nothing, while the son "hath omitted all, and that Moses left all things perfect but Christ either began them not or did not finish what he began."[7] Based on the premises that Travers allowed, he could only conclude that Christ left a perfect rule and discipline "which is common and general to all the Church and perpetual for all times."[8]

The Puritan understanding and interpretation of Scripture had a direct bearing on their attitude toward church government, discipline, worship, and every other issue over which they came into conflict with the authorities of the Church of England. In *An Adomonition to the Parliament*, attributed to Thomas Wilcox, which was published together with *A View of Popishe Abuses yet remaining in the Englishe Church*, attributed to John Field, the Puritan complaints are clearly outlined. Throughout the pamphlet the criticism leveled at the Church of England is its failure to conform to the biblical model of a church. The Puritans insisted that reformation had a positive as well as a negative dimension. Avoiding what is forbidden by Scripture was

3. Everett H. Emerson, ed., *English Puritanism from John Hooper to John Milton* (Durham, N.C.: Duke University Press, 1968), 27.

4. Ibid., 90.

5. Ibid., 91.

6. Ibid.

7. Ibid., 92.

8. Ibid.

not sufficient for them. True religion consisted in also doing only what Scripture commanded. Herein lies the fundamental cleavage between the Puritans and the Elizabethan Settlement with respect to the authority of Scripture:[9]

> They hould and mainetaine that the word of God contained in the writings of the Prophets and Apostles, is of absolute perfection, given by Christ the head of the Churche, to bee unto the same, the sole Canon and rule of all matters of Religion, and the worship and service of God whatsoever. And that whatsoever done in the same service and worship cannot bee instified by the same word, is unlawful.[10]

The General Intent of Scripture. Puritans also stressed the general intent of Scripture. Cartwright stressed the general intent of Scripture in the Admonition controversy with Whitgift following Whitgift's *Answer to the Admonition.*[11] In Cartwright's *Reply to an Answer* he said that "many things are both commanded and forbidden, for which there is no express mention in the word, which are as necessarily to be followed or avoided as those whereof express mention is made."[12] The difference consists in the double negative formula of authority (not contrary to) that the established church followed and the positive formula (according to) that the Puritans advocated.

Negative or Positive Authority? John Coolidge considers this subtle difference in formulation to be the crucial issue in the attitude of the Puritans toward the Scripture. Though there may be no difference in the logical equivalence of the expressions, there is a world of difference "in the way in which the mind is conscious of being affected in its operations by the Bible."[13] The matter at issue is the conception of obedience to God that each formulation suggests. The Puritans could not accept ceremonies or anything else introduced into the church that did not come as a positive response of obedience to God through the guidance of the Scriptures. For the Puritan, the avoidance of wrongdoing was not the same as seeking to do the will of God, and in Cartwright's estimation, the formulation of scriptural authority that Archbishop Whitgift defended implied an indifference to Scripture.[14] The Puritans were not content in not violating the Word of God; they were zealous to follow the

9. Ibid., 45.

10. William Bradshaw, *English Puritanism and Other Works*, ed. R. C. Simmons (Westmead, England: Gregg International, 1972), 1.

11. Cf. William Ames, "The Dispute about Humane Ceremonies," in *A Fresh Suit against Human Ceremonies*, ed. R. C. Simmons (Westmead, England: Gregg International, 1871), 18.

12. John Whitgift, *The Works of John Whitgift, D.D.*, ed. John Ayre (Cambridge: The Parker Society, 1860), 1:176. Whitgift included a full transcript of Cartwright's *Reply* in his own *Defense of the Answer.*

13. Coolidge, *Pauline Renaissance*, 11.

14. Thomas Cartwright, *The Second Replie* (1575), cited by Coolidge, *Pauline Renaissance*, 10.

counsel and direction of the Word of God and do so with the expectation that God had given direction for those who seek direction. Yet even their interpretation of the Scriptures depended upon the degree to which the Puritans stressed the rule of Christ in the church. The more a Puritan stressed the kingdom as the rule of Christ in the church, the less willing he was to conform in the matter of indifferent things.

Discipline as Government. Cartwright protested against the distinction Whitgift drew between matters of faith necessary to salvation and those things of indifference introduced into the church:

> But you say that in matters of faith and necessary to salvation it holdeth: which things you oppose after and set against matters of ceremonies, orders, discipline, and government; as though matters of discipline and kind of government were not necessary to salvation and of faith.[15]

He continued by arguing that church government; excommunication, censures, and other matters of discipline; and the sacraments and other ceremonies are all matters of faith and necessary to salvation. This conviction led to a stream of thought within Puritanism that considered church government, or submission to the kingly rule of Christ, as a fundamental element of the gospel.[16] The stress on the kingdom as the essence of the gospel reappeared with devastating consequences in the 1630s. This stress was a prime motivation for separation and tended to divert men from the work of preaching for conversion to the work of erecting the true church.

The Rule of Christ in the Heart

As presbyterianism came to an end in the late 1580s as a result of persecution by the authorities, William Perkins was developing a form of discipline that concentrated on the individual believer and pastoral care by the pastor.[17] Perkins was arguably the most influential of all the Puritans in terms of theology. For decades his books far exceeded in circulation those of Calvin or any other theologian in England. His model provided the pattern for Puritan ministry from the late 1590s until the mid 1630s. Perkins's construction of a Puritan casuistry provided a framework of

---

15. Whitgift, *Works*, 1:181.

16. Emerson, *English Puritanism*, 87–88. A point Walter Travers made clear in his appeal for the institution of a presbyterian form of church government in *A Full and Plaine Declaration*: "yet could not England be brought to leave that form of governing the Church whereunto it had been accustomed under popery, but divided and separated as under the doctrine and discipline of the Gospel, two things which both by their own nature and also by commandment of God are to be joined together."

17. For discussions of Perkins's casuistry, see Elliot Rose, *Cases of Conscience* (Cambridge: Cambridge University Press, 1975), 185–213; Ian Breward, "William Perkins and the Origins of Reformed Casuistry," *The Evangelical Quarterly* 49 (1968): 3–20.

personal discipline for those who sought to live a godly life. Godly living had a profound relationship to salvation for the Puritans who believed that the assurance of salvation grew out of one's godly life. Perkins's approach to discipline reflects a concept of the gospel rooted in the hyper-Calvinistic interpretation of Reformed theology. His approach consisted of offering cases whereby one might determine if they were elect or reprobate. This stream of thought about the essence of the gospel gained popular expression in the Calvinistic context of the church and served as a framework for presenting Christ, but after the rise of Arminianism in the late 1620s it quickly became the body of the gospel rather than the frame. In this reactionary situation, the concern for conversion turned into polemical controversy.

The development of casuistry as a source of personal discipline coincided with the imprisonment of the remaining leaders of the presbyterian movement but it also coincided with Whitgift's own efforts at reform of abuses in the church. The articles passed by the Convocation of 1585 aimed at some of these abuses. Pluralities were restricted to within thirty miles of each other, and a program for improving the biblical learning and preaching skills of the clergy began that promoted study and the writing of essays under supervision. The articles further enjoined the bishops to report on the morals and the learning of the clergy, while efforts were made to make the ecclesiastical courts more effective. By allowing a more modified form of subscription whereby Puritans agreed to use the Book of Common Prayer "and none other," Whitgift opened a way for moderate Puritans to conform without swearing that the Prayer Book was according to the Word of God.[18]

Collinson says that the "temporary exhaustion of old controversies" in the 1590s "brought the essential matter of salvation to the forefront."[19] Indeed, salvation had been and would remain the essential matter, but it tended to beget controversy. The political circumstances of the 1590s and the creativity of the new generation of Puritans provided a basis for a temporary peace that saw Puritans and Whitgift joined in defending Calvinistic orthodoxy, while the concern for salvation kept the subsidiary issues of biblical interpretation, church government, and worship in the background. For the time being, under a modified conformity the Puritans tried to accomplish their purposes through preaching and casuistry, but when pressed to strict conformity the subsidiary issues affecting salvation would rise to the front, overshadow the Puritans' primary concern about salvation, and redirect their energies toward theological controversies.[20]

---

18. Patrick Collinson, *The Elizabethan Puritan Movement* (London: Jonathan Cape, 1979), 264.

19. Ibid., 434.

20. Cf. J. B. Marsden, *The History of the Early Puritans*, 3d ed. (London: Hamilton, Adams, 1860), 293. Marsden charged the Puritans with a "mischievous diversion of the common people from the great and sanctifying doctrines of personal religion, to discussions (which to the multitude must always be unprofitable) upon recondite questions of church government."

Richard Sibbes was perhaps the most prominent of Puritan preachers in the generation after Perkins. Master of Catherine Hall in Cambridge and lecturer at Gray's Inn in London, he took a leading role in the project to buy back the lands originally attached to parish churches that had been intended to provide clergy with an income. Over the centuries since the Norman conquest, many of these lands had fallen into the hands of monasteries, and after the dissolution of the monasteries, into private hands. The Feoffees for the Purchase of Impropriations intended to place preachers in churches and provide them with a living wage. Sibbes and the Feoffees were prosecuted by the attorney general for usurping the royal prerogative in this matter. Nonetheless, Sibbes continued to conform to the Church of England.

The unity of the church had a strong relationship to salvation in Sibbes's thought because he believed that conversion took place in the context of the church and that

> Christ conveyes spirituall life and vigour to Christians, not as they are disjoyned from, but as they are united to the mysticall body, the Church.[21]

He warned that separation from the church would not bring the peace of mind to consciences offended by ceremonies that many Puritans sought. On the contrary, he warned that faction and separation would produce a "grand enormity" and a heinous sin.[22] As an eschatological category in the Calvinist system of the Puritans, salvation came at the end to the elect who, of course, would have persevered, but to leave the church would endanger the possibility of one's sanctification. Sibbes wrote that "it is no better than soulemurder for man to cast himself out of the Church, either for reall or imaginall corruptions."[23] Sibbes did not deny the presence of corruptions, but he lamented the growing preoccupation that Puritans had for ceremonies. He wrote in the preface to *The Soul's Conflict* in 1635, "What unthankfulness is it to forget our consolation, and to look only upon matter of grievance! to think so much upon two or three crosses as to forget a hundred blessings!"[24]

Sibbes insisted that the problems of the Church of England could not be solved by conflict and controversy, for

> Corruption will hardly yield to corruption in another. Pride is intolerable to pride. The weapons of this warfare must not be carnal, 2 Cor. x. 4.[25]

21. Richard Sibbes, *The Complete Works of Richard Sibbes, D.D.*, ed. Alexander Balloch Grosart (Edinburgh: James Nichol, 1862), 1:cxv.

22. Ibid.

23. Ibid., cxvi. Sibbes does not deal with the seeming representation that one of the elect could choose to be damned. He keeps his discussion at the level of peace and assurance.

24. Sibbes, *Works*, 1:123.

25. Ibid., 57.

While neither party could acknowledge their own faults, Sibbes saw the conflict as essentially spiritual in nature. He feared any attempt to resolve the struggle politically. Instead, he encouraged the Puritans to forget their discouragement and consider all the promises of God to the church of the last days, turning these into prayers for fulfillment. If the Puritans were right, then Sibbes demanded to know,

> why do we make God in his rich promises a liar? Strive against thyself, the greatest enemy. Why do we fear the conquered world, that have the conqueror himself on our side?[26]

Sibbes challenged the Puritans to believe in the sovereignty of God and accept the condition of the church, praying that the Lord would change it by his return.[27] Sibbes placed his hope for the final reformation of the church in the second coming of the Lord and could imagine no condition on earth in which the church would be anything but imperfect.[28] This understanding of the church only intensified Sibbes's exhortation to be saved immediately and begin enjoying the presence of God until Christ comes. Rather than speculate on the proper form of government in the visible church, Sibbes stressed the importance of submitting to Christ's government over one's heart:

> Because if judgment should prevail in all other about us and not in our own hearts, it would not yield comfort to us; hereupon it is the first thing that we desire when we pray, "Thy kingdom come," that Christ would come and rule in our hearts. The kingdom of Christ in his ordinances serves but to bring Christ home into his own place, our hearts.[29]

Just as salvation for a soul involved a process of sanctification, the consummation of the church awaited the end when Christ would rule no longer "in the midst of enemies," but only "in the midst of his friends."[30] Until then, Sibbes would stress the conversion of individual sinners and Christ's government in their hearts rather than in the outward form of the church.

Pressing for attention to the spiritual nature of the conflict within the Church of England, Sibbes pleaded for Christians to "have nothing to do with carnal shifts and politic ends."[31] Instead, they should rely on God's provi-

---

26. Ibid., 126.
27. Ibid., 5:142.
28. Ibid., 2:517.
29. Ibid., 1:78, 374.
30. Ibid., 2:516; 5:141–42.
31. Ibid., 1:416.

dence, trusting his judgment about what happened to and within the church.[32] Sibbes insisted that salvation remained the primary concern of Christians for which they should strive, but in all other things they should trust God:

> Indeed, we should indent with God, and tie him to look to the salvation of our souls; but for other things leave them to his own wisdom, both for the time, for the manner and measure, do what he will with us.[33]

Sibbes looked for God's hand in the state of the church, and though he avoided the intricate Calvinistic theological speculation in his sermons that characterized other Puritan preaching, still he exercised an abiding faith in the Sovereign God of Calvin, determining that whether "religion flourish or goes downward" that he would "rely on him still."[34]

Seeing the growth of dissension in the church, Sibbes feared what course it might take. He warned:

> For the most part, ecclesiastical dissension end in civil; and therefore we see, before the destruction of Jerusalem, what a world of schisms and divisions were amongst the Jews. . . . It is a fearful sign of some great judgment to fall upon a church, when there is not a stopping of dissension.[35]

His statement partially justifies Laud's fear of the political consequences of Puritan resistance to conformity, though his opposition tended to intensify the resistance. Placing the blame did not concern Sibbes, however. He desperately sought to avoid a further split in the church because of what he feared the end result would be. When he looked at the Church of England he asked, "What is the glory of England? Take away the gospel, and what have we that other nations have not better than ourselves?"[36]

Sibbes most feared that God in his sovereignty would take away the gospel from England as he had taken it from the Jews and from Rome.[37] He believed that dissension would bring judgment as the people turned away from their "first love," the gospel, to fight about other matters.[38] For this reason, Sibbes exhorted Puritans and Laudians alike to "esteem the treasure of the gospel at a higher rate than ever we have done."[39] He warned that "if we suffer that [the

32. Ibid.
33. Ibid., 422.
34. Ibid., 422–23.
35. Ibid., 379.
36. Ibid., 382.
37. Ibid., 375, 380.
38. Ibid., 380.
39. Ibid., 382.

gospel] to be shaken any way, our peace and prosperity will then leave us, and judgment upon judgment will come upon us,"[40] because "God cannot endure his glorious gospel should be slighted, as not deserving the richest strain of our love."[41]

The Example Set by Sibbes

With his position clearly set forth, Sibbes proceeded to draw closer to the Church of England than he had been since the beginning of his Gray's Inn ministry. In 1633, the same year as the dismantling of the Feoffees, Richard Sibbes accepted the vicarage of Trinity Church, Cambridge, that Thomas Goodwin had resigned.[42] The appointment seems all the more remarkable since the presentment lay within the patronage of King Charles and Laud administered the royal ecclesiastical preferments. Sibbes kept the terms of conformity, however, even to the extent of avoiding controversial topics in his preaching. He punctuated his sermons with such remarks as, "I will not speak by way of controversy,"[43] and "I am sorry to mention these things, in a point tending more to edification."[44]

The Rule of Christ on Earth

An increasing number of Puritans began to disagree with Sibbes in his conviction about the unity of the church during the reign of King Charles. Unlike his father, James I, who had a personal representative at the Synod of Dort, Charles embraced the Arminianism of William Laud, whom Charles appointed archbishop of Canterbury. In addition to his objectionable theology, Laud also had a preference for the ceremonies that so offended the Puritans.

Thomas Goodwin represents that type of Puritan who could no longer conform to the Church of England during the reign of Charles I. Goodwin had been a student at Cambridge and disciple of Sibbes. He would eventually come to prominence as a leader of the Independent churches, president of Magdalen College (Oxford), and chaplain to Oliver Cromwell. His shift from conformity to independency also involved a change in perspective from concern about the reign of Christ in the heart to the return of Christ to reign on earth.

The most telling allusions to the growing troubles of the kingdom came, not in reference to the church, but to the state. One might wonder if Goodwin already anticipated the struggle of the 1640s when he wrote *The Happinesse of*

---

40. Ibid., 383.
41. Ibid., 380.
42. Sibbes, *Works*, 1:cxi. Cf. Robert Halley, "Memoir of Dr. Thomas Goodwin," in *The Works of Thomas Goodwin, D.D.*, ed. John Miller (Edinburgh: James Nichol, 1861), xxiv.
43. Sibbes, *Works*, 6:499.
44. Ibid., 2:242.

the Saints in Glory in which he made such statements as "Kingdoms in this life are taken away, Kings deprived of their dignities,"[45] "the glory of Kingdoms decay daily, and Monarchies fall"[46] and "the Kingdoms of this world were brave places if they might have no end, the Kings of them exceeding happy if they might never die."[47] Still, these passages are rare and brief and could easily apply to the struggles of the Thirty Years' War on the Continent. These passages do indicate, however, that Goodwin was thinking of the fleeting nature of earthly kingdoms in comparison with Christ's kingdom as early as 1637, when the treatise was licensed.[48]

Richard Sibbes had tried to calm the Puritans' anxiety over conformity by preaching that the condition of the church would remain partially corrupt until the return of the Lord. Until then, Sibbes pleaded for attention to the preaching of the gospel and prayer for the Lord's return. As the Laudian innovations increased in the 1630s and the terms of conformity became more offensive, Goodwin must have turned increasingly to a contemplation of when the Lord would return. Increasingly, Goodwin thought of the message of the gospel as living under the kingly rule of Christ, but Laud's innovations and restrictions violated the royal commands of Christ. This concern for Christ's rule turned to millenarianism as Goodwin saw the dreams of the Puritans thwarted. Sibbes had said that final reformation must wait for Christ's return. Therefore, Goodwin turned to millenarianism for hope. Goodwin's concept of the gospel as the preaching of the kingdom paved the way for his millenarianism, which in turn produced his radicalism. In this transition, as Goodwin's millenarianism began to play a greater part in his activity, his mind turned from a concern for conversions to the establishment of the kingdom of Christ.

From Nonconformity to Independence

The watershed in Goodwin's movement away from the Church of England came in 1639 when he fled to Holland. Until then his writings avoided discussion of church government, but in that year he wrote a lengthy exposition of Revelation. In this treatise he declared his expectation that Christ would soon return and establish his kingdom on earth.

Goodwin believed that the prophecy in the eleventh chapter of Revelation contained a clue for computing when the downfall of the fourth monarch and the advent of "Christ's visible kingdom" should come.[49] Based on Daniel's vi-

---

45. Ibid., 89.
46. Ibid., 86.
47. Ibid., 82.
48. Ibid., imprimatur.
49. Goodwin, *Works*, 3:20. Cf. Fienberg, "Thomas Goodwin's Scriptural Hermeneutics," 40–49. Fienberg discusses Goodwin's millenarianism in relation to his hermeneutics and his view of church government.

sion of the Four Monarchies, Goodwin and many other Puritans believed that when the last of these fell, then Christ would institute the "Fifth Monarchy." The first three monarchies (Assyria, Persia, and Greece) had already fallen, but the fourth, Rome, survived in the form of the Roman church and the beast who ruled in the form of the pope.[50] No doubt, Revelation gave men like Goodwin the only peace they could find in their time of trial and afflicted conscience, for they saw in the prophecy a word for their time,

> so the church might have both warning, and not think it strange at the fiery trial which at last was to come upon them; as also to be comforted, for it should be the last. . . .[51]

In the vision of the vials, Goodwin found the clue that indicated to him the coming ruin of the beast. The vials represent the judgments of God seen in Europe since the Reformation began. Four vials are poured out before the end of the fourth monarchy.[52] Before the beast's time expires, he will "scatter the holy people," which will be the immediate sign of the ruin of the fourth monarchy.[53]

The two witnesses accomplish the "work of finishing the temple" and their work precipitates the pouring of the fourth vial.[54] Goodwin believed that the two witnesses

> are the churches themselves, as chap. i. 20. So that both eminent persons, and likewise churches themselves, the purest of them, are the witnesses against the false church that are here spoken of.[55]

Goodwin believed these churches were called "candlesticks," in the plural, because in the New Testament "there is not one church only" but many "particular congregations."[56]

In his treatment of the two witnesses, Goodwin first began to explore the idea of congregational church polity. He decided that properly instituted churches consist of "congregations of true public worshippers."[57] He concluded that in the New Testament, believers worshipping are the churches.[58] Goodwin also ex-

---

50. Ibid., 21–24. Goodwin quoted Joseph Mede, Thomas Brightman, Johann Heinrich Alsted, Sir Henry Finch, Melchior Adamus, and William Wood who had also sought to interpret Revelation.

51. Ibid., 20.

52. Ibid., 109.

53. Ibid., 111–12.

54. Ibid., 144.

55. Ibid., 151.

56. Ibid.

57. Ibid., 125.

58. Ibid., 126.

pressed his belief that the "radical power" in the church belonged to the brethren rather than to the elders, who were but servants of the church.[59] This treatise presents only a vague, undeveloped picture of the polity of a congregation, but it does classify the elders of the church into four categories: ruling elders, pastors, deacons and widows, and teachers. Goodwin based this understanding of the church on his interpretation of the vision of the throne, the four living creatures, and the elders in which the throne represents Christ, the creatures represent the four offices of elders, and the elders represent the congregation.[60]

Goodwin also believed that, while each country where the gospel had been preached had its own true witnesses, the prophecy of the killing of the two witnesses referred specifically to England or the island of Britain. He said that

> Only in the witnesses of Great Britain both the light and heat of religion have been kept up and increased; and among them only hath the profession of the power of godliness been continued, with difference from the crowd of common professors.[61]

The place of the mount and the temple "Between the seas" appeared as a clear reference to the true witnesses who had erected the temple in England.[62] Goodwin mused, "It is but a little resting till our brethren, (it may be ourselves,) the witnesses, are killed; and then down goes Rome, and the hierarchy with it."[63] In this final episode, Christ will come to establish his kingdom on earth and the saints shall reign with him.[64]

Impact on Evangelistic Fervency. Until 1639, Goodwin had devoted himself to preaching the gospel to enlarge the church, but with his new preoccupation with the coming Fifth Monarchy, Goodwin entered a period during which he saw the church's role as isolating itself from the world and caring for itself. The time for the proclamation of the gospel had passed. In *The Return of Prayers* Goodwin had mentioned that where God sends the gospel, there he intends to save someone. Now the same logic that compelled the English Calvinists to affirm the negative of the doctrine of predestination also compelled Goodwin to affirm the negative of his proposition. Where God takes away the gospel, as he had been doing in England through Laud, he does not intend for anyone to be saved. Goodwin believed that preaching the gospel laid the foundation for the coming kingdom and that Christ had first offered peace through the gospel for those kingdoms that would submit to him.[65] In the white horse of the vision,

59. Ibid., 5.
60. Ibid., 3–6.
61. Ibid., 177.
62. Ibid., 126.
63. Ibid., 41.
64. Ibid., 15.
65. Ibid., 33–34.

Goodwin saw the peace offered by the gospel, but following it came the red horse, symbolizing the blood of war; "and civil war it is, as those words note out, that 'men should kill one another . . .'" because of their contempt for the gospel.[66] Once the time of preaching had passed, the time of judgment came and Goodwin warned his generation to "expect judgments where the gospel has been preached; for the quarrel of the covenant must be avenged and vindicated."[67]

The "quarrel of the covenant" covers the controversies that engaged the Puritans and the establishment from the time of Elizabeth until Goodwin's writing.[68] Human inventions, particularly the innovations of Laud, brought about Goodwin's nonconformity. To the offense of inventions Goodwin added:

> Or else the quarrel hath been about God's own election of a few to be priests unto him . . . . This was the quarrel then; and these now plead the cause of all mankind in universal grace and redemption.[69]

The introduction of Arminian theology amounted to the preaching of false doctrine. How could anyone be saved with superstitious ceremonies and false preaching? The true witnesses had the task in this situation of preaching the gospel and giving people a means, by way of the casuistry introduced by Perkins, of judging their state of grace or reprobation.[70]

After the peace of the preaching of the gospel follows the devastation of war and famine as God's judgment upon those who did not respond. In the intensity of ecclesiastical and political events that began unfolding with the Scottish rebellion in 1638, Goodwin believed that the time for preaching the gospel had passed in England and Scotland.[71] Goodwin came to accept the Laudian innovations as the curse of God upon the carnal professors of the gospel by turning them back to Rome.

Goodwin's calculation of the date of the killing of the witnesses and the establishment of the Fifth Monarchy probably accounts for the resolve with which he abandoned his primary emphasis on preaching for conversion and turned toward the more exclusive task of marking "out whom God hath chosen, and who only are true priests and worshippers of him in spirit and truth."[72] The subtlety of the shift in emphasis from drawing people into the church to excluding people from the church grew out of Goodwin's belief

66. Ibid., 35.
67. Ibid., 38.
68. Ibid., 147.
69. Ibid.
70. Ibid., 130–31.
71. Ibid., 90.
72. Ibid., 147.

that the killing of the witnesses would take place between 1650 and 1656.[73] In the time immediately preceding the killing, God would be at work cutting people off from the church, as the vision of the measuring of the temple without the outward court had indicated to Goodwin. The task of the church or true witnesses during this period "is to finish what was before left incomplete, and to begin to make a further and purer edition of churches according to the pattern."[74]

Goodwin believed that war would rage prior to the killing of the witnesses. While the killing of the witnesses would not take place until the 1650s, the war would last long before that killing. Rome's advancement to the outward court corresponds to the war Goodwin foresaw.[75] The erection of stone altars in the cathedrals and parish churches by Laud heralded these events as the "abomination of desolation."[76] With such a scenario in his mind, Goodwin warned that the time had come to flee.[77] He also reasoned that Holland was the only safe refuge. Since it had been the last country to receive the gospel, Holland would be the last one to receive the judgment of war.[78] Goodwin wrote confidently of the coming catastrophe. He said,

> Fear not the cause of God in England; there is a battle to be fought: Christ in his angels growing more and more holy, and fuller of light; and Satan in his growing worse and worse, deceiving, and being deceived.[79]

Goodwin saw the coming years as a time of judgment and desolation and not a time of preaching the peace of the gospel. At the end of the three and a half years of the witnesses' death when an earthquake occurred, God would cause a "mighty commotion of the state of things and of the people's hearts," whereupon the people would rise up in insurrection and cast off the beast's power in England.[80] When the insurrection comes, the "false names and titles of church-officers which Christ appointed not" would be rooted out of "this one king-

---

73. Ibid., 197–98. The 1290 days or years of Dan. 11:11 provides the key to the time of the killing of the witnesses, while the 1260 years referred to the ruin of the beast. By dating the reign of the beast from 406, Goodwin concluded that his ruin would occur in 1666, a year which conveniently contained the number of the beast. By placing the killing of the witnesses 1290 years after the persecution of Julian, Goodwin concluded that the event would occur between 1650 and 1656. Using the 1335 years from the time of Julian till the final accomplishment of the whole prophecy that he found in Dan. 11:12, Goodwin believed Christ would establish his kingdom between 1690 and 1700.

74. Ibid., 150.
75. Ibid., 162.
76. Ibid.
77. Ibid.
78. Ibid., 38.
79. Ibid., 35.
80. Ibid., 185.

dom."[81] Goodwin condemned the bishops as the servants of Antichrist in Rome who had opposed the saints' preaching because it threatened their own power.[82] The bishops were the agents of Rome and Spain, wallowing "in the blood of the saints."[83] In his invective against the bishops who allowed the ceremonies of Rome, Goodwin declared that those who cleaved to Rome's superstitions would "be certainly damned, and go to hell."[84]

Under the increased pressure of Laudian innovations, Goodwin became more concerned about the damnation of the reprobate than the salvation of the elect, whom he thought had already been gathered into the true witness. The church, in Goodwin's understanding of the period prior to the establishment of the Fifth Monarchy, was in a defensive position, an embattled fortress, struggling to survive. Goodwin anticipated a siege mentality that was not so much interested in making new converts as in excluding those that did not meet his criteria for true believers. The time for conversions must wait for the Fifth Monarchy, when great numbers of people, particularly the Jews, would be converted.[85]

Conclusion

Goodwin's writings in the 1630s indicate that his concern about church government came as a derivative of his concern about worship and that his concern about worship originated in his concern for conversion that found expression in the preaching of the gospel. The innovations of Laud, which Goodwin considered a reintroduction of popish superstition, perverted the free grace of the gospel, and Goodwin resigned his positions rather than be a party to the proclamation of a false gospel that the ceremonies symbolized for him. The crisis of worship precipitated the crisis in government as Goodwin relived all the old Puritan complaints against bishops. The undeveloped understanding of congregational polity in the *Exposition of the Revelation* indicates that government had not occupied his interest as a primary concern, but his apocalyptic inquiry initiated Goodwin's concern for the institution of true churches. This shift in emphasis away from conversions proved to be one of the major internal factors that tore the Puritans apart. The course of action that prompted independency created an ecclesiological issue that permanently split the Puritans.

The final sad story of millenarianism among the Puritans would play itself out during Cromwell's regime, when even he was considered impure to the true believers. After Cromwell dissolved the Barebones Parliament in 1653,

81. Ibid., 188.
82. Ibid., 191.
83. Ibid., 41.
84. Ibid., 88.
85. Ibid., 29, 170, 201.

the Fifth Monarchy Men began to plot the violent overthrow of the government to make way for Christ's kingdom. Thomas Venner, the leading voice of the Fifth Monarchists, was discovered and went to the Tower until after Cromwell's death. At the Restoration of Charles II, Venner resumed his activities and attempted an overthrow of Charles. As a result of this millenarian adventure, the Clarendon Code was enacted that placed nonconformists under a severe persecution that would last until the Reform Bill of 1832.

Part 4

Theological Perspectives on Eschatology

11

Hope: The Heart of Eschatology

J. Lanier Burns

Dallas Theological Seminary

Nadine Gordimer, recipient of the 1991 Nobel Prize in Literature, has summarized the twentieth century as a time of challenged hope, because "humankind has not known how to control the marvels of its achievements":

> Now that the deeds are done, the hundred years ready to seal what will be recorded of us, our last achievement could be in the spirit of taking up, in the "ceaseless adventure of man," control of our achievements, questioning honestly and reflecting upon the truth of what has been lived through, what has been done. There is no other base on which to found the twenty-first century with any chance to make it a better one.[1]

Gordimer's list of "moral complications" includes medical discoveries, atomic potentials, industrial advances, space explorations, and democratization of media with concomitant compression of time and space into an "Age of Impatience" and the expectation of "instant gratification." Advances are shaded by the unspeakable shame and horror of the Holocaust and Hiroshima, the rise and fall of Communism, and the waning of Eurocentric colonialism, she emphasizes in order of importance. Gordimer is joined in her concerns by her fellow laureates Kenzaburo Oe and Elie Wiesel. Like Gordimer, they have addressed our century's postwar, elusive search for hope. In his *The Crazy Iris and Other Stories of the Atomic Aftermath*, Oe states: "The fundamental condition in life [after Nagasaki and Hiroshima], then, is that we are assailed by overwhelming fear, yet, at the same time,

---

1. Nadine Gordimer, *Living in Hope and History: Notes from Our Century* (New York: Farrar, Straus and Giroux, 1999), 236.

beckoned by the necessity to rebuild hope, however difficult, in defiance of that fear."[2] Wiesel similarly responded: "When I look around the world I see nothing but hopelessness. And yet I must, we all must, try to find a source for hope. We must believe in human beings, in spite of human beings."[3] These critics of the century share a fear of war, a cynicism about technology's direction, and a thoroughly humanistic "hope-against-hope." Their experiences in the "trenches of despair" taught them to distinguish between hope and optimism, a distinction too frequently ignored by people whose belief in progress has not been touched by world wars or apartheid. The cautionary tone of a Gordimer, Oe, or Wiesel makes them apropos for keynoting a paper about hope at the end of the century.[4] Thinkers like these often have tried to discuss hope in contexts of atheistic despair, thus undermining its effectiveness in spite of their stated desires for a better future.

One must note, however, that their views have been shared by some prominent American evangelicals. Philip Edgecombe Hughes described in his *Hope for a Despairing World* how "each new conquest of man extends the range of his propensity for evil."[5] Elton Trueblood, in a similar vein, wrote about "the paradoxical nature" of the century:

> We now know that it is at once more sordid and more wonderful than any of the prophets of fifty years ago supposed it could be. . . . It is the century of starvation, of concentration camps, of widespread famine, of unexampled terror. . . . One does not have to be a philosopher to realize that there can be bitterness in air-conditioned houses and that there can be gross injustice among people who go to the courtroom in fenderless cars. Even the unreflective must notice that trivialities are just as trivial when they are transmitted by the wonders of television. The more thoughtful are beginning to suspect that there may be a genuine connection between our inventive cleverness and our human difficulties, in that the same techniques by which we have overcome the perils of nature have, by their very character, increased the perils of history.[6]

2. Kenzaburo Oe, *The Crazy Iris and Other Stories of the Atomic Aftermath* (New York: Grove, 1985), 16. Gordimer, *Hope and History*, 83–102, esp. 99. Gordimer and Oe, in correspondence, agreed that the banalization of violence is the greatest threat to hope at the end of the century.

3. Ekkehard Schuster and Reinhold Boschert-Kimmig, *Hope against Hope: Johann Baptist Metz and Elie Wiesel Speak Out on the Holocaust* (Mahwah, N.J.: Paulist, 1999), 63.

4. The spirit of this introduction is expressed in Nadezhda Mandelstam's *Hope against Hope: A Memoir* (New York: Modern Library, 1999), chap. 45, "Hope," which begins, "M.'s three-year term of exile was supposed to end in the middle of May 1937, but we did not attach too much significance to this . . . full of the rosiest hopes, quite forgetting how insidious and delusive is the one whose name I bear . . . ." In those settings, hope seemed to have no certain object.

5. Philip E. Hughes, *Hope for a Despairing World: The Christian Answer to the Problem of Evil* (Grand Rapids: Baker, 1977), 10.

6. Elton Trueblood, *Signs of Hope in a Century of Despair* (New York: Harper, 1950), 13, 16–17, 19.

All of these scholars underscore our century's easily besetting reversals and despair.

Hope has had pervasive roles on the stages of our lives, from the above concerns to mundane daily worries. Newspapers characteristically headline "hope" in contexts of illnesses, poverty, international crises, and polls about quality-of-life issues. In its initial feature of the new millennium, the *Dallas Morning News* featured "Let's Begin with Hope." Beatriz Terrazas described it as "clear and shapeless as water—you can see it and feel it. But try to explain or hold it, and it slips away." Various contributors proceeded to apply hope's "infinite possibilities" to every area of life.[7] Internet searches hit hundreds of sites from a wide variety of book titles to music, toys, and games. Studs Terkel discovered that people were most concerned about the loss of meaningful relationships, the human touch, in the mechanicalness of their technological world. His interviews reiterated the promiscuous use of the machine, the loss of personal connection, the decline of traditional skills, the rise of a competitive edge rather than a cooperative center, the corporate credo as all-encompassing truth, the sound bite as instant wisdom, the acceptance of trivia as substance, and the denigration of language. A painter told him, "I feel as long as there's one person or two aware of our capacity to feel, think, and remember, we're on pretty sound ground . . . . I hope so."[8]

The Bible centralizes "hope" from Job's futile expectation of wise comfort from his friends (6:14–23), to Emmaus's disillusioned pair who "had hoped that [Messiah] was the one who was going to redeem Israel" (Luke 24:21), to the removal of despair in the fulfillments of the new Jerusalem (Rev. 21:3–4). The juxtaposition of historical crises, daily wishes, and biblical dilemmas suggests an important point of penetration for Christian ministry in human experience.[9]

This paper is about "Hope: The Heart of Eschatology." It will seek to relate theological eschatology to biblical hope and contemporary needs. Eschatology has often been trivialized by sensationalistic connections with apocalyptic issues that range from "Y2K readiness" to the identity of Antichrist. Sensationalism erodes credibility in eschatology's contribution to Christian thought by redirecting biblical emphases about the past and future to headliner events.

---

7. Beatriz Terrazas, "Let's Begin with Hope," *Dallas Morning News* (January 1, 2000), C1.

8. Studs Terkel, *My American Century* (New York: New Press, 1997), 480.

9. Gerhard Sauter ("Hope—The Spiritual Dimension of Theological Anthropology," in *Spirituality and Theology: Essays in Honor of Diogenes Allen,* ed. Eric Springsted [Louisville: Westminster John Knox, 1998], 105) observes: "It is remarkable that a word from everyday speech [hope] appears to be able to suffice, without any specific context, in speaking about something so wide-stretching and many-sided as God's dealings with humans and the world; about God's hiddenness and revelation; about his grace and judgment; God's Spirit and the human condition in all its tensions; about distress and happiness, temptation and certainty, death and life."

Thus, it tends to replace divine promises with faddish speculations. Charles Hardwick represented a number of academicians when he wrote, "At no point is contemporary theology more lacking in candour than in its pronouncements about the 'last things.'"[10] In fact, practical needs and biblical doctrine, in transtemporal perspectives, meet at hope. Brian Dailey defines eschatology insightfully in terms of comprehensive fulfillment and vindicated faith:

> Eschatology is the hope of believing people that the incompleteness of their present experience of God will be resolved, their present thirst for God fulfilled, their present need for release and salvation realized. . . . So eschatology includes, among other things, the attempt to construct a theodicy: a justification of faith in God, a hope in the final revelation of God's wise and loving activity throughout history, with a longing for final reckonings. It is the logical conclusion of the biblical doctrine of creation, in the attempt to fulfill creation's purpose.[11]

Stanley Grenz argues as well that eschatology as hope is central to the fulfillment of God's purpose in the new creation of the heavens and earth:

> It cannot be relegated to the fringes of biblical proclamation. . . . The centrality of John's vision of a future eon characterized by a new order of reconciliation and harmony indicates that what theologians call "corporate eschatology"—the consummation of human history—lies at the heart of the concern of the Bible.[12]

In short, hope is the heart of eschatology in the biblical sense of the focusing center of the subject. As Andrew Delbanco has expressed the concept, "When I say 'center,' I mean it in the gravitational sense of the word—the point around which we orbit, and toward which, if we lose velocity, we fall."[13] This paper will maintain that eschatology can maintain its important contribution to biblical thinking if it is anchored to hope in its biblical-emphasis-with-human-need connections.

We do not advance the hope and eschatology connection as a self-evident theme, as if contemporary studies have not raised significant questions at precisely this point. For example, is talk about hope necessarily eschatological? Is eschatology strictly about hope? If eschatology is "realized" in an ultimate sense, do hopes in mundane affairs reduce the subject in terms of its

---

10. Charles Hardwick, *Events of Grace: Naturalism, Existentialism and Theology* (Cambridge: Cambridge University Press, 1996), 267.

11. Brian Dailey, *The Hope of the Early Church: A Handbook of Patristic Eschatology* (Cambridge: Cambridge University Press, 1991), 1–2.

12. Stanley Grenz, *Millennial Maze: Sorting Out Evangelical Options* (Downers Grove, Ill.: InterVarsity, 1992), 27–28.

13. Andrew Delbanco, *The Real American Dream: A Meditation on Hope* (Cambridge, Mass.: Harvard University Press, 1999), 3.

exalted christological expectations? Is eschatology "this worldly" or "other worldly," continuous or discontinuous, with the present order of the world? If eschatology is "other worldly," how does it lend purpose or relevance to our present activity? If an eschatological future is in some sense related to the fulfillment of present conditions, then on what factors can we base the certainty of a better future, a central aspect of meaningful hope, as opposed to a mere dream about what a utopian world might be like? Such questions raise assumptions that form the paper. With Dailey and Grenz, and in agreement with traditional eschatologies, we assume that eschatology is about the last things as they fulfill human aspirations and history under the providential hand of the Creator. The questions will resurface in the paper as appropriate, but we are working with eschatology and hope as biblically presented and as broadly described in Christian traditions.

The paper will describe hope in terms of the biblical concept in comparison with some important twentieth-century writers on the subject. Neither as human trait nor biblical emphasis is hope controversial in itself. The connection, however, is particularly edifying at our juncture of history. At times, we can emphasize a distinctively Christian expectation of the Lord's return to the neglect of daily concerns, thus narrowing the impact of eschatology for the public that we serve. Also, hope can be trivialized as "daily wishes" without long-term comfort in perilous times. Lewis Smedes was confronted by "the foul stench of despair" in the wake of the Los Angeles riots of 1992. When tempted to retreat into a "comfortable cocoon," he was jolted into writing his insightful *Standing on the Promises* by an alarming sign on Airport Boulevard, proclaiming "KEEP HOPE ALIVE." Consequently, he began his book with the words, "Hope is so close to the core of all that makes us human that when we lose it we lose something of our very selves. . . . Let me put it as baldly as I can: there is nothing, repeat nothing, more critical for any one of us, young or old or anything in between, than the vitality of our hope."[14]

An important preliminary problem is the meaning of hope, a definition that is usually assumed to be self-evident or commonly understood. Our English term developed from Saxon and Low German roots like the substantival *hoop* and *hopa* or verbal *hopian*, later spreading into High German and Scandanavian usages. Its customary nuance has been "expectation of a desire" that is based on a personal promise, but the notion of desire sometimes faded to a mere prognostication about the immediate future.[15] Hope's expectation or desire is distinctively positive and forward-

---

14. Lewis Smedes, *Standing on the Promises* (Nashville: Thomas Nelson, 1998), ix–x. Karl Menninger referred to hope as our "life instinct," with the implication that we die when we stop hoping ("Hope," in *The Nature of Man,* ed. Simon Doniger [New York: Harper & Row, 1962], 186).

15. *Oxford English Dictionary*, compact ed., s.v. "Hope," 1:379–80.

looking, offering comfort or encouragement for a better future in relation to suffering or misfortune or the successful outcome of present effort.[16] Antonyms can clarify hope's meaning as well. For example, hope is focused on a desirable and uplifting outcome as opposed to melancholic or depressing situations. The Latin root for *depression* is *de primere*, meaning "to press down" with the burdens of life.[17] Though positive, hope is "object dependent": it is only as strong or reliable as the source of comfort or encouragement. Thus, as a working definition, hope is the positive expectation (or desire) for deliverance from negative (or unfulfilling) circumstances, ordinarily based on a trusted source.

We will trace the mood of hopelessness and the definitional "expectation of deliverance from a despairing present" through a circle of intellectually related European thinkers with a characteristic vocabulary. Their exposure to the cataclysmic wars and the erosion of optimism prompted them to analyze hope with extraordinary depth and vividness. The primary thinkers are Bloch, Marcel, and Moltmann, with secondary remarks about Pannenberg and Nabert. Their writings revolve around concepts that lend themselves to dialectical counterpoints: meaning, being, memory, alientation, community, apocalypse, eschaton, trauma, trivia, the relationship of present and future, and a tension between a human and/or divine basis for hope. We self-consciously move in this discussion from an atheistic approach to positions that approximate biblical hope.

In the wake of the Enlightenment, notably the thought of Hegel and Feuerbach, Ernst Bloch (1885–1977) wrote as a Marxist who was interested in aspects of religious hope. His utopian commitments led him to apocalyptic Christianity in the tradition of radical reformers like Thomas Muntzer and the possibility of an ideal society.[18] A devout Stalinist who taught at Leipzig, Bloch wrote his three-volume *Das Prinzip Hoffnung* between 1954 and 1959.[19] Bloch belonged

16. The nuance of desire can be negative. We can say, "We hope that our enemies will be punished or killed." But our intent is an imprecatory desire that is properly vengeance rather than hope.

17. Gabriel Marcel used *désespérance* for "despair" or "hopelessness." The French term is a contraction of the preposition *de*, the definite article *les*, and the noun *espérance*. Hence, it literally means "out of + the + hope." Despair had its practical expression in suicide. "Desperado" is another case in point. It stems from the Old Spanish *desperar* from the Latin *desperare* (*de* = without + *sper* = hope), thus a fugitive from desirable circumstances. Cf. Joseph Shipley, *Dictionary of Word Origins* (New York: Philosophical Library, 1945), 114.

18. Ernst Bloch, *Geist der Utopie Urste Fassung*, GA 16 (Frankfurt Am Main: Suhrkamp, 1977). "Munzer is for Bloch the prototypical religious man, who, having repudiated the security of Luther's understanding of faith, prefigures Kierkegaard through the reinstatement of a real 'spiritual yearning' (*geistlicher Sehnsucht*)." (Richard Roberts, *Hope and Its Hieroglyph: A Critical Decipherment of Ernst Bloch's "Principle of Hope"* [Atlanta: Scholars, 1990], 14.

19. *Das Prinzip Hoffnung* was published in East Berlin and is accessible in the collected edition of Suhrkamp Verlag (1977). The work has been translated into English by Neville Place, Stephen Plaice, and Paul Knight (Oxford: Basil Blackwell, 1986).

to a circle of thinkers who rejected the personalness, transcendence, and infinity of God in behalf of the infinity and freedom of humanity. His atheistic "philosophy of hope" rejected the "God-hypostasis" of the Judeo-Christian tradition. Its messianic axis, he thought, was progressively humanized until it was dissolved (*aufgehoben*) in the consubstantiality of the Christ with God. Christ's ideal from manger to cross did not survive in Christian traditions. Instead, it became localized in the community of the apocalyptic Christ. The utopian kingdom, on the other hand, abides as the valid hope of humankind's "venturing beyond" oppressive social structures.

Wolfhart Pannenberg (b. 1928) noted that "Bloch has taught us about the overwhelming power of the still-open future and of the hope that reaches out to it in anticipation for not only the life and thought of man but also the ontological uniqueness of everything in reality."[20] In other words, an ideal future must exist for the present to have any meaning. As one would expect from a Marxist, Bloch thought that the transcendent ideal of humanity lies in its potential to achieve a classless society. Humankind will somehow achieve the hope of the "not-yet" out of the being of the present by revolutionary means.[21] Bloch's thesis blended apocalypticism and messianic Marxism.

Pannenberg perceptively asked, in his critique of Bloch, how the present aspirations of men and women with their imperfections can be projected into an ideal future. How can Bloch's "potencies and latent aspects" of material processes effect or result in a novel future that transcends the human condition, past and present? Are not people content with a self-satisfied present? Does the utopian impulse of his transcendent humanity not disenchant hopeful people with the certainty of death and the uncertainty of merely possible processes?[22] Is Bloch's view simply implausible without an an irruption of God's kingdom "from without" to bring in a solution for overweening aspirations? Pannenberg realized that Bloch was aware of this yawning gap between his rejection of God and his future kingdom.[23]

For his part, Pannenberg affirms that "the hope of Christians for themselves has a place only in connection with hope for others in light of the inbreaking of the eschatological future of God. . . . The future of God's kingdom for whose coming Christians pray in the words of Jesus (Matt. 6:10) is

---

20. Wolfhart Pannenberg, *Basic Questions in Theology* (Philadelphia: Westminster, 1971), 2.238.

21. In addition to the *Principle of Hope*, Bloch discussed the ideal of social process in *Man on His Own* (New York: Herder, 1970).

22. Wolfhart Pannenberg, *Systematic Theology* (Grand Rapids, Edinburgh: Eerdmans and T & T Clark, 1998), 3:175.

23. Pannenberg, *Basic Questions*, 2:239–41.

the epitome of Christian hope."[24] He frequently reaffirms the biblical triad of faith, hope, and love in affirming God's promised kingdom as a resurrectional triumph over death.

Two themes are noteworthy in Pannenberg's position. First, he inextricably connects faith in God's promises with hope, the two being joined in the concept of trust. The object of faith-hope must be God, involving a reliance on a person and a reference to the future. Hope is "an essential part of being human, a primal trust that is at work in human behavior from birth."[25] However, the fulfillment of hope requires a "self-transcendence" that is directed to God and grounded in him. This basis is the uniqueness of Christian hope as distinct from mere human aspiration and expectation.

Second, he answers Feuerbach's charge that Christian eschatological hope is merely a self-seeking projection of this life into the future. Pannenberg's answer is that Christian hope is corporate rather than individual and involves the salvation of all people as well as the totality of earthly existence. How the human Jesus can be the ultimate revelation of God remains incomprehensible apart from eschatological expectation.[26] Furthermore, an understanding of the significance of history in its wholeness requires a comprehensive future. He summarized his position as follows:

> Faith thus gives rise to a hope that is concerned not merely about one's well-being but is bound up with the cause of God in the world that has the salvation of all humanity as its goal and embraces the believer's I only in this broad context. . . . Eschatological hope casts its light already on the present life and protects it against despair but also against an illusory overvaluing or even absolutizing of finite goals of hope. This applies both to hopes of individual fulfillment of life in this world and to hopes of bettering the social order and its institutions.[27]

In a word, there is a christological over-spilling of history into God's comprehensive fulfillment of his creation.

The universalism of Pannenberg is possible because of his ambivalence about historical facts. He affirms scientific investigation of history, yet rejects a literal understanding of resurrection because we have no analogy for it in our common historical experience. Facts require analogical proofs. An evangelical is left with objections to Pannenberg's otherwise helpful insights if the uniqueness of Christ and an exclusive Christian faith are imprecise uncertainties.

24. Pannenberg, *Systematic Theology*, 3:211, 527, cf. 608–9.
25. Ibid., 3:173–74.
26. Wolfhart Pannenberg, *Jesus: God and Man*, 2d ed. (Philadelphia: Westminster, 1977), 82–83.
27. Pannenberg, *Systematic Theology*, 3:179, 181.

Gabriel Marcel (1889–1973), Bloch's contemporary, developed an open-ended "metaphysic of hope" that contrasted with the latter's atheistic utopianism. His position has been called an "ontological personalism," his response to what he perceived were the horrors of war and technology.[28] In his autobiographical statement, he described the earlier part of the century as times of

> exhausting sacrifices—exhausting far beyond the powers of recuperation—the war had cost my country and more generally what we then called the civilized world. . . . I see myself walking up the Champs Elysees on a magnificent day and scanning with a sort of despair the carefree faces of all those passers-by who seemed to show not the slightest awareness of an approaching catastrophe. Yes, I am certain that on that day I had a distinct foreboding of imminent disaster. . . . Something irrational in us, which should not be confused with Hope, tended to persuade us that the worst was not a certainty.[29]

His walk on that day was like his philosophical position. "Viator," a traveler on the way of life, permeates his pilgrimage and writings: "He is best described as a *Philosophe Viator*—a Philosopher-on-the-Way seeking truth, beauty, goodness, and being."[30]

Hope, he emphasized, is a "mystery" as distinct from a "problem," thus ultimately ineffable. It is inextricably linked to the mystery of love, the subordination of self to others as "the essential ontological datum."[31] In love, hope is "a concept in my work dominating all others."[32] He came closest to a definition in *Homo Viator*: "Hope is . . . essentially the availability of a soul which has entered intimately enough into the experience of communion to accomplish in the teeth of will and knowledge the transcendent act—the act establishing the vital regeneration of which experience affords both the pledge and the first-fruit."[33] In short, hope is a matter of life rather than intellectual analysis, an entry into and response to meaningful relationships. As a person lives in hope, he or she lives in being and Infinite Being. Hope is the purposeful experience that gives *homo viator* the resolve to continue beyond despair. Its substance is purpose in life that is nurtured by abiding commitments to God and other people.

28. John Macquarrie, *Twentieth-Century Religious Thought: The Frontiers of Philosophy and Theology, 1900–1980*, rev. ed. (New York: Scribner, 1981), 359–61.

29. Gabriel Marcel, "An Autobiobraphical Essay," in *The Philosophy of Gabriel Marcel*, ed. P. A. Schilpp and L. E. Hahn (LaSalle, Ill.: Open Court, 1984), 3, 37–38, also 20–21.

30. Albert Randall, *The Mystery of Hope in the Philosophy of Gabriel Marcel 1888–1973: Hope and "Homo Viator"* (Lewiston, N.Y.: Edwin Mellen, 1992), 39.

31. Gabriel Marcel, *Being and Having* (New York: Harper, 1965), 167.

32. Gabriel Marcel, *Philosophical Fragments* (South Bend, Ind.: University of Notre Dame Press, 1965), 19.

33. Gabriel Marcel, *Homo Viator* (New York: Harper, 1965), 10.

Problems form the background of hope from its starting point in the hope-lessness of suicide. They are limited in scope and can be objectively analyzed and solved by empirical means. By research in the public domain, the questioner is able to separate self from the data and to manipulate it into manageable form. This "spirit of abstraction" strives for scientific objectivity. In the same vein as objective analysis, Marcel also critiqued producers and consumers as the idols of success, a world of "having" where profit replaces people in industrial systems that grind on for their own sake. In a world of technical problems, human dignity is vested in the function that we perform rather than the inherent worth of our relationships under God. As bonded agents in a nomadic world of endless options, technocrats mortgage themselves to the highest bidder at the cost of familial cohesiveness and community. "Having" is the primary barrier to hope, and its domain of inductions and statistics leads to the brokenness of the world:

> Don't you feel sometimes that we are living . . . in a broken world? Yes, broken like a broken watch. The mainspring has stopped working. Just look at it, nothing has changed. Everything is in place. But put the watch to your ear, and you don't hear any ticking.[34]

The most devastating sign of brokenness is the loss of a feeling of "togetherness" or "fellow feeling." This can be experienced as the absence of common human courtesy whereby one person affirms the value of another. Consequently, the world has become lonely, devoid of meaning, and hopeless for masses of people.

Despair, on the other hand, is the condition of hope rather than its end; hope is "the act by which the temptation [to despair] is actively and victoriously overcome."[35] Similarly, pessimistic thinkers like European existentialists are valuable because they remind us of the need for hope and authenticity in life in opposition to superficial optimisms where the thrill of possessions wears thin.[36]

The arenas of hope are relationships that are concrete and open to change in the journey of life. Kindred mysteries are love, faith, and freedom as characteristics of "being." These qualities concern meaningful presences rather than manipulated objects. Mystery can be known only by a personal involvement, as a lover with a beloved, in which subject and object are inseparably committed in fidelity to one another.[37] The entry

34. Gabriel Marcel, *The Mystery of Being* (Chicago: Gateway, 1960), 1:27–28.
35. Marcel, *Homo Viator*, 36.
36. A similar emphasis is found in Jacques Ellul, *Hope in Times of Abandonment* (New York: Seabury, 1973), 229.
37. Marcel's emphasis on mysterious, meaningful relationships in an alienated world is strikingly similar to Martin Buber's "I-Thou" principle.

into being is an act of commitment to the transcendent God as inexhaustible Presence that effects an openness to his redemptive purpose for people. Being is a state of transformation that is synonymous with the human quest for salvation.[38] It is a direct participation of one life with another, beginning with a "we are" rather than "I am." Marcel expressed this hope as a union between "person—engagement—community—reality."[39] Thus, hope is a concrete "act of faith" that forms meaningful relationships in God. It is the symphonic harmony of relationships amid tensions in the drama of life, amounting to a priority (or "disposability") for others in life as we "concretely" live it. In his self-styled "authentic formula of hope," "'I hope in thee for us,' is perhaps the most adequate and the most elaborate expression of the act which the verb 'to hope' suggests in a way which is still confused and ambiguous."[40] He meant that the "formula" is the communion of mutual fidelity that modestly awaits an open-ended future.

The vanity of Marcel's "having" manipulated possessions is developed by Jean Nabert. Drawing on the contrast between *espoir* and *espérance*, Nabert points beyond the mundane, daily wishes of *espoir* to the deeper, fulfilling perspectives of *espérance*, which is a fixation of faith on higher promises as a guide through the maze of earthly realities. Both kinds of hope are inherently human and universal. All people have been created hopeful with physical and spiritual appetites, living with a frustrating "is" (the present) in view of their roots (past) and their sense of what "ought to be" (future). Nabert emphasizes the dialectical character of hope; namely, every action is driven by a need to fulfill unreachable needs and ideals, an "enigmatic insatiability."[41] In other words, every action carries the seeds of its own frustration in the perpetual inabilites of people to attain their ideals and dreams except in imperfect ways. Our accomplishments never satisfy our insatiable desires. Each time we do something, we discover that the action is a springboard for a new desire that pushes us toward a theoretically perfect goal. For Nabert, this "lever of meaning" is a "regenerative desire" that characterizes the insatiability of humanity through history.[42]

Finally, Jürgen Moltmann (b. 1926), Pannenberg's peer and his complement in christocentric hope, wrote his *Theology of Hope* in 1974. The work

---

38. Marcel, *Being and Having*, 74–75.
39. Marcel, *Homo Viator*, 22.
40. Ibid., 60. Cf. Francisco Peccorini, *Selfhood as Thinking Thought in the Work of Gabriel Marcel: A New Interpretation* (Lewiston, N.Y.: Edwin Mellen, 1987), 71–72.
41. Jean Nabert, *Eléments pour une éthique* (Paris: Aubier, 1943), 19–20.
42. Ibid., 26.

put the theme of hope in the forefront of discussion as an encounter between Christian faith and dialectical philosophies.[43] In his words,

> In actual fact, however, eschatology means the doctrine of the Christian hope, which embraces both the object hoped for and also the hope inspired by it. From first to last, and not merely in the epilogue, Christianity is eschatology, is hope, forward looking and forward moving, and therefore also revolutionizing and transforming the present. The eschatological is not one element of Christianity, but it is the medium of Christianity as such, the key in which everything in it is set, the glow that suffuses everything here in the dawn of an expected new day. . . . Eschatology is the passionate suffering and passionate longing kindled by Messiah.[44]

The statement expresses the core of his view of eschatology as it formed his theology: the God of hope (the future as mode of God's being), history as God's future (the future as history), the advent of God's future in Jesus (Jesus' Lordship, Jesus as Son of God, and the meaning of the crucifixion and resurrection).[45] He accepted Bloch's principle of *futurum* in the sense of the Greek idea of *physis* as a transcendent becoming. However, he distinguished himself by saying that God is not *futurum* as a mode of being (Bloch), but rather with *Zukunft* (future) as his mode of acting upon the present and the past (*adventus Dei*).[46] Thus, we are to read time from the future into the present in terms of the God of hope:

> From the God of whom we hear in the context of historical persons and events, all things are experienced with a view to the future, that is, eschatologically. As

43. In his 1984 Ingersoll Lecture, Pannenberg attributed recent eschatological interest to the impact of Moltmann's *Theology of Hope*. Pannenberg's affirmation should remove any reservation about Moltmann's contribution. See Pannenberg, "Constructive and Critical Functions of Christian Eschatology," *Harvard Theological Review* 77 (1984): 119.

44. Jürgen Moltmann, *Theology of Hope on the Ground and the Implications of a Christian Eschatology* (Minneapolis: Fortress, 1993), 16. His *Theologie der Hoffnung* was published in 1964, and the first English edition appeared in 1967. In his "An Autobiographical Note" (in *God, Hope, and History: Jurgen Moltmann and the Christian Concept of History*, ed. A. J. Conyers [Macon, Ga.: Mercer University Press, 1988], 208), Moltmann states with the same emphasis: "The theology of hope is thus theology of the modern age. As I worked, though, hope became ever more strongly for me a subject of theology. I was theologizing no longer *about* hope, but from hope. . . . A proper theology should therefore be constructed beginning with its future goal. Eschatology should be not its end, but its beginning."

45. Jürgen Moltmann, Harvey Cox, Langdon Gilkey, Van Harvey, and John Macquarrie, in *The Future of Hope: Theology as Eschatology*, ed. Frederick Herzog (New York: Herder & Herder, 1970), 1–50. In the chapter, Moltmann acknowledges "a certain harmony of ideas" with J. B. Metz and W. Pannenberg in their joint work in *Ernst Bloch zu ehren: Beiträge zu seinem Werk* ([Frankfurt am Main]: Suhrkamp, 1965), 9 n. 11.

46. Ibid., 11–14.

the God of the promises and the historical guidance toward fulfillment, that is, as the God of the coming kingdom, he has shaped the experience of the historicity of the world and man that is open towards His future. The place where God's existence and communion are believed and hoped for is the place "in front of us" and "ahead of us."[47]

Moltmann, like his European counterparts, owed his appreciation of hope to his "certain situation" in war:

I lived through the destruction of Hamburg by firestorm, while in an antiaircraft battery in the central part of the city. In 1944 I went to the front, and in 1945 I was captured; I returned three years later, in 1948. In the camps in Belgium and Scotland I experienced both the collapse of those things that had been certainties for me and a new hope to live by, provided by the Christian faith. . . . I came back a Christian, with the new "personal goal" of studying theology, so that I might understand the power of hope to which I owed my life. . . . Of what else after all should one speak after Auschwitz, if not of God?! Keeping silence brings no salvation, for all other talk fails to be even a solution for the heavy depression. This condition of being unable to speak any longer of God, but all the while being compelled to speak of him—as the result of concrete experiences of an overwhelming burden of guilt and of ghastly absurdity in my generation—would seem to be the root of my theological endeavors, for reflection about God is continually reducing me to this perplexity.[48]

In the wake of the war, he separated himself from Bloch's atheism as the basis of social messianism.[49] The underlying reason, he held, was the question of one's identity in terms of one's relationship to history and the possibility of community. A direct connection of God with the dilemmas of humanity makes God responsible for the human experiment. This blame, in turn, leads

47. Moltmann, "Theology as Eschatology," 10. At this point, he enters discussion of the dynamic relationship of God and the future. Moltmann comes close to a panentheism that was characteristic of the day. Cf. E. Schillebeeckx, *God—the Future of Man* (New York and London: Sheed and Ward, 1968/1969), 144; Karl Rahner as discussed by Peter Phan, *Eternity and Time: A Study of Karl Rahner's Eschatology* (Selinsgrove, Pa.: Susquehanna University Press, 1988), 195; and Tim Bradshaw, *Trinity and Ontology: A Comparative Study of the Theologies of Karl Barth and Wolfhart Pannenberg* (Edinburgh: Rutherford, 1988), 402. Stanley Grenz (*Reason for Hope: The Systematic Theology of Wolfhart Pannenberg* [New York and London: Oxford University Press, 1990], 211), disclaims panentheistic implications: "For Pannenberg, then, God is affected by the world process but not in the sense that this process adds to the divine reality. Rather, the effect of the process lies in the demonstration of the relationship of God over creation, without which God would not be God and cannot be 'all in all.'"

48. Moltmann, "Autobiographical Note," 203–4.

49. "I had no designs on a role for myself as Ernst Bloch's heir. I did not want to be his follower. I most certainly did not want to give his 'Prinzip Hoffnung' a Christian baptism, which is what Karl Barth suspected at that time, from his base in Basel" (ibid., 207).

to atheism: If there is no God, then everything is permitted; in such a world man becomes god with infinite freedom and self-definition. With these assumptions, hope collapses in a self-defeating spiral. No, he affirmed, hope requires a christocentric theology that brings promise to bear on seemingly hopeless conditions in the world: "It is a thinking between cross and parousia and holds up the hope for God's coming in the painful realities of this world."[50]

Two features distinguished Moltmann's theology of hope for our purposes. First, he takes the eschatological character of Christianity with utmost seriousness as opposed to dismissing it as part of an antiquated worldview. Hope for him meant prioritizing promise rather than the earlier focus on the validity of revelation: "Hope is nothing else than the expectation of those things which faith has believed to have been truly promised by God."[51] History, the matrix of tradition and the time of hope, is the key to "the process of identification." In this perspective, the Exodus event, the crucifixion, and the parousia form the axis of meaning. In the Exodus God was understood as creator and deliverer from darkness and chaos, while protology and eschatology universalized Yahweh who alone is God over everything. The "Christ event," the passion and resurrection of Jesus, is the "eschatological event," the presence of God whose future is our present and whose presence is our future. The chapter titles of his *Theology of Hope* resonate with promise as hope: Promise and the Revelation of God, The Word of Promise, Promise and the Eschatology of the Prophets, Gospel and Promise, The God of the Promise, etc. The promise, *par excellence*, is the power of resurrection, a transformation of the human condition. This hope of transformation from above is what distinguishes eschatology as kingdom from humanistic utopias. The supreme promise is a general resurrection of the dead that inspires social action. The church must be dissatisfied with present injustices as compared with just promises, thus motivating its participation in God's future: "As a result of this hope in God's future, this present world becomes free in believing eyes from all attempts at self-redemption or self-production through labour, and it becomes open for loving, ministering self-expenditure in the interests of a humanizing of conditions and in the interests of the realization of justice in light of the coming justice of God."[52]

50. Moltmann, "Theology as Eschatology," 8.
51. Moltmann, *Theology of Hope*, 20.
52. Ibid., 338. Nicholas Lash (*A Matter of Hope: A Theologian's Reflections on the Thought of Karl Marx* [London: Darton, Longman & Todd, 1981; Notre Dame, Ind.: Notre Dame University Press, 1982], 161) refers to eschatology as a stimulant rather than a narcotic. The comment rebuts the Marxist critique of religion as an opiate of the people and makes us think indirectly of Bloch.

Second, Moltmann related Christian hope to social situations like post-colonial oppression in our century. The subject of present "injustices" is where his *The Crucified God* fits, and relates his eschatological thinking to the work of liberation and political theologians of the day like Metz, Cone, Gutierrez, Alves, Bonino, Reuther, and Russell among others.[53] He also argues with kinship, albeit Christian, to Bloch, who held that the lowly, suffering Jesus marked the exception to gods of power who sponsored ideologies of oppression in their representative empires. In brief, Moltmann identified himself with hope as a this-worldly ideal, an attainment of cross-identification for theology, church, and society. The hope of resurrection is contingent upon the church's identification with the pathos of God by breaking its alliance with the powerful and entering into solidarity with the oppressed of the world. He cites Luther's theology of the cross as well as contemporaries like Kitamori and Sobrino for support on the power of redemptive suffering.[54] Moltmann's position amounts to a countercultural resistence to a crucifying world, a crossing over to a more just future with hope in God's promises.

Finally, in his recent book *The Coming of God*, Moltmann concluded his thinking on the new creation by claiming that the Christian millenarian hope is necessary for interpreting history and is a crucial element in eschatology.[55] Moltmann is not concerned with a futurist millennium that separates the present and the future and relegates the church to mere hope and prayer for a supernatural event.[56] Neither is it epochal millenarianism, the secularized dreams of the post-Enlightenment world that has justified catastrophic violence to achieve domination.[57] Rather he defends an eschatological millenarianism in which ecclesial resistance to the powers of the world effects an alternative reign of Christ and an end of history in the new creation.[58] Like Bloch, Moltmann was indebted to the Joachimist tradition that restored the idea of kingdom to the historical process, an activist tradition that was present from the patristic period to the fourth century. This

53. Jürgen Moltmann, *The Crucified God* (New York: Harper & Row, 1974). *Der gekreuzigte Gott* was published by Christian Kaiser in 1973. Moltmann was accused of bypassing a sociopolitical analysis that identified concretely with the oppressed of the world. Moltmann replied that liberation theologians neglected a comprehensive goal in their diverse agendas, but that they were all headed in the same direction anyway. Cf. Rubem Alves, *A Theology of Human Hope* (Washington, D.C.: Corpus, 1969).

54. Moltmann, "Autobiographical Note," 209–11.

55. Jürgen Moltmann, *The Coming of God: Christian Eschatology* (Minneapolis: Fortress/London: SCM, 1996). *Das Kommen Gottes: Christliche Eschatologie* was published by Christian Kaiser in 1995.

56. Ibid., 147–53.

57. Ibid., 134–35, 184–92.

58. Ibid., 139–46, 152–59, 194–96.

was a time when the forward look of earthly activism replaced the upward (heavenly) look.[59]

The journey from war-torn Europe to the affluence of contemporary technological societies may seem disconnected. However, it is as close as early warnings about the emptiness of finding hope in "having" things as manipulated objects or caveats about the loss of community when self-gratification becomes the dominant ethos. Andrew Delbanco and Christiaan Beker are representative of a number of scholars who discern a hopelessness at the end of the century and millennium in spite of "epochal" peace and prosperity that should have diminished the horrors of war at the beginning of the century.

Delbanco argues that there has been a "diminution of hope" in America. His thesis is based on the premise that people find hope in cultural stories that give them personal meaning through collective purposes.[60] Contemporary America is experiencing melancholy of despair, because its collective purpose has dissolved in the acids of self-gratification. The Puritans grounded hope in their higher commitment to God, a love that was manifested in a love of neighbor. This "spiritual longing" was translated into a sacred hope for social freedom and equality, a universal distribution of rights by a redeemer nation between Abraham Lincoln and Lyndon Johnson. From the 1960s, Delbanco argues,

> the reform impulse subsided in solipsism, and in the 1980s—two phases of our history that may seem far apart in political tone and personal style, but that finally cooperated in installing instant gratification as the hallmark of the good life, and in repudiating the interventionist state as a source of hope. . . . The history of hope I have tried to sketch in this book is one of diminution. At first, the self expanded toward (and was sometimes overwhelmed by) the vastness of God. From the early republic to the Great Society, it remained implicated in a national ideal lesser than God but larger and more enduring than any individual citizen. Today hope has narrowed to the vanishing point of the self alone.[61]

59. As early as 1991, Moltmann had sought a balance between Joachim's immanent, messianic, and millenarian kingdom and Thomas's transcendent and heavenly eschatology (*History and the Triune God: Contributions to Trinitarian Theology* [London: SCM, 1991/New York: Crossroad, 1992], 91–109). His inclination was to see the new creation as more transcendent and other-worldly. A helpful summary of Moltmann's intellectual heritage can be found in Robert Walton, "Jurgen Moltmann's *Theology of Hope*—European Roots of Liberation Theology," in *Liberation Theology*, ed. Ronald Nash (Milford, Mich.: Mott Media, 1984), 145–74. A postmillenarian critique of Moltmann can be found in Richard Bauckham, "Must Christian Eschatology Be Millenarian? A Response to Jurgen Moltmann," in *Eschatology in Bible and Theology: Evangelical Essays at the Dawn of a New Millennium*, ed. Kent Brower and Mark Elliott (Downers Grove, Ill.: InterVarsity, 1997), 263–77.

60. Delbanco, *Real American Dream*, 1, 103.

61. Ibid., 96–97, 103. Perhaps one can argue that Delbanco could have said that the basis of hope, a human trait and need, had been transferred from God to nation to self. However, one must remember that he argued that America is in a period of self-absorbed melancholy rather than hope of any meaningful kind.

Elsewhere, he concludes that our society suffers from "an ache for meaning that goes unrelieved."[62] Possessive individualism tries to compensate with competitive self-display, but its storyless charade breaks down.

Delbanco recognizes that a self-absorption with one's limitless possibilities without a larger vision was incipient in the beginnings of the republic. With prescient insight, Alexis de Tocqueville realized that the things of the world cannot satisfy the human heart. Accordingly, he wrote in his classic *Democracy in America* after his tour in the 1830s that "men never attain as much as they desire . . . that is the reason for the strange melancholy that haunts inhabitants of democratic countries in the midst of abundance."[63] There is no higher purpose at the borders of the recreational self beyond the instant desire to be seen at "golden arches" in "swooshes," with lizards and ferrets as companions in consumption. Image, in every sense of the technological self, has become the message. The world-at-large now collapses despair, deity, and hope incoherently in a collective self. Tocqueville's old "melancholy" is a synonym for the despairing emptiness of materialistic fulfillments, the inadequacy of transient pleasures for enduring purposes. It is an unrelieved "ache for meaning" that we addictively refuse to treat lest we lose the mirage in the process. Conspicuous consumption at "temples" like stadiums, theatres, corporate headquarters, and bars has caused the self to become everything and nothing at the same time.[64]

Beker analyzes the same milieu in terms of a precarious balance between suffering and hope that has been lost. Despair in times of affluence and self-absorption, for Beker, can be explained by global suffering that overwhelms us with its unparalleled scope and intense urgency. We are increasingly aware, in the information revolution, that all of life stands or falls in an apocalyptic

---

62. Ibid., 107.

63. Alexis de Tocqueville, *Democracy in America* (New York: Vintage, 1990), 2.138–39.

64. One of the best indicators of the narcissism of the times is the sexual revolution Walker Percy describes as modern self-absorption as an "endemic Cartesianism" that was observed by Tocqueville and that has left twentieth-century people without a coherent theory of transcendence (Lewis Lawson and Victor Kramer, eds., *More Conversations with Walker Percy* [Jackson, Miss.: University of Mississippi Press, 1993], 232–33). In his *Love in the Ruins: The Adventures of a Bad Catholic at a Time Near the End of the World* (New York: Farrar, Straus, and Giroux, 1971), 116–21, Percy juxtaposes Max Gottlieb, a psychiatrist for whom sex without guilt is the essence of the good life, with Dr. Tom More, an anachronistic believer and an abandoned husband whose three paramours have caused him to feel lost to God: "The problem is that if there is no guilt, contrition, and a purpose of amendment, then sin cannot be forgiven" (117). Sin?! According to Percy, in a self-gratifying world sex is "a debased sacrament," no longer a meaningful sign of the sacramental life. Guiltless, safe, sexual pleasure between consenting adults is a symbol of the fact that all notions of true meaning, purpose, and commitment have been lost. Cf. Jay Tolson, *Pilgrim in the Ruins: A Life of Walker Percy* (Chapel Hill: University of North Carolina Press, 1992), 349–51.

climate where inexplicable, fateful suffering eclipses legitimate grounds for authentic hope. Suffering without transcendent meaning leads to "hope" for short-term escapes at the cost of long-term cynicism and despair. Sensing uncertainty and doom, masses of people have embraced egocentric projects of survival. These are "false hopes" that generate large industries of self-help gurus who pander to fabricated potentialities of wounded people, often with quasi-Christian rationales. Secularity has nurtured apocalyptic dramas with no sense of deity other than ourselves. Thus, we are dealing with many nefarious human agents who produce Armageddons with no exit. In contrast to biblical suffering that is transformed by hope into character and maturity, today's climate only evaporates it:

> And so in our time apocalyptic social disorder is conjoined and correlated with the private world of suffering within us. For instance, our computer-society, which aggravates an already impersonal bureaucratic way of behaving, treats people as items in a statistical column and can only worsen the personal needs of people in distress. . . . Social interpersonal confusion and psychic intrapersonal disorder about the meaning of suffering join to increase the apocalyptic sense of doom and drive us from expectations of hope into hopelessness and despair. We are increasingly aware that those forms of suffering preoccupy us which, because of their scope, gravity, and seeming senselessness, destroy hope.[65]

Thus, the Christian task is to incarnate authentic hope in a provident God who punishes, teaches, or tests in the extraordinary variety of life's experiences.

We have traced hopelessness in this century from a European despair over war and oppressive technologies to the trivia of the self-obsessed vanities of contemporary America. These representative despairs and melancholies of the century are best viewed against the backdrop of biblical hope. The Bible gravitates to 1 Corinthians 13:13: "And now these three remain: faith, hope and love." The nuance of trust connects faith and hope in an emphasis on God and his promises:

> What all this comes down to is that our "sure and certain" hope of eternal life is a special, personal, and unprovable kind of certainty we call trust. We know it will happen because we trust someone to make it happen. We stand on the promises. . . . We are sure of God only if we have learned to trust Him.[66]

---

65. J. Christiaan Beker, *Suffering and Hope: The Biblical Vision and the Human Predicament* (Philadelphia: Fortress, 1987), 20.
66. Smedes, *Standing on the Promises*, 161–62. Also see Rudolf Bultmann, "ἐλπίς," *TDNT* 2:522.

The connected themes staccato through Scripture as keynoted in passages like 1 Peter 1:21 ("Through him you believe in God, who raised him from the dead and glorified him, and so your faith and hope are in God"); Titus 1:2 ("A faith and knowledge resting on the hope of eternal life, which God, who does not lie, promised before the beginning of time . . ."); and Hebrews 10:23 ("Let is hold unswervingly to the hope we profess, for he who promised is faithful").

The roots of this uniquely personal confidence in God and his future are found in the Old Testament's patriarchal revelations. Hope there was founded on promises that promoted a confident waiting in spite of implausible circumstances.[67] Walther Zimmerli states: "'The fear of God' is a matter of confident waiting . . . the hope that is present.' Here 'hope' shades into 'trust' (*biṭṭaḥon*) and 'confidence' (*kishah*)."[68] Also see Psalm 27:13–14 ("I am confident of this: I will see the goodness of the LORD in the land of the living. Wait for the LORD; be strong and take heart and wait for the LORD") and Jeremiah 29:11 ("'For I know the plans I have for you,' declares the LORD, 'plans to prosper you and not to harm you, plans to give you hope and a future'").

Everett Harrison summarizes the Old Testament vision: "The crowning feature of the prophetic message of hope was the promise of a messianic king (Isa. 11:1, etc.)."[69] Accordingly, biblical hope was incarnated in the Messiah. Our Lord as hope shades toward apposition in phrases like "Christ in you, the hope of glory" (Col. 1:27) and "Jesus Christ our hope" (1 Tim. 1:1). Our hope in Christ is vested not only in his resurrection as firstfuits but also in his priestly ministry at the right hand of the Father. In Hebrews 2:10–18, he incarnately shared our humanity, so that in his death he could free believers from their fear of death. Being like his brothers, Abraham's seed of faith, he is an empathetic and faithful High Priest. In Hebrews 12:1–3, believers are exhorted to persevere by following Christ "who for the joy set before him endured the cross, scorning its shame, and sat down at the right hand of the throne of God." We should consider him "who endured such opposition from sinful men, so that [we] will not grow weary and lose heart."

With the transbiblical messianic hope is the example of Abraham as pilgrim. In Abraham, faith, hope, and promise converge in a context of the divine monologue in Genesis 15: "Against all hope, Abraham in hope believed [or, as sometimes paraphrased, "hoped against hope"] and so became the father of many nations" (Rom. 4:18), even as he "tented" in his forward quest

---

67. Smedes (*Standing on the Promises*, 42) notes insightfully, "Waiting is the hardest work of hope." Also see Eugene Peterson, *A Long Obedience in the Same Direction: Discipleship in an Instant Society* (Downers Grove, Ill.: InterVarsity, 1980), chap. 12.

68. Walther Zimmerli, *Man and His Hope in the Old Testament* (Naperville, Ill.: A. R. Allenson, 1968/London: SCM, 1971), 9–10.

69. E. F. Harrison, "Hope," *ISBE* 2:752.

for a city, whose architect and builder is God" (Heb. 11:9–10). Promises had been given, but their accompanying hopes were necessarily unseen and unpossessed (Rom. 8:24–25) because faith "is the assurance of things hoped for" (Heb 11:1 RSV).

The agony is that our wait may involve holocaust, indignity, or an ungodly, self-absorbed society. Examples of faith in settings like these died without the promises and still await their anticipated destiny (Heb. 11:39). History's lesson is that the Christian's "blessed hope" transcends self and society and is "anchored" in the accomplishments of the Melchizedekian Priest-King (Heb. 6:19–20). The "blessed hope" purifies us with a love of "the glorious appearing of our great God and Savior, Jesus Christ" (Titus 2:13) as opposed to a hatred of our inabilities to rise above death, even in a corporate, utopian sense. This is doxology instead of despair.

I would draw four conclusions from this study that address the balance that a believer should sustain between the God in whom we believe and the world in which we live. First, we should understand the condition of our world (space) and our century (time). Christians tend to avoid the inconvenient and the uncomfortable, and like their fellow citizens they passionately pursue the advantages of progress and prosperity that technology has provided. Hope therefore is not a concern, because the certainty of what we have seems more important than the sometimes uncomfortable (com)mission of the God that we serve. Our century has been characterized as one of despair, or perhaps disillusionment, by thoughtful critics in spite of revolutionary scientific discoveries and technological advances.

This paper began with Gordimer's observation that we do not know how to control the marvels of our achievements. Perhaps this is true because we like to enjoy the marvels without the risks and sufferings that they pose in this fallen world. One of the newest summaries of the century is a thirteen-pound collage entitled *Century: 100 Years of Human Progress, Regression, Suffering and Hope*.[70] Its apt title covers a long parade of events and people that shaped the most chronicled period of history. The century's initial optimisms were crushed by the world wars that have persisted in localized conflagrations. As noted by Hughes and Trueblood, the promises of technology created a coexisting capacity for unparalleled prosperity and destruction. A post-sixties period of relative peace, potential globalization, exploding markets, and informational overload has led to widespread apocalypticisms at millennium's end.

This paper demonstrates a scholarly consensus that present trends have important precedents, and that history has been saturated with various kinds of pains and pleasures that undermine a biblical kind of hope in God's future. At the same time, knowledgeable commentators of our day recognize that tech-

---

70. Bruce Bernard, ed., *Century: One Hundred Years of Human Progress, Regression, Suffering and Hope* (London: Phaidon, 1999).

nology has compressed the world, that change for good and evil has escalated beyond our ability to control it. As we examine the mirror of our times, we see a desire to satiate appetites of the moment—to the neglect of past and future—in a parade of status symbols, fads, and lists of "the best, brightest and most beautiful." Entertainment has taken the place of higher purposes, and we strive with nerve-crunching anxiety for the economic means to sustain them. Global spiritualities are one of these means. So, secular humanism has yielded to cosmic humanism; namely, New Age, new world order mysticisms of the divine Self as a means of spirituality, stress management, and coping without moral accountability. In such a world, the cries for hope are ubiquitous, but their substance is only as deep as the objects of their desires. Furthermore, the apocalyptic implications of the new century and millennium tend to diminish the eschatological hope of the return of the Lord for his people.

Second, the century has taught us that hope is the heart of eschatology. The laureates and informational sources have underlined the pervasiveness of hope in human life, "enigmatically insatiable" in Nabert's terms. Like its intangible kins, faith and love, hope cannot be quantified, which is frustrating in a statistically driven world. But it can be qualified by its object. So, Terkel's subjects realized that technology lacks a comforting "touch." And, without a personal God like Christ, people's anxieties become apocalypses without exits. The concern of the century has been resources rather than resurrection, so its leaders have usually solved its "ache for meaning" with an imminently defined "hope against hope."

Eschatology's resurgence in academia has had hope at its heart. Even the atheist Bloch turned to "the principle of hope" to formulate his utopian possibilities. Marcel's "open-ended personalism" centered hope in meaningful relationships with God and humankind to counter autonomous selves in an increasingly alienated technological world. Marcel, among others, has reminded us that hope is mysteriously communitarian, a shared virtue instead of an individual achievement. We are to hope in Thee for us. Pannenberg and Moltmann theologically tethered hope to a forward-looking faith in God's future, the latter "identifying" hope and dynamic eschatology in the promises of God. Surprisingly, "authentic hope" is as problematic in self-centered secularism as suicidal war zones. Delbanco argued that the melancholy of despair proliferates in societies without higher purposes, connecting hope with a transcendence that unites people. Beker interpreted egocentric affluence as a mask for pervasive suffering, leaving a hopeless world in the grip of an apocalyptic sense of doom. If eschatology concerns the "last things" in God's purposes for his creation, then authentic hope is truly the heart of a biblical eschatology that would meet the needs of contemporary criteria like a sense of fulfillment of higher promises and purposes, meaningful commitments and relationships, and biblical fidelity.

Third, the century has debated the "God of hope" on its center stage. Theological academies (evangelicals "hopefully" excepted) have roller-coastered from immanence to transcendence, settling on a "transcendence within" that accords with the globalizing world and its corporate need for everyone to be "OK." Is this not the answer to the wars of this inhumane century and the goal of prosperity that can bring us happiness and an earthly heaven now? Have not exclusive religions been one of the greatest causative factors in the century's bad news? Thus, in a seemingly endless variety of movements, the tenets of biblical faith have been redefined to remove incorrect edges, hoping to form inclusive smooth stones that will not cause stumbling on the offense of the cross. The cost is a world in which we only go around once, so we need "all the gusto that we can get." Immortality, accordingly, is reduced to a notion of human memory that anesthetizes painful departures. We can hardly see beyond the meditations, hypnoses, magical incantations, and endless therapies that have renewed the church's awareness that it may be more of a statistical remnant than the "majority." Evangelicals should be wise, lest they obscure biblical faith with cultural hopes. A diminished biblical hope in God and his future is expensive, because it entails loss of confidence, assurance, comfort, and godliness (Rom. 5:2–5; Eph. 1:13–14; 1 Thess. 1:3–10, 5:4–24; 1 Peter 1:6–16; 1 John 3:3).

Fourth, believers should understand that their hope is one of their most precious possessions and, potentially, one of their greatest gifts to the world. In the latent hopelessness of the century, there is a muffled cry for "a hope in Christ that is larger than the transitory desires of this life only" (1 Cor. 15:19). "The testimony of Jesus," the angel reminded John, "is the spirit of prophecy" (Rev. 19:10). Of course, there are multitudes who expound the Word and glorify Christ, who is virtually synonymous with hope in the New Testament. All of this means that theology has the distinguished task of studying and communicating resurrection as the only worthy object of peoples' hopes. By the same token, it means that hope is a foundation stone in the maintenance of a vital eschatology.

This is not a paper about doom. It is a call to hope in Christ that has reverberated across a century characterized by despair. We tend to speculate about details and neglect the forest that shades us from worldly challenges: from loss of relationships, from loss of jobs, from inexplicable traumas and tragedies, and from the sheer trivia of competitive greed. Hope is what keeps an enduring eschatology from dissolving into faddish apocalypses that sometimes inveigle even the church from its eternal promises.

12

The Place of Imminence in Recent Eschatological Systems

Robert L. Thomas

The Master's Seminary

Throughout the church's history imminence has been a prominent part of her teaching about events connected with the second advent of Jesus Christ. It began with the church's earliest writers[1] and continues to the present day. Expectation of an imminent happening was seemingly universal among the fathers, even though their writings do not express complete agreement about what that happening would be. In supporting the posttribulational stance among early church writers, Ladd wrote, "The expectation of the coming of Christ *included the events which would attend and precede His coming*."[2] Lea concludes regarding the fathers that the expectancy of the early church was a series of events that would precede and surround Christ's actual advent.[3] Walvoord saw in these early writings a form of "incipient" pretribulationalism with its associated idea of imminence.[4]

---

1. *First Epistle of Clement* 23; *Epistle to Polycarp* 1, 3; Ignatius, *Ephesians* 11 (shorter and longer versions); *Teaching of the Twelve Apostles* 16; *Pastor of Hermas*, vision 4, chap. 2; Irenaeus, *Against Heresies* 5.29.1; 5.35.1; Hippolytus, *Treatise on Christ and Antichrist*; Tertullian, *Apology*, part 1, chap. 21; *On Repentance* 1; *The Shows* 30; Cyprian, *On the Unity of the Church* 27; *Treatises of Cyprian* 7.2; 12.3.89; *Constitutions of the Holy Apostles* 7.2.31; 7.2.32; Tertullian, *On the Resurrection of the Flesh* 41; cf. Thomas D. Lea, "A Survey of the Doctrine of the Return of Christ in the Ante-Nicene Fathers," *JETS* 29 (1986): 170–72.

2. G. E. Ladd, *The Blessed Hope* (Grand Rapids: Eerdmans, 1956), 20.

3. Lea, "Survey of the Doctrine," 172.

4. J. F. Walvoord, "A Review of the *Blessed Hope* by George E. Ladd," *BSac* 113 (1956): 291–92; cf. Robert H. Gundry, *The Church and the Tribulation* (Grand Rapids: Zondervan, 1973), 179.

Both amillennialists and premillennialists endorse the teaching that the Lord could return virtually at any time.[5] They may differ regarding the imminence of what, but they agree that either the personal coming of Christ or the events associated with his coming could come at any moment. Postmillennialists are alone in denying the New Testament doctrine of imminence in the present day.[6]

The reason for widespread belief in the imminence of end time events and Christ's return is, of course, the teaching of the New Testament. The last book of the New Testament builds its case around the imminence of Christ's return. In the book's very first verse, the *en tachei* ("soon") offers encouragement to the faithful among the readers that their predicted deliverance is very close.[7] Long ago, Moffatt appropriately called this focus on immediacy "the hinge and staple of the book."[8] Revelation fulfils this emphasis on Jesus' imminent coming with repetitions of *en tachei* and other literary indications that relief for the faithful from persecution along with judgment to the rest of the world may happen at any moment. Additional references to imminence in Revelation include the following: (1) *en tachei* again in 22:6; (2) *tachy* in 2:16; 3:11; 22:7, 12, 20; (3) the use of *engys* in Revelation 1:3 and 22:10; (4) the "thief" simile in 3:3 and 16:15; (5) the futuristic use of the present tense of *erchomai*[9] in 1:7; 2:5, 16; 3:11; 16:15; 22:7, 12, 20; (6) the metaphor of the judge at the door in 3:20; and (7) the use of *mellō* in 3:10, 16.[10] Compounded with many references to imminence in other books of the New

5. Millard J. Erickson, *A Basic Guide to Eschatology: Making Sense of the Millennium* (Grand Rapids: Baker, 1998), 75.

6. Ibid.

7. Cf. Robert L. Thomas, *Revelation 1–7: An Exegetical Commentary* (Chicago: Moody, 1992), 54–56. Stanton has cited some of the arguments used by opponents of imminence to disprove that NT teaching (Gerald B. Stanton, "The Doctrine of Imminency: Is It Biblical?" in *When the Trumpet Sounds*, ed. Thomas Ice and Timothy Demy [Eugene, Ore.: Harvest House, 1995], 229–32). If the last book of the Bible teaches the imminence of Christ's coming and of the beginning of other end-time events, certain arguments against the NT's teaching of imminence disappear. Opponents of imminence have cited the necessity of intervening events such as the death of Peter, the plan and content of Paul's ministry, and the destruction of Jerusalem (cf. Robert G. Gromacki, "The Imminent Return of Jesus Christ," *Grace Theological Journal* 6/3 [fall 1965]: 14–16). All those lay in the past by the time Revelation was written, and so were no obstacle to understanding the book's emphasis on imminence.

8. James Moffatt, "The Revelation of St. John the Divine," in *The Expositor's Greek Testament*, ed. W. Robertson Nicoll (Grand Rapids: Eerdmans, 1956), 335.

9. Cf. Robert L. Thomas, *Revelation 1–7*, 82. Wallace notes that the futuristic present denotes either immediacy or certainty, depending on the context in which it appears (Daniel B. Wallace, *Greek Grammar beyond the Basics* [Grand Rapids: Zondervan, 1996], 535–36). In the context of the Apocalypse its obvious connotation is immediacy.

10. H. B. Swete, *The Apocalypse of St. John* (London: Macmillan, 1906), 55; Isbon T. Beckwith, *The Apocalypse of John* (New York: Macmillan, 1919), 490; Walter Scott, *Exposition of the Revelation of Jesus Christ*, 4th ed. (Grand Rapids: Kregel, n.d.), 112; cf. Thomas, *Revelation 1–7*, 289–290, 309.

Testament,[11] these literary devices show why the church from its beginning until the present has viewed end time events including the coming of Christ as something that could occur or begin to occur at any moment.

This present study will survey and evaluate how three recent eschatological schemes have responded to this New Testament teaching about the imminence of Christ's return and its surrounding events. These responses have attracted special attention in evangelical churches of recent days, to the point that leaders in those churches are asking how to advise their people regarding them. Preterism will be the first to be examined, then two non-imminent-advent views, and finally a view that combines preterism, idealism, and futurism.

Preterism

Recently R. C. Sproul has adopted a view that Greg Bahnsen held before his death, namely, that most of Jesus' predictions about his future coming referred to the destruction of Jerusalem in A.D. 70 and the events leading up to it.[12] The position understands the "soon" of Revelation 1:1 in light of Matthew 24:34 where Jesus promised, "This generation will not pass away until all these things take place." It accepts Jesus' teaching of an imminent return, but also stipulates a time limit within which the predicted events must occur, a limit that came in forty years.

Gentry reasons this way: "If, as it seems likely, Revelation is indeed John's exposition of the Olivet Discourse, we must remember that in the delivery of the Discourse, the Lord emphasized that it . . . was to occur in His generation (Matt. 24:34)."[13] From that point Gentry proceeds with a chapter on the temporal expectation of the Apocalypse.[14] Sproul has a similar chapter on Revelation, but has noted regarding Matthew 24:34 that "this generation" limits the period during which Jesus' coming must transpire to thirty or forty years,[15] a limitation similar to that of Gentry.[16] DeMar follows essentially the same approach regarding the meaning of "this generation,"[17] as does Mathison.[18]

---

11. Cf. Matt. 24:42–25:13; Mark 13:32–37; Luke 12:39–40; 21:34–36; Rom. 13:11–12; 1 Cor. 1:4–7; 15:51–53; 16:22; 2 Cor. 5:6–10; 1 Thess. 4:15; 5:2–3; 2 Peter 3:10.

12. See R. C. Sproul, *The Last Days according to Jesus* (Grand Rapids: Baker, 1998); cf. Greg L. Bahnsen, "The Prima Facie Acceptability of Postmillennialism," *Journal of Christian Reconstruction* 3 (winter 1976–77): 48–105.

13. Kenneth L. Gentry Jr., *Before Jerusalem Fell: Dating the Book of Revelation* (Tyler, Tex.: Institute for Christian Economics, 1989), 131.

14. Ibid., 133–45.

15. Sproul, *Last Days*, 56–57.

16. Gentry, *Before Jerusalem Fell*, 131.

17. Gary DeMar, *Last Days Madness: The Folly of Trying to Predict When Christ Will Return* (Brentwood, Tenn.: Wolgemuth & Hyatt, 1991), 100.

18. Keith A. Mathison, *Postmillennialism: An Eschatology of Hope* (Phillipsburg, N.J.: Presbyterian & Reformed, 1999), 111–12.

The above-named individuals fall into the camp of moderate or partial preterism. Because of a few passages such as 1 Thessalonians 4, they support the teaching of a future resurrection and kingdom.[19] They distance themselves from full or plenary preterism, which has no place for a future bodily resurrection in its doctrinal system.[20] Sproul, Gentry, and company do allow for a future bodily resurrection and kingdom in the eternal state.

At least three reasons negate the handling of Matthew 24:34 by both plenary and partial preterism. (1) The first is that the gospel of the kingdom had not been preached to all nations as Jesus said it would be by the time of the end (Matt. 24:14). Sproul responds to this objection by his claim that the gospel had been preached throughout the Roman Empire by A.D. 70,[21] but "all nations" (*pasin tois ethnesin*) in Matthew 24:14 covers more than just the Roman Empire. It covers the entire world composed of the Gentile nations. The gospel had not spread that far by the time Jerusalem was destroyed by the Romans.

(2) Another shortcoming of the preterist handling of Matthew 24:34 is the obvious fact that Christ did not personally return in the clouds as he promised he would in Matthew 24:30. In response to this obstacle, Sproul approvingly cites J. Stuart Russell, who says Matthew 24:29–31 is poetic and symbolic in keeping with Old Testament passages that speak of the coming of God to judge.[22] Gentry's response is the same, as he states emphatically: "*No scriptural statement is capable of more decided proof than that the coming of Christ is the destruction of Jerusalem, and the close of the Jewish dispensation.*"[23]

Such answers furnish an excellent example of resorting to a nonliteral interpretation whenever a literal interpretation does not fit into the eschatological system being espoused. In his Olivet Discourse Jesus plainly promised the Jewish nation that at some time in the future he would personally return to pass judgment on their response to his plea for repentance. The judgment against Jerusalem through the Romans in A.D. 70 plainly does not fulfil that promise.

(3) The third obstacle to the preterist understanding of Matthew 24:34 is the most formidable. That is the fact that Jesus could not have been stipulating a 30-to-40-year period in which his promised return would occur. Just two verses later he informed his listeners that no one, including himself, knew *when* all his predictions would come to fruition: "But of that day and hour no

19. E.g., Sproul, *Last Days*, 167–70.

20. See e.g., J. Stuart Russell, *The Parousia: A Critical Inquiry into the New Testament Doctrine of Our Lord's Second Coming* (1887; reprint, Grand Rapids: Baker, 1983), and Max R. King, *The Cross and the Parousia of Christ: The Two Dimensions of One Age-Changing Eschaton* (Warren, Ohio: Writing and Research Ministry, 1987).

21. Sproul, *Last Days*, 48.

22. Ibid., 41–48.

23. Gentry, *Before Jerusalem Fell*, 131 (emphasis in original).

one knows, not even the angels of heaven, nor the Son, but the Father alone" (Matt. 24:36 RSV). If he did not know the time, as he states, he could not have set a time period within which his coming must occur.

Sproul responds to this obstacle thus: "Because the day and hour are not known does not preclude the application of a time-frame as lengthy as a human generation. Someone, for example, could predict that an event will take place in the next forty years, and then qualify the prediction by saying, 'I don't know the particular day or hour' within that span of time."[24] His response is remarkable in light of the preterists' criticism of contemporary date setting for the return of Christ. DeMar is particularly critical of modern-day date setters, and subtitled his volume voicing that criticism *The Folly of Trying to Predict When Christ Will Return.* Yet he, Sproul, and other preterists are guilty of the same practice in their analysis of the first-century outlook. Just as some recent students of prophecy have suggested forty years from the establishment of the Jewish state in 1948 as a date for Christ's return,[25] so preterists claim that Christ had to return within forty years of uttering Matthew 24:34. Just as recent date setters have said, Christ's declaration that no one knows the day or hour of his return does not preclude a knowledge of the general time period, preterists are currently interpreting his words in the same way in reference to a first-century situation.

Clearly such was not the intent of Matthew 24:36. The same Person who said of that day and hour no one knows said less than two months later that no one knows "the times or the seasons" (Acts 1:7 RSV). He thus answered his disciples' question about the time of restoration for Israel's kingdom. In conjunction with his comment about the day and hour, Jesus clarified his meaning with three parables—those of the householder (Matt. 24:43), of the wicked slave (Matt. 24:48), and of the foolish virgins (Matt. 25:5).[26] The behavior of guilty characters in these parables makes no sense if they had known the general time period during which the thief, the master, or the bridegroom would arrive. They would not have grown tired of waiting if they had known that the time of arrival was no more than forty years away. The householder would not have been caught unaware by the thief, the wicked slave by his master, or the foolish virgins by the bridegroom. Jesus' words about the day and the hour include ignorance of the general time period of his return, not just the day and hour. No one knew or knows when it will be.

24. Sproul, *Last Days*, 42.
25. Hal Lindsey with C. C. Carlson, *The Late Great Planet Earth* (Grand Rapids: Zondervan, 1970), 53–54.
26. Regarding these parables Charles L. Holman observes, "In the parables which exhort the disciples to watchfulness for the parousia (24:45–51; 25:1–13; 25:14–30) the idea of imminence is implicit; otherwise, why would the disciples need to watch for His coming?" ("The Idea of an Imminent Parousia in the Synoptic Gospels," *Studia Biblica et Theologica* 3 [March 1973]: 17).

If "this generation" in Matthew 24:34 did and does not refer to a stipulated period of time, to what does it refer? Jesus' use of the expression earlier in the same day as his Olivet Discourse is important in answering that question. Matthew records it as part of Jesus' seventh woe against the scribes and Pharisees in Matthew 23:36: "All these things will come upon this generation" (NASB). A careful tracing of Jesus' words in Matthew 23:29–39, observing the interchangeability of "this generation" with the second-person-plural pronouns will show that "this generation" is a qualitative expression without chronological or temporal connotations.[27] It refers to a kind of people Jesus encountered at his first advent and also to the same kind of people who rebelled against God's leadership throughout the Old Testament. It refers to the kind of people who will not see Jesus again and who will continue to predominate in their rejection in the future until the nation Israel repents and says, "Blessed is [the one] who comes in the name of the Lord" (Matt. 21:9; 23:39). In other words, "this generation" set no time deadlines by which Jesus must return.

The preterist relegation of imminence to a prescribed period in the first century A.D. does not satisfy the criteria of the text, particularly its focus on imminence throughout the period of Christ's absence.

A Non-imminent Advent

A relatively recent view called "the pre-wrath rapture" of the church fits under the above heading. The idea is that the tribulation or seventieth week of Daniel is imminent or almost imminent, but that prophesied events within that week must occur before the personal coming of Christ.[28] The view therefore opposes the teaching of Christ's imminent return and in that regard is closely akin to a posttribulational view of his coming.[29] Both positions place the day of the Lord at the end of Daniel's seventieth week and then proceed to point out various prophesied events that must precede that day.[30] The only difference between the two views is slight and pertains to the duration and exact location they assign to the day of the Lord. Prewrath rapturism conceives of the day as a period of undefined length toward the end of the tribulation,

27. Cf. Evald Lövestam, *Jesus and "This Generation": A New Testament Study* (Stockholm: Almqvist & Wiksell, 1995), 81–87.

28. Robert Van Kampen, *The Sign of Christ's Coming and the End of the Age*, 2d ed. (Wheaton, Ill.: Crossway, 1992), 98–99, 185.

29. Robert Gundry has recently reaffirmed his posttribulantional stance in *First the Antichrist* (Grand Rapids: Baker, 1997). That, along with other works such as Millard J. Erickson, *A Basic Guide to Eschatology: Making Sense of the Millennium* (Grand Rapids: Baker, 1998), allows consideration of that view under the heading of "recent" also.

30. Cf. Marvin Rosenthal, *The Pre-wrath Rapture of the Church* (Nashville: Nelson, 1990), 115–61, with Robert H. Gundry, *The Church and the Tribulation* (Grand Rapids: Zondervan, 1973), 89–99.

during which the trumpet and bowl judgments are fulfilled, while posttribulationism identifies the day as a brief, undefined period of divine judgment after the tribulation. Arguments to support the two positions are quite similar, however. Both deny the imminence of Christ's coming for the church, the former by substituting imminence of the day of the Lord within the seventieth week and the latter by substituting expectancy for imminence,[31] though in some instances both talk about expectancy rather than imminence.[32]

The Handling of Revelation 6:17

An exegetical point the two views have in common is their handling of Revelation 6:17. The key word in the verse is *ēlthen* in the statement "the great day of their wrath has come." Both the prewrath and the posttribulational positions understand that aorist indicative verb not to refer to past action (as is normally true of aorist indicatives). They rather refer it to action that is about to begin by calling it either an ingressive aorist,[33] a dramatic aorist,[34] or proleptic aorist.[35] They then theorize that the seventh seal in Revelation 8:1 begins the day of the Lord with the initiation of his wrath either at his second coming (posttribulationalism) or at a time shortly before his second coming (pre-wrath rapturism). These two systems depend heavily on identifying that aorist verb in one of those three ways rather than calling it a constative aorist, which summarizes events that have taken place in the past.

All three alternatives rule themselves out, however. The ingressive aorist would indicate that the wrath of God begins with the sixth seal, contrary to the theories of both systems. The dramatic aorist would have the force of depicting an event that has happened just recently, that is, the wrath has come *just now*.[36] Another grammarian says the dramatic aorist states "a present reality with the certitude of a past event."[37] Either meaning would stifle both the posttribulational and the prewrath views. Besides this, usage of the dramatic aorist in the New Testament is relatively rare. The proleptic aorist would project the writer's perspective to a time in the future from which he is looking back on the completed wrath. That is not the meaning that the two

31. Rosenthal, *Pre-wrath Rapture*, 166, 285; also Gundry, *Church*, 29–37.

32. Van Kampen, *Sign*, 274–78; Gundry, *Church*, 29–43.

33. Van Kampen, *Sign*, 294–95; idem, *The Rapture Question Answered* (Grand Rapids: Revell, 1997), 153–54; Gundry, *Church*, 76.

34. Gundry, *Church*, 76; Rosenthal, *Pre-wrath Rapture*, 165.

35. Van Kampen, *Sign*, 295, citing Paul Feinberg, *The Rapture: Pre-, Mid-, or Post-Tribulational* (Grand Rapids: Zondervan, 1984), 59.

36. Daniel B. Wallace comments regarding the dramatic aorist, "The aorist indicative can be used of an event that happened rather recently. Its force can usually be brought out with something like *just now*, as in *just now I told you*" (*Greek Grammar beyond the Basics*, 564).

37. H. E. Dana and Julius R. Mantey, *A Manual Grammar of the Greek New Testament* (n.p.: Macmillan, 1955), 198.

views under discussion are seeking either. In 6:17 they want a wrath beginning with the seventh seal, not a summarization of the whole package of wrath. Besides this, proleptic aorists in Revelation characterize the words that originate with heavenly singers or voices, not words from other sources.[38]

A burning question persists for those who want to begin the wrath of God with the seventh seal: How can an unbelieving world whose cries are recorded in Revelation 6:16–17 know that the wrath of God is about to fall on them at the time represented by the sixth seal? The day of God's wrath will catch them by surprise, as a thief catches his victims at night (Rev. 3:3; 16:15; cf. 1 Thess. 5:2–3). The wrath to which these earth-dwellers refer must be something that has already begun, and now for the first time they recognize it while experiencing the afflictions of the sixth seal.

To sustain the position that the wrath of God does not begin until the seventh seal judgment, the pre-wrath rapturist must adopt two key teachings: (1) He or she must dispense with the doctrine of Christ's imminent return and be satisfied with substituting expectancy of Daniel's seventieth week, but not of an imminent return of Christ.[39] (2) He or she must define the day of the Lord as God's climactic judgment, excluding the period of the seals.[40] He or she holds these two distinctives in common with posttribulational rapturists.[41]

In response to the first tenet, one may note Christ's coming to inflict wrath is simultaneous with his coming to deliver the faithful (Rev. 3:10–11). In response to the second is the clear word of Isaiah 2:17–21 and other Old Testament prophecies that events of the first six seals are part of the day of the Lord. Those events cannot coincide with the personal return of Christ in judgment because at that time men and women will not have opportunity to hide in the caves. The cosmic upheavals of the sixth seal are preliminary to the cosmic upheavals Jesus spoke of as coming after the tribulation of those days (Matt. 24:29).

Dispensing with the Imminence of Christ's Return

About imminence Gundry writes: "*By common consent imminence means that so far as we know no predicted event will necessarily precede the coming of Christ.*"[42] He continues, "The concept [of imminence] incorporates three essential ele-

---

38. The proposed supporting usages of *ēlthen* as the dramatic aorist in Mark 14:41 and the proleptic aorist in Rev. 19:7 (Rosenthal, *Pre-wrath Rapture*, 165–66) come from different contexts. In Mark 14:41 "the hour has come" means that the period of crucifixion, not the very moment of crucifixion that was yet to come, had already arrived. In Rev. 19:7 the aorist is proleptic as is often the case with heavenly singing in Revelation. Revelation 6:17 is not heavenly singing, however.

39. Van Kampen, *Sign*, 276–77.

40. Rosenthal, *Pre-wrath Rapture*, 117–34.

41. E.g., Gundry, *Church*, 29–43, 89–99.

42. Ibid., 29 (emphasis added). By including only the italicized words, one has a more accurate definition of imminence.

ments: suddenness, unexpectedness or incalculability, and a possibility of occurrence at any moment. . . . Imminence would only raise the possibility of pretribulationism on a sliding scale with mid- and posttribulationism."[43] Carson writes regarding imminence, " '[T]he imminent return of Christ' then means Christ may return at any time. But the evangelical writers who use the word divide on whether 'imminent' in the sense of 'at any time' should be pressed to mean 'at any second' or something looser such as 'at any period' or 'in any generation.' "[44]

Trying to understand what representatives of this "not imminent but imminent" group mean by imminence or expectation is extremely difficult. Carson says, "Yet the terms 'imminent' and 'imminency' retain theological usefulness if they focus attention on the eager expectancy of the Lord's return characteristic of many NT passages, a return that could take place soon, i.e., within a fairly brief period of time, without specifying that the period must be one second or less."[45] Erickson puts it this way: "It is one thing to say we do not know when an event will occur; it is another thing to say that we know of no times when it will not occur. If on a time scale we have points 1 to 1,000, we may know that Christ will not come at points 46 and 79, but not know at just what point He will come. The instructions about watchfulness do not mean that Christ may come at any time."[46] Erickson's reasoning is difficult to follow here. Witherington's wording is different: "In short, one cannot conclude that 1 Thessalonians 4:15 clearly means that Paul thought the Lord would definitely return during his lifetime. Possible imminence had to be conjured with, but certain imminence is not affirmed here."[47] From a practical standpoint, possible imminence is tantamount to certain imminence. Witherington's distinction is hard to grasp. Beker clarifies Paul's attitude more accurately:

> Thus delay of the parousia is not a theological concern for Paul. It is not an embarrassment for him; it does not compel him to shift the center of his attention from apocalyptic imminence to a form of "realized eschatology," that is to a conviction of the full presence of the kingdom of God in our present history. It is of the essence of his faith in Christ that adjustments in his expectations can occur without a surrender of these expectations (1 Thess. 4:13–18; 1 Cor. 15:15–51; 2 Cor.

43. Ibid.

44. D. A. Carson, "Matthew," in *The Expositor's Bible Commentary*, ed. Frank E. Gaebelein (Grand Rapids: Zondervan, 1984), 490.

45. Ibid. Carson's reference to "one second or less" vividly recalls 1 Cor. 15:52, where Paul prophesies that Christ's coming will be "in a moment [or flash], in the twinkling of an eye."

46. Millard J. Erickson, *A Basic Guide to Eschatology*, 181.

47. Ben Witherington III, "Transcending Imminence: The Gordian Knot of Pauline Eschatology," in *Eschatology in the Bible and Theology* (Downers Grove, Ill.: InterVarsity, 1997), 174.

5:1–10; Phil. 2:21–24). Indeed, the hope in God's imminent rule through Christ remains the constant in his letters from beginning to end. . . . [48]

All these "nonimminence" scholars must mean imminent within a limited period of time, because all would agree that events of the tribulation period will be recognizable. If that is their meaning, Christ's warnings to watch for his coming are meaningless until that future period arrives. And even then, imminence cannot have its full impact because his coming will not be totally unexpected. It will have specified events to signal at least approximately, if not exactly, how far away it is.

Saying the New Testament teaching of imminence has become garbled in the systems of pre-wrath rapturism and posttribulationism is probably not an overstatement. According to different advocates, it may mean at any moment within the last half of the seventieth week, at any moment after the seventieth week, at any time rather than any moment, at an unexpected moment with some exceptions, possibly at any moment but not certainly at any moment, or as many other meanings as there are other advocates.

In the midst of their dilemma, pre-wrathers and post-tribs have to talk around the plain meaning of Christ's words in Matthew 24:36 just as the preterists do. In that comment, that is, Jesus' words about no person knowing the day or the hour, Gundry says of those in the tribulation that they will not be able to count seven years from the beginning or three and a half years from "the abomination of desolation," because Jesus says the days will be shortened in Matthew 24:21–22.[49] He allows that they will know the general time period, but not the exact time. According to his theory, the watchfulness urged by Jesus applies only to saints in the tribulation who will be able to set an approximate date for the Lord's return. That is the same type of date-setting engaged in by the preterists and the type so strongly criticized in recent years. To do justice to Jesus' words in Matthew 24:36, one must acknowledge that he meant that no one would know even the general time period.

That is confirmed in Jesus' statement to the disciples in Acts 1:7: "It is not for you to know the times or the seasons which the Father has fixed by his own authority" (RSV). Gundry responds to the Acts 1:7 statement by claiming that Jesus is brushing aside the question of his disciples in order to emphasize to the disciples that they should evangelize all peoples of the world (Acts 1:8) and not be thinking about the future kingdom.[50] That, however, attributes wrong interpersonal techniques to the Lord. When asked questions, he answered them forthrightly. He did not for unspoken reasons shuttle them aside by changing the subject. Acts 1:7 was another way he had of stating that no man knows the day or hour of his return.

48. J. Christiaan Beker, *Paul's Apocalyptic Gospel* (Philadelphia: Fortress, 1982), 49.
49. Gundry, *First the Antichrist*, 26–27.
50. Ibid., 32.

The Restricting of the Day of the Lord

Gundry goes to great lengths to demonstrate that the day of the Lord does not include the tribulation period.[51] Rosenthal and Van Kampen do the same.[52] Both systems restrict the day to a relatively brief period of God's judgment against the world at the end of the tribulation. To restrict the day in this manner and place it at the end of the seventieth week is impossible, however. The day could not in that case come as a thief as both Paul and Peter say it will (1 Thess. 5:2; 2 Peter 3:10). That definition and placement of the day would leave it with easily recognizable signs to precede it, thus removing it from the "complete surprise" category of an unexpected burglar.

Furthermore, Isaiah 2:17–21 makes clear that at least the sixth seal is part of the day of the Lord. A good case exists for paralleling earlier seals with known day-of-the-Lord events. So on these grounds too, that the seventh seal is the beginning of the day of the Lord is improbable.

A passage that always enters the discussion at this point is 2 Thessalonians 2:1–3, where some have supposed that Paul names recognizable events that will precede the day of the Lord. In fact, Robert Gundry apparently looks to this passage for the title of his recent book, *First the Antichrist: Why Christ Won't Come before the Antichrist Does*.[53] That view is oblivious to what the passage teaches, being based on the way most English translations have rendered 2 Thessalonians 2:3. Three features related to the verse deserve emphasis.

(1) In the verse just before (2 Thess. 2:2) the verb *enestēken* is present in meaning even though its form is perfect tense. It combines the prepositional prefix *en* with the frequent verb *histēmi*, which in all of its New Testament usages in the perfect tense is intransitive and intensive in emphasizing existing results.[54] That the perfect tense of *enistēmi* means "is present" cannot seriously be doubted in light of its usage elsewhere in the New Testament (Rom. 8:38; 1 Cor. 3:22; 7:26; Gal. 1:4; Heb. 9:9).[55] Recognition of this fact indicates that the false information among the Thessalonians that Paul was

---

51. Gundry, *Church*, 89–93.

52. Rosenthal, *Pre-wrath Rapture*, 115–61; Van Kampen, *Sign*, 348–52.

53. Gundry writes, "Paul says not only that 'the Day of the Lord' won't arrive unless that evil figure 'is revealed' but also that 'the rebellion' which he will lead against all divinity except his own (claimed falsely, of course) 'comes first' (2 Thess. 2:1–4)" (20). See also Erickson, *Basic Guide to Eschatology*, 175.

54. A. T. Robertson, *A Grammar of the Greek New Testament in the Light of Historical Research* (Nashville: Broadman, 1934), 881; G. Abbott-Smith, *A Manual Greek Lexicon of the New Testament* (Edinburgh: T. & T. Clark, 1937), 219; James Hope Moulton, *A Grammar of New Testament Greek*, 3d ed., vol. 1, *Prolegomena* (Edinburgh: T. & T. Clark, 1908), 147–48; Wallace, *Greek Grammar beyond the Basics*, 579–80.

55. F. F. Bruce, *1 & 2 Thessalonians*, Word Biblical Commentary (Dallas: Word, 1982), 165; D. Michael Martin, *1, 2 Thessalonians*, New American Commentary (Nashville: Broadman & Holman, 1995), 227–28.

combating was the teaching that "the day of the Lord is present," not that it "has already come" (ICB, NIV) or that it "is at hand" (KJV) nor that it "is just at hand" (ASV) or that it "has come" (NASB, NASBU, RSV) or that it "had come" (NKJV). I have found only three versions that render the verb correctly. Darby renders, "the day of the Lord is present"; Weymouth has, "the day of the Lord is now here"; and the NRSV gives, "the day of the Lord is already here." Either of these captures the intensive force of the perfect tense of *enestēken*.

The day of the Lord is a complex idea, including a number of events as evidenced from various passages of Scripture that refer to it.[56] Because of the increased severity of their persecutions, some were trying to convince the Thessalonians that they were already in that period of woes, a part of the day of the Lord, that will precede the personal return of the Messiah.

(2) The second feature of 2 Thessalonians 2:3 to notice is the suppressed apodosis that must be supplied with the conditional clause begun by *ean*. Clearly the apodosis to be supplied comes from the end of verse 2. Translations that have missed the sense of the end of verse 2 supply the wrong apodosis: "that day shall not come" (KJV); "it will not be" (ASV); "That day of the Lord will not come" (ICB); "it will not come" (NASB, NASBU); "that day will not come" (RSV, NIV); "that Day will not come" (NKJV). But even the three versions that render 2:2 correctly supply the wrong apodosis: "that day cannot come" (Weymouth); " that day will not come" (NRSV); "it will not be" (Darby). Some versions indicate the absence of an explicit apodosis, but others do not.

To be faithful to the context, the understood apodosis should be "the day of the Lord is not present."[57] Complying with the context in this manner yields grammatical criteria for labeling the last half of verse 3 as a present general condition. Most clauses with *ean* and the subjunctive in the New Testament are more probable future conditions, but when the verb of the apodosis has the force of a present indicative, that makes it a present general condition. Such a construction often expresses a maxim,[58] a generic condition in the present time.[59] It expresses a principle or a proverb.[60] In such cases the protasis makes an assumption in the present time, and the apodosis gives a conclusion in the form of a general rule.[61] Therefore, the sense of Paul's statement in verse 3b is as follows: "If the apostasy does not come first and the man of lawlessness

56. Leon Morris, *The First and Second Epistles to the Thessalonians*, ed. Gordon D. Fee, rev. ed. (Grand Rapids: Eerdmans, 1992), 216.

57. R. L. Thomas, "A Hermeneutical Ambiguity of Eschatology: The Analogy of Faith," *JETS* 23 (March 1980): 51–52; cf. G. Lunemann, *The Epistles to the Thessalonians*, Commentary on the New Testament, ed. H. A. W. Meyer (Edinburgh: T. & T. Clark, 1880), 208.

58. Robertson, *Grammar*, 1019.

59. Wallace, *Greek Grammar*, 696–97.

60. Ibid., 698.

61. Hardy Hansen and Gerald M. Quinn, *Greek: An Intensive Course* (New York: Fordham University Press, 1992), 1:95.

is not revealed, the day of the Lord is not present. That is a proverbial truth you can count on."

(3) The third feature of 2:3 relates to the adverb *prōton* ("first") in the first half of the protasis. Two possible meanings present themselves. It can mean that the day of the Lord is not present before the coming of the apostasy and the revelation of the man of lawlessness, or it can mean that within the day of the Lord the apostasy will come first, followed by the revelation of the man of lawlessness.[62] Stated another way, does the "first" compare to the apodosis or does it compare to the last half of the protasis?

A close parallel to this set of criteria occurs in John 7:51, where there is (1) present action in the apodosis, (2) a compound protasis introduced by *ean mē* with the action of both verbs included in the action of the apodosis, and (3) *prōton* in the former member of the compound protasis. John 7:51 reads thus: "Our Law does not judge the man unless it first hears from him and knows what he is doing, does it?" (NASB). The judicial process (present indicative of *krinei*) is not carried out without two parts: hearing from the defendant first, and gaining a knowledge of what he or she is doing. Clearly in this instance, hearing from the defendant does not precede the judicial process; it is part of it. But it does precede a knowledge of what the person does. Here the *prōton* indicates the first half of the compound protasis is prior to the last half.

Another verse relevant to this set of criteria is Mark 3:27: "No one can enter the strong man's house and plunder his property unless he first binds the strong man, and then he will plunder his house" (NASB). Here the apodosis is present indicative followed by *ean mē* and a compound apodosis. Because of the *tote* in the last half of the protasis, the *prōton* clearly evidences the priority of the first half of the protasis over the last half, that is, the binding of the strong man prior to the plundering of his house. It does not indicate that the whole protasis is prior to the apodosis, that is, the binding of the strong man and the plundering of his house prior to entering the house. In other words, it indicates that the binding precedes the plundering, but not the entering, and the entering includes both the binding and the plundering.

Application of these data to 2 Thessalonians 2:3 results in the following: "The day of the Lord is not present unless first in sequence within that day the apostasy comes, and following the apostasy's beginning, the revealing of the man of lawlessness occurs." Rather than the two events preceding the day of the Lord, as has so often been suggested, these are happenings that comprise conspicuous stages of that day after it has begun. By observing the nonoccur-

---

62. Martin (*1, 2 Thessalonians*, 232) notes, "Its [i.e., the adverb *prōton*] placement in the sentence slightly favors the understanding that the apostasy comes 'first' and then the lawless one is revealed," and goes on to say the adverb could indicate that the arrival of apostasy and the revelation of the man of lawlessness before the day of the Lord.

rence of these, the Thessalonian readers could rest assured that the day whose leading events will be so characterized had not yet begun.

This meaning of 2 Thessalonians 2:3 frees Paul from the accusation of contradicting himself. In 1 Thessalonians 5:2 he wrote that the day of the Lord will come as a thief. If that day has precursors, as 2 Thessalonians 2:3 is often alleged to teach, it could hardly come as a thief. Thieves come without advance notice. Neither does the day of the Lord have any prior signals before it arrives.[63] Paul does not contradict that meaning in 2 Thessalonians 2:3.

We have seen now how the preterists and the non-imminent adventists dispense with the New Testament emphasis on imminence, by sidestepping Jesus' clear teaching in Matthew 24:36. They limit the period of imminence to either the forty years between A.D. 30 and A.D. 70 or to the seven years of future tribulation. Those limitations are untenable, however, because Jesus placed no such limitations. Specifically, the comparison of his coming to that of a thief (Matt. 24:43–44) allows for no such time restrictions. Thieves do not give notice of a block of time in advance of their burglarizing visits. Had Jesus intended to designate a specific date within a certain period for his return, he would not have chosen an illustration that covers not only a specific date but also a broader period such as the centuries that have elapsed since he spoke the words.

Preterist-Idealist-Imminent Advent View

One final eschatological scheme of recent vintage is that of progressive dispensationalism (PD), a system that attempts to combine preterism, idealism, and imminence into itself. It approaches the Book of Revelation from an eclectic perspective.[64] Combining three such divergent approaches to the book inevitably creates a complex mixture of hermeneutical principles.

Such an explanation violates grammatical-historical rules of interpretation in several respects:

(1) It neglects the principle of limiting each passage to a single interpretation. Years ago Terry wrote, "A fundamental principle in grammatico-historical exposition is that the words and sentences can have but one significance in one and the same connection. The moment we neglect this principle we drift out upon a sea of uncertainty and conjecture."[65] More recently, Ramm has written, "But here we must remember the old adage: 'Interpretation is

---

63. To this effect J. Christiaan Beker writes, "Paul emphasizes the unexpected, the suddenness and surprising character of the final theophany (1 Thess. 5:2–10)" (*Paul's Apocalyptic Gospel*, 48).

64. C. Marvin Pate, "A Progressive Dispensationist View of Revelation," in *Four Views on the Book of Revelation*, ed. C. Marvin Pate (Grand Rapids: Zondervan, 1998), 146.

65. Milton Terry, *Biblical Hermeneutics*, 2d ed. (reprint; Grand Rapids: Zondervan, n.d.), 205.

one, application is many.' This means that there is only one meaning to a passage of Scripture which is determined by careful study."[66] Summit II of the International Council on Biblical Inerrancy concurred with this principle: "We affirm that the meaning expressed in each biblical text is single, definite and fixed. We deny that the recognition of this single meaning eliminates the variety of its application."[67]

An example of PD's compounding of meanings for a single passage comes from Revelation 3:21, where Christ promises the overcomer the privilege of sitting with him in his throne as he overcame and sits with the Father in his throne. The PDs would have Christ occupying David's throne in the present while he is in heaven and also in the future when he returns to earth. The throne, they say, is both identical with the Father's throne in heaven and distinct from it as an earthly throne.[68]

A further illustration of this hermeneutical diversity comes from PD's handling of Babylon in Revelation 17–18. Proponents of this system contend that Babylon stands for both Rome and a rebuilt Babylon, plus any city in "the sweep of history."[69] They join the idealist in this explanation of Babylon. They also match the preterists in identifying Babylon as Jerusalem of the past.[70] Such conclusions run roughshod over rational principles of hermeneutics.

(2) PD neglects the principle of *tabula rasa* ("clean slate") interpretation. It not only allows but also encourages the incorporation of the interpreter's preunderstanding as the first step in the interpretive process.[71] Pate exemplifies the violation of this principle in his preunderstanding of an "already/not yet" key to interpreting Revelation.[72]

That approach to the interpretive process runs counter to what traditional grammatical-historical principles dictate. Terry describes the latter thus:

> In the systematic presentation . . . of any scriptural doctrine, we are always to make a discriminating use of sound hermeneutical principles. We must not study them in the light of modern systems of divinity, but should aim rather to place ourselves in the position of the sacred writers, and study to obtain the impression their words would have made upon the minds of the first readers. . . . Still less should we allow ourselves to be influenced by any pre-

66. Bernard Ramm, *Protestant Biblical Interpretation: A Textbook on Hermeneutics*, 3d ed. (Grand Rapids: Baker, 1970), 113.
67. Article VII, "Articles of Affirmation and Denial," adopted by the International Council on Biblical Inerrancy, November 10–13, 1982.
68. Pate, "Progressive Dispensationalist View," 138, 170.
69. Craig Blaising and Darrell Bock, *Progressive Dispensationalism* (Wheaton, Ill.: Victor, 1993), 93–96.
70. Pate, "Progressive Dispensationalist View," 153–56, 160–61.
71. Blaising and Bock, *Progressive Dispensationalism*, 35–36.
72. Pate, "Progressive Dispensationalist View," 135–36.

sumptions of what the Scriptures *ought* to teach. . . . All such presumptions are uncalled for and prejudicial.[73]

Ramm expressed the same principle this way:

It is very difficult for any person to approach the Holy Scriptures free from prejudices and assumptions which distort the text. The danger of having a set theological system is that in the interpretation of Scripture the system tends to govern the interpretation rather than the interpretation correcting the system. . . . Calvin said that the Holy Scripture is not a tennis ball that we may bounce around at will. Rather it is the Word of God whose teachings must be learned by the most impartial and objective study of the text.[74]

Pate's assumption of an "already/not yet" key for interpreting Revelation clearly violates the *tabula rasa* principle in grammatical-historical hermeneutics.

(3) PD neglects the principle of rationality. It understands some of the prophecies in Revelation to be predicting *past* events, a scheme that defies logic.

The aspect of assigning a date to the book is relevant here. Pate assigns two dates, that preferred by the preterists during the reign of Nero from 54 to 68, and the date traditionally preferred during the reign of Domitian between 81 and 96.[75] That double-dating of the book's composition in itself defies rationality, but even worse is the system's handling of prophetic portions.

Regardless of which date PD assigns, PD understands a fulfillment of prophetic events that occurred before the book's writing. Examples are numerous. Even if written in the sixties, fulfillment of the second seal judgment of Revelation 6:3–4 between A.D. 41 and 54[76] looks back to a time prior to the prophecy. The same is true regarding the claim of fulfillment of the third seal (Rev. 6:5–6) in A.D. 42, 45–46, 49, and 51.[77] The same applies to the suggestion that the fifth seal (Rev. 6:9–11) found fulfillment in the persecutions described in Acts 4:1–12; 6:8–7:60; 8:1–4; 12:1–2; 16:22–30; 21:27–23:35.[78] All these alleged fulfillments predate even the earlier time for the writing of the book.

---

73. Terry, *Biblical Hermeneutics*, 595.

74. Ramm, *Protestant Biblical Interpretation*, 115–16. Ramm also quotes Luther to emphasize this point: "The best teacher is the one who does not bring his meaning into the Scripture but gets his meaning from Scripture" (ibid., 115, citing F. W. Farrar, *History of Interpretation*, 475).

75. Pate, introduction to *Four Views on the Book of Revelation* (Grand Rapids: Zondervan, 1998), 14.

76. Pate, "Progressive Dispensationalist View," 151.

77. Cf. ibid., 152–53.

78. Cf. ibid., 154–55.

That type of irrationality directly violates the insistence on reasonableness by the grammatical-historical method of interpretation. According to Terry, the method rests on the foundation of the rational nature of humans.[79] He adds, "The use of reason in the interpretation of Scripture is everywhere to be assumed. The Bible comes to us in the forms of human language, and appeals to our reason and judgment. . . ."[80] PD's handling of Revelation's prophecies is woefully insulting to human reason.

The absence of rationality in PD's interpretations and its other hermeneutical shorcomings are conspicuous, but the point at issue in the present discussion is what that has to do with the imminence of Christ's return. It may not eliminate that teaching completely, but it substantially weakens it. The following remarks illustrate this weakening.

Robert Saucy has written:

While most dispensationalists probably hold to a pretribulation rapture of the church as being in certain respects more harmonious with dispensationalism in general, many would not desire to make this a determining touchstone of dispensationalism today. For these the broad dispensational interpretation of biblical history does not ultimately stand or fall on the time of the rapture.[81]

In softening his position regarding the pretribulation rapture of the church, Saucy makes no allowance for how alternative positions alter the New Testament teaching regarding the imminence of Christ's return.

Blaising and Bock are equally soft in advocating a pretribulation rapture: "This deliverance, or rapture, *would appear to* coincide with the inception or coming of the Day of the Lord, since that is the focus in 1 Thess. 5:2–4."[82] Neither do they pursue the matter further to discuss how other positions would affect the teaching of Jesus' imminent return.

This change in perspective has been sufficient to attract the attention of at least one nondispensational scholar. Elwell notes what a remarkable change this amounts to for dispensational scholars, that they would "only say the Rapture 'would appear to be pretribulational.'"[83]

So PDs have not fully dispensed with the doctrine of imminence, but they have tempered the teaching through their suspect hermeneutics and their

79. Terry, *Biblical Hermeneutics*, 173–74.
80. Ibid., 153.
81. Robert L. Saucy, *The Case for Progressive Dispensationalism* (Grand Rapids: Zondervan, 1993), 8–9.
82. Blaising and Bock, *Progressive Dispensationalism*, 264; cf. also 317 n. 15 (emphasis added).
83. Walter A. Elwell, "Dispensationalists of the Third Kind," *Christianity Today* 38, no. 10 (12 September 1994): 28.

highlighting of a continuity from Israel to the church. That tempering of continuity brings Blaising to the point of contending that the church will be in the tribulation, even though it will be raptured before the tribulation.[84] Though professing to uphold a distinction between Israel and the church, PDs have difficulty in maintaining that distinction consistently.

What Is Left of Imminence?

The doctrine of imminence has fallen on hard times in contemporary evangelicalism. Preterism has relegated imminence to a thirty- to forty-year span in the first century A.D. Pre-wrath rapturism and posttribulationism have limited it to a period of seven years or less in the future. Progressive dispensationalism has weakened it to the point of "we can do without it if we have to."

The imminence of Christ's return, including his coming to deliver the faithful and his coming to begin inflicting wrath of the rest of the world, is the repeated teaching of the Apocalypse as well as the rest of the New Testament. No prophecy of Scripture remains to be fulfilled before either of these events occurs. The church needs to be watching so as not to be lulled into lethargy by thinking some other predicted event will signal the approach of his return. It may come at any moment in any hour, day, week, month, year, decade, and century. Only with this attitude can the church have the right motivation for repentance, holy living, and zealous activity. Beker uses Paul to portray the balance between anticipating the imminent coming of Christ and remaining busy in reaching the world with the gospel:

> For how is it possible for Paul to be engaged in two seemingly opposite activities? How can he simultaneously long for the future reign of God and yet be occupied with missionary strategy for the long run? How do this impatience and this patience cohere in his life? . . . Passion and sobriety go hand in hand in Paul's life because the necessity of the imminent end is directly related to its incalculability. This gives Paul the freedom to be committed simultaneously to the imminence of the end and to the contingencies of historical circumstance. He . . . is able to allow God the freedom to choose the moment of his final glorious theophany, whereas he strains in the meantime to move God's world into the direction of its appointed future destiny.[85]

That is the attitude that Scripture prescribes for all Christians.

---

84. Craig A. Blaising, "Premillennialism," in *Three Views on the Millennium and Beyond,* ed. Darrell L. Bock (Grand Rapids: Zondervan, 1999), 209–10 n. 74.
85. Beker, *Paul's Apocalyptic Gospel,* 51–52.

13

Incarnational Explanation for Jesus' Subjection in the Eschaton

GARY W. DERICKSON

Western Baptist College

A renewed interest in the doctrine of the Trinity has arisen within orthodox Christianity in recent years, especially as it has impacted the issues of equality and subordinationism within the body of Christ, specifically with regard to evangelical feminism or egalitarianism. One issue that seems to be critical to the debate concerns the nature of Jesus' subordination along with its extent in time. This article shall address the issue by examining the affirmations of three key passages of Scripture as they impact the two issues mentioned above.[1]

To begin with, Paul clearly teaches in 1 Corinthians 15:24–28 that at the end of time, when all things, including death, have been subjected to Christ, that he, in turn, will be subjected to the Father "that God may be all in all." This, along with other statements of Jesus' relationship of obedience to the Father, led to the doctrine of his subordination, with the problem of his equality naturally arising. The church's response through the centuries, and today, has been to affirm the eternal existence of God the Son whose essence is identical to that of God the Father and God the Holy Spirit. Bauman provides an excellent summation of the doctrine of Jesus' subordination as the church's "effort to understand the hierarchical differentiation that exists within the God-

---

1. It is not the purpose of this article to address any particular feminist or non-feminist theologian or issue, but, rather, to examine passages related to the issue of Jesus' submission to the Father.

head," which is conceived "primarily in the sense of administration within the Trinity," with each person sharing an identical essence while voluntarily relating to one another differently.[2] But this summary fails to do justice to the variation within orthodox and evangelical Christianity that presently exists. In answering problems raised by the doctrine, the church has not responded with a unified voice even among those viewed as orthodox.[3] This has been evident in recent years within the Evangelical Theological Society, as reflected in the article by John Dahms that elicited a response from Gilbert Bilezikian, and most recently by Kovach and Schemm.[4]

Evangelical Views

A review of evangelical theological works reveals a variety of views on Jesus' relationship to the Father as a coequal person within the Trinity, past, present, and future.[5] Generally, systematic theologies do not address the issue of Jesus' subordination to the Father in much other than a cursory manner, if at all. The basic approach of these theologians has been to affirm the essential equality of the Godhead and some form of economic or functional hierarchy, either eternally existing or existing for a season, such as during Jesus' two messianic ministries and his present role in heaven as High Priest.

One of the best treatments comes from Charles Hodge, who sees the Son and Spirit subordinate to the Father only regarding their "mode of subsistence and operation," without implying inferiority or posteriority on the basis of their shared essence.[6] Berkhof affirms eternal subordination, with different roles being played within the "economic Trinity."[7]

Grudem represents recent developments in evangelical theology as we enter a new millennium. In his systematic theology he rejects both Arianism and what he terms subordinationism on the basis of God the Son's shared nature with God the Father. His definition of subordinationism, which he rejects, is "that the Son was eternal (not created) and divine, but still not equal to the Father in being or attributes—the Son was inferior or 'subordinate' in being

2. M. E. Bauman, "Milton, Subordinationism, and the Two-Stage Logos," *WTJ* 48 (1986): 177–78.

3. This issue becomes more significant in light of the recurrence of Arianism in various cults today, such as the Jehovah's Witnesses, The Way International, and the Christadelphians, who deny both Jesus' deity and eternality. Arius taught that only the Father is God, Jesus was created by him, and the Holy Spirit is impersonal.

4. J. V. Dahms, "The Subordination of the Son," *JETS* 37 (1994): 351–64; G. Bilezikian, "Hermeneutical Bungee-Jumping: Subordination in the Godhead," *JETS* 40 (1997): 57–68; and S. D. Kovach and P. R. Schemm Jr., "A Defense of the Doctrine of the Eternal Subordination of the Son," *JETS* 42 (1999): 461–76.

5. Those discussed below are not exhaustive of evangelical works.

6. Charles Hodge, *Systematic Theology* (Grand Rapids: Eerdmans, n.d.), 1:460–61.

7. Louis Berkhof, *Systematic Theology* (Grand Rapids: Eerdmans, 1939, 1941), 95.

to God the Father."[8] Yet he affirms functional differences within the God-head, with 1 Corinthians 11:3 "indicating a distinction in role in which primary authority and leadership among the persons of the Trinity has always been and will always be the possession of the Father."[9] Thus he appears to want to affirm eternal equality while denying it.[10]

Dahms seems to agree with Grudem when he argues for eternal subordination of the Son to the Father. He addresses the more classic, functional/economic formulation and rejects the separation of "Christ's being from his work," though, arguing that "Paul speaks of the subjection of the Son, not merely the subjection of the work or office of the Son."[11] His argument flows from the doctrine of the eternal generation of the Son.[12] He says that "if there is not essential subordination of the Son" Jesus would be "misrepresenting deity" when he "speaks of the Father as 'my God'" in John 20:17 as well as when he "speaks of being sent by the Father," and when he "prays to the Father."[13] In anticipation of objections to his view, he also asserts that "eternal subordination need not imply an Arian view of the Son of God."[14] This is certainly a necessary caveat.

In response to Dahms and Grudem, Bilezikian rejects the idea of eternal subordination but, rather, affirms that subordination within the Trinity did not precede the incarnation. Further, Jesus' subordination will end once he completes his work and delivers the kingdom over to God the Father. His reasoning is that since "there was no order of subordination within the Trinity prior to the Second Person's incarnation, there will remain no such thing after its completion."[15] He says further that "both God the Father and God the Son occupy the same throne for eternity" and they will be "equal in power and glory."[16] The philosophical-theological basis for his conclusion, contra Dahms, is that "since the attribute of eternity inheres in the divine essence,

---

8. Wayne Grudem, *Systematic Theology* (Grand Rapids: Zondervan, 1994), 245.

9. Wayne Grudem, *Recovering Biblical Manhood and Womanhood* (Wheaton, Ill.: Crossway, 1991), 457.

10. It seems that Grudem's view on Jesus' eternal functional subordination and eternal distinction in roles in the Godhead is closely tied to his view on the role of women in the church. This being recognized, it in no way lessens the importance of his position, nor weakens his other arguments in the present debate.

11. Dahms, "The Subordination of the Son," 353.

12. Ibid., 363.

13. Ibid., 364. Jesus' affirmation must be understood in light of his relationship to the Father as a result of his humanity rather than his deity.

14. Ibid., 363.

15. Bilezikian, "Hermeneutical Bungee-Jumping," 60.

16. Ibid., 63. His view should then interpret the last phrase of 1 Cor. 15:28 to mean a cessation of Jesus' temporary subordination and a return to the status of full equality in power and glory and no aspect of his being or activity reflecting a subordinate role or relationship ever again.

any reality that is eternal is by necessity ontologically grounded. Eternity is a quality of existence. Therefore if Christ's subordination is eternal . . . it is also ontological."[17] With him Erickson concurs, viewing Jesus' subordination as a temporary state taken to accomplish a specific task. He says, "Each of the three persons of the Trinity has had, for a period of time, a particular function unique to himself. This is to be understood as a temporary role for the purpose of accomplishing a given end, not a change in his status or essence."[18] He describes Jesus' earthly obedience to the Father in terms of his "functional subordination during the incarnation."[19]

Kovach and Schemm object to Erickson's view, classifying it as a "modern" development, and therefore suspect.[20] They assert that "there are at least two main categories that affirm eternal subordination: the Son's relation to the Father and the Son's role on behalf of the Father."[21] While the Son's subordination is voluntary, it is economic and eternal because of the eternal nature of both his mission and function.[22] They correctly caution that "the idea of subordination does not necessarily entail inferiority. As applied to the Trinity, the term subordination does not always amount to a heretical distinction of worth and dignity between the Father and the Son."[23] But, the idea that "God the Father planned the sending of his only begotten Son (John 3:16, 17) from eternity because he was eternally the Son" in a subordinate sense is a leap of logic, not an affirmation of Scripture.[24] An *eternal plan* is very different from an *eternal existence*. Though the incarnation was planned from eternity past, and thus the role and title of "Son" applied to the One we know as the Second Person of the Godhead, it does not follow that Jesus was eternally incarnate. In the same way, the decision of the Godhead to have one member, God the Son, take a subordinate role in his incarnation need not require that he already had a subordinate role within the Godhead from eternity past. That is a theological deduction, a construct, not a direct or indirect affirmation of Scripture. The problem raised by this construct can be illustrated from Kovach and Schemm's handling of Hebrews 5:8:

> While it is true that he learned obedience, it was in the context of his earthly life that he had never before experienced. With respect to his human nature, he had to learn obedience to God in the conditions of human life on earth. While the Son had an eternal role as the agent of God, he had never experienced human

17. Ibid., 64.
18. Millard Erickson, *Christian Theology* (Grand Rapids: Baker, 1989), 338.
19. Ibid., 698.
20. Kovach and Schemm, "A Defense of the Doctrine," 470.
21. Ibid., 462.
22. Ibid., 463.
23. Ibid., 464.
24. Ibid., 471.

nature until he came to earth. In this new experience, not in a changed eternal position, the Son learned obedience.[25]

Thus, they see Jesus learning obedience in only one of his two natures, the human one. But, though Jesus has two natures, he remains eternally one person and acts as a single person, not two. Jesus is not bipolar in his person. This explanation of Hebrews 5:8 fails to acknowledge what the author of Hebrews clearly asserts: that it was *the begotten Son* learning obedience "in the days of his flesh." It is not just the human side of his being, since the divine side had already known obedience prior to the days of his flesh. In Jesus' one person, his one consciousness, his one will, both natures act simultaneously and without conflict. Further, the passage where this statement occurs has the time period of incarnation in view, not eternity past or future. It makes better sense to say that if Jesus was not subordinate prior to his incarnation, he would have learned obedience in all of his person, both divine and human natures being represented, not just his human one.

Each of these theologians, in attempting to understand key biblical passages and avoid Arianism, are correct in certain aspects of what they say. None is completely correct or completely wrong. And, if 1 Corinthians 15:28 is understood in light of a few other key passages, the view that follows will make better sense of the data, as well as exposing their errors. This verse, and the question of Jesus' subordination to the Father, must be understood in light of Jesus' own assertion in John 17 and Paul's affirmation in Philippians 2. So, to better understand Paul's statement, John 17:5 must be addressed first.

Key Passages

John 17:5

Jesus made a statement during his High Priestly prayer that cannot be ignored in this discussion. He said to his heavenly Father, of whom he had repeatedly affirmed his dependence and obedience, "And now, O Father, glorify Me together with Yourself, with the glory which I had with You before the world was."[26] In light of what God said twice in Isaiah 42:8 and 48:11, namely, "I will not give My glory to another," Jesus must have assumed his deity and equality with the Father to make such a request.[27] Otherwise, his

25. Ibid., 472.
26. John 5:30; 7:18; 8:28–29, 42, 55; 10:18; 12:49–50; 15:10 all precede Jesus' request of the Father.
27. Jesus uses the aorist active imperative of "to glorify" to request the return of his glory. In view of his subordination to the Father at this time in his ministry, we see this not as a command, but as an imperative of entreaty (R. A. Young, *Intermediate New Testament Greek* [Nashville: Broadman & Holman, 1994], 144–45).

request could only be seen as presumptuous. But, in praying this he affirmed three things. First, he shared glory with the Father in eternity past. Second, he was not sharing that glory while on earth. And third, he intended to share it again, following his crucifixion and resurrection.

His prayer has been answered. He is sharing glory with God the Father at this very moment, as Paul affirms in Philippians 2:9–11. This is confirmed in such passages as Revelation 5:13 and 7:10, where Jesus is worshipped and praised together with God the Father. Dahms is therefore correct when he says Jesus' "final relationship to the Father will not be inferior to the relationship he had with the Father in his preexistent state."[28] And, Erickson initially seems correct in his view that Jesus' subordination extends only during his earthly ministry, though he also seems to imply that his incarnation is a temporary state, rather than continuing into eternity.[29] And, Scripture affirms that Jesus has *already* begun to share the Father's glory. He is exalted already by the Father. But, and this is important to note, he still has more time to spend on earth fulfilling his human role as Messiah during his millennial reign that precedes the eternal state wherein he both will be sharing glory with *and* will be submitting to the Father.

Still, there is the problem of his subjection in 1 Corinthians 15:28 following his millennial reign and extending into eternity, which must accord with Paul's affirmations in Philippians 2.

Philippians 2:5–11

Christ's subjection in 1 Corinthians must be viewed in light of Paul's statement in Philippians 2:5–11.[30] The role Jesus' incarnation plays there can aid in making sense of how he can be subordinate to the Father while remaining eternally his true equal, never less God than he ever was but still in subordination to him without being his subordinate.

The key to understanding the incarnation's impact on Jesus' relationship to the Father is found here in Paul's affirmations, all given to illustrate Jesus' humble attitude that caused him to look out for the interests of others rather than his own interests and *rights*. First, Paul affirms that Jesus existed in the form of God prior to his incarnation, declaring that he was fully God.[31] Sec-

---

28. Dahms, "The Subordination of the Son," 352.

29. Erickson, *Christian Theology*, 338.

30. Though the context of the passage is instruction on humility, and Paul's description of Christ is presented as an illustration of the kind of humility he was calling his readers to emulate rather than an intended theological treatise on the incarnation, Paul's affirmations are, nonetheless, theologically significant. And, while recognizing that what is discussed in this paper does not lie in the realm of Paul's purpose in the passage, it is still relevant to doctrinal development since what is discussed fits in the realm of Paul's assumptions from which the illustration of Christ's humility arises.

31. E. C. Beisner, *God in Three Persons* (Wheaton, Ill.: Tyndale, 1984), 30.

ond, he affirms that Jesus willingly *took* the form of a servant, with all that entailed, including crucifixion. And, this choice was made at the time he was existing solely in the form of God. These actions occurred because Jesus "did not consider it robbery to be equal with God." That Jesus continues throughout his incarnation to remain fully God is affirmed by Paul in Colossians 2:9: "For in Him dwells all the fullness of the Godhead bodily" (NKJV). This is Paul's description of Jesus in his present state, not just during his first earthly ministry.

Critical to understanding the kenosis is the need to recognize the union of the two natures, divine and human, without their admixture nor diminishment. The self-emptying of Christ was not a loss of deity, but an addition of humanity.[32] The means of taking the form of a servant was to "make himself of no reputation." This "emptying" has to do with humbling himself, not losing himself.

Grudem correctly understands Paul's point with regard to Jesus' deity when he notes that "the context itself interprets this 'emptying' as equivalent to 'humbling himself' and taking on a lowly status and position.... The emptying includes change of role and status, not essential attributes or nature."[33] Further, he notes that Christ "put the interests of others first and was willing to give up some of the privilege and status that was his as God."[34] He says this with the balancing recognition that "Jesus speaks elsewhere of the 'glory' he had with the Father 'before the world was made' (John 17:5), a glory that he had given up and was going to receive again when he returned to heaven. And Paul could speak of Christ who, 'though he was rich, yet for your sake he became poor' (2 Cor. 8:9), once again speaking of the privilege and honor that he deserved but temporarily gave up for us."[35] But Grudem incorrectly goes on to describe Jesus as having two wills as well as two natures, and therefore two "centers of consciousness," and that he could act on the basis of either will or nature.[36] Still, he correctly affirms that whatever either nature does, "the person of Christ does" and so "we must affirm that everything that is true of the human or the divine nature is true of the person of Christ."[37]

Dahms gives a different understanding to the passage. Focusing on verses 10–11, he says "it is implied that the glorification of the Son is subordinated to the glorification of the Father."[38] He argues further that these verses can be seen "as descriptive of his eternal state of exaltation when his triumph has had

32. L. S. Chafer, *Chafer Systematic Theology* (Dallas: Dallas Seminary Press, 1947), 1:378–79.

33. Grudem, *Systematic Theology*, 550.

34. Ibid., 551.

35. Ibid.

36. Ibid., 561.

37. Ibid., 562.

38. Dahms, "Subordination of the Son," 355.

its full effect." And, he concludes his discussion of Philippians 2 with, "I submit that a responsible reading of Phil. 2 finds the doctrine of the eternal subordination of the Son implied in it."[39] But, Dahms fails to consider Jesus' sharing all the glory he shared previously in eternity (John 17:5), as well as his return to it.

Bilezikian does not see it as a description of an eternal condition. Rather, he says, "Within the context of Christ's ministry to the world, and in this context alone, Scripture indeed teaches the complete humiliation of the Son. From the position of equality with the Father, at the pinnacle of divine glory, the Son descended. . . ."[40] He notes that "during his earthly life Christ remained a full participant in the Godhead, thereby retaining his divine subsistence. Paradoxically he also made himself subject to the Father when he assumed human personhood."[41] He concludes correctly from this, "The Biblical definition of the *kenosis* as the Son's refusal to exploit the status of equality he had with the Father attests to the fact that there was no subordination prior to the *kenosis*."[42]

Erickson understands the passage much differently. He sees Jesus giving up equality in his kenosis without losing his divine nature. Interestingly, he limits the loss of equality to the period of his incarnation. He argues, "While he did not cease to be in nature what the Father was, he became functionally subordinated to the Father for the period of the incarnation." And, "he accepted certain limitations upon the functioning of his divine attributes."[43] Contra Grudem, he does not see the natures functioning independently, but concurrently, with his humanity imposing "functional limitations" on his divinity.[44] He correctly argues that "Christ's incarnation was a voluntary, self-chosen limitation. He did not have to take on humanity, but he chose to do so for the period of the incarnation. During that time his deity always functioned in connection with his humanity."[45] Still, he seems to see Jesus' incarnation as a limited experience and something that will not continue into eternity.

As can be seen from the various interpretations of this passage and its theological implications, a uniformity of opinion within evangelical scholarship does not exist. Rather, almost as many views exist as there are commentaries and works on theology. Why? Either because of the paucity of revelation or the failure to synthesize key passages that clarify Paul's understanding of the kenosis.

The key to understanding Paul's meaning and discerning the truth or error in these various and conflicting views may be found, again, in the

---

39. Ibid., 356.
40. Bilezikian, "Hermeneutical Bungee-Jumping," 58.
41. Ibid., 59.
42. Ibid., 64.
43. Erickson, *Christian Theology*, 735.
44. Ibid.
45. Ibid., 736.

Gospel of John. In describing his actions during supper, as he moves to wash the disciples' feet, John notes, "Jesus, knowing that the Father had given all things into his hands, and that he had come from God and was going to God, rose from supper and laid aside his garments, took a towel and girded himself" before washing his disciples feet (John 13:3 NKJV). Jesus takes the *form* of a bondservant to serve, though without forgetting who he is and where he is going (from the Father and to the Father), and without ceasing to be who he is (their teacher and Lord as he affirmed in John 13:13). He takes the actions and assumes the role of a servant precisely because he is humbling himself in order to serve them, because he loves them completely (John 13:1), and because he is teaching them to live out love for one another through humble service. Not only do his actions embody the attitude Paul describes, but his "appearance" as a bondservant parallels his "likeness" and "appearance" as a man. Thus, taking on humanity can be an act of God the Son that need not diminish his deity, nor change his status. Acting like a servant need not reduce him to a servant.

Further, fulfilling the role of a servant need not require that he always was subordinate or will remain subordinate. The best illustration of this is the change in roles of the Holy Spirit with relation to Jesus. While on earth Jesus remained dependent on the Holy Spirit, who led him (Matt. 4:1; Mark 1:12; Luke 4:1) and empowered him (Luke 4:14), as is evident in his warning about blasphemy against the Holy Spirit (Matt. 12:22–32). When accused of casting out demons by Beelzebub, Jesus first stated that he cast out demons "by the Spirit of God" (v. 28). This demonstrated the truth that Jesus was empowered by, and therefore dependent on and subordinate to, the Holy Spirit. It was this truth that made their accusation blasphemy against the Spirit and not against him.

Following Jesus' ascension, the Spirit's relationship/role within the Godhead is that of subordination to the Son. Where he led Jesus before, Jesus now sends him (John 16:7). He does not proceed just from God the Father, but also is sent by God the Son (John 15:26).[46] He glorifies

---

46. I concur with Ryrie that the doctrine of the eternal generation of the Son based on Psalm 2:7 and of the Spirit based on John 15:26 is less an "exegetically based" doctrine and more a theological construct (C. C. Ryrie, *Basic Theology* [Wheaton, Ill.: Victor, 1986], 54–55). And, though Scripture is clear that each member of the Godhead has different roles in relation to creation, that need not require One be less than the Other. As Ryrie says, "The concept of the economical Trinity concerns administration, management, actions of the Persons, or the *opera ad extra* ('works outside,' that is, on the creation and its creatures). For the Father this includes the works of electing (1 Peter 1:2), loving the world (John 3:16), and giving good gifts (James 1:7). For the Son it emphasizes His suffering (Mark 8:31), redeeming (1 Peter 1:18), and upholding all things (Heb. 1:3). For the Spirit it focuses on His particular works of regenerating (Titus 3:5), energizing (Acts 1:8), and sanctifying (Gal. 5:22–23)."

Jesus and communicates what Jesus wants the disciples to know because "he will not speak on His own authority, but whatever He hears He will speak" (John 16:13 NKJV). Thus, God the Holy Spirit presently takes a subordinate role to God the Son that he did not have during the Son's earthly sojourn.

But, how do all these elements fit into our understanding of what Paul is saying about Jesus and his relationship to the Father in eternity future? How do various theologians handle 1 Corinthians 15:28? The gap between the two major views is wide. Either this verse teaches essential subordination or it only refers to a subordination that ends with the inauguration of the eternal state.[47]

1 Corinthians 15:28

This verse states that Jesus will be subjected to the Father after everything has been subjected to him. In it Paul describes Jesus' subjection to the Father by using the future passive form of the verb "to subject" with respect to Jesus.[48] This is done in light of the description of whom he submits to, namely, the One subjecting (aorist active participle) "all things" to Jesus, not himself. And with regard to everything that is subjected, the use of the passive form of "subject" portrays clearly the Father actively promoting Jesus' rule over creation in that "all things" will be "made subject to him." Paul's repeated use of the same Greek verb in the passage, especially in choosing to describe God the Father as the one subjecting everything to Jesus, with himself excepted, and then Jesus being subjected to him, must be seen as deliberate and significant. Paul wants us to recognize the truth that Jesus will be subject to the Father in the eschaton.[49]

47. Gordon D. Fee, *The First Epistle to the Corinthians,* NICNT (Grand Rapids: Eerdmans, 1987), 760.

48. Mare sees the future tense form as significant, saying, "If there were inherent inferiority, the present tense would be expected—i.e., 'he is ever subject to the Father.' But the future aspect of Christ's subjection to the Father must rather be viewed in the light of the administrative process in which the world is brought from its sin and disorder into order by the power of the Son, who died and was raised and who then, in the economy of the Godhead, turns it all over to God the Father, the supreme administrative head" (W. H. Mare, "1 Corinthians," in *Expositor's Bible Commentary* [Grand Rapids: Zondervan, 1976], 286). Godet saw this as a second aorist passive and argued from that that it had a more "reflective sense" than if it had been a first aorist (F. L. Godet, *Commentary on First Corinthians* [Grand Rapids: Kregel, 1977], 796).

49. Godet's understanding of the last phrase, "that God may be all in all," is well stated (*First Corinthians*, 801). He says, "He did not here wish to designate God specially as Father, in opposition to the Son and the Spirit, but God in the fulness of His being, at once as Father, the source of all, both in Himself and in the universe, as Son, revealing Him, and as Spirit communicating Him. It was in this fulness that God dwelt in the man Jesus, and it is with the same fulness He will dwell in every man who has become in Him His child and heir."

Dahms describes this verse as the "*locus classicus* for the doctrine of the essential subordination of the Son."[50] For him it further implies "that the last of the eschatological events prior to the eternal state will be the subjection of the Son to the Father and that this will be the condition forever thereafter. And surely his final relationship to the Father will not be inferior to the relationship he had with the Father in his preexistent state."[51] Thus Jesus has eternally been subordinate in essence as well as position. Barackman uses strong language to describe the relationship between God the Father and Son that results from Jesus' continued humanity. "As man and Messiah, the Lord Jesus will always be subject to the Father's authority and will serve him. . . . Continuing his messianic work as the Father's *Slave*, the Lord Jesus will rule until he has achieved the divine objectives of his present messianic work."[52] He says further that God the Father "will supremely rule over all things forever, with the Lord Jesus as his *Viceroy*, or *Assistant*."[53] The use of such terms as "slave" when describing Jesus' eternal relationship with the Father is quite disturbing and stands in conflict with Jesus' own words. Slaves do not share glory with their masters. Only equals share glory. And Jesus will share glory, as affirmed by his request in John 17, as seen in the Father's response in Philippians 2, and described repeatedly in Revelation. Further, the relationship of a slave to his master is very different from a son to his father. Significantly, neither Jesus nor the apostles ever describe his relationship to the Father as anything other than that of Son. It would be appropriate to say, rather, that every one of the apostles would have viewed such as description of Jesus as abhorrent and degrading. The very point of Hebrews 1–2 is that Jesus is superior in his person to the angels and Moses precisely in that he is a son and *not* a slave or servant in God's program.

A second approach to this passage is not to see it affirming essential subordination. For example, Bilezikian says, "Any inference relative to an eternal state of subjection that would extend beyond this climactic fulfillment is not warranted by this text or any other Biblical text."[54] And with him Erickson concurs.[55] Jesus' subordination is the direct result of his fulfilling the *role* of a

---

50. Dahms, "Subordination of the Son," 351. With him stands Godet, who rejects the idea of one of Jesus' natures (human) being subordinate while the other (divine) "remains free and self-sufficient" (*First Corinthians*, 796–97). He says the language of subordination "does not bear only on the function of the Son, but also on His personal position" (798). He then deals with the problem of Christ's place in the Trinity by saying, "As the word is subordinate to the thought, and yet one with it, so in the notion of Son there are united the two relations of subordination and homogeneity."

51. Dahms, "Subordination of the Son," 352. He throws out the bugbear of Nestorianism for those who would disagree with him.

52. F. H. Barackman, *Practical Christian Theology* (Grand Rapids: Kregel, 1998), 99 (emphasis mine).

53. Ibid., 131 (italics mine).

54. Bilezikian, "Hermeneutical Bungee-Jumping," 60.

55. Erickson, *Christian Theology*, 698, 735.

servant by humbling himself, not by being humbled. Bilezikian is correct in noting that concerning the phrase "he humbled himself" in Philippians 2, "it is much more appropriate, and theologically accurate, to speak of Christ's self-humiliation rather than of his subordination. Nobody subordinated him, and he was originally subordinated to no one. He humbled himself."[56] He chose a relationship and role. It was not forced on him. And, in Paul's assertion here that he will be subjected to the Father, there is no indication of unwillingness on the part of Jesus. He will do it because he wants to do it, not because it is forced on him.[57]

Kovach and Schemm see it otherwise. Somehow this subordination must reflect the status of the Son's relationship with the Father in eternity past as well as future without a surrender of his status as Deity. They conclude, "Having brought all powers under his domain, the Son will voluntarily surrender his authority, power and prerogatives to God the Father. The purpose is that God may be all in all (1 Cor. 15:28)." They caution correctly that they do not mean by this "that Christ and mankind will be absorbed into God." And then they conclude that "the unchallenged reign remains with God the Father alone."[58] But having said all this, it must be remembered that their view is developed in light of their belief that passages such as 1 Corinthians 8:6 and 11:3 teach that "God is the eternal origin of all things and Christ is the eternal agent" and that "the Son is eternally subordinate to God the Father both in relation and role."[59] It also assumes that "God" in the last phrase of the verse refers to God the Father and not to all three members of the Trinity together. But another option would be to see Paul's use of "God" here not to refer solely to the Father.[60] And so the idea of Jesus' subordinate role ending at the start of the eschaton might be inferred from such an interpretation. Further, Kovach and Schemm's view ignores the reality that Jesus is described as taking the servant's form (and so role) in the incarnation (Phil. 2) and reigning *with* the Father in Revelation, evidenced by his reception of *equal* worship and his own affirmation that he sits *on* his Father's throne, not beside it (Rev. 3:21). To sit *on* his Father's throne is to rule, to share authority. Jesus' promise to us

56. Bilezikian, "Hermeneutical Bungee-Jumping," 59.

57. Godet, *First Corinthians*, 798.

58. Kovach and Schemm, "Defense of the Doctrine," 472.

59. Ibid. Yet, 1 Cor. 8:6 only affirms a distinction in functions—who did and does what—rather than a distinction in status. The assumption that one role is superior to the other is an assumption, not an affirmation of Scripture. It thereby fails to account for the reality that Scripture only reveals a glimpse of the Divine Godhead's inner workings as each member of the Trinity relates to each other. Similarly, 1 Cor. 11:3 is better seen as a description of the present relationship Jesus has while fulfilling the role of Son in the Godhead in the present dispensation of God's program without requiring it be a description of their relationship before his incarnation or in the eschaton.

60. H. A. Ironside, *Addresses on the First Epistle to the Corinthians* (New York: Loizeaux, n.d.), 488–89.

to sit on *his* throne is clearly a reference to the Davidic throne of the Messianic (Millennial) Kingdom, not his Father's throne, which is identified as distinct from his own in Revelation 3:21.

Does 1 Corinthians 15:28 infer or require that Jesus' self-humiliation continue into the eschaton? Certain factors should help explain the passage and answer this question. First, Jesus' self-humiliation involved adding humanity to his deity from the point in time of his conception. He did not share in humanity prior to his incarnation, even though in his Old Testament appearances he assumed human forms.[61] His conception began a new relationship with humanity, as a partaker of it, sharing in flesh and blood, and thereby becoming qualified to represent us before the Father (Heb. 2:14–17). Second, with acceptance of humanity came certain human responsibilities that Jesus willingly accepted in his choice to experience incarnation. These responsibilities, shared by every human being equally, include submission and service, worship, to God only. Jesus expressed this clearly in his response to Satan on the Mount of Temptation, "You shall worship the LORD your God, and Him only you shall serve" (Matt. 4:10 NKJV). This human aspect of Jesus' relationship to the Father was expressed repeatedly by him with such statements as, "I am ascending to My Father and your Father, and to My God and your God" (John 20:17 NKJV). Yet, third, his deity was never forgotten nor abrogated, as evidenced by his response to Thomas's cry, "My Lord and my God!" Instead of following the pattern of Paul in Acts 14 and an angel in Revelation 19 and 22, rejecting worship and commanding worship of God, Jesus responded to Thomas with "because you have seen Me, you have believed. Blessed are those who have not seen and yet have believed" (John 20:28–29). He accepted and affirmed Thomas's new understanding and declaration. But, even as Jesus did that, he was still obedient to his Father, and therefore functioning in a servant, subordinate role. And so the question remains, will that continue?

Jesus' self-humiliation will continue through eternity and will include subordination to the Father as God, contra Erickson and Bilezikian. Bilezikian errs when he says, "The humiliation of the Son was an interim or temporary state. It was not, nor shall it be, an eternal condition. Christ's humiliation was essentially a phase of ministry coincidental with the need of his creatures."[62] First, this subjection of Jesus occurs at the end of his earthly ministry and precedes the eternal state. And second, he will remain a human eternally, as affirmed in Psalm 110 (per Heb. 5:6), by his eternal designation as a priest ac-

---

61. Though some appearances of God in the Old Testament were in dreams and visions, his preincarnate physical presence occurred in places such as Gen. 18 where God (preincarnate Jesus) ate and conversed with Abraham, Gen. 32 where he wrestled with Jacob, Exod. 24 when he ate with Israel's elders, Josh. 6 as the Commander of the Lord's army, and Judg. 13 with Samson's parents.

62. Bilezikian, "Hermeneutical Bungee-Jumping," 59.

cording to the order of Melchizedek. And, since he will never cease being a human, he will never cease having certain responsibilities that come from being a human. This being said, Jesus may still fulfill this role through willing submission that need not detract from his deity or equality.

But, if as God he is equal to the Father, and therefore need not be subject, why is he *subjected*? Why is the subjection something he receives (passive voice) rather than something he does (middle voice)? And if he is subjected, is it in just one of his natures or both? He in his single person, sharing two natures, can freely choose to respond as God, precisely because he is humble, in the manner appropriate to humanity and fulfill the role as the head of the human race that includes being made subject to God. This subjection of humanity to God is necessary to complete the process of restoring humanity, including those who are still in rebellion, to a state of submission following the fall. In that context, though Jesus will willingly lead humanity in worshipping and submitting to the Father, all of humanity will be being made subject to God in the process. And, as a human, his willing subjection will not lessen the reality that all of humanity is made subject and that he will be sharing in humanity at the time that subjection is brought about. It is a responsibility and a future destiny he freely accepted when he chose to become incarnate. But, it is a responsibility and destiny he freely chose while "being in the form of God." And, he made the choice and accomplishes his will without any diminishment of his essential nature as God, or his eternal relationship to the Father as his equal. This is no more a lessening of his divine status than a loss of position as their Lord when he washed the disciples' feet.

Back to Philippians 2

Jesus' continued status as equal to the Father while being subject to him in his role as a servant is evidenced further in Philippians 2 by the action of the Father in exalting him. The context of that exaltation is the unity of the Godhead as an expression of the humility of not just Jesus, but also God the Father. Interpreters often miss the point of those eleven verses. The illustration of Jesus' humble submission and sacrifice (vv. 5–7) is the model the readers are to follow in pursuing the unity commanded in verses 1–4. And, it is the unity within the Godhead that is demonstrated in the illustration and serves as the model for the church.

We focus on Jesus' humble submission (vv. 6–8), and then puzzle over the last verses (9–11), wondering how they illustrate the point Paul is making to his readers about their need to humbly serve one another in pursuit of unity. The answer is not that God will exalt the readers at the proper time and reward them if they humbly serve. The answer lies in its expression of the unity within the Trinity, the unity of the members of the Godhead. Jesus, though fully equal, chooses to humble himself. God the Father responds to Jesus' self-humiliation with exaltation, inviting (insisting?) Jesus to share his glory, to be treated by all sentient beings as his equal, to be worshipped.

Paul's point in including this response by the Father to the Son is not to promise us that we will be rewarded for submitting. His point is that the Father is as humble as the Son, and considers the Son more important than himself, just as the Son considered us more important than himself. And so the unity within the Godhead results because both members involved in the incarnation consider others more important than themselves and take those actions appropriate to meeting others' needs. That unity is expressed in equality, even within the context of the incarnation and its implications. Jesus "needs" to be worshipped by every sentient being precisely because he is God. It is the only proper response of humanity and the angelic host. The Father exalts him to his rightful place of worship and shares the glory he set aside in his obedience to death on humanity's behalf in order to meet that very legitimate need/right that Jesus did not consider it robbery to give up. The same will happen at the threshold of the eschaton when everything and every one has been subjected to Jesus, who in turn will be subjected to the Father, "that God may be all in all."

So, in understanding the issue, the kind of response Jesus receives now from the Father and will receive in the eschaton must be taken into account. As evidenced by the Father's exalting him (Phil. 2) and his reclaiming the glory he shared with the Father in eternity past (John 17), in his single person, Jesus still exercises those rights belonging to him as God. He will receive the worship of every sentient being in heaven, on earth, and under the earth (Phil. 2), God the Father and God the Holy Spirit being the only exceptions. All the saints worship him along with the Father (Rev. 5:13).

But, he will also worship the Father, because he will remain a human as well as God. He will do so of his own volition, not under compulsion, in the same way that every saint will willingly bow before the Father while every condemned creature will bow under compulsion. And Jesus will do this without feeling or being slighted. God the Father will accept his submission, as he leads us all in bowing before him, while exalting him to his rightful place of shared worship, shared glory. Both natures will thereby be expressed fully in eternity without either being sacrificed, in that Jesus, as God, can still choose to subject himself to the Father without denying or reducing their equality. He will participate fully in the rights and responsibilities of both natures eternally in his one person as a consequence of his humble choice, willingly made.

Conclusion

Though orthodox Christianity affirms Jesus' deity and shared essence with God the Father, its handling of the question of his subordination has not led to consensus. Generally the difference arises with the question of how long his subordination has and will last, as well as how deeply it penetrates his nature, whether it is essential or functional. Jesus' subordination involves willing submission in that he made the choice prior to his incarnation. This submission is his own response to his incarnation, which in no way violates his divine nature or prerogatives, in no way changes his essential nature as God, nor changes his essential, ontological, relationship to the Father as a member of the Godhead. This submission, which began with his incarnation, will continue into eternity in that Jesus will never cease sharing in humanity and willingly doing those things every human being is obligated to do. As modeled in the upper room, he does this, and will continue to do it, without lessening his position in the Godhead. It is a part of the divine mystery that we mere humans will never fully understand.

How can God become a man? How can God worship God? How can God submit to God and still be equal to God? We do not have the explanations, just the affirmations of Scripture. He has. He will. And we marvel.

14

The Pretribulation Rapture: A Doubtful Doctrine

T. Van McClain

Mid-America Baptist Theological Seminary

The purpose of this paper is twofold: to encourage others to reconsider the truthfulness of the pretribulation rapture doctrine and to make a defense of the posttribulation rapture position. Various arguments in favor of the pretribulation rapture will be examined, and weaknesses to those arguments will be demonstrated. Then some of the strengths of the posttribulation position will be stated.

John F. MacArthur Jr. has recently written a book entitled *The Second Coming*.[1] His book will be used to represent the pretribulation position for several reasons. First, he is a popular writer who is well respected in the evangelical community. Second, MacArthur actually gives several reasons for his belief in the pretribulation rapture, unlike many books that simply assume the pretribulation position. Third, while his book is written on a popular level, it is still written by the president and founder of a fine evangelical seminary. All of this indicates the scholarly underpinnings of the book.

MacArthur began his book by distancing himself from the paperback eschatology of Hal Lindsey. Hal Lindsey believed the rapture and the start of the Great Tribulation would occur in the 1980s.[2] However, the truth is that Lindsey's position is basically the same as MacArthur's, except that Lindsey was not as cautious in his interpretation, particularly in the area of setting dates.

---

1. John F. MacArthur, *The Second Coming: Signs of Christ's Return and the End of the Age* (Wheaton, Ill.: Crossway, 1999).

2. Hal Lindsey, *The 1980s: Countdown to Armageddon* (New York: Bantam, 1980), 12, cited by MacArthur, *Second Coming*, 15.

Evidence for the Pretribulation Position

The Imminent Return of Christ

MacArthur began his discussion of the pretribulation position with what is probably the most cited argument: the imminent return of Christ, which for him means an "at-any-moment" return. It should be agreed by all that the clear teaching of the New Testament is that Christ is coming soon. In Revelation 3:11 Jesus says, "I am coming soon. Hold on to what you have, so that no one will take your crown."[3] Many other passages can affirm that the coming of Christ is at hand, but does this mean that he can come at any moment? Well, of course, Christ *can* come at any moment. He can do whatever he wants. However, there is good reason to believe that certain things must happen before he returns, as 2 Thessalonians 2:1–4 says.

Of course, the key question with this passage concerns the timing of the rapture and the second coming. The passage does not explicitly state that the two events are separated by seven years. In fact, a straightforward reading of the passage suggests that the two events occur at the same time. The phrase, "Concerning the coming of our Lord Jesus Christ and our being gathered to him," more naturally would be understood to refer to two events occurring at the same time, unless there is a compelling reason from context to consider the two events as being separate in time. Of course, there is no compelling reason to separate these two events in time within the context of the passage.

It is instructive to note how the Old Testament refers to the first coming of Christ. In Malachi 3:1 God speaks of God coming "suddenly." Just as the Lord is promised to come suddenly by Malachi, so he is promised to come suddenly by the New Testament writers. Nevertheless, even though Malachi said that the Lord would come suddenly, he still would be preceded by a special messenger, as Malachi 4:5–6 also makes clear.

Before the first coming of our Lord, certain events had to occur. Even if one claims that the previously mentioned reference in Malachi actually refers to the second coming, the argument presented here is only strengthened. Likewise at the second coming, the Lord will come suddenly, but certain signs will precede that coming.

If the second coming of the Lord is an event separated by the space of seven years from the rapture, then, why not speak of a second coming and a third coming? Of course, hardly anyone wants to affirm three separate comings of Christ, but the truth is that the pretribulation position requires three separate comings of Christ to earth. The first coming, of course, is our Lord's coming to earth in the womb of a virgin to die for our sins and be resurrected for our salvation. The second coming, then, would be our Lord's coming *for* the saints. After seven years, the Lord would then come for the third and final

---

3. The NIV is cited throughout this essay unless otherwise noted.

time, and his coming would be *with* the saints. Instead of speaking of three separate comings, MacArthur said that the second coming would occur in two stages, "Scripture suggests that the Second Coming occurs in two stages—first the Rapture, when He comes *for* the saints and they are caught up to meet Him in the air (1 Thess. 4:14–17), and second, His return to earth, when He comes *with* the saints (Jude 14) to execute judgment against His enemies."[4]

However, if both the rapture and the second coming are referred to as "comings" (and they are), and if they are separated by a period of seven years, then it makes little sense to say that the two separate comings are actually only one coming. Of course, if the two comings actually occur at the same time, then it would be appropriate to speak of the one coming of our Lord. That one coming, then, would be both *for* the saints, and then, after they rise to meet him, *with* the saints, as our Lord returns to earth.

My mother lives in Texas. One year, she visited with me during the middle of October, and she also visited with me during the summer. Those two visits, those two comings, were at two separate times; but it would be nonsense to refer to those two comings as one coming in two stages. Of course, if she were driving from Texas to New York, and she stopped in Pennsylvania; and if I drove to Pennsylvania to meet her and escort her back to New York (which is exactly what I did several years ago), then I would not refer to that coming as two events, but as truly two stages of one event, or as two events involved in her one coming.

It should be noted that MacArthur stated that the Scripture only "suggests" the pretribulation rapture. While he often seems dogmatic and certain in his book, it appears that he realizes that Scripture does not explicitly teach his view; in his view it is only suggested by the biblical material.

Again, the doctrine of imminence does not have to mean "any moment." Yet, MacArthur's question should be answered: "How can we cultivate a daily expectation of Christ's return if these preliminary signs must yet be fulfilled before He returns?"[5] It is a fair question, and the answer is actually quite simple. Before the first coming of Christ, it is clear that many were looking forward to the coming of the Messiah, even though they had not yet seen the messenger who was to be sent before him. However, even more importantly, the early church was looking forward to the second coming of Christ, even though many signs (many more signs than now) had yet to be fulfilled. Every day they looked forward to our Lord's coming, but that does not mean that they thought that his coming could happen on just any day, except for one group of Christians at Thessalonica (2 Thess. 2:1–4).

Now, if the rapture was the next event on the eschatological horizon, it seems strange that Paul did not mention that. Instead, he indicated that the

4. MacArthur, *Second Coming*, 87.
5. Ibid., 54.

arrival of the man of sin, the antichrist, would come before the day of the Lord. Of course, MacArthur is aware of this passage, and he says of it, "They [the Thessalonians] obviously feared they had missed the Rapture and were about to be swept away in the final and epochal judgments of the Day of the Lord."[6] If MacArthur is right, then, one would expect that the phrase "the day of the Lord" must refer to the rapture. After all, Paul indicates that the Thessalonians had feared that the day of the Lord had already come. Strangely enough, MacArthur does not believe that the day of the Lord refers to the rapture; he apparently believes it refers to a period of judgment before the return of Christ. If that is really to what the day of the Lord refers, then, the Thessalonians did not fear that the rapture had taken place; they feared only that the earth had entered into apocalyptic judgment.

It is believed that the real meaning of this passage is not so difficult to understand if one has not already assumed that the rapture and second coming are two separate events in time. Quite simply, MacArthur is correct when he says that the "coming of our Lord Jesus Christ and our gathering together to Him" is the rapture, but it is believed that the truth is that the rapture occurs at the same time as the second coming of Christ. What MacArthur seems to lose sight of is that Paul is writing "concerning" the rapture, as he says in verse one; and since he is writing concerning the rapture, he tells them not to be alarmed at some report that the day of the Lord has come; that is, the day of the Lord must refer back to the rapture, since that is expressly what Paul is writing about. (Whether the day of the Lord is one day or a period of time at this point is irrelevant.)

Christ's coming will be sudden, and it will be unexpected, as Paul says in 1 Thessalonians 5:1–3. He continues with something that would startle many Christians today, if they really understood it, by saying, "But you, brothers, are not in darkness so that this day should surprise you like a thief" (1 Thess. 5:4). In other words, the second coming of Christ will not be unexpected for Christians, because Christians are not in the darkness. Those who are Christians will see the signs, and they will be expecting the Lord's return. His coming for *us* will not be like that of a thief coming in the night. It will *not* be unexpected. Of course, this does not mean that any Christians should be setting dates for our Lord's return, but it suggests that Christians will know when they have entered the tribulation period.

By the way, when Paul says that the day of the Lord will be like a thief coming in the night, this does not mean that his coming will be a secret coming, like a rapture before the tribulation period. No! It is not sneakiness that is the point of this analogy; it is the unexpectedness of the coming which Paul has in mind. Jesus makes the analogy clear in Matthew 24:42–44.

6. Ibid., 55.

A thief in the night would not sneak through a window, he would break through the door and take anything of value that was in sight. So if you knew when to expect the coming of the thief, you could be prepared. The point of the analogy is that the coming of the Lord will be a surprise, that is, to everyone but Christians.

Another statement of MacArthur deserves comment:

> If the apostle now meant to teach them that all the events of the Tribulation must be fulfilled *before* Christ could return for them, that would be scant "comfort" indeed. In fact, it would overturn everything the New Testament has to say about Christ's return being imminent, comforting, and helpful.[7]

Actually, nothing in the New Testament would be overturned if the events of the tribulation had to occur before the rapture and second coming, only the doctrine of the pretribulation rapture would be overturned. It would actually be of great comfort to believers in the tribulation to know that Christ was coming soon.

Christ's return will be soon, it is imminent, but it is not likely to happen at any moment, because certain things must happen before his return that have not happened yet.[8] However, since there is a possibility that this writer is wrong, it is enough to say that the any-moment return of Christ is "not likely" but still possible. He also wishes that some pretribulationists could admit that they might be in error, instead of making the pretribulation position a test of orthodoxy.

In the conclusion of his study on imminence, MacArthur posed a question that a skeptic might ask, "Does the passing of 2,000 years indeed prove that Christ's coming was not imminent in the early church era and that the apostles were mistaken?"[9] Of course his answer is that the passing of 2,000 years does not disprove the imminent return of Christ; in fact, nor would the passing of 2,007 years disprove the imminent return of Christ. MacArthur believes that all of the general signs given in the New Testament have been fulfilled,[10] but is it likely that all of the general signs had been fulfilled in the apostolic period? It is not likely. This author can think of several general signs that probably had not been fulfilled by the end of the apostolic period, and, if this is true, then the apostles believed in the imminent return of Christ, even though all the signs had not yet been fulfilled.[11]

---

7. Ibid., 56.

8. According to *Webster's Ninth New Collegiate Dictionary* (Springfield, Mass.: Merriam Webster, 1990), the word *imminent* means "ready to take place; *esp.*: hanging threateningly over one's head." However, it can also mean "coming on shortly," according to *The Compact Edition of the Oxford English Dictionary* (New York: Oxford University Press, 1971).

9. MacArthur, *Second Coming*, 57.

10. Ibid., 54.

11. One such sign would have been the end of the times of the Gentiles (Luke 21:20–24), which, in this writer's view, has not yet happened.

God Will Preserve His People from Wrath

Another argument cited by MacArthur in favor of the pretribulation rapture relates to the preservation of God's people from wrath during the Great Tribulation. MacArthur said, "God did not appoint us to wrath. The day of wrath that will come in the Tribulation is not what we are to be preparing for. The sudden appearing of Christ to take us to glory is our hope."[12]

One might assume that those who reject the pretribulation rapture doctrine further believe that the church will suffer God's wrath during the Tribulation. Nonsense! One wonders if MacArthur simply has not read other views, or if he simply imagines what others believe. Paul D. Feinberg, himself a pretribulationist, *has read* what others believe, and so he correctly stated, "It might be wondered if there is anything that the participants of this debate agree upon. Surprisingly enough, I think there is. All agree that God has exempted the church from divine wrath."[13]

The question then, is not *whether* the church will be exempt from divine wrath, but *how* the church will be exempted. Feinberg argued that the church would be exempt from the tribulation by virtue of the fact that the church would be in heaven during the tribulation period. Others, who do not hold to the pretribulation rapture position, would argue that God preserves his people from his wrath by some other means, just as he has in the past. During the ten plagues of Egypt, for example, God's people experienced the first three plagues along with the Egyptians, but they were preserved from the last seven plagues by supernatural means.

Assume for a moment that the pretribulation position is correct. Will there not be believers in Christ present during the great tribulation period? Of course there will be. Even if the church is raptured out of the tribulation period, there will still be many who will stand for Christ during that period of time (having decided to follow Christ after the rapture). So then, will those people be protected from the wrath of God? Certainly, but they will not be protected from the wrath of humanity, generally speaking; just as today, Christians are not protected from the wrath of humanity (more Christians have died for their faith in the last century than have died for their faith in the previous nineteen centuries combined). Therefore, the argument that there must be a pretribulation rapture to protect the church from God's wrath is a bogus argument. While on the subject of believers in Christ who will be present during the tribulation, Matthew 24:30–31 notes what happens to them at the end of the tribulation period. MacArthur argued that the great tribulation mentioned in Matthew 24:21 is *the* great tribulation that is still to

---

12. MacArthur, *Second Coming*, 63.

13. Paul D. Feinberg, "The Case for the Pretribulation Rapture Position," in *The Rapture: Pre-, Mid-, or Post-Tribulational?* (Grand Rapids: Zondervan, 1984), 50.

occur in the future. This great tribulation will be "cut short," however, as Matthew 24:22 says. So then, it is for the sake of the elect (the phrase normally refers to the church in the New Testament, but here, for the sake of argument, it will be agreed with MacArthur that the elect must refer to saints in the great tribulation after the time of the rapture).

According to Matthew 24:29–31, it is after the distress of the tribulation period, or at the end of it, that the sign of the Son of Man appears, at which time he sends his angels to gather the elect, remembering that the elect in this context is not the church, but the saints of the tribulation period. It is the tribulation saints, then, who are gathered from one end of the heavens to the other; in other words, they are raptured up into heaven to meet Christ. Of course, one may argue that it is the saints in heaven who are called to accompany Christ to earth, but the context favors the tribulation saints.

In other words, it can be argued that the pretribulation position actually affirms a belief in three comings of Christ, and two raptures of the saints.

Evidence for the Posttribulation Rapture

The Parousia of Christ

One word Paul uses to describe the coming of Christ is *parousia* or "coming" (1 Thess. 4:13–5:4). Of course, in this passage Paul is not stating that he would survive until Jesus returned. The meaning is that those who are still living at the time of the coming of Christ, and who are Christians, would be caught up with Christ in the air (Paul includes himself in the "we").

The word for "coming" in verse 15 is the word *parousia* that occurs some twenty-four times in the New Testament. In two instances it is translated as "presence," while the rest of the time it is translated as "coming." At the coming (the *parousia*) of Christ, Paul says that we will meet the Lord in the air (1 Thess. 4:15–17). This passage is referring to the rapture. In fact, the Latin word *rapio*, from which we get the word *rapture*, is the Latin Vulgate's translation of "caught up" in verse 17.

Notice in verse 16 that the Lord himself comes down from heaven, "with a loud command, with the voice of the archangel and with the trumpet call of God." This description could hardly be considered a "secret" coming. As someone once joked, "the shout and the trumpet sound will be loud enough to wake the dead." This same word, *parousia*, is used to refer to the second coming in Matthew 24:3 and 27.

So, then, the word *parousia* refers both to the rapture and to the second coming of Christ. If *parousia* refers to both, and the two are separated in time, then there would be two comings. If so, there should be some passage that clearly indicates that the two events are separate; but since there is none, *parousia* refers both to the rapture and the second coming as two aspects of the same event that will occur almost simultaneously.

Furthermore, the *parousia* is to occur at the end of the great tribulation period. Second Thessalonians 2:8 says, "And then the lawless one will be revealed, whom the Lord Jesus will overthrow with the breath of his mouth and destroy by the splendor of his coming [*parousia*]."

In the first four centuries after the resurrection of Christ, the early church believed basically as follows: (1) the Antichrist would be an evil ruler of the end times who would persecute the church and afflict her with great tribulation; (2) the church would be purified through suffering; (3) Christ would, at the end of the tribulation period, destroy the Antichrist, deliver the church, and set up the millennial kingdom.

This view of the second coming has been called the historic premillennial view. It was historically the view of the early church, and it affirms the existence of a millennial reign of Christ on earth that will follow his second coming. In his discussion of the eschatological views of the early church, George Ladd wrote, "We can find no trace of pretribulationism in the early church; and no modern pretribulationist has successfully proved that this particular doctrine was held by any of the church fathers or students of the Word before the nineteenth century."[14] A recent dispensational writer called Ladd's view "extreme" but did not offer any rebuttal. Instead, he said, "It should be noted that dispensationalists have neither said that the early church was clearly pretribulational nor that there are even clear individual statements of pretribulationism in the fathers."[15]

The early church fathers believed the Antichrist to be an evil ruler of the end times who would persecute the church and afflict her with great tribulation. There is biblical evidence for this claim in 2 Thessalonians 2:1–2. If the rapture and second coming of Christ are separated by seven years, could not someone say that the day of the Lord had already come (2 Thess. 2:3–12)?

From this passage it can be clearly seen that there will be a great rebellion just previous to the coming of Christ. At that time, a "man of lawlessness" will be revealed. He will be the Antichrist who will oppose the true God and actually set himself up as God. The Antichrist will display numerous types of counterfeit miracles, signs and wonders, and he will deceive many. He will persecute the church.

Some believe that it is the church who is holding back the Antichrist. Hence, the church must be removed at the beginning of the great tribulation period. However, there is nothing in this passage to indicate that it is the church who is the restrainer. Nor did anyone in the early church consider the

---

14. George E. Ladd, *The Blessed Hope: A Biblical Study of the Second Advent and the Rapture* (Grand Rapids: Eerdmans, 1956), 31. Ladd's book presents a good defense of the historic premillenial position.

15. Larry V. Crutchfield, "The Early Church Fathers and the Foundations of Dispensationalism," *Conservative Theological Journal* 3 (August 1999): 196.

church to be the restrainer. Tertullian was explaining why Christians should pray for the emperor, when he wrote:

> For a stupendous shock impends over the whole world and the very ending of the age threatening terrible sufferings; and this we know is only retarded by the respite won by the Roman Empire. . . . We have no wish to experience these calamities and as we pray that they may be delayed we favour the long-continued existence of Rome.[16]

Bettenson further stated that the view that the "restraining power" was the Roman state was also held by Cyril of Jerusalem, Jerome, and Augustine.[17]

Interestingly enough, even John MacArthur cited one of the church fathers who believed that the Antichrist would persecute Christians. MacArthur began by stating that Justin Martyr was probably born in the first century and knew many of the believers who had lived during the apostolic period. Then MacArthur quoted from Justin Martyr's *Dialogue with Trypho*:

> Two advents of Christ have been announced: the one, in which He is set forth as suffering, inglorious, dishonoured, and crucified; but the other, in which He shall come from heaven with glory, when the man of apostasy, who speaks strange things against the Most High, shall venture to do unlawful deeds on the earth against us the Christians. . . . The rest of the prophecy shall be fulfilled at His second coming. (chap. 110)[18]

One should not be surprised that the church will be persecuted by the Antichrist, for already many antichrists have come, as John says in 1 John 2:18. The Antichrist will be one who denies that Jesus is the Christ, as 1 John 2:22 and 4:3 say.

This coming Antichrist will persecute the church. However, it is often maintained that the church will not be present during the tribulation period, especially since the word "church" is not found after the third chapter of Revelation, and this fact supposedly indicates that the church has been raptured out of the world. However, Revelation 7:9–8:1 describes those who *are* left here during the tribulation and persecuted by the forces of evil, including the Antichrist.

The description of these saints is exactly identical to how one could identify Christians: having their robes washed in the blood of the Lamb, with the

---

16. Tertullian, *Apologeticus* 32; cited by Henry Bettenson, ed. and trans., *The Early Christian Fathers: A Selection from the Writings of the Fathers from St. Clement of Rome to St. Athanasius* (New York: Oxford University Press, 1956), 219.

17. Henry S. Bettenson, *Early Christian Fathers*, 219 n. 1.

18. MacArthur, *Second Coming*, 124.

Lamb at the center of their throne, who is promised to be their Shepherd. Is one to imagine that Jesus is the Shepherd of those who are not Christians?

From Revelation 12:9–11, one would think that those who have been washed in the blood of the Lamb and who testify of Jesus would be none other than Christians. Again, Revelation 12:17 speaks of war against "her off-spring—those who obey God's commandments and hold to the testimony of Jesus" and Revelation 17:6 refers to the saints in the tribulation as those "who bore testimony to Jesus."

Again, who else but those who are a part of the church bear testimony to Jesus, obey God's commandments, and have been washed in the blood of the Lamb? Furthermore, Revelation 19:10 clearly ties the saints in the tribulation period to the saints in the early church.

Those in the church are brothers and sisters of those saints who hold to the testimony of Jesus during the tribulation. They are brothers because the church, just as the tribulation saints, has been washed in the blood of Christ. Furthermore, they share a common confession of faith—the testimony of Jesus. It seems odd that many who would insist that it is only the true church who holds to the testimony of Jesus would also insist that the saints of the tribulation period who held to the testimony of Jesus could not and would not be a part of the church. Of course, if it is claimed that the saints of the tribulation actually are members of the church, then we must affirm that a part of the church goes through the tribulation, or to be more specific, those saints who waited until after the rapture to make their profession of faith have to go through the great tribulation. Again, it seems ridiculous to say that people who die while testifying of their faith in Christ are not really Christians.

Will anyone be saved during the tribulation period, except by repentance from sin and faith in Christ? To suggest that someone could be saved in the future outside of the cross of Christ is to denigrate the wondrous sacrifice of Christ. Again, is it possible that someone could place their faith in Christ, and not become a part of the church? No. Anyone who genuinely repents of their sin and calls upon Christ as Savior will be saved (Rom. 10:13). There is no hint in Scripture that there will ever be some other means of salvation outside of the sacrifice of Christ.

Furthermore, anyone who is genuinely saved also becomes a part of the universal church. Of course, it is possible that someone could be saved and not become part of a local church, but there is a spiritual baptism that occurs at the moment of salvation and it happens to every believer (1 Cor. 12:13). Each believer is baptized into the body of Christ, the church. The word "into" is the English translation of the Greek preposition *eis*. It is possible that *eis* has a purposive usage here, so that believers are all baptized for the purpose of making one body. However, it is believed by this writer that the spatial usage fits best, in other words, at the moment of conversion believers are placed into the body of Christ by spiritual baptism. Either usage ends up with the same spiritual reality—those who are spiritually baptized at the moment of conversion then become a part of the body of Christ.[19]

If anyone is to be saved during the tribulation period, it must be by repentance from sin and faith in Christ. And those who are saved will be led to faith by those who already believe in Christ, and will be drawn by the saving work of the Holy Spirit. Those who believe in Christ will become Christians; they will be spiritually baptized into the body of Christ. There is no reason to think that people may be saved some other way with some other end result. Christians will be present during the tribulation period.

The coming of Christ will be sudden and unexpected to an unbelieving world, but those who know Christ will not be caught by surprise at our Lord's coming. Why will believers not be surprised at Christ's coming? Because certain definite signs will precede that coming (2 Thess. 2:1–4). The next thing to expect before the return of Christ is the coming of the Antichrist. Is it possible that the Antichrist has already come? Probably not. It seems likely that many Christians would have recognized his coming. The coming of the Antichrist will not be welcome, but there is no need for Christians to fear. Christians will be protected from the wrath of God, and he will be with true believers when they are overtaken by the wrath of humanity.

Is it possible that the posttribulation position is wrong and that Christ will come and rapture the church before the beginning of the tribulation period? Yes! This writer does not claim to be inerrant in interpretation and is willing to admit that the historic premillennial view could be wrong. As a matter of fact, this writer hopes that he is wrong. He hopes that the church is raptured out of the tribulation period.

Paul says that the remnant will "meet [*apantēsis*] the Lord in the air" (1 Thess. 4:17). This Greek word is used three times in the New Testament (here, Matt. 25:6, and Acts 28:15).

Vine indicated its importance from the historical perspective when he said, "It is used in the papyri of a newly arriving magistrate. It seems that the special idea of the word was the official welcome of a newly arrived dignitary."[20]

Peterson says it is to be understood "as a technical term for a civic custom of antiquity whereby a public welcome was accorded by a city to important visitors." The rabbis adopted the word as a loan word for use in a phrase such as, "The great of the city moved out to meet the king."[21] In other words, if any dignitary was arriving at an ancient city, many of the people of the city

19. For a helpful discussion, see Gordon D. Fee, *The First Epistle to the Corinthians*, NICNT (Grand Rapids: Eerdmans, 1987), 603–6.

20. Biblesoft Ver. 3.0b (Seattle: Biblesoft, 1998), "Moulton, Greek Test. Gram. Vol. 1, p. 14," cited in *Vine's Expository Dictionary of Biblical Words* [CD-ROM] (Nashville: Nelson, 1985).

21. Erik Peterson, "ἀπάντησις," *Theological Dictionary of the New Testament*, ed. Gerhard Kittel, trans. Geoffrey W. Bromiley (Grand Rapids: Eerdmans, 1964), 1:380–81.

would go out to meet him and escort him back into the city. They were rolling out the red carpet. This type of meeting is what is described in the three passages in the New Testament.

Matthew 25:6 speaks of virgins going out to meet the bridegroom and escorting him to the wedding. In his comments on this parable, MacArthur is helpful in his description of how this part of the marriage ceremony occurred: "At the start of the celebration, the bridegroom and his groomsmen would go to the bride's house. His arrival was a ceremonial event, heralded by the bridesmaids, who would come out to meet the bridegroom and escort him to the bride's house."[22]

So here is an accurate picture of the second coming: the bridegroom (Jesus) will leave his house (heaven) and come to the bride's house (earth). On the way to the bride's house, the bridesmaids (Christians) will come out to meet the bridegroom and escort him to the bride's house for the marriage supper of the Lamb. The fact that the bride and bridesmaids are similar in identity does not take away from the truth of the picture. The bridesmaids would actually be the Christians who are raptured, while the bride would likely be all believers in Christ.

In Acts 28:15 Paul is met while approaching Rome and escorted there. In other words, in both Acts 28:15 and Matthew 25:6 we have a picture of an important person who is going toward a destination. As he approaches his destination, others come out to meet him and continue the journey with him toward the destination he is approaching.

There is no reason why 1 Thessalonians 4:17 should not be translated with the same understanding. At the time of Christ's return to earth, "we which are alive and remain shall be caught up together with them in the clouds, to meet the Lord in the air: and so shall we ever be with the Lord" (KJV). Christians will be raptured up to meet him, and then they will escort him back to earth.

This argument does not prove the posttribulation rapture, but it does give strong evidence for it. J. Barton Payne stated the argument very well when he said that 1 Thessalonians 4:17 was

> Scripture's most explicit presentation of the rapture of the living saints. . . . Specifically, the church is to go up *eis apantesin, to* the *meeting,* of the Lord. That is, the Lord descends from heaven, and the church ascends from earth to meet Him. But when they meet (since they do not stay in midair), one party must therefore turn about; and it would hardly be the Lord. For in the usage of *eis apantesin* elsewhere in Scripture, the contexts consistently describe how the ones who do the meeting then turn around and accompany the one who is met for the remainder of his journey . . . the church is to meet Christ in the air and thus join in His triumphant procession down to earth.[23]

22. MacArthur, *Second Coming,* 153.
23. J. Barton Payne, *Encyclopedia of Biblical Prophecy: The Complete Guide to Scriptural Predictions and Their Fulfillment* (Grand Rapids: Baker, 1973), 560–61.

In 1 Corinthians 15:50–57, the dead are raised and the living are changed. This passage is referring to the rapture. Paul uses the word "we" to include himself, just in case he is around when this event occurs. Notice that this event occurs at the *last* trumpet. It must be the same event or after the event that is mentioned in Matthew 24:30–31and 1 Thessalonians 4:16–18. The last trumpet will signal the end of this age, the rapture of the church, and the second coming of Christ.

If there is even the slightest possibility that the pretribulation rapture doctrine is erroneous, then belief in that doctrine should not be a test of one's orthodoxy. Instead, the following statement of faith emphasizes what is important and omits what is not essential:

God, in His own time and in His own way, will bring the world to its appropriate end. According to His promise, Jesus Christ will return personally and visibly in glory to the earth; the dead will be raised; and Christ will judge all men in righteousness. The unrighteous will be consigned to Hell, the place of everlasting punishment. The righteous in their resurrected and glorified bodies will receive their reward and will dwell forever in Heaven with the Lord.[24]

May our Lord come quickly!

---

24. *The Baptist Faith and Message: A Statement Adopted by the Southern Baptist Convention* (Nashville: Sunday School Board, 1963), 15.

Part 5

Eschatology and an Open View of God

15

Toward a More Inclusive Eschatology

CLARK H. PINNOCK

McMaster Divinity School

Christian hope is filled with glorious themes: parousia, resurrection, kingdom, new creation, etc. We look forward with joy and a hope inspired by the Holy Spirit to the time when life will truly begin. But our hope is shadowed somewhat by a nagging concern about the fate of the unevangelized that refuses to go away. The eschatological outlook is hopeful for those who have participated in God's covenants with Israel and the church, but what about the innumerable others whose lives have been lived outside these spheres? Theological tradition has often (though not always) taken a hardline position that outsiders to these covenants cannot be saved, which very likely means that a large proportion of humanity cannot be saved because (through no fault of their own) they have not been part of these arrangements. This can be enormously vexing. First-generation Christians (for example) often agonize over the question in relation to the destiny of their ancestors.[1]

1. Mark Mullins discusses the issue in the Japanese context: "What about the Ancestors? Japanese Responses to Protestant Individualism," *Studies in World Christianity: The Edinburgh Review of Theology and Religion* 4 (1998): 41–64. Here is part of a letter I received from an Asian American pastor: "As you articulated in your book [*A Wideness in God's Mercy*], a growing number of people today especially Asian Americans with no ties to Christianity, are deeply troubled with the predominant teaching that all of their unsaved loved ones—dead or alive—are automatically going to go to hell. So why should we be excited about going to heaven, if everyone we love is going to hell? What kind of good news is this? Being able to assure them that Jesus will make the right call at least gives them some measure of hope. For them, without this kind of hope, becoming a believer seems to demand not only the loss of unsaved loved ones but the loss of our own humanity." Welcome is Richard J. Plantinga, *Christianity and Plurality: Classic and Contemporary Readings* (Oxford: Blackwell, 1999).

Because eschatology is a concern on the minds of many, inside and outside the churches, I thought it was an issue to be touched upon in this essay and possibly one that ought to be treated more often and with greater sensitivity in evangelical systematic theologies.[2]

It is not everybody's problem, certainly not in the same way, and therefore might not be part of everyone's eschatology. Soteriological monergists, for example, do not have the problem of eschatology that synergists do—for them, God himself decides who will be saved and lost before the creation of the world. There is little left to worry about (eternal destiny being a foregone conclusion) except perhaps in reference to the goodness of God.[3] Nevertheless, the issue can surface even in this context if we suppose that some of God's elect live their lives out in pagan societies apart from Christian influences and need to be saved by other means. Augustine himself entertained such an idea and used it in his reply to Porphryry: "From the beginning of the human race, whoever believes in him, and in any way knew him, and lived in a pious and just manner according to his precepts, was undoubtedly saved by him, in whatever time and place he may have lived."[4] Thus it would not seem to follow even from soteriological monergism that the axiom "Outside the church, no salvation" is necessarily true. Indeed it seems as if, before the church spread widely and became established, that the axiom had reference to apostates who left the church, but as time went on, it began to be applied more and more harshly to any and all who had not joined the church for any reason, the assumption being that the gospel had been proclaimed everywhere and anyone who had not joined the church was culpable.[5]

---

2. It is treated among the topics of eschatology (for example) by Wolfhart Pannenberg, *Systematic Theology* (Grand Rapids: Eerdmans, 1998), 3:615–17, and by Hendrikus Berkhof, *Christian Faith: An Introduction to the Study of the Faith* (Grand Rapids: Eerdmans, 1979), 528–33. But it is not found among the topics of eschatology in Millard Erickson, Wayne Grudem, or Bruce Demarest/Gordon Lewis, though one can find it in their work under the topic of general revelation (Erickson, *Christian Theology* [Grand Rapids: Baker, 1983], 172–73; in Grudem, *Systematic Theology: An Introduction to Christian Doctrine* [Grand Rapids: Zondervan, 1994], 121–22; and in Demarest, *General Revelation: Historical Views and Contemporary Issues* [Grand Rapids: Zondervan, 1982], 259–61). One can also find it under soteriology in A. H. Strong, *Systematic Theology* [Philadelphia: Fleming Revell, 1907], 842–44).

3. Roger E. Olson speaks of the problem Augustine had with affirming the goodness of God if God is in total control of the destiny of creatures (*The Story of Christian Theology: Twenty Centuries of Tradition and Reform* [Downers Grove, Ill.: InterVarsity, 1999], 275–77). Terry Tiessen relieves tension somewhat by maintaining that God makes himself known to everyone in a manner adequate to solicit saving faith in them and that this revelation is accompanied by an inner work of grace to enable everyone to respond ("Divine Justice and Universal Grace: A Calvinistic Proposal," *Evangelical Review of Theology* 21 [1997]: 63–83).

4. From Augustine's letters in *Nicene and Post-Nicene Fathers*, first series, 1:417.

5. On the history and meaing of the axiom, see Francis A. Sullivan, *Salvation outside the Church? Tracing the History of the Catholic Response* (New York: Paulist, 1992), and Jacques Dupuis, *Toward a Christian Theology of Religious Pluralism* (Maryknoll, N.Y.: Orbis, 1997), chap. 3.

It is safe to say, however, that those who feel the problem most keenly among the topics of eschatology are the evangelical (and other) synergists who comprise a good proportion of the world's Christian people: including the Eastern Orthodox, Roman Catholics, Wesleyans, the free churches, Pentecostals, etc. By synergists, I mean people who believe that God's agency and human agency cooperate in some way in salvation and in history.[6] For them, there is a real problem, since they view it as essential that sinners somehow have an opportunity to respond to the grace of God. If God loves the whole world, they reason, there must be an opportunity for all people to participate in God's salvation. The latter cannot lack opportunity merely because the gospel did not reach them. If everyone has been provided for in the redemption of Christ, it must be possible for every person to be eligible at some point to receive that provision, regardless of his or her circumstances. As I have written elsewhere: "We cannot reasonably suppose that a failure of evangelization that affects many millions would leave them bereft of any access to God."[7]

As a result, there have been numerous attempts to explain how such an opportunity is afforded by way of typologies of a wider hope: (1) God may provide opportunities in this life for people to know him and his Spirit wherever they live; (2) God may get the message to those seeking God before they die; (3) God may calculate what the response of unevangelized persons would have been had they heard the gospel; or (4) God may provide a universal opportunity at or after death to be saved.[8]

In this paper, I want to explore the biblical basis of the first option, the "catholic" option, sometimes termed inclusivism, which is reflective of the thinking of some of the early fathers, of select individuals over the centuries (including evangelicals), and which more recently has become the official position of the Roman Catholic Church. In dialogue with Donald G. Bloesch, who opts for postmortem evangelization as a solution, Avery Dulles presents this contemporary Catholic thinking that picks up on the idea of "seeds of the Word" found in the reflections of certain patristic writers, which was taken over by Vatican II and occurs frequently in the writings of John Paul II. Quoting Dulles, "According to this view, the philosophies and religions that have arisen prior to, or independently of, biblical revelation may be salvifically oriented to Christ in a hidden way that is manifest to the eyes of God. By adhering to this seminal divine revelation, persons ignorant of God's full revelation in Christ may be associated with Christ and the church in a measure sufficient

---

6. On evangelical synergism, Olson, *Story of Christian Theology*, 256, 267–77, 280; and John Sanders, *The God Who Risks* (Downers Grove, Ill.: InterVarsity, 1998), 237–51.

7. Clark H. Pinnock, *A Wideness in God's Mercy: The Finality of Jesus Christ in a World of Religion* (Grand Rapids: Zondervan, 1992), 157–68.

8. John Sanders, *No Other Name: An Investigation into the Destiny of the Unevangelized* (Grand Rapids: Eerdmans, 1992).

to them to attain eternal life."[9] The appeal of inclusivism is that it retains the unique centrality of Christ as the sole source of salvation, while at the same time not requiring us to believe that God consigns to perdition the majority of the race who are not Christians through no fault of their own.

In search of a biblical basis, I will appeal to a number of scriptural themes that orient theology in this more hopeful direction and speak of a universal divine saving economy. I will refer to (1) God's cosmic covenant with humankind; (2) the universal economy represented by categories like God's wisdom, spirit, and word; (3) the significance of pagan saints; (4) Jesus' attitude toward believers outside Israel; and (5) the openness of early Christians to God's work among the heathen before their evangelization. I am aiming at a theological perspective that would, while holding fast to faith in Jesus Christ as traditionally understood, be able to recognize the grace of God at work beyond the church. I am aware of a prevalent negative assessment of these matters among evangelicals and would wish to orient us (if I can) toward a more positive evaluation of the workings of grace outside the church. I seek what I have called elsewhere a hermeneutics of hopefulness.[10]

The Appeal to Scripture

In recognition of the fact that no one comes from nowhere and everyone comes from somewhere, let me begin by referring to three hermeneutical presuppositions in the paper. First, I recognize that the biblical writers feature as their main theme what God is doing through Abraham and his seed and that the testimony to the wider work of God, though it exists, is not their primary focus. I see myself exploring a subplot of God's dealings with the nations, prior to Abraham, and alongside the history of Israel and church. Scripture concentrates on the ingathering of the nations through the salvation history that begins with the call of Abram. However, there is also a subplot that deals with what God is doing in the wider world. What God is doing in salvation history in the narrow sense does not entail the notion that this is the only divine initiative God has going on anywhere. Though one is struck by the Abrahamic covenant and its subsequent developments, it does not exhaust what the Bible has to say about salvation. This means that material I am able to appeal to is less ample than I could wish, and therefore the use that I make of it

9. Avery Dulles interacting with Bloesch in *Evangelical Theology in Transition: Theologians in Dialogue with Donald Bloesch*, ed. Elmer M. Colyer (Downers Grove, Ill.: InterVarsity, 1999), 73–74. The Doctrine Commission of the Church of England has recently aligned itself with this viewpoint: *The Mystery of Salvation: The Story of God's Gift* (London: Church House, 1995), chap. 7.

10. Pinnock, *A Wideness in God's Mercy*, 20–35. On the biblical teaching I found two books particularly helpful: Donald Senior and Caroll Stuhlmueller, *The Biblical Foundations for Mission* (Maryknoll, N.Y.: Orbis, 1983), and Dupuis, *Toward a Christian Theology of Religious Pluralism*, chap. 1.

can be readily questioned. Critics might think that the evidences that I cite in support of the wider work of God are too imprecise and/or flimsy to make the point I have in mind. In reply, I would say that I do not wish to exaggerate the evidence that I find, but that I also do not want to see important data swept under the rug. For example, I should not exaggerate the significance of God's covenant with Noah or the speech on the Areopagus, but neither should anyone else underrate such matters.

Second, I find the Bible to be a complex book, on this as on other subjects, and I do not assume only a single line of testimony on this or other questions. Neither my position or any other can be established by "proof texting" that assumes a flat uniformity of biblical teaching, because of the dialectical quality in the material. I see a complexity in Scripture with its tensions and complementary elements. Take, for example, Paul's attitude in Romans 1 compared with his approach in Acts 17. On the one hand, in Romans, discontinuity with the stress on the radical newness of Christ in contrast to pagan darkness—on the other hand, in Acts, continuity between the gospel and the Greek world waiting for the unknown God to be revealed, prepared by their own poet-theologians. Are there not two tendencies here, of continuity and discontinuity, which create a dialectical tension that is not to be suppressed? Or, to take another example, there is the Word made flesh, but also the Word present from the beginning. There is the active presence of the Logos not yet incarnate in the world and the event of incarnation, which is the culmination of God's revelation. Recognizing the dialectical nature of the Bible forces us to go deeper and to search for directions in texts—not just statements. We must ask: where are we being led? We need to be open to the dialogical nature of this biblical witness, open to its overall drift, and sensitive to the struggle for truth in the Bible itself. The Bible is a complex book, and reading it can be like listening to a conversation. Not to see this feature can lead to a depreciation of the complex canonical witness that often presents testimony and counter-testimony and requires us to "tack" between them. If we disregard the testimony to continuity, we end up in restrictivism; if we disregard the testimony to discontinuity, we end up in religious pluralism.[11]

Third, I am also influenced in my reading of the Bible by a Wesleyan/Arminian type of orientation to the gospel that leads me to favor a hermeneutic of hopefulness and to view God as a serious and inclusive lover. God loves his enemies and is kind to the ungrateful and wicked (Matt. 5:45; Luke 6:35). Jesus proclaims God's acceptance to the riff-raff—to outcasts, sinners, renegades, prostitutes. He did not wait for them to make themselves respectable but preached good news to them. God's love toward the race is radical, his

---

11. Walter Brueggemann structures his *Theology of the Old Testament* (Minneapolis: Fortress, 1997) around Israel's core testimony and counter-testimony and urges us to maintain the tensions; otherwise, we may miss the biblical teaching altogether (400–402).

generosity overflowing. I believe God wants everyone to be saved and come to a knowledge of the truth (1 Tim. 2:4), that Jesus was lifted up to draw everyone to himself (John 12:32), and that God is not willing that any should perish (2 Peter 3:9). God's grace abounds more than sin (Rom. 5:20) and God sent his Son as last Adam, signaling the desire to turn things around on a large scale. It is inconceivable to me to imagine that this God who seeks out one lost sheep would leave millions without hope of salvation. In short, I read the Bible in relation to what God has revealed in Jesus, which means (for example) that I read the early chapters of Genesis hopefully and notice clues of divine generosity sometimes passed over in other places. I read the Old Testament with liberty as Scripture that has reached its goal in Jesus Christ. From this point of view, it is hard for me to believe that God first thought of saving humankind when Abram came along or that he would be content with saving only Abram's seed. Like the interpreters of the New Testament, I do not treat the Old Testament as a text that contains unchangable truths to which the readers and the readers' community make no contribution as to their meanings. These texts have meaning as they are read and used by the people of God. We have a measure of interpretive freedom and ought to read all Scripture as a witness to the gospel of Jesus.[12]

Five Interpretive Themes

1. Christian theology after New Testament times, perhaps surprisingly, began with a concept of a universal divine saving economy. With insight Irenaeus wrote not only of God's covenants with Abraham and Moses, but also of his covenants with Adam and Noah. Along with other church fathers, he did not limit the history of salvation to the chosen people, but saw it extended to all humankind and to all human history. Using a kind of dispensational theology, they distinguished different ages or phases designed by divine pedagogy. These ages were progressive, organically connected, and part of the history of salvation. "Particular" salvation history operates in the wider context of "universal" salvation history, that is, God's dealing with the nations before Abram and later alongside Israel. Thus God's mission is broader than the mission assigned to us—our mission is caught up in a larger mission. Irenaeus wrote: "Four covenants were given to the human race: one, prior to the deluge, under Adam; the second, after the deluge, under Noah; the third, the giving of the law; the fourth, that which renovates the human being, and sums up all things in itself by means of the Gospel, raising and bearing human beings upon its wings into the heavenly kingdom."[13] Just as there are four Gos-

---

12. Richard B. Hays argues that this was Paul's practice: *Echoes of Scripture in the Letters of Paul* (New Haven: Yale University Press, 1990), chap. 5.
13. Irenaeus, *Against Heresies* 3.11.8.

pels, so are there four covenants struck with humanity. Evidently God has more than one covenant and more than one people.

God's covenants are with the whole of humanity. God's care for the nations is obvious from the call of Abram, which issued in a history of salvation that looked forward to a new covenant including all nations. But before the Abraham cycle of stories, there are the Adam and the Noah cycles. God's dealings with Adam are symbolic of a universal cosmic covenant with the human race, and in the Noah cycle, a covenant is struck with all creation through him with the promise that cosmic order will endure thanks to the faithfulness of God. This covenant does not belong to another order of significance than the other covenants. In it God is manifesting himself to Noah and through him to the nations. Though the revelation remains simple, it is integral to the saving acton of God in the world. It is not simply a revelation of God in nature but, I suggest, a move of God in the history of the nations previous to later covenants with the chosen people.

What we seem to have here is a variety of divine manifestations in the unity of God's saving plan. The plan is neither monolithic nor piecemeal, but single and complex at the same time. Salvation history is coextensive with history itself—it begins with creation and goes on to the end of the world. The history of salvation should not be reduced to the Hebrew-Christian traditions when it coicides with the history of the world. It is a mistake to reduce its value as just "general" revelation or "reduced" salvation or "common" grace. We can and ought to speak of the universal presence of Word and Spirit in extrabiblical traditions as we do in our own. The Bible sets the story of God's redemptive activity in the history of Israel within a framework of God's universal activities beyond the bounds of Israel. God does not limit his activity to Israel, because he is the Lord of universal history. Election does not cut Israel off from the nations, but situates Israel in relation to them and looks forward to the day when the nations will know the Lord along with Israel.

In the Old Testament, Israel is certainly presented as God's preferred and privileged partner, but the nations are also related to the Lord and live under the large horizon of God's rule. Hence they are challenged: "Say among the nations, 'the Lord reigns'" (Ps. 96:10). Yahweh is sovereign over the nations and they ought to accept his rule. "All the nations you have made shall come and bow down before you, O Lord, and shall glorify your name" (Ps. 86:9–10). Therefore, the psalmist cries out: "Praise the Lord, all you nations! Extol him, all you peoples!" (Ps. 117:1 NRSV). They are called to join Israel in praising God's mighty works: "Clap your hands, all peoples; shout to God with loud songs of joy" (Ps. 47:1 NRSV). Indeed the expection is that one day they will come—gladly, willingly, and expectantly—and serve the Lord (Isa. 2:2–5). Amos even declares: "'Are you not like the Ethiopians to me, O people of Israel?' says the LORD. 'Did I not bring Israel up from the land of Egypt, and the Philistines from Caphtor and the Arameans from Kir?'" (Amos 9:7 NRSV).

These other nations have also experienced God's saving grace—Israel has no monopoly on the Lord! Though she is a recipient of God's favor, her claim on God is not exclusive. God has blessed other nations too. How glorious will be the day when God will dwell with them and they will be his peoples (plural, Rev. 21:3) and when all the kings of earth will bring the glory of their nations into the new Jerusalem (Rev. 21:26).[14]

2. God's universal divine saving economy is also indicated by three biblical terms—*wisdom*, *spirit*, and *word*—that refer to ways in which God reveals himself beyond, as well as within, the boundaries of Israel. These terms witness to God's dealings with humanity from the beginning of history until now and in the definitive event of the incarnation. They were seen first as dynamic expressions of God's activity in history pending their realization in the Word/ Wisdom made flesh and in the outpoured Spirit.

First, Wisdom was present when creation first unfolded and she teaches humans everywhere to be wise (Prov. 8:22–36; parallels in Sirach 24 and Wis. 6–13). "I was beside him, like a master workman; I was daily his delight, rejoicing before him always, rejoicing in his inhabited world and delighting in the sons of men." Wisdom describes her as "the breath of the power of God and a pure emanation of the glory of the Almighty" (Wis. 7:25). Like a preacher standing at the crossroads, she calls on passersby to heed God's self-manifestation in the beauty and order of the divine plan. "Listen to me, my children," she calls. With God at creation, Wisdom brings God's works to realization and spells life to the persons who find her. Wisdom has a special work among the elect people of God, but not exclusively, since she is present everywhere. The Wisdom of God operated effectively in history before she became incarnate in Jesus. Her action toward Israel was unique but not exclusive, since she is universally present in history. In the New Testament, the theme develops into a wisdom Christology in John and Paul.

Second, the Holy Spirit, God's energy and power, is also active in creation, hovering over the primeval waters (Gen. 1:2) and renewing the face of the land (Ps. 104:30). Present in human beings as life giving and present in creation, Spirit will be present also in the new creation, being poured out upon all flesh. Again, the Spirit is active in the history of Israel and also universally. In the history of Israel, the Spirit lays hold of human beings to transform them into instruments of God's action among his people and will rest upon the Messiah and servant of God (Isa. 42:1). But, at the same time, the Spirit fills the world (Ps. 139:7; Wis. 1:7). In Job we read: "If [God] should take back his spirit to himself and gather to himself his breath, all flesh would perish together and man would return to dust" (Job 34:14–15 RSV). Like Wisdom, Spirit is both universal and particular. It is both present in history before Christ and oriented to these eschatological events. Unlike the economy of

14. Brueggemann, *Theology of the Old Testament*, chap. 16.

Christology, unavoidably limited by the particularity of history, the economy of the Spirit knows no bounds of space and time. Free of constraints, the Spirit can blow where it wills and be present throughout history. Jesus has opened the gate for all to enter in—the Spirit knows how to lead them to the door even if they die unexposed to Christ. There is room in God's house for many other sheep.[15]

Third, there is the Word that goes forth out of God's mouth. It is the Word that is spoken in creation and that speaks the divine law—which interprets the meaning of God's historical activities and that is efficacious of God's designs (Isa. 55:11). Primarily this is in reference to God's interventions in the history of Israel, but also in cosmic actions and universally (Ps. 33:6–9). The universal presence of the Logos before the incarnation does not replace the incarnation, the latter being the event in which God's plan for the world reaches climax in Christ. The Word that was made flesh in Jesus of Nazareth is present in the entire world as cosmic Christ and in the whole of human history, enlightening people prior to the incarnation (John 1:9). The Word itself anticipates its own decisive action in Jesus. It is a source of light and life for all human beings throughout history. The illuminating power of the Logos, operative in all of history, accounts for the salvation of human beings before its manifestation in the flesh. The centrality of the act of incarnation must not obscure the abiding action of the Word that transcends the bounds of time and space.

Wisdom-Spirit-Word witness to God's dealings with the whole of humanity from the beginning of time. They tell us that history is a history of salvation and does not just contain one way in which salvation is brought about. They confirm a dialogue initiated by God with humankind from the dawn of time and that through distinct phases leads humanity to God's appointed fulfilment. They allow us to speak of the various paths to Jesus Christ.

3. The universal divine saving economy is also indicated by the biblical phenomena of pagan saints, who responded to God and lived by faith outside the dispensation of the chosen people. The existence of such people is what we would expect if there were a cosmic covenant with humanity and a universal saving economy. We do not know how many of them there have been or are, but we do know they form a part of the great cloud of witnesses surrounding us (Heb. 11:1). By faith they were acceptable to God, a faith that was possible to have beyond the boundaries of Israel (Heb. 11:6).

First, I note a group of them that preceded Abraham. There is Abel, who inaugurated the line; Enoch who walked with God; and Noah who heeded God's word about the coming judgment. Second, I see a group contemporary with the Jewish dispensation. There is righteous Job; Melchizedek, the priest of God Most

---

15. The unbound action of the Spirit is a theme emphasized by Pope John Paul II because it helps him explain how elements of grace and truth come to be present in human cultures. See Dupuis, *Toward a Christian Theology of Religious Pluralism*, 173–79.

High, to whom Abraham paid the tithe; Abram's nephew Lot; Abimelech; Jethro; Rahab; Naaman; Ruth; the Queen of Sheba; the Magi; and Cornelius—"what more shall I say?" (Heb. 11:32).

Here were people who responded to the light they received.[16] Israel knew that not everyone among the nations were idolaters. They knew how the city of Nineveh turned in repentance to the God of Israel under the name of Elohim. A. H. Strong conjectures:

> The patriarchs, though they had no knowledge of a personal Christ, were saved by believing in God so far as God had revealed himself to them; and whoever among the heathen are saved, must in like manner be saved by casting themselves as helpless sinners upon God's plan of mercy, dimly shadowed forth in nature and providence. But such faith, even among the patriarchs and heathen, is implicitly a faith in Christ, and would become explicit and conscious trust and submission, whenever Christ were made known to them.[17]

Here we have outsiders, beyond the confines of Israel and church, who knew God and who require us to broaden our idea of the horizon of God's people. The Spirit of God is at work in the lives of those who are not yet incorporated into the zone of the explicitly sacred. Though we know little about it, it appears that God paints on a broad canvas and is ever reaching out. The Bible contains both positive and negative material—we do not have to disregard either. I think that the recent statement, "The Gospel of Jesus Christ: An Evangelical Celebration" (June 1999), is too limiting when it says: "The Bible offers no hope that sincere worshippers of other religions will be saved without personal faith in Jesus Christ."

4. Jesus himself interacted with pagan saints. Though sent to the lost sheep of the house of Israel himself, he was open to God's activity outside Israel and recognized faith among Gentiles. He was conscious of a universal divine saving economy. We read of his admiration for the faith of the centurion. "Not even in Israel have I found such faith" (Matt. 8:10 RSV). This faith stirred within him the announcement that many Gentiles from all over the world would come into the kingdom of God. Later another officer would say, "Truly this man was the Son of God" (Mark 15:39 RSV). Similarly, in trips through

---

16. Morimoto points in Jonathan Edwards to his dispositional view of salvation. Just as the Old Testament faithful were saved on account of their disposition for God, so non-Christians may be saved in the same way. So long as anyone has the disposition, they will be saved, whether or not they have the opportunity to exercise that disposition. Apparently one can include in the ranks of inclusivists both Edwards and Strong (see the next note). Anri Morimoto, *Jonathan Edwards and the Catholic Vision of Salvation* (University Park, Pa.: Pennsylvania State University Press, 1995), 60–61, 82, 113, 115, 153. See also Gerald R. McDermott, *Jonathan Edwards Confronts the Gods: Christian Theology, Enlightenment Religion, and Non-Christian Faiths* (Oxford: Oxford University Press, 2000).

17. Strong, *Systematic Theology*, 842.

Syro-Phoenician territory, he came into contact with persons who did not belong to the chosen people. Once more he was astounded by their faith. There he healed the possessed daughter of a Canaanite women and marveled: "O woman, great is your faith! Be it done for you as you desire" (Matt. 15:28 RSV). Jesus could see that the kingdom of God was already at work among outsiders. On another occasion, returning from Judea, Jesus passed through Samaria and conversed with a Samaritan woman at Jacob's well in Sychar. This was surprising in itself, but Jesus marveled at her thirst for living water. He did not reject her or her faith, but spoke of true spiritual worship that would transcend both Jewish and pagan worship. In the Good Samaritan, he also saw a "heretic" with a heart for the kingdom of God and used him as an example of one who was a true neighbor. We also read about a faithful leper cleansed by Jesus who was a Samaritan and who returned to give thanks (Luke 17:11–19). Jesus asked: "Was no one found to return and give praise to God except this foreigner?" I sense that for Jesus, saving faith is not only remotely possible to pagans but is operative among them. Many already belong to the kingdom of God. Grace and faith were operating already among them.

Jesus was looking for more than faith alone in people. For him, the message of the kingdom was to be the standard of divine judgment and the norm by which God judges both his people and also those who have not heard of Jesus. He looked then not only for faith in people but for the cup of cold water and the outstretched hand (Matt. 25:31–46). The issue for Jesus was not so much calling him "Lord" verbally as it was doing the will of the Father (Matt. 7:21). He says, "Here are my mother and my brothers! Whoever does the will of God is my brother and sister, and mother" (Mark 3:34–35 RSV). Jesus had an eye not only for those with the right lineage and correct profession but for co-builders of the kingdom of God. The criterion of judgment is the self-giving love of God made known in Jesus. The judgment is therefore not so much a matter of doctrine as it is about how people respond to God's mercy. What is important is participation in Christ's loving way of life that manifests itself in the service of others. What is all-important are kingdom acts and the kind of faith that is revealed in works. As with the father's two sons, it was not so much what they professed that they would do at first, but what they did in the end. Jesus asked, "Which son do you think pleased God?" As John the Baptist said: "Being a descendant of Abraham is neither here nor there. Descendants of Abraham are a dime a dozen. What counts is your life. Is it green and blossoming? Because if it's deadwood, it goes into the fire" (Matt. 3:9 *The Message*). There is salvation for those who, without knowing God as revealed in the gospel, showed justice to the oppressed and acted in accordance with God's purposes. Not everyone can have a personal relationship with Jesus Christ because many have not been reached by the proclamation. In their case what counts is whether their conduct agrees with the will of God as Jesus explained it. Agape is the sign of the operative presence of the mystery of salvation in any and every person. Jesus says that people can meet him in the poor, the sick, and the dying and find the door to eternal life. Not just the name of Jesus but the spirit of Jesus, the spirit of love, matters on the day of judgment. We evangelicals too, with all of our theological correctness, will be measured by the same standard.

Pannenberg writes:

> The message of Jesus is the norm by which God judges even in the case of those who never meet Jesus personally. As the parable of the sheep and goats shows, this means that those who have never known Jesus but who have done works of love that are in accord with his message will in fact participate in the salvation of God's kingdom and will be pronounced innocent at the judgment of God, while those who are only nominal Christians are excluded from salvation.[18]

Further he says,

> If we consider that the primary significance of Jesus Christ at the last judgment is that of being the criterion of God's relation to us, to all of us, this means that God sees and judges all people, not just Christians, from the standpoint of their explicit or implicit relation to the teaching and destiny of Jesus, and especially with the merciful love in view that found expression in the sending of Jesus. Thus God's relation to all people, not just Christians, is different from what it would have been without the sending of Jesus. Even those who have not become confessing members of the Christian church can have a share in the new life manifested in Jesus Christ if their hearts are open to the nearness of God and his kingdom that Jesus proclaimed.[19]

I think that Jesus could take such a liberal stance because he believed that God's kingdom was larger than the Israel. The community may be a sacrament of the kingdom, but the kingdom is larger than that. People outside church can also share in its reality and foster its values. Jesus cared less about orthodoxy, I think, and more about whether religion enslaves people or sets them free. He cared about whether it fosters love and compassion.

5. A fifth clue indicating belief in a universal divine saving economy can seen in the attitude of the apostolic church to the as-yet unconverted Gentiles. After the resurrection, the early church proclaimed the good news but needed to grow in its awareness of the universality of its mission. Specifically it had to get over a Jewish distaste for Gentiles. After that, it had to think about common ground with Gentiles and how to reach them. In Romans, as I have said, Paul places emphasis on discontinuity with the past, but in the Book of Acts the emphasis is on continuity. Discontinuity stresses the radical newness of

18. Pannenberg, *Systematic Theology*, 3:615.
19. Ibid., 639.

Christ and the condemnation of Jew and Gentile alike, while continuity underlines the homogeneity of salvation as it unfolds under God's plan. In Acts I find an open attitude to the prior spiritual condition of non-Christians. At Lystra Paul comments on the religion of the Gentiles now being superseded: "In past generations God allowed all the nations to walk in their own ways; yet he did not leave himself without witness, for he did good and gave you from heaven rains and fruitful seasons, satisfying your hearts with food and gladness" (Acts 14:17 RSV). His speech in Athens is also affirmative. There he praises the religious spirit of the Greeks and announces to them the "unknown God" whom they worship without knowing it. He depicts the Greek world as waiting for God and as being prepared by its own poet-theologians to meet him (Acts 17:22–31). He seems to suggest that even the religions of the Gentiles are not bereft of value and may find in Jesus Christ the fulfilment of their aspirations.

A remarkable statement about the breadth of salvation history is found in the prologue to John's Gospel. Long before the incarnation, John writes, the Word was already present in the world, giving light and life. He speaks of God's universal involvement with humanity and the incarnation of the Word that was a culmination of the ministry of the Word, which encompasses the history of the world. Before the incarnation, the Word was actively present in the world as the source of light and life. This links up with what we noted in the Old Testament of God's Wisdom and Word, which John sees present in Jesus. In this Logos/Wisdom theology, we have what may be the widest perspective on God's universal and continual involvement with humanity.

Conclusion

The Christian faith projects a glorious future for those who have come to know God along the path of Israel and the church. But what, we ask, of the innumerable others who have lived their lives outside these covenantal relationships? Is it really true that the majority of humanity will perish because the opportunity of such a relationship was never a real possibility? And, if so, what has become of God's reconciling of the whole world and his desire to set the oppressed multitudes free? Do the inequalities that stalk the world in this old aeon follow us into the everlasting future too? It is easy to accept that God will sweep away in judgment true enemies of his kingdom, but does he also plan to sweep away all those who might have become his friends had they had half a chance? Admittedly, God's ways are higher than our ways (Isa. 55:6–9) and we bow to that, but are they not higher precisely in respect to showing mercy?

I think they are higher than what our theologies sometimes propose, and I have sought to give flesh to a more generous interpretation. I have sought to show that there is at work in the world according to the Scriptures a universal divine salvific economy that points us to a more inclusive eschatology. My belief is that a high Christology does not entail a narrowness of hope. It is not necessary to construe the good news of Jesus Christ in ways that do not reflect its true breadth and grandeur. Some believe that it is dangerous to entertain too much hope. What will it do to missions if everybody is not going to hell? But to me hope is a motivator. I delight to reflect on the fact that God is a serious lover and I bless him for it. I cherish the thought that, wherever I, or we, take the good news, the Holy Spirit is already there, in advance of evangelists bringing the definitive proclamation of the Word made flesh. This would imply too that messengers would be sensitive and watchful for signs of a true knowledge of God among non-Christians. Who knows but there might be a wisdom and charity that would challenge even Christ's witnesses to repentance?

I am aware of a possible problem. If I stress the importance of believing in God's prevenient grace, I may leave the impression that the urgency of missions is threatened. Why go to the ends of earth to preach the gospel if people can enter God's house without knowing Jesus? I say that we must go to share with everyone the abundant love and hope, the joy and peace that Jesus brought. We take news of the unsearchable riches of Christ and invite everyone to view the plan of the mystery hidden for ages in God who created all things (Eph. 3:8–9). What we have received is so beautiful that we cannot keep it to ourselves, but are compelled to bring it to everyone we meet. On the matter of mission and hope, I take comfort in remembering that John Stott, a great evangelist and promoter of world missions, hopes for the salvation of the majority of the human race, and I notice that this hope did not squelch his passion for missions. May it not squelch our own.[20]

20. Stott made his remarks in David L. Edwards with John Stott, *Evangelical Essentials: A Liberal-Evangelical Dialogue* (Downers Grove, Ill.: InterVarsity, 1989/London: Hodder & Stoughton, 1988, where it is entitled simple *Essentials*), 327.

16

God as Omnicompetent Responder? Questions about the Grounds of Eschatological Confidence in Open Theism

STEVEN C. ROY

Trinity Evangelical Divinity School

In contemporary evangelical theology, a significant new proposal has been circulating, calling for a substantial revision in classical Christian theism's understanding of the nature of God. This view has been variously called "free-will theism,"[1] "the openness of God,"[2] "Consistent Arminianism,"[3] and a form of "relational theism."[4] The contours of this view, which I will call "open the-

1. Clark H. Pinnock, "From Augustine to Arminius: A Pilgrimage in Theology," in *The Grace of God, the Will of Man*, ed. Clark H. Pinnock (Grand Rapids: Zondervan, 1989), 23–26; Richard Rice, *God's Foreknowledge and Man's Free Will* (Minneapolis: Bethany House, 1980) and "Divine Foreknowledge and Free-Will Theism," in *The Grace of God, the Will of Man*; and David Basinger, *The Case for Freewill Theism: A Philosophical Assessment* (Downers Grove, Ill.: InterVarsity, 1996).

2. Notably in Clark H. Pinnock, Richard Rice, John Sanders, William Hasker, and David Basinger, *The Openness of God: A Biblical Challenge to the Traditional Understanding of God* (Downers Grove, Ill.: InterVarsity, 1994).

3. Rice, "Divine Foreknowledge and Free-Will Theism," 123. Rice's use of this term clearly indicates that he views classical Arminianism (which differs from open theism most notably in its view of God's foreknowledge) as inconsistent.

4. John Sanders, *The God Who Risks: A Theology of Providence* (Downers Grove, Ill.: InterVarsity, 1998), 12. Sanders uses this term as an umbrella term for "any model of the divine-human relationship that includes genuine give-and-take relations between God and humans such that there is receptivity and a degree of contingency in God." Under the umbrella of relational theism, he specifically includes open theism.

ism" throughout this essay, have become well known in recent theological discussions. One general description will suffice to give a broad overview of the position. In his chapter in the seminal book *The Openness of God*, David Basinger describes open theism in terms of five basic characteristics:

(1) God not only created this world *ex nihilo* but can (and at times does) intervene unilaterally in earthly affairs.

(2) God chose to create us with incompatibilistic (libertarian) freedom—freedom over which he cannot exercise total control.

(3) God so values freedom—the moral integrity of free creatures and a world in which such integrity is possible—that he does not normally override such freedom, even if he sees that it is producing undesirable results.

(4) God always desires our highest good, both individually and corporately, and thus is affected by what happens in our lives.

(5) God does not possess exhaustive knowledge of exactly how we will utilize our freedom, although he may well at times be able to predict with great accuracy the choices we will freely make.[5]

In addition, open theists also affirm a high degree of confidence that God's ultimate purposes will be achieved in the end. The eventual outcome of history does not remain in doubt. God's kingdom will ultimately triumph over the powers of evil. For example, Clark Pinnock confidently asserts, "Evil may have its day, but it will not finally triumph."[6] It is the purpose of this paper to evaluate this eschatological confidence and to determine whether or not it is consistent with the fundamental convictions of open theism.

Central Theological Convictions of Open Theism

At first glance, this high level of eschatological confidence seems unwarranted in light of certain fundamental theological convictions of the open theist position. This is particularly due to the nature of divine sovereignty, divine foreknowledge, and divine risk-taking proposed in the model. And in turn, each of these positions are grounded in God's free decision to create a world inhabited by creatures possessing libertarian freedom.

Since God has decided to create a world inhabited by significantly free creatures, he has voluntarily decided to limit himself,[7] to pull back, as it were, so as to honor the freedom of his creatures. Pinnock says,

---

5. David Basinger, "Practical Implications," in *The Openness of God*, 156. See also the summary statement of Clark H. Pinnock, "Systematic Theology," in *Openness of God*, 103–4.

6. Ibid., 116.

7. Pinnock argues, "Upholding God's power, [open theism] understands God to be voluntarily self-limited, making room for creaturely freedom" (ibid., 117).

The Bible presents God as the superior power who does not cling to his right to dominate but steps back to give the creatures room. . . . The Bible gives us the picture, not of an all-determining God, but of one who gives room to human beings and accepts the consequences, good and bad, of that policy. . . . God surrenders the exercise of some of his power in order to gain the voluntary partnership with us he so much desires. We may speak of a voluntary self-limitation of God in the decision to create our kind of world.[8]

This means, according to Richard Rice, that God's sovereign rule over his world is "flexible." His sovereign plans are not fixed from all eternity. No, they are always open to modification in his genuine give-and-take relationship with his creatures.

In short, God must "improvise" as circumstances change if He wishes to reach His objectives. This does not mean that God lacks a plan and simply must make do. Instead, it means that God's plans must be sufficiently comprehensive and flexible to include a variety of possible courses of action.[9]

John Sanders says that God's plan is not an exhaustive blueprint or a detailed script of history written in advance. Rather, he likens God's work with creation to jazz, "a melody with a good deal of improvisation."[10] He argues that this divine improvisation does not occur at the level of God's primary or overall purpose, but rather in the means he employs to get there. He calls this flexibility within God's sovereign rule a "divine purpose with open routes." Thus, for Sanders, "God remains faithful to his original purpose even while adjusting plans to take into account the decisions of his free creatures."[11]

God's free decision to create human and angelic[12] beings possessing libertarian freedom also impacts the way open theists understand the nature of

---

8. Clark H. Pinnock, "God Limits His Knowledge," in *Predestination and Free Will: Four Views of Divine Sovereignty and Human Freedom*, ed. David Basinger and Randall Basinger (Downers Grove, Ill.: InterVarsity, 1986), 151. Pinnock also states that "God gives a degree of reality and power to the creation and does not retain a monopoly of power for himself. His sovereignty is not the all-determining kind, but an omnicompetent kind" (ibid., 146). The implications of Pinnock's description of God as "omnicompetent" will be addressed below.

9. Rice, *God's Foreknowledge and Man's Free Will*, 63. Pinnock also speaks of God's flexibility: "Divine sovereignty involves flexible outworking of God's purposes in history. It refers to his ability, as the only wise God, to manage things, despite resistance to his will. . . . The future is determined by God not alone but in partnership with human agents. . . . He is flexible and does not insist on doing things his way. God will adjust his own plans because he is sensitive to what humans think and do" ("Systematic Theology," in *Openness of God*, 116).

10. Sanders, *God Who Risks*, 231.

11. Ibid.

12. The vast implications of the libertarian freedom possessed by angelic and especially demonic beings are explored in Gregory A. Boyd, *God at War: The Bible and Spiritual Conflict* (Downers Grove, Ill.: InterVarsity, 1997).

God's knowledge. It is this reality of creaturely, libertarian freedom that leads open theists to affirm that God's foreknowledge is non-exhaustive, that he does not know certainly and infallibly the future free decisions made by his creatures. Pinnock says,

> If choices are real and freedom significant, future decisions cannot be exhaustively foreknown. This is because the future is not determinate but shaped in part by human choices. The future is not fixed like the past, which can be known completely. The future does not yet exist and therefore cannot be infallibly anticipated, even by God. Future decisions cannot in every way be foreknown, because they have not yet been made. God knows everything that can be known[13]—but God's foreknowledge does not include the undecided.[14]

Richard Swinburne adopts a similar understanding of the extent of God's foreknowledge, arguing that God's inability to know infallibly the future free decisions of human beings is a "limitation which results from his own choice to create human beings with free will. Choosing to give others freedom, he limits his own knowledge of what they will do."[15]

This voluntary self-limitation of God and flexible sovereignty that he exercises so as to respect and honor the significant freedom with which he has en-

---

13. Thus open theists insist that they understand God to be fully omniscient. For example, David Basinger says that "to say that God is omniscient is to say simply that God knows all that can be known." ("Can an Evangelical Christian Justifiably Deny God's Exhaustive Knowledge of the Future?" *Christian Scholars Review* 25/2 [1995]: 133). Richard Swinburne draws a commonly cited parallel between the extent of God's omniscience and the extent of his omnipotence. "Just as omnipotence must be regarded as the power to do what is logically possible, so omniscience must be regarded as knowledge of what is logically possible to know" (*The Coherence of Theism*, rev. ed. [Oxford: Clarendon, 1993], 180). See also William Hasker, *God, Time, and Knowledge* (Ithaca, N.Y.: Cornell University Press, 1989), 73; Richard Rice,"Divine Foreknowledge and Free-Will Theism," 128; and John Sanders, *The God Who Risks*, 199. The point of all of these authors is that future decisions made by indeterministically free moral agents are not logically possible for God to know.

14. Pinnock, "Systematic Theology" in *Openness of God*, 123.

15. Swinburne, *Coherence of Theism*, 181. Other statements from open theists show that it is the need to maintain libertarian freedom that drives this new understanding of the extent of God's foreknowledge. For example Richard Rice says "*In order to affirm creaturely freedom*, the open view of God maintains that certain aspects of the future are as yet indefinite. Therefore they are unknowable. And this means that God's knowledge of the future cannot be exhaustive" (*God's Foreknowledge and Man's Free Will*, 53 [italics mine]). Rice also says that "several recent thinkers [including Rice himself] redefine omniscience *in order to allow for a strong sense of creaturely freedom*." ("Divine Foreknowledge and Free-Will Theism," 130 [italics mine]). And Pinnock says, "An important implication of this strong definition of freedom is that reality is to an extent open and not closed. . . . It implies that the future really is open and not available to exhaustive foreknowledge, even on the part of God. It is plain that *the biblical doctrine of creaturely freedom requires us to reconsider the conventional view of the omniscience of God*" ("God Limits His Knowledge," 150 [italics mine]).

dowed his human image-bearers, coupled with his lack of exhaustive fore-knowledge, has inclined open theists to speak in terms of God as a risk-taker. This is most clearly seen in John Sanders's very significant recent study of divine providence, which he entitles *The God Who Risks*. Sanders sees the crucial feature that distinguishes views of God's providence in which God takes risks, and those in which he takes no risks, to be the nature of the sovereignty that God chooses to exercise.[16] Only a God who foreordains all that will happen can legitimately be said to take no risks at all. Any form of nondeterminist divine sovereignty renders God to be a risk-taker.[17] David Basinger is another open theist who argues that a non-determining God must be a risk-taker:

> The fact remains that freewill theists, unlike theological determinist, must ultimately view God in a very real sense as a risk-taker. The God of freewill theism hopes that individuals will always freely choose to do what he would have them do. But for the freewill theist there can be no assurance that they will do so.[18]

Can Open Theists Be Eschatologically Confident?

Given these affirmations of open theism, we must return to our original question. Does the nature of God's sovereignty, his foreknowledge and his risk-taking mean that the fulfillment of his ultimate purposes is uncertain? Do these realities mean that the eventual outcome of history remains in doubt? Open theists argue no. They assert that we can be confident of the final triumph of God's kingdom and his ultimate victory over sin and evil.

Open theists affirm two primary arguments for this high degree of eschatological confidence. First of all, God is viewed to be "omnicompetent" in his ability to anticipate what his creatures will freely choose to do and to respond appropriately. It is God's omnicompetent response in any and every circumstance that guarantees the accomplishment of his ultimate purposes. And secondly, God in his sovereignty retains the right to intervene in human history and, on rare occasions, to overrule human freedom to ensure the ultimate accomplishment of his purposes.

God as Omnicompetent Responder

In support of this line of argument, Richard Rice says,

---

16. Sanders, *God Who Risks*, 12, 195.

17. Paul Helm also uses the issue of risk as the key distinguishing characteristic of views of divine providence. But for Helm, what makes a particular view of God's providence "risky" or "risk-free" is the exhaustiveness of God's knowledge of the future. See Paul Helm, *The Providence of God* (Downers Grove, Ill.: InterVarsity, 1994), 41–42.

18. Basinger, *Case for Freewill Theism*, 36. For other open theists who affirm God to be a risk-taker on the basis of his non-exhaustive foreknowledge, see Hasker, *God, Time, and Knowledge*, 197, and Boyd, *God at War*, 57.

The open view of God does not render God helpless before a dark and mysterious future. Nothing can happen that He has not already envisioned and for
which He has not made adequate preparations. Consequently, although God
does not know the future absolutely, He nevertheless anticipates it perfectly. . . .
God knows what could happen as the result of creaturely decisions. And He
knows just what course of action He will take in response to each eventuality.[19]

Pinnock agrees that God is able to bring his will to pass in the ultimate
sense even in a world in which finite agents are free to resist him:

He can do it because of his ability to anticipate the obstructions the creatures
can throw in his way and respond to each new challenge in an effective manner.
. . . It is possible to grant a sphere of significant freedom in the world without
fearing that God's basic goals will be realized. Nothing can happen which God
has not anticipated or cannot handle.[20]

Often cited in support of this position is Peter Geach's illustration of a
game of chess played between a Grand Master, who represents God, and a
novice, who represents humans in their freedom. While Grand Master cannot
determine every move the novice makes, he or she has sufficient skill and resourcefulness to respond to whatever the novice does so as to guarantee victory. Geach explains the illustration as follows:

God and man alike play in the great game. But God is the supreme Grand Master
who has everything under control. Some of the players are consciously helping his
plan, others are trying to hinder it; whatever the finite players do, God's plan will be
executed . . . . God cannot be surprised or thwarted or cheated or disappointed.
God, like some grand master of chess, can carry out his plan even if he has
announced it beforehand. "On that square," says the Grand Master, "I will promote
my pawn to Queen and deliver checkmate to my adversary": and it is so. No line of
play that finite players may think of can force God to improvise: his knowledge of
the game already embraces all the possible variant lines of play, theirs do not.[21]

Most open theists are not as confident as Geach that God can necessarily
win the game on any square he chooses. They would affirm that human free
choices may rule out some options that God might otherwise have pursued.
But they are agreed that no matter what humans choose to do, individually or
collectively, God will still win in the end. Thus Greg Boyd argues:

19. Rice, *God's Foreknowledge and Man's Free Will*, 58.
20. Pinnock, "God Limits His Knowledge," 146. Hasker argues in the same vein, saying
that "we certainly should not underestimate the tremendous resourcefulness of God in adapt-
ing his responses to human actions—even willful and disobedient human actions—so as to
achieve his wise and loving purposes" ("A Philosophical Perspective," in *Openness of God*, 153).
21. Peter Geach, *Providence and Evil* (New York: Cambridge University Press, 1977), 58.

[God] is an omni-resourceful God who can creatively and ingeniously work around any situation. Like a master chess player, he may not know exactly what moves his opponents will make—for he is playing persons, not a preprogrammed computer. And so he may not know exactly how many moves he will have to make, or what moves he will have to make, or even what players he may have to sacrifice in order to checkmate his opponent. But being the supreme chess player he knows the game so well, and his novice opponents so well, that he can guarantee victory.[22]

Because of this, Rice argues that

the final outcome of history is a practical certainty. God's objectives for mankind will be realized, whatever the actual course of events may be. Because God's resources are infinitely superior to those of His creatures, He can respond to all their decisions with complete adequacy.[23]

John Sanders is less confident, however, that the Grand Master analogy can adequately illustrate the personal nature of the relationship between God and his human creatures.[24] He argues that future reality is not as closed as Geach seems to suggest and that the reality of libertarian human freedom eliminates the kind of total and complete control of the game that Geach postulates (down to the very square on which God will win the game). Indeed, Sanders says that "God cannot win every move on account of human sin and evil."[25] He argues that we must distinguish between God's overall goal in creation and his specific desires for specific individuals. God's specific desires for individuals may not be accomplished: "If God does not force the creatures to reciprocate his love, then the possibility is introduced that at least some of them may fail to enter into the divine love, and thus certain of God's specific desires might be thwarted."[26]

When Sanders looks to the ultimate fulfillment of God's overall goals and objectives (asking "Will God win in the end?"[27]), he does not feel able to give

22. Gregory A. Boyd, "The Bible and the Open View of the Future" (unpublished paper, 8 July 1999).

23. Rice, *God's Foreknowledge and Man's Free Will*, 66–67.

24. Sanders, *God Who Risks*, 229–30. Sanders suggests that better analogies include that of the leader of a climbing party, who is responsible to plan for routes and supplies but who on the journey has to make ad hoc decisions along with the other members of the party, and that of a theater director directing actors and actresses in a play who also play a significant part in how the play goes (216–17, 230).

25. Ibid., 230.

26. Ibid., 229. Sanders argues that while "God's overarching intentions cannot fail in that God establishes the boundaries in which the world will operate; but God's detailed or particular desires can fail in that God may not achieve all he wants for every individual. . . . Unless one affirms either universalism or double predestination, it must be concluded that God's project ends in failure for some" (230).

27. Ibid., 234.

the kind of rational certainty Geach offers. Sanders argues that we must trust in the living God for the fulfillment of his promises. But he offers substantial hope for this ultimate victory, on much the same grounds as do other open theists—on God as the omnicompetent responder.

> We should not underestimate God's ability or overestimate our own in this enterprise. God is omnicompetent, resourceful and wise enough to take our moves into account, mighty enough to act and faithful enough to persist. If one of God's plans fails, he has others ready at hand and finds other ways of accomplishing his objectives.[28]

God's Sovereign Intervention in Human History

The other primary line of argument offered by open theists for confidence in the ultimate triumph of God over sin and evil involves his sovereign right to intervene in human history. As the Creator of the universe, God retains that right. And although God will intervene only very rarely because of his desire to respect libertarian human freedom, he will do it in order to assure that his ultimate purpose stays on track. Thus David Basinger's five-point summary of open theism, cited at the beginning of this paper, begins with the affirmation that "God not only created this world *ex nihilo* but can (and does) intervene unilaterally in earthly affairs."[29] This, Basinger says, is a crucial way in which open theism differs from process theism:

> Unlike proponents of process theism, we maintain that God does retain the right to intervene unilaterally in earthly affairs. That is, we believe that freedom of choice is a gift granted to us by God and thus that God retains the power and moral prerogative to inhibit occasionally our ability to make voluntary choices to keep things on track.[30]

John Sanders agrees that this is a powerful reason for eschatological confidence and hope for the people of God.

> God has not given everything over to us. . . . There are some things that the almighty God retains the right to enact unilaterally in the future. If the divine wisdom decides it is best to bring about some specific event in history, then God can do so.[31]

William Hasker compares God's "control" over the lives of people with the "control" that parents exercise in the lives of their small children.

28. Ibid.
29. Basinger, "Practical Implications," in *Openness of God*, 156.
30. Ibid., 159.
31. Sanders, *God Who Risks*, 234.

The parents of small children certainly desire to be "in control" of what happens in their children's lives, and often manage this to a considerable degree. But they do not, if they are wise, attempt to exercise this control by determining every detail of what their children do and experience. On the contrary: in large measure, they seek to create suitable conditions for the child to explore for itself the possibilities of life, and to encourage it to take advantage of those opportunities. Their policy could well be described as the deliberate and intensive application of "persuasive power"—though to be sure, coercive power is there in reserve, should the child start to run out into a busy roadway. Should not a similar account be given of God's control over us?[32]

Thus Hasker seems to be allowing for the possibility that should God's overall purpose start to get off track, he can intervene unilaterally and coercively (i.e., overruling libertarian human freedom) to keep things on track.

Thus for both of these reasons—God being an omnicompetent responder, and God being the sovereign God who retains the right to unilaterally intervene in human history if need be—open theists argue for a strong sense of eschatological confidence. While they may differ as to whether this eschatological confidence rises to the level of "practical certainty" (e.g., Geach, Boyd, Rice) or remains at the level of confident hope (e.g., Sanders), they are united in the conviction that God will ultimately win in the end. Jesus Christ will return and will bring the kingdom of God to its ultimate and eternal triumph. Sanders's ultimate expression of confidence is representative of this eschatological hope:

God makes promises, and we may have confidence that God will keep them even though the exact way and form in which God elects to bring them about may surprise us. Though we do not know precisely what the prophets meant by the new heavens and the new earth, we long for and expect the new and greater things that he who creates *ex nihilo* and redeems through Jesus will bring forth.[33]

Evaluation

It is the opinion of this writer that the level of eschatological confidence espoused by open theists cannot be coherently sustained within this model. Given the central theological assumptions of the open view (e.g., libertarian human freedom, God's actions being contingent upon and responsive to free human decisions, and God's non-exhaustive foreknowledge), a high level of eschatological confidence cannot stand. In fact, I will argue, there is an inverse relationship between eschatological confidence and these central, core doctrines of the openness view. The more strongly these are affirmed, the less es-

---

32. Hasker, "A Philosophical Perspective," in *Openness of God*, 142.
33. Sanders, *God Who Risks*, 235.

chatological confidence is warranted. Conversely the greater the level of eschatological confidence, the more compromises will need to be made in these core doctrines. To make this case, let me point to six observations—three of which relate to the first ground of eschatological confidence appealed to by free-will theists (God as omnicompetent responder) and three that relate to the second (God's retained right to sovereignly intervene in human affairs).

The Omnicompetent God

(1) One of the reasons why Richard Rice believes that God can omnicompetently respond to everything humans freely choose to do is that he is able to perfectly anticipate their actions in the future. As quoted earlier in this paper, Rice says

> The open view does not render God helpless before a dark and mysterious future. Nothing can happen that He has not already envisioned and for which He has not made adequate preparations. Consequently, although God does not know the future absolutely, He nevertheless anticipates it perfectly.[34]

While Rice explicitly differentiates God's "perfect anticipation" from his "absolute knowledge" of the future, it is not at all clear how a divine anticipation of future human decisions that is "perfect" is different from the classical view of divine foreknowledge. Rice goes on to acknowledge that in practical terms the results of God's perfect anticipation look to be identical with his having exhaustive foreknowledge. But he argues that with respect to creaturely freedom, there is a world of difference. Exhaustive divine foreknowledge, according to Rice, eliminates the possibility of genuine human freedom, while God's anticipation, even if it is perfect, gives room for creaturely freedom to function.[35]

Yet to this writer, Rice seems to be longing to have both sides of an incompatible combination. To ensure that the future is not determinate and definite and fixed in such a way as would eliminate the reality of libertarian human freedom, Rice seeks to downgrade God's beliefs about the future from that of certain and infallible knowledge to "anticipations" that are potentially fallible. To show that there are times when God's beliefs about the future are, in fact, mistaken, open theists often point to Jeremiah 3:6–7, 19–20:

> During the reign of King Josiah, the LORD said to me, "Have you seen what faithless Israel has done? She has gone up on every high hill and under every

34. Rice, *God's Foreknowledge and Man's Free Will*, 58.
35. Rice says, "The open view of God, then, views the future as partly definite and partly indefinite from God's perspective. His relation to the future is one of perfect anticipation. This understanding allows for creaturely freedom" (ibid., 59).

spreading tree and has committed adultery there. I thought that after she had done all this she would return to me but she did not. . . . I thought you would call me 'Father' and not turn away from following me. But like a woman unfaithful to her husband, so you have been unfaithful to me, O house of Israel," declares the LORD.

Greg Boyd says that in this text "the Lord can be heard expressing his surprise at [this] improbable happening," for even though the Lord thinks it most likely that Israel will return to him, yet something else altogether occurred. Boyd argues that this divine surprise and disappointment can only be authentic if the future is at least partly a realm of possibilities and probabilities, not settled certainties that are foreknown infallibly.[36] Terence E. Fretheim argues that these verses depict God as being overly optimistic about Israel's response to him: "The people did not respond as God thought they would. God's knowledge of future human action is thus clearly represented as limited."[37] John Sanders argues that God's knowledge of the future in this text is not just limited. He says that, "God himself says that he was mistaken about what was going to happen."[38]

But if God's "anticipation" of the future could be mistaken and wrong in this case, could it not be wrong in other more serious cases as well? It's hard to see how this kind of fallible anticipation can enable God to omnicompetently respond to whatever humans freely decide to do (how could a false anticipation help God cope with the future challenges of human history?). On the other hand, if God's anticipation of the future is perfect enough and accurate enough to provide the basis for God to make adequate preparations for his future responses, it implies just as great a fixity of future events as does exhaustive divine foreknowledge. Thus it seems that the eschatological confidence that Rice desires can only be achieved by ascribing to God's anticipations of the future a degree of accuracy that in turn undermines libertarian human freedom and the contingency of God's responsiveness to it.

(2) If human freedom is truly libertarian, how can God guarantee that he will be able to respond to every move freely made by humans in the cosmic chess game? Sanders seems to grant the force of this objection in his statement quoted above: "God cannot win every move on account of human sin and evil."[39] But if God cannot win every move, how can we be sure that he will inevitably win the decisive moves that determine the outcome of the game?

---

36. Boyd, "The Bible and the Open View of the Future," 11.

37. Terence E. Fretheim, *The Suffering of God: An Old Testament Perspective* (Philadelphia: Fortress, 1984), 46.

38. Sanders, *God Who Risks*, 74. Sanders cites Jer. 3:6–7, 19–20 as an example of "several biblical texts that seem to affirm that what God thought would happen did not come about" (ibid., 205).

39. Sanders, *God Who Risks*, 230.

Granted that God's wisdom and skill and resourcefulness are infinitely greater in comparison to ours than that of the greatest Grand Master compared to the novice chess player, but what guarantee is there that the novice will not stumble by blind chance into the one in a million move that the Master cannot respond to? As long as humans have libertarian freedom, that is always possible.

Consider, for example, God's judgment of the world through the flood. According to Genesis 6, when the Lord saw the depth and pervasiveness of human evil, he "was grieved that he had made man on the earth and his heart was filled with pain" (Gen 6:6). This is one of the divine repentance verses that are frequently appealed to by open theists to argue that God is in fact responsive to human decisions and that the give-and-take in the divine-human relationship is genuine in both directions. And free-will theists argue that for this divine repentance to be real and authentic, the depth and pervasiveness of human sin must not have been foreseen, and certainly not planned, by God.[40] Thus in genuine responsiveness to unforeseen and freely chosen human decisions, God undertakes a new and different course of action (judging the world through the flood).

But the question must be asked: what is to prevent there from being another future degeneration of the human race into sin that is even greater than that which precipitated the flood? What is to prevent an outbreak of human sin and evil that is so great and so pervasive that in response God will abandon his prior plans and destroy the human race completely in his judgment? Most open theists will argue that this kind of universal judgment will not happen, for God has promised in the Noahic covenant that it never will (Gen. 8:21–22). While God does not foreknow the free decisions of creatures possessing libertarian freedom, he can and he does know what he will unilaterally choose to do in the future.[41]

But can the God of open theism really know that? I would argue that if God is indeed genuinely responsive to humans and if God cannot infallibly know the future free decisions of humans, then it is in principle impossible for God to know infallibly what he will do in the future as well. Might there not be a future, unforeseen occurrence that would lead God to reconsider his previously planned and previously announced course of action? God could not infallibly know such an eventuality in advance. And should it occur, it is certainly possible that a genuinely responsive God would decide to change his

---

40. For example, Sanders says that the depth and pervasiveness of human sin and evil shows that "creation has miscarried." In light of that reality, "God regrets his decision to go ahead with creation in light of these tragic developments. He is extremely disappointed at how things are turning out" (*God Who Risks*, 49).

41. For example, Rice argues that God can know his future actions "that are not dependent upon circumstances in the creaturely world but arise solely from God's personal decision" (*God's Foreknowledge and Man's Free Will*, 56–58). In addition, God knows all that will happen in the future as a deterministic result of present and past factors (ibid.).

plans. This is what happened when God reconsidered his announced intention to destroy Nineveh after the Ninevites had repented in response to the preaching of Jonah. Open theists (and classical Arminians and Calvinists alike) consider God's statement of impending judgment to fall upon Nineveh to include an implicit, though unstated, condition.[42] But how do we know that God's promise never again to destroy all living creatures (Gen. 8:21) is not similarly conditional? The point is that the mere statement of the God of open theism that he will never do something in the future (or a positive statement that he will most assuredly do something in the future) cannot be taken as an absolute guarantee. There is always the possibility that some unforeseen event in the future would move this genuinely responsive God to change his announced plans and do things differently. Thus even God's knowledge of his own actions in the future is at best probabilistic.[43] And so God's statement that he will ultimately triumph over sin and evil is no necessary guarantee. As Grudem says,

> How can we be sure that God will triumph over [evil] in the end? Of course, God *says* in Scripture that he will triumph over evil. But if he was unable to keep it out of his universe in the first place and it came in against his will, and if he is unable to predict the outcome of any future events that involve free choices by human, angelic, and demonic agents, how then can we be sure that God's declaration that he will triumph over all evil is itself true? Perhaps this is just a hopeful prediction of something that. . . . God simply cannot know.[44]

(3) While the distinction that Sanders draws between God's overall goals and objectives for his creation project and his specific desires for individual persons is necessary if one seeks to hold to both overall eschatological confidence and the libertarian freedom of individual human beings, it comes with a very heavy price to pay. Sanders's distinction assumes that it is possible for

---

42. Rice, *God's Foreknowledge and Man's Free Will*, 79–80; Pinnock, "God Limits His Knowledge," 158; Hasker, *God, Time, and Knowledge*, 194–95; Sanders, *God Who Risks*, 70, 131. For examples of non-open theists who understand God's statement to Nineveh as including an implicit condition, see William Lane Craig, *The Only Wise God: The Compatibility of Divine Foreknowledge and Human Freedom* (Grand Rapids: Baker, 1987), 41–44, and Wayne A. Grudem, *Systematic Theology: An Introduction to Biblical Doctrine* (Grand Rapids: Zondervan, 1994), 164–65.

43. Richard Swinburne argues that God cannot know what he will do in the future. He grounds this, however, not in God's responsiveness to unforeseen, freely chosen actions of humans, but rather in the nature of God's own libertarian freedom. Just as exhaustive divine foreknowledge is incompatible with libertarian human freedom, so it is incompatible with libertarian divine freedom. "I conclude that it seems doubtful whether it is logically possible that there be both an omniscient person and also free men; but that it is definitely logically impossible that there be an omniscient person who is himself perfectly free" (*Coherence of Theism*, 177).

44. Grudem, *Systematic Theology*, 350.

God's ultimate purposes in history to be fulfilled in history even while many individuals reject God's grace in Christ and end up in hell. If this is the case, then God's ultimate purposes must be separated from the welfare of individual human beings. God's ultimate purposes must be cosmic and racial rather than individual. This reality, then, would go against the claim that open theism magnifies the love of God for individuals.[45] In reality, it seems to do the opposite.[46]

God's Sovereign Intervention

(4) If one of the crucial grounds for eschatological confidence is that God retains the right to intervene unilaterally (and coercively) in human history to keep things on track, the question must be raised: On what basis does God decide when and if he should intervene? Sanders said, as we saw above, "If *the divine wisdom* decides it is best to bring about some specific event in history, then God can do so."[47] But on what basis does this divine wisdom operate? Certainly it is not on the basis of his infallible foreknowledge of human decisions. Open theism is insistent that God does not possess such exhaustive foreknowledge. And God's probabilistic beliefs or anticipations about the future can be wrong (so open theists argue from Jer. 3:6–7, 19–20). Without such foreknowledge, how can God be confident that any particular occasion is decisive enough to call for his unilateral intervention to "keep things on track"? If God cannot know infallibly or accurately predict the future free decisions of human beings, he cannot know when it would be necessary for him to intervene. And he cannot know the ultimate impact of his intervention, for he cannot know how humans will choose to respond to his actions in human history. Thus God is forced to make his decisions about whether and how to intervene based on incomplete knowledge. This hardly seems to be the exercise of divine wisdom that Sanders understands it to be.

(5) If and when God does intervene, two crucial questions must be raised. Does that divine intervention into human affairs overrule and eliminate human freedom? Clearly the answer is yes. The libertarian view of human

---

45. Richard Rice is perhaps representative of open theists in emphasizing the love of God. "From a Christian perspective, *love* is the first and last word in the biblical portrait of God. . . . Love is central, not incidental, to the nature of God. Love is not something God happens to do, it is the one divine activity that most fully and vividly discloses God's inner reality. Love, therefore, is the very essence of the divine nature. Love is what it means to be God" ("Biblical Support," in *Openness of God*, 18–19).

46. For if God's overall purposes can still be accomplished with many individual humans spending eternity in hell, his overall purposes cannot be tied to love of specific individuals. They can only be tied to a general purpose such as that of giving libertarian freedom to each person and then respecting his or her ultimate choice.

47. Sanders, *God Who Risks*, 234 (italics mine).

freedom asserted in open theism could be characterized as an "either/or" kind of position. Either a particular human action is divinely determined (as when God intervenes in human history to keep things on track) or it is free. This is opposed to a compatibilist understanding of freedom that is "both/ and." Compatibilism affirms that every free human action is both divinely determined and humanly free. But unlike compatibilism, open theism has no place for divine determination to exist along with human freedom. Thus if God intervenes, it by definition eliminates human freedom.[48] That is why Hasker labels such intervention "coercive." Again this is different than its compatibilist counterpart, which asserts that God determines human actions non-coercively.[49] Millard Erickson points out the implications of this fact:

> If I understand Hasker correctly, he seems to be suggesting that, in a situation of extremity, God may use "coercive power" to exercise his "control over us." But is this not the very thing with which the free will theists have charged the classical view: of holding that God coerces, or works irresistibly, thus robbing humans of their freedom? If he is actually suggesting this, however, then the difference between this view and the classical view is one of degree, not of kind.[50]

A second question that follows is whether God's unilateral intervention, which overrules human freedom, also eliminates human moral responsibility. Again the answer is yes. Open theists affirm that libertarian freedom is the necessary prerequisite for moral responsibility. Pinnock says:

> The idea of moral responsibility requires us to believe that actions are not determined either internally or externally. The Bible agrees with our intuitions about choosing and moral behaving. The love God wants from us is a love we are not compelled to give. The sin God condemns us for is a sin we did not have to commit. They are actions for which there are not prior conditions which render

48. For example, David Basinger says that proponents of the open view "deny that God can unilaterally control human decision-making that is truly voluntary but affirm that God can unilaterally intervene in human affairs" ("Practical Implications," *Openness of God*, 160). But because of the great value that God puts on freedom, "he does not normally *override* such freedom, even if he sees that it is producing undesirable results" (ibid., 156).

49. For example, compatibilist John Feinberg says, "According to determinists such as myself, an action is free even if causally determined so long as the causes are nonconstraining. This view is often referred to as *soft determinism* or *compatibilism*, for genuinely free human action is seen as *compatible* with nonconstraining sufficient conditions which incline the will decisively in one way or another" (John Feinberg, "God Ordains All Things," in *Predestination and Free Will*, 24–25).

50. Millard J. Erickson, *God the Father Almighty: A Contemporary Exploration of the Divine Attributes* (Grand Rapids: Baker, 1998), 91.

them certain—actions which result from the genuine choices of historical agents.[51]

Thus when God unilaterally intervenes in human affairs, which open theists affirm he does occasionally to ensure his ultimate and final triumph over sin and evil, he eliminates human freedom and moral responsibility. This means that at the most crucial points in all of human history, where the key decisions have to be made that will be decisive for the final outcome, God effectively takes humans out of the picture, turning them into "robots," as it were, devoid of freedom and moral responsibility in these decisions. Ultimately, then, open theism, which seeks to elevate the reality and the importance of libertarian human freedom and of human moral responsibility, ends up minimizing these realities. For at the crucial decisive moments in human history, God is willing to dispense with both freedom and moral responsibility.[52]

(6) If the God of open theism retains the right to intervene in human history to control and/or overturn human decisions so as to ensure that his project stays on track, this causes great problems with respect to the problem of evil.[53] Simply put, if God can intervene sometimes, why not at other times? Even if we agree with Basinger and affirm that God intervenes only very rarely (say 1 percent of the time or even 0.1 percent), the question can still be raised: Why this 0.1 percent and not some other? For example, the question might be asked: why did God not intervene to stop the Holocaust? If God is as good a predictor as open theists like Rice and Pinnock claim that he is, he certainly could have seen it coming and intervened to prevent it. Or even if he could not have foreseen it, he certainly would have been aware of the Holocaust once it started, and he could have intervened and minimized the suffering and death.

51. Pinnock, "God Limits His Knowledge," 149. Bruce Reichenbach (not an open theist, but one who is also committed to libertarian human freedom) also argues that this kind of freedom is an indispensable requirement for moral responsibility. "If persons are to be held morally accountable for their actions, they must have been able to have acted differently." (Bruce Reichenbach, "God Limits His Power," in *Predestination and Free Will*, 104).

52. Again, the contrast with a compatibilist view is important to see. Compatibilists say that in every free decision that God determines non-coercively, the human actor remains both genuinely free and morally responsible.

53. This charge, if it can be substantiated, is a serious one for open theism, for they regularly assert that one of the primary benefits of their position is its greater ability to deal with the problem of evil in an adequate way. See, for example, Hasker, "A Philosophical Perspective," in *Openness of God*, 152, and Basinger, "Practical Implications," in *Openness of God*, 168–71. Other examples of an appeal to the free-will defense by theologians sympathetic to open theism include Peter Geach, *Providence and Evil*, and Michael Peterson, *Evil and the Christian God* (Grand Rapids: Baker, 1982). For an argument that open theism does not do a better job of dealing with the problem of evil than does classical theism, see Paul Helm, "The Philosophical Issue of Divine Foreknowledge," in *The Grace of God, the Bondage of the Will*, ed. Thomas R. Schreiner and Bruce A. Ware (Grand Rapids: Baker, 1995), 485–97.

It seems that at this point, open theists are in worse shape than are Calvinists.[54] The God of Calvinism has reasons (shrouded in mystery, to be sure) as to why he would allow any particular evil and how it would fit into his overall plan. But the God of open theism hates evil and is unalterably opposed to it. Yet he allows it to occur in his universe when he could have prevented it.[55] Again the argument that only very minimal divine intervention is possible so that God can preserve libertarian human freedom doesn't work, for the question can still be raised why this particular evil should be the one that God prevents and not another.

Conclusion

My goal in this essay has been to evaluate the grounds of eschatological confidence proposed by open theists. After examining the arguments of God as omnicompetent responder and of God's right to sovereignly and unilaterally intervene, I conclude that neither argument warrants such eschatological confidence in light of certain central, core convictions of open theism. In the end, I affirm that there is an inverse relationship between the level of eschatological confidence that is possible and the reality of human libertarian freedom, the genuine responsiveness and contingency of God in his relationships with his human creatures, and God's inability to infallibly know future free decisions of humans, angels, and demons. To the extent that one is elevated, the other is diminished. To quote Erickson again, the God of open theism

> does not coerce or override free human will. Further, he does not even know what humans are freely going to choose and do. How, then, can he really know how best to go about eliminating evil? Although there is strong confidence that this will happen, it is not at all clear that such confidence is really warranted. To be sure, God will ultimately overcome evil, according to his view. But to do so, he may have to make one of his last-resort coercive efforts.[56]

Thus in the final analysis, according to Erickson, open theists are confronted with the dilemma of "either the loss of human freedom or of certainty of the ultimate outcome."[57]

---

54. This is not to say that Calvinists do not have many difficult issues that arise in their own system with regard to the problem of evil. I am only trying to argue that open theists are in no better shape, and arguably in worse shape, on this particular point.

55. Thus open theists end up asserting some type of permissive will of God. To be sure, Sanders argues strenuously against any kind of view that asserts "two wills in God" (*God Who Risks*, 217–20). Yet when he allows for the possibility of God intervening at certain points in history but says that he doesn't always intervene, he seems to be allowing for another, permissive, sense of God's will. Whenever there are evil acts of free human beings that God chooses to allow rather than intervening to stop, he is exercising a form of permissive will.

56. Erickson, *God the Father Almighty*, 289.

57. Ibid., 92.

In the end, I would argue, open theists must come face to face with this very choice: either they can give up a high degree of eschatological confidence and assurance, or they can give up or limit key elements of their position. But they cannot have both.

17

The Openness of God and the Assurance of Things to Come

John Sanders

Huntington College

"Now faith is the assurance of things hoped for, the conviction of things not seen" (Heb. 11:1 NASB). Biblical figures looked forward to the fulfillment of what God had promised. Some of these promises have come to fruition, while others await fulfillment. Christians are to look forward in confidence to God's bringing about the final victory over evil. However, some object that proponents of the openness of God cannot have assurance that God will accomplish what has been promised either because of libertarian freedom or because God does not have exhaustive definite foreknowledge of contingent events. In order to answer this objection, this paper will first summarize the openness model, state the objection, and then respond to the objection by articulating and answering five related questions.

Summary of the Openness Model

The understanding of divine providence from the openness of God model may be summarized as follows. First, the *triune* God of love has, in *almighty* power, created all that is and is *sovereign* over all. In *freedom* God decided to create beings capable of experiencing the triune love. God loves us and desires for us to enter into reciprocal relations of love with him and our fellow creatures. In creating us, the divine intention was that we would come to experience the triune love and respond to it with love of our own and freely come to collaborate with God toward the achievement of God's goals. Second, God

281

has, in *sovereign freedom*, decided to make some of his actions contingent upon our requests and actions. God establishes a project and elicits our free collaboration in it. Hence, there is conditionality in God for God truly responds to what we do. Third, the only *wise* God has chosen to exercise general rather than meticulous providence, allowing space for us to operate and for God to be creative and resourceful in working with us. Fourth, God has granted us the libertarian freedom necessary for a truly personal relationship of love to develop. Despite the fact that we have abused our freedom by turning away from the divine love, God remains *faithful* to his intentions for creation. Finally, the *omniscient* God knows all that is possible to know. God knows the past and present with exhaustive definite knowledge and knows the future as partly definite and partly indefinite. God's knowledge of the future contains knowledge of what God has decided to bring about unilaterally (that which is definite) as well as knowledge of possibilities (that which is indefinite) and those events which are determined to occur (e.g., an asteroid hitting a planet).

In bringing about the divine project, God established a covenant with the creation, making a fundamental commitment to its well-being and to seeing the project through to completion. The commitment to love his creatures and bring them into a reciprocal relationship of love is fundamental to God. Once sin enters the scene, God does not give up on his covenantal commitment but, instead, responds to this development with a strategy for redeeming the situation.[1] The flexibility of the divine strategies does not imply a change in the fundamental commitment, but it does mean that God reacts to contingencies, taking them into account in order to fulfill the goal of his project.[2] God remains faithful to his original purpose even while adjusting plans to take into account the deci-

1. Even those who affirm timeless knowledge or simple foreknowledge have to say that God atemporally either planned ahead for this contingency or responded to it in this way once God in foreknowledge "saw," and thus "learned," sin would occur, which implies that God is conditioned by creatures.

2. For a helpful discussion of this notion see Eugene TeSelle, *Christ in Context: Divine Purpose and Human Responsibility* (Philadelphia: Fortress, 1975), 148–55. Wolfhart Pannenberg (*Systematic Theology,* trans. Geoffrey Bromiley [Grand Rapids: Eerdmans, 1991], 1:380, 388) disagrees with this approach, saying that the concept of a goal implies a difference between the goal and its fulfillment. God, according to Pannenberg, can have no goals because a God with goals left to fulfill is a finite God. This point was made earlier by Plato, who claimed that God could not love or desire something, for that would indicate a lack in God (an imperfection), and Spinoza, who held that God could not pursue purposes since this would imply that God lacks (a deficiency) what he purposes to achieve. For Pannenberg, God does not have unfinished goals because God experiences all time at once (simultaneity). Consequently, God does not have an open future at all! This is quite contrary to what many have thought Pannenberg was saying regarding God's actual experience in history. His use of simultaneity (following Boethius and Plotinus) and his disavowal of talk of God as an agent leads me to suspect that Pannenberg is uneasy, at best, with the notion of a personal God working with us in history toward an open future.

sions of his free creatures. God establishes general commitments and is free to decide some specific future actions that he will undertake. Hence, the future is partly open or indefinite and partly closed or definite. It is not the case that just anything may happen, for God has acted in history to bring about events in order to achieve his unchanging purpose.

Furthermore, the covenant or general commitment God makes is not a detailed script, but a broad intention that allows for a variety of options regarding precisely how it may be reached. "The divine plan," says Jacques Maritain, "is not a scenario prepared in advance, in which free subjects would play parts and act as performers. We must purge our thought of any idea of a play written in advance."[3] Some things are fixed while others are contingent. At creation God establishes a general purpose that, as history progresses, becomes more specific. God decides on certain routes in connection with human choices such that the specifics of the final destiny, as well as the path to it, take on greater definitiveness as the relationship unfolds. What God and people do in history matters. Had Jacob's family returned to Canaan after the famine was over, there would have been no bondage in Egypt and no need for an exodus. God would have continued working with them, but history would have been very different. If the midwives had feared Pharaoh rather than God and killed all the baby boys, it would be a different story than the one we have. That God resorts to plan B, allowing Aaron to do the public speaking instead of Moses, altered what God had in mind. If the Jewish leaders had come to accept Jesus as God's way in the world, we would have had a very different Book of Acts and subsequent history than we do. What people do and whether they come to trust God makes a difference concerning what God does.[4] This does not mean that God is helpless in the face of human sin. "God is not," says Brian Hebblethwaite, "stumped by men's failure to co-operate. There are things that God can do to bring good out of evil—the paradigm being the incarnation and the cross of Christ. But at every point, we realize that God does not fake the story of human action and human history."[5]

Objection

Proponents of specific sovereignty, however, object to this open-ended view of history. Paul Helm explains specific sovereignty thus: "God does not,

---

3. Jacques Maritain, *Existence and the Existent*, trans. Lewis Galantiere and Gerald Phelan (New York: Random House, 1966), 116.

4. Proponents of specific sovereignty can say that what people do matters in the sense that God is using people as secondary causes. But they cannot say that it makes a difference for God, since every single detail God wants to happen does happen according to specific sovereignty.

5. Brian Hebblethwaite, "Some Reflections on Predestination, Providence and Divine Foreknowledge," *Religious Studies* 15, no. 4 (December 1979): 437.

then, exercise providential control in a way that leaves two or more possible ways of achieving some goal. Nor does he will the end but leave the means to others. . . . Rather, the providence of God is fine-grained; it extends to the occurrence of individual actions and to each aspect of each action."[6] For Helm, God has an exhaustive *blueprint* for everything: an eternal plan that contains all the details which will ever occur. R. C. Sproul adds, "If there is one single molecule in this universe running around loose, totally free of God's sovereignty, then we have no guarantee that a single promise of God will ever be fulfilled. . . . Maybe that one molecule will be the thing that prevents Christ from returning."[7] Will God win in the end? Is it simply unwarranted posturing for proponents of relational theology to claim that God will achieve victory? Where is our security if God does not guarantee every single detail? What guarantee is there that God will prevail if humans have libertarian freedom? If any of God's promises depend upon contingent decisions, what security do we have that God's ultimate purpose will not be thwarted?

Response to the Objection

In response, let me make two observations. First, the only ones, to my knowledge, raising these questions are proponents of specific sovereignty. I am not aware of any Arminian, Wesleyan, or other freewill theist raising these objections; the reason for this will be spelled out below. The second observation has to do with the core beliefs of Christian eschatology. Though many evangelicals have developed elaborately detailed eschatological schemes, most Christian eschatology has been far more modest. The Apostle's Creed affirms that Jesus will return to judge the living and the dead and that there will be a resurrection of the flesh. The Scriptures speak of God bringing about a new heaven and earth and Revelation refers to this as a place wherein God dwells and there is no darkness (21:25), curse (22:3), sea (21:1), death (21:4), or temple (21:22). We shall be like him, for we shall see him as he is (1 John 3:2). Finally, God will achieve his purpose: we shall be his people and he shall be our God, dwelling among us (Rev. 21: 3, 7). There is nothing in the openness model incompatible with these claims or the assertion that God can bring these about. To see why this is so, five related questions will be examined: (1) Can a God who grants libertarian freedom and does not foreordain all things give us assurance? (2) Can a God without exhaustive definite foreknowledge give us assurance? (3) Does God have a blueprint for the future? (4) What is the nature and ground of our assurance? (5) Will the possibility of evil come to an end?

6. Paul Helm, *The Providence of God* (Downers Grove, Ill.: InterVarsity, 1994), 104.
7. R. C. Sproul, *Chosen by God* (Wheaton, Ill.: Tyndale, 1986), 26–27.

Can a God Who Grants Libertarian Freedom and Does Not Fore-ordain All Things Give Us Assurance?

According to proponents of specific sovereignty, who claim God foreordains all things, we have no grounds for trusting that God will bring the future about as promised unless God controls every single detail of history. Luther writes: "If you doubt, or disdain to know that God foreknows and wills all things, not contingently, but necessarily and immutably, how can you believe confidently, trust to, and depend upon his promises?"[8] If God's knowledge is not based upon his foreordination of all things, but, instead, upon what he simply foresees contingent beings doing in the future, then the future is not secure and we cannot trust God to fulfill his promises. John Feinberg focuses on libertarian freedom (the ability to do otherwise than you did): "I wonder how God can guarantee that his ends will be done in virtue of contra-causal freedom. Given such freedom, it must always be possible for someone to overturn God's plans by choosing to do otherwise than God wants."[9] If the divine will can be resisted and thwarted, then how can we have any assurance that the eschaton will come about as promised?

The first point to notice is that this is not an objection against the openness model only, but against *all classical freewill theists*, including Arminians. Although contemporary theological determinists are shouting this objection most vociferously against proponents of openness, it applies just as much to all who affirm libertarian freedom. So, how can freewill theists have any assurance? To begin, Feinberg has misstated the freewill theist's position.[10] We do not maintain that humans have an "absolute" freedom, but freedom within limits—we are not unconditionally free. God has sovereignly established the rules of the game by which the divine-human relationship shall operate. We simply do not have the freedom to do anything we wish. God has not given everything over to us. God is the one who established the conditions, and so his overarching purposes cannot be thwarted. Whatever ability we have to thwart God's more specific plans is given us by God. Moreover, there are some things that the almighty God retains the right to enact unilaterally in the future. If the divine wisdom decides it is best to bring about some specific event in history, then the almighty God can do so. Feinberg asserts that all freewill theists are committed to the belief that we can *always* "overturn God's plans." This is simply incorrect, for some of God's plans involve God's performance of certain actions regardless of what humans want to do (e.g., creating the new heavens and earth or bringing about a final judgment). Moreover, although

8. Martin Luther, *The Bondage of the Will*, quoted in Alan Johnson and Robert Webber, *What Christians Believe* (Grand Rapids: Zondervan, 1989), 91.

9. John Feinberg, "John Feinberg's Response," in *Predestination and Free Will: Four Views*, ed. David Basinger and Randall Basinger (Downers Grove, Ill.: InterVarsity, 1986), 125.

10. I would like to thank Kevin Gilbert for bringing this to my attention.

we affirm that God does not normally override human freedom, we do believe God can do so. R. K. McGregor Wright is incorrect when he asserts that all Arminians believe that "God never overrides our free will."[11] David Basinger explains: "Freewill theists do not deny that God has the capacity (power) to keep a person *in every case* from acting out her intentions and/or to prohibit undesired consequences. . . . Nor do freewill theists deny that God might in some cases be justified in intervening in this manner. Freewill theists believe that God does unilaterally control some things."[12] God can, and does, intervene when he deems it necessary to accomplish his purposes. Though freewill theists agree that God can and has overridden human freedom, we do not all agree as to when in Scripture God has done so. Nevertheless, the openness and Arminian contention is that, as a general rule, God does not normally override the freedom he has given us.[13] Consequently, God's ability to control the events of history—including the movement of molecules—is limited only by God's sovereign restraint, not by his inability to do so.[14]

Can a God without Exhaustive Definite Foreknowledge Give Us Assurance?

Although proponents of simple foreknowledge reject divine foreordination of all things, they believe there is a way to affirm both that God has granted us libertarian freedom and that God can guarantee the promised future.[15] According to simple foreknowledge, God simply perceives all of time at once (without causing it) and so, when God proclaims that thus and such will occur in the future (the end from the beginning), we can be absolutely sure that it will. Moreover, they claim that the openness of God position cannot have assurance regarding the fulfillment of divine promises, since a God without exhaustive definite knowledge of all future contingent events is unable to guarantee the future because God does not know for sure what humans will do. According to Jack Cottrell: "Because it is by this means that God can allow

11. R. K. McGregor Wright, *No Place for Sovereignty: What's Wrong with Freewill Theism* (Downers Grove, Ill.: InterVarsity, 1996), back cover.

12. David Basinger, *The Case for Freewill Theism* (Downers Grove, Ill.: InterVarsity, 1996), 34.

13. Freewill theists do not all agree as to how often or precisely where in biblical history God has overridden human freedom (e.g., Peter's denial, the crucifixion, etc.).

14. Michael Horton defectively states our position when he says we believe God is "intrinsically" dependent upon creation. If it is God's sovereign choice to be dependent, for some things, upon creatures, then it is most certainly not an intrinsic dependence. See his "Challenges to the Classical Doctrine of God," *Modern Reformation* (September 1999): 2.

15. Simple foreknowledge is the belief that God's eternal knowledge of all future contingent events is *dependent* upon what contingent beings decide to do in the future. Proponents claim that foreknowledge does not imply determinism, and they reject the notion that God foreknows the future because God foreordains the future.

man to be truly free in his choices, even free to resist his own special influences, and at the same time work out his own purposes infallibly. For if God foreknows all the choices that every person will make, he can make his own plans accordingly, fitting his purposes around these foreknown decisions and actions."[16] Cottrell believes God can use foreknowledge to either permit or prevent human choices.

Unfortunately, proponents of simple foreknowledge have failed to realize that this model cannot deliver the desired result. Having discussed this extremely important point in some detail elsewhere, I will here simply summarize why this theory cannot provide any guarantees about the future.[17] Can a God with simple foreknowledge prevent certain evil choices? No, for the simple reason that if what God *foreknows* is the *actual* world, then God foreknows (in exhaustive detail) the births, lives, and deaths of actual events in people's lives—not what *might* happen to them. Once God has foreknowledge of actual events, he cannot change what will happen, for that would render his foreknowledge incorrect (i.e., God would foreknow what does not actually happen). God cannot make actual events "deoccur." If God foreknows (has knowledge of the actual occurrence) that Adam will freely choose to mistrust God, then God cannot intervene to prevent Adam from this mistrust. Hasker correctly observes that:

> It is clear that God's foreknowledge cannot be used either to *bring about* the occurrence of a foreknown event or to *prevent* such an event from occurring. For what God foreknows is *not* certain antecedents which, unless interfered with in some way, will *lead to* the occurrence of the event; rather, it is *the event itself* that is foreknown as occurring, and it is contradictory to suppose that an event is *known* to occur but then also is *prevented* from occurring. In the logical order of dependence of events, one might say, by the "time" God knows something will happen, it is "too late" either to *bring about* its happening or to *prevent* it from happening.[18]

If God has simple foreknowledge of future contingent events and sees that humans will do what God desired, it will be so because God was fortunate enough that free beings decided to do what God wanted. It will not be because foreknowledge enabled God to do something which otherwise would not have

16. Jack Cottrell, *What the Bible Says about God the Ruler* (Joplin, Mo.: College Press, 1984), 208.

17. See my "Why Simple Foreknowledge Offers No More Providential Control than the Openness of God," *Faith and Philosophy* 14, no. 1 (January 1997): 26–40, and my *God Who Risks: A Theology of Providence* (Downers Grove, Ill.: InterVarsity, 1998), 200–206.

18. Hasker, *God, Time, and Knowledge* (Ithaca, N.Y.: Cornell University Press, 1989), 57–58. This same point was made in 1843 by Billy Hibbard, *Memoirs of the Life and Travels of B. Hibbard*, 2d ed. (New York: self-published), 387, and is also discussed by Keith Ward, *Rational Theology and the Creativity of God* (New York: Pilgrim, 1982), 152.

happened. Simple foreknowledge simply does not guarantee the future—it is an illusory solution to the problem. A God with simple foreknowledge is not able to guarantee *on the basis* of simple foreknowledge, from before creation, that God's plans would be successful in every detail. If a God with simple foreknowledge promises his ultimate triumph over evil, it will be due to the divine *almightiness, not foreknowledge.* Hence, a God with simple foreknowledge has no more ability to guarantee the success of his plans than does the God of the open view because simple foreknowledge is simply useless for providential control. Adherents of both simple foreknowledge and the openness model have precisely the same sort of assurance regarding the fulfillment of the eschaton. Thus, Arminians and proponents of openness are in the same boat.

In order for proponents of simple foreknowledge to have assurance of the fulfillment of God's promises in the future, they have to appeal to the *divine power*, rather than simple foreknowledge, to bring about such events. It is divine power over the forces of evil, rather than exhaustive definite foreknowledge of their defeat, that is the basis for our hope. Arminians have emphasized the wrong divine attribute for this issue. Consequently, theological determinists, Arminians, and proponents of the openness of God all affirm (or should affirm) that God guarantees the future judgment, new heaven and earth, and resurrection of the body, not because he sees these events ahead of time, but because he has preordained to bring these events to fruition. All that is required is that God have the requisite power to bring them about, and freewill theists affirm that he does.[19]

Does God Have a Blueprint for the Future?

Though some forms of popular evangelicalism have elaborate formulations of the "end times," I read biblical prophecies to be about the overall trajectory of God, rather than predictions of precise details regarding the future. Although "inquiring minds want to know," God has chosen not to provide details relevant only for those alive at the very end. Instead, God provides a vision of the victory over the powers of evil and the full manifestation of the divine presence in the new creation. When one examines the prophecies in the Old Testament about the redemption of Israel, it becomes clear that it was not possible to deduce from God's initial covenant purpose exactly how God would seek to accomplish his project. It was not possible

---

19. Proponents of middle knowledge believe it offers a way in which God can exercise meticulous control over all events while (supposedly) retaining libertarian freedom, and can thus provide us with assurance that what God has promised, he is able to accomplish. Most Calvinists, however, reject middle knowledge because the so-called counterfactuals of freedom are not under God's control and thus compromises God's absolute independence. See William C. Davis, "Does God Know the Future via Middle Knowledge?" *Modern Reformation* (September 1999): 24–25.

for anyone to predict that God would elect the people of Israel for a special task. Nor was it knowable just how the people would respond and how God would react to them in the course of the covenant relationship. Nobody expected the particular kind of Messiah Jesus chose to be. Who would have thought that God would "overrule" sin by the redemptive grace of the cross? The disciples certainly did not! The crucifixion crushed their hopes that Jesus was the Messiah (Luke 24:21). Who could have known that God was going to bring the Gentiles into the people of faith as he did? That the early Christians did not is demonstrated by the pervasive turmoil over this issue in much of the New Testament literature.

The path God takes to achieve his purpose is not a detailed, pre-planned, route, but, as seen in the biblical story, is an unpredictable zigzag course. Van de Beek puts it well: "the way of God to Christ was not an established road. It is a way which can only be read in retrospect in the light of Christ, not guaranteed in advance. It is a way on which God went past many dead ends."[20] Just as there is no way to deduce what God must do in carrying out his purpose, so there is no infallible way of predicting what God will do in the future. Just as the disciples had to undergo a paradigm shift in order to understand what God had done in Jesus, so we may be quite surprised as to the precise nature of the new creation. Nevertheless, God does provide us some clues about his ultimate direction based on the way God has chosen to work in history—especially in the life, death, and resurrection of Jesus. Wherever the Holy Spirit blows he seeks to take people in the trajectory of Jesus. Jesus points us toward the future which the Father wants to establish. Christology informs eschatology.[21]

God has established some definite events and states of affairs for the future, yet the specific nature as well as the route God takes to reach these states of affairs is not yet entirely definite. Paul Fiddes is on track when he says,

> Decisions and experiences in this life matter: they are building what we are. Since God's aim is the making of persons, he has the certain hope that we will be "glorified," but the *content* of that end depends upon human responses, for the content of the end is persons. . . . Thus the risk upon which God is embarked is real and serious, though not a total one. He has a certain hope of the fact of the end, but there is a genuine openness about the route and therefore the content of the end.[22]

20. A. van de Beek, *Why? On Suffering, Guilt, and God*, trans. John Vriend (Grand Rapids: Eerdmans, 1990), 300.

21. This is a point badly neglected in many discussions of eschatology. See Adrio König, *The Eclipse of Christ in Eschatology: Toward a Christ Centered Approach* (Grand Rapids: Eerdmans, 1982).

22. Paul S. Fiddes, *The Creative Suffering of God* (New York: Oxford University Press, 1988), 105.

It is like a "Choose Your Own Adventure" novel in which there are a number of story lines, and the particular story that develops depends upon the choices one makes. The possible story lines are set by the author, but the reader becomes active in the determination of which line is actualized. Similarly, God has established the possible story lines along with a definite ending, but which paths are taken to that ending and some of the specific content of the ending are the results of the decisions taken in the course of the divine-human interaction.

God is able to bring about the specifics he chooses even though he has granted us libertarian freedom. Yet, someone may object that if so much depends upon individual human decisions, what assurance do we have that God will be successful? Can we prevent God from bringing about the eschaton? Might nuclear or biological warfare, for instance, place God's plans in jeopardy? A variety of responses are available to the freewill theist. To begin, who knows whether such things might not be God's way of bringing about the end? If they are not, God might intervene to disrupt such plans or God would be ready with contingency plans—God will not be caught off guard. Think for a moment about the nature of the world according to many contemporary scientists who affirm that nature is partially definite and partially indefinite—there are determinate boundaries as well as indeterminate specifics. This is as true in quantum physics as it is in sociology or the animal kingdom.[23] Insurance companies, for example, accurately predict death and accident rates in various parts of the population. Sociologists can predict what portion of a given population will become alcoholics. Scientists can predict what a colony of ants will do. What they cannot predict, however, is what any one individual in the group will do. Which individual will be in an accident this year, which individual will become addicted, and which ant will move a particular grain of sand, are not predictable. If humans are able to bring about states of affairs utilizing such unpredictability, what is to preclude God from doing so? God need not meticulously control every detail in order to bring about certain states of affairs. If God has been able to work in human history given its partially determinate and partially indeterminate nature, and we have seen what God has accomplished thus far, we ought to have great confidence in God's ability to bring about the type of future he desires. We should not underestimate God's ability, as does Sproul, to cope with contingencies. God is omnicompetent, resourceful, and wise enough to take our moves into account, mighty enough to act, and faithful enough to persist. According to Gabriel Fackre, "The foreknowledge of God is grounded in the confidence God has

---

23. I thank Gregory Boyd for some of these illustrations. For a study of how humans and God make use of unpredictability, see D. J. Bartholomew, *God of Chance* (London: SCM, 1984).

in the Power of God, the Holy Spirit, to fulfill the eternal purpose of God."[24] This leads to the next point.

What Is the Nature and Ground of Our Assurance?

Regarding the nature of assurance, many evangelicals seem to equate assurance with rational certitude—the end of a process of reasoning such that we cannot be wrong. Much of evangelical apologetics, in both its rationalist and empiricist forms, is given over to the quest for absolute certainty and is driven by the acceptance of the Enlightenment criteria for knowledge. Many evangelicals have decided to play by the rules of the game established by modernity, with its requirement of an absolutely secure foundation in order to have rational certainty. This has led, in my opinion, to grounding our hope in some sort of "system" of thought (e.g., impassibility) so that we are able to see God operating according to that system and thus guarantee the outcome we long for. Instead, we need to trust in God, not in a system we have constructed for God's way of working in the world.[25] We are assured in our hope by the work of the triune God in history.

Our assurance is grounded in the character of God, as revealed in Scripture, and in what God has done in human history. Abraham, for example, was promised a son through his old and barren wife, Sarah. According to Paul, Abraham understood his own old age and Sarah's barrenness, yet he believed that what God had promised, God was able to perform (Rom. 4:19–20). It is doubtful that Abraham placed his assurance of this promise in divine foreknowledge. Rather, his confidence was grounded in God's previous work in his own life and in the almighty and faithful character of God. God has a proven track record demonstrating his resourcefulness in fulfilling his promises. This is especially so in relation to Jesus Christ, whom Paul says is our hope (1 Tim. 1:1; Col. 1:27). It is our privilege to *hope* in the living God (1 Tim. 4:10). We, who have a taste of the victory of God, look forward to our own salvation as well as the redemption of the cosmos (1 Thess. 5:8; Rom. 8:18–23). We hope in the revelation of the glory of God (Rom. 5:2), and we must wait eagerly for it (Rom. 8:24–25). God makes promises, and we may have confidence that God almighty will keep them, even though the exact way and form God elects to bring them about may surprise us. Though we do not

---

24. Gabriel Fackre, *The Christian Story*, rev. ed. (Grand Rapids: Eerdmans, 1984), 257.

25. Donald Bloesch, following the Reformers, affirms that we have a "certainty of faith . . . a spiritual, not a rational, certainty" produced by the inward confirmation of the Holy Spirit and grounded in the work of Jesus Christ. Bloesch distinguishes between certainty (firm belief in something), assurance (confidence), and security (protection or guarantee from doubt), and he concludes that "there is certainty and assurance in the Christian faith but not security" (*The Ground of Certainty* [Grand Rapids: Eerdmans, 1971], 68). See also Bloesch, *A Theology of Word and Spirit: Authority and Method in Theology* (Downers Grove, Ill: InterVarsity, 1992), 202.

know the precise nature of the new heavens and new earth, this should not prevent us from assurance of the new and greater things that he who creates *ex nihilo* and redeems through Jesus will bring forth. Sproul's claim that one molecule not under God's meticulous control could ruin God's redemptive plans shows little confidence in almighty God's ability to cope with contingencies. God's ultimate victory is not in doubt, but the precise way in which God will triumph is not something we can describe in detail. The almighty, faithful, loving, and wise God, who has repeatedly demonstrated his ability to fulfill his promises in a world of contingent creatures, is the solid source of our assurance.

The assurance that God will bring his redemptive project to fruition is centered in the divine wisdom, power, and faithfulness manifested in the resurrection of Jesus Christ. The creator of the world is the author of the new creation in Christ as well. Israel was called to remember God's mighty hand in the exodus, and this was their basis for hope. Christians are called to remember the power of God in raising Jesus from the dead, and this is our basis for hope. Thomas Finger puts it well: "One's faith is based not on what has not yet happened but on what has already occurred."[26] If God created the present world and raised Jesus from the dead, then we ought to have confidence that God can bring about a new creation in Christ that overcomes suffering and death. In light of what God has done, we have assurance that nothing can happen that our wise, almighty, faithful, and loving God cannot handle. With Christ as our hope we can, with consistency, say with Paul: "I am convinced that neither death nor life, nor angels, nor principalities, nor things present, *nor things to come* . . . will be able to separate us from the love of God, which is in Christ Jesus our Lord" (Rom. 8:38–39 NASB, italics added).

Will the Possibility of Evil Come to an End?

Despite all that has been said, our detractors see a problem in our affirmation of both libertarian freedom and God's ultimate victory over evil. Given the fact of our ability to choose otherwise, will we be able to sin in heaven? How can God guarantee the absence of sin if being sin-free is contingent upon human choices? Could we, as Origen speculated, fall away from the divine glory in the new creation? Several points may be made in response. To begin, it needs to be pointed out again that this is not just a problem for the openness view, but for all who affirm libertarian freedom, including the early fathers, Eastern Orthodox, Arminians, Wesleyans, and other freewill theists. In light of this, one wonders why the charge is being directed so narrowly and vituperatively at the proponents of openness: have the theological determinists forgotten about the Arminians? Second, we

---

26. Thomas Finger, *Christian Theology: An Eschatological Approach* (Nashville: Nelson, 1985), 1:124.

should recall that in the new heaven and earth God will dwell with us and be among us in a way we presently do not experience (Rev. 21:3). God will make "all things new" (Rev. 21:5), and part of making all things new will involve a powerful divine disclosure—we shall see the face of God (Rev. 22:4). Moreover, God's name shall be on our foreheads (Rev. 22:4)—we will not need phylacteries any longer (Exod. 13:16). We shall be like him for we shall see him as he is (1 John 3:2). Hence, we shall experience life with God as we never have.

This reality would seem to be so far beyond what we now experience that it is difficult for us to say precisely what will happen. Nevertheless, I shall venture some options that have been put forth by proponents of libertarian freedom (some of the proposals differ only in matters of emphases). One suggestion is that we will retain our libertarian freedom in heaven but we will not be tempted to do evil, and so sinning will not be a possibility for us. Peter van Inwagen suggests that in heaven we shall have both the Beatific Vision and the memories of the hideousness of our existence prior to our restoration to God. Such knowledge will prevent us from sinning.[27] A second possibility, put forth by Gary Habermas and J. P. Moreland, holds that the glorification process involves the free choice to attain the state where we are either unable to sin or consistently able not to sin.[28] Perhaps we shall freely choose to be so conformed to the image of Christ and our love for God so deepened that we freely never sin. This would be something like a furthering of the Wesleyan understanding of entire sanctification. Putting this in older theological terms, we might say that our material freedom (the freedom to love God) becomes so confirmed and pervasive that we freely never use our formal freedom to sin. One might connect this to the Eastern Orthodox notion of *theōsis*, whereby we are incorporated into the divine nature (or image of Christ) such that we never desire to sin.

A final possibility is that we shall no longer have libertarian freedom to sin. Gregory Boyd, for instance, believes the reason why God granted us libertarian freedom—a probationary period in which to make the choice to enter into a loving relationship with God—will have been fulfilled and so there will no longer be need of it. We freely give God our permission to finish the conformation of our character toward Christlikeness. In this view, we are becoming irreversibly confirmed in our character by the choices we make. James Sennett asks: "What does it take for a character to be formed appropriately?" It requires "that an agent must be responsible for his character formation—*choosing* it by performing certain undetermined actions at certain points in his life.

---

27. Peter van Inwagen, *God, Knowledge and Mystery* (Ithaca, N.Y.: Cornell University Press, 1995), 112–13.

28. Gary Habermas and J. P. Moreland, *Immortality: The Other Side of Death* (Nashville: Thomas Nelson, 1992), 150–51.

A character that is libertarian freely chosen is the only kind . . . ."[29] We are freely choosing to develop our characters either toward or away from God. Our freedom to do otherwise diminishes as we become increasingly godly or demonic. Over time we become permanently one or the other "until our *doing* has determined our *being*."[30] Thus, we will find that although we could have been otherwise had we chosen a different path, we now have become what we chose to be.[31]

Hence, all freewill theists, including proponents of openness, have plausible explanations as to why there will be no moral evil in heaven and why they may have assurance of God's triumph over sin and the eradication of evil.

Conclusion

The openness model has been accused of forfeiting any confidence we might have in God's ability to deliver on his eschatological promises. We have seen that, despite appearances to the contrary, all other varieties of freewill theism (including Arminians and proponents of simple foreknowledge) may be accused of the same thing, since foreknowledge does not solve the problem. The Arminian and other freewill models are in no better, or worse, position to handle this objection than the openness of God model. Moreover, just like other freewill theists, proponents of openness may have the same degree of confidence that the almighty, wise, faithful, and loving God will be able to bring it about that he shall be our God and we shall be his people in the eschaton. Our assurance for this is firmly based on the resurrection of Jesus from the dead. It is with great confidence that we look forward to the time when Jesus will return to judge the living and the dead, bring about the resurrection of the flesh, and consummate the new heaven and earth.

29. James F. Sennett, "Is There Freedom in Heaven?" *Faith and Philosophy* 16, no. 1 (January 1999): 74. Sennett argues that the character formed by libertarian freedom eventually becomes compatibilist freedom. In heaven we shall be confirmed in character and never desire to sin, but this requires libertarian freedom to form it or we sacrifice a number of positions we cherish such as the freewill defense for the problem of evil.

30. Gregory Boyd, "Satan and the Problem of Evil" (unpublished manuscript).

31. A variation of this last position draws upon Alvin Plantinga's distinction between morally significant freedom (the ability to sin or not to sin) and libertarian freedom (the freedom to do otherwise in all areas but sin). According to this view, in the new creation we shall lose our morally significant freedom but retain our libertarian freedom. Consequently, in heaven we shall make lots of free choices, just not choices to sin. See his *God, Freedom and Evil* (Grand Rapids: Eerdmans, 1977), 29–30.

18

Theodicy, Eschatology, and the Open View of God

STEVEN R. TRACY

Phoenix Seminary

Theodicy is arguably the most formidable theological challenge Christians face as we begin the twenty-first century. Many atheistic philosophers argue that the presence of evil and suffering give powerful evidence that God does not exist.[1] Some theists, on the other hand, maintain that evil is best explained not by denying God's existence, but by denying his goodness.[2] Other theists, particularly process theologians, validate God's goodness, but deny his omnipotence. Charles Hartshorne, who is largely responsible for the formulation of process theodicy, argues that God's power is not the power of deterministic omnipotence, but the "appeal of unsurpassable

---

1. J. L. Mackie has given one of the classic articulations of this in "Evil and Omnipotence," *Mind* 64 (1955): 200–212. Mackie argues that religious beliefs do not lack all rational support, but rather they are positively irrational in view of conflicting postulates regarding God and evil (God exists and is omniscient and omnipotent; a perfectly good being would eliminate evil as far as possible; there are no limits to what an omnipotent being can do; evil exists). William Rowe modifies this argument by asserting that a good God would eliminate all pointless suffering, "The Problem of Evil and Some Varieties of Atheism," *American Philisophical Quarterly* 16 (1979): 335–41.

2. For example, Richard Rubenstein declares that the Holocaust has rendered the "Father-God" of traditional theology dead, yet he affirms the existence of a divine "Holy Nothingness" that is described as a "cannibal mother" (*After Auschwitz: Radical Theology and Contemporary Judaism* [Indianapolis: Bobbs-Merrill, 1966], 198). See also Elie Wiesel, *Night* (New York: Avon), 42.

love."[3] It is not coercive, but persuasive power. God is not responsible for good or evil, but rather for the possibility of both good and evil. Evil and suffering result from creaturely autonomy and are by-products of the natural laws that support life.[4] While many theists have found the process theodicy quite convincing,[5] others have found this solution far too radical, and have countered with a multitude of theodicies that affirm both the goodness and the omnipotence of God.

Theodicy and Eschatology

Central to much of the theodicy debate has been the role of eschatology. Ivan Karamazov is the often-cited spokesman for those who assert that one can only rebel against a theodicy that somehow seeks to explain present evil based on future blessedness. After citing various hideous examples of child abuse, Ivan mercilessly queries his religious brother Alyosha:

> Let's assume you are called on to build the edifice of human destiny so that men would finally be happy and find peace and tranquility. If you knew that, in order to attain this, you would have to torture just one single creature, let's say the little girl who beat her chest so desperately in the outhouse, and that on her unavenged tears you could build that edifice, would you do it? ... And do you find acceptable the idea that those for whom you are building that edifice should gratefully receive a happiness that rests on the blood of a tortured child and, having received it, should continue to enjoy it eternally?[6]

In other words, how can anyone accept a future blissful existence in heaven that is built on the earthly suffering of children? Similarly, process

---

3. Charles Hartshorne, *Omnipotence and Other Theological Mistakes* (Albany, N.Y.: SUNY Press, 1984), 14.

4. Hence, ultimately a theologically interpreted evolutionism is said to do more to explain human evil than anything else written in the last 2,000 years (Hartshorne, *Omnipotence*, 126–30).

5. David Ray Griffin draws heavily on Hartshorne, but offers a more refined process theodicy. See his *Evil Revisited: Responses and Reconsiderations* (Albany, N.Y.: SUNY Press, 1991) and *God, Power, and Evil: A Process Theodicy* (Philadelphia: Westminster, 1976). Barry Whitney affirms a process theodicy, but questions whether Hartshorne has underestimated the coercive aspect of God's persuasive influence (*Evil and the Process God* [New York: Edwin Mellen, 1985], 88–141). Tyron Inbody draws heavily on process theology and believes the best response to suffering is not to affirm "raw divine omnipotence" but to build a trinitarian theology which highlights divine passibility, and the transforming power of God, evidenced in the incarnation and the crucifixion of Christ (*The Transforming God: An Interpretation of Evil and Suffering* [Louisville: Westminster/John Knox, 1997], 167–69).

6. Fyodor Dostoevsky, *The Brothers Karamazov* (New York: Bantam, 1970), 296. For a bold response to Dostoevsky, see Thomas Tracy, "Victimization and the Problem of Evil: A Response to Ivan Karamazov," *Faith and Philosophy* 9 (1992): 301–19.

theodicies expressly deny that present suffering can be satisfactorily justified eschatologically, for if God is omnipotent, why would he establish
justice in the next world but not this one? Furthermore, how do we even
know that he will establish justice in the next world when we have no evidence of him doing so in this world?[7] John Hick, on the other hand, has
very influentially argued the opposite position, reasoning that suffering is
integral to the perfection of the soul, and most of this takes place eschatologically in the future eternal state: "Theodicy cannot be content to look
to the past, seeking an explanation of evil in its origins, but must look towards the future, expecting a triumphant resolution in the eventual perfect fulfillment of God's good purpose."[8] Indeed, much of the theodicy
debate hinges on how present evil and suffering are related to God's future
eschatological work.

Open View Theodicy

Recently several "open view" theologians have offered a rather novel theodicy that is ostensibly given from within the evangelical tradition, and yet significantly deviates from the historical evangelical understanding of the divine
attributes.[9] While the open view theodicy places pivotal emphasis on theology
proper, not eschatology, I will argue that some of the most serious weaknesses
of the open view theodicy are eschatological.

Richard Rice proposes two chief characteristics of an "open view" of God.[10]
First of all, love is the definitive divine attribute, and involves not just care and
commitment, but genuine responsiveness. God's interaction with the world is
dynamic, not static. He influences the world, yet he is truly influenced by it.
Hence "the course of history is not the product of divine action alone. God's
will is not the ultimate explanation for everything that happens."[11] This di-

---

7. Inbody, *Transforming God*, 68. Whitney argues that from a process perspective, belief in
a conscious existence in the afterlife is not essential for Christianity or for the theodicy (*Evil
and the Process God*, 158).

8. John Hick, *Evil and the Love of God*, 2d ed. (New York: Harper & Row, 1978), 340.

9. One of the first broad explanations of an open view was a work coauthored by Clark
Pinnock, Richard Rice, John Sanders, William Hasker, and David Basinger, entitled *The
Openness of God: A Biblical Challenge to the Traditional Understanding of God* (Downers Grove,
Ill.: InterVarsity, 1994). The fullest treatment of the open view to date is given by John Sanders
in *The God Who Risks: A Theology of Providence* (Downers Grove, Ill.: InterVarsity, 1998). David Basinger gives a philosophical treatment of an open view model in *The Case for Freewill
Theism: A Philosophical Assessment* (Downers Grove, Ill.: InterVarsity, 1996). Gregory Boyd,
while not formally calling himself an "open view" theologian, is strongly sympathetic with this
view of God in *God at War: The Bible and Spiritual Conflict* (Downers Grove, Ill.: InterVarsity,
1997). John Boykin also offers a model very similar to the open view in *The Gospel of Coincidence: Is God in Control?* (Grand Rapids: Zondervan, 1986).

10. Richard Rice, "Biblical Support for a New Perspective," in *Openness of God*, 15–16.

11. Ibid., 15–16.

vine interaction with creation is such that God in some ways is conditioned by the creatures he created. He takes risks because things do not always turn out as he plans or desires.[12] Secondly, God's knowledge is dynamic, for he knows and learns as events take place in history. This is called an "open view" of God since he is "receptive to new experiences" and "flexible in the way he works toward his objectives in the world."[13]

An open view of God is said to be particularly helpful for the problem of suffering and evil. This is said to be shown in several ways: (1) Evil and suffering can be understood to be the gratuitous byproducts of a world containing freedom, byproducts that we and God wished had not occurred. Suffering is not part of a divine plan, and it does not necessarily lead to a greater good. This is said to be a far healthier understanding than the traditional view of meticulous sovereignty that must explain even the most horrendous evil as the outworking of a specific divine plan.[14] (2) God is relieved of the responsibility for evil and suffering, for he is not their immediate or remote cause. On the other hand, with the traditional model of meticulous divine sovereignty, "the human agent is the immediate rapist and God is the mediate rapist."[15] (3) Because God does not have simple foreknowledge and only knows the past and the present, he did not know that evil and suffering would result from his creation of the world. He only knew that it might occur. In other words, "the present world is something of a divine adventure or experiment, the results of which were not foreknown when God decided to create."[16] Hence God cannot be indicted for creating beings who failed to love him or who turned out evil, since he did not know for certain that this would happen. (4) We can take seriously the biblical statements regarding God being grieved and angry at sin, for it is not part of his plan. On the other hand, those who hold the traditional view must deny divine displeasure over sin and suffering, for in their model "God gets precisely what he intends in each and every situation."[17]

12. Sanders, *God Who Risks*, 10–11.

13. Ibid., 16.

14. Basinger, "Practical Implications," in *Openness of God*, 170–71. Similarly, Boyd mocks what he calls the traditional "divine blueprint" view of divine sovereignty that affirms "a cosmos that is being coercively run by a supreme being who secretly wills the torture of little girls—'for his glory'" (*God at War*, 292).

15. Sanders, *God Who Risks*, 255–56.

16. Ibid., 260; cf. also Basinger, "Can an Evangelical Christian Justifiably Deny God's Exhaustive Knowledge of the Future?" *Christian Scholars Review* 25 (1995): 133–45. John Cowburn, who is not an open view theologian but draws on Augustine and Teilhard de Chardin (a most unlikely synthesis), makes a similar argument about God's foreknowledge of evil. He states, "When a young person dies or a deformed child is born, and people ask, 'Did God want this to happen?,' the best short answer is 'No—he didn't even know it was going to happen'" (*Shadows and the Dark: The Problems of Suffering and Evil* [London: SCM, 1979], 37).

17. Ibid., 257.

Strengths of Open View Theodicy

Suffering and Evil Are Taken Seriously

Many Christian theodicies are rightfully criticized for minimizing the nature or extent of human suffering and evil. Sometimes this results from suffering and evil being analyzed in a largely theoretical manner. For example, Alvin Plantinga's Free Will Defense is a tightly argued rebuttal to Mackie's atheistic theodicy.[18] At the same time, explaining the logical necessity for evil as the price for a universe that contains free moral good without evaluating the extent and nature of specific human evil is quite unsatisfying in post-Holocaust history. Marilyn McCord Adams's criticism of Plantinga's theoretical Free Will Defense is appropriate. She writes "Plantinga explicitly hopes that the problem of horrendous evils can thus be solved without being squarely confronted."[19]

Other theodicies also suffer from the temptation to soften the reality and extent of suffering by appealing to a higher good. For example, Paul Helm argues for an *o felix culpa* (happy fault) view of theodicy via the fall of Adam. Since the fall brought about the great blessings of redemption, it can be considered a "happy fault."[20] This approach necessarily minimizes the agony of evil and suffering that resulted from the fall and cannot be reconciled with God's agony and displeasure at human suffering (Hos. 11:8; Matt. 9:36; John 11:35). Nor can this view be reconciled eschatologically with the Pauline understanding of death as the last great enemy to be conquered at Christ's return (1 Cor. 15:26). Additionally, it cannot be harmonized with the cosmic reconciliation of Christ found in Colossians 1:20, in which everything, particularly the demonic spirits, will be put back in their proper place under the lordship of Christ (cf. Phil. 2:9–11; Rom. 8:18–24).[21]

Many other theodicies seek to affirm the sovereignty and goodness of God in the face of human suffering, but fail to account for the extent and severity of human suffering and evil. Evil haunts real places at real times and destroys real people. Kenneth Surin recounts the many Jewish children not only gassed but

---

18. Alvin Plantinga, *God, Freedom, and Evil* (Grand Rapids: Eerdmans, 1977). Plantinga demonstrates that, logically, there is a different kind of good (freely chosen moral good) that God cannot bring about without permitting evil.

19. Marilyn McCord Adams, "Horrendous Evils and the Goodness of God," in *The Problem of Evil: Selected Readings*, ed. Michael L. Peterson (Notre Dame, Ind.: University of Notre Dame Press, 1992), 213. See also Kenneth Surin, "Theodicy," *HTR* 76 (1983): 230–32.

20. Paul Helm, *The Providence of God* (Downers Grove, Ill.: InterVarsity, 1994), 214–15. This type of logic leads Helm elsewhere to state that there is no real tragedy in the life of a believer (141).

21. Steven Tracy, "Living under the Lordship of Christ: The Ground and Shape of Paraenesis in the Epistle to the Colossians" (Ph.D. diss., University of Sheffield, England, 1995), 96–99.

burned alive in Nazi furnaces. He reminds the would-be theodicist to "take burning children seriously."[22] Only when suffering is taken seriously will the eschatological promises receive their full import. Because suffering is so real and destructive, the believers' great hope is that some day God shall wipe away every tear and remove all suffering, mourning, and death (Rev. 21:4).

Open view theologians do take burning children seriously and squarely confront the problem of horrendous evil. Boyd, for example, uses the hideous story of the mutilation and murder of Zosia by the Nazis to frame the discussion of his entire book. Other open view theologians are also forthright in their consideration of the reality of human evil and horrible suffering.[23] This is a significant strength of their theodicy.

God Is Not Responsible for Suffering and Evil

One of the driving objectives of open view theodicy is the attempt to clear God of responsibility for suffering and evil. This objective must be seen in the light of the traditional Calvinistic explanation that all suffering and evil is a necessary part of the divine decree. Since in Calvinism the decree is understood to be absolute (unconditional), universal (all-comprehensive), efficacious, and immutable, everything that happens, including sin and evil, is ultimately the will of God and happens because God sovereignly determined that it should happen.[24] Gordon Clark is so bold as

22. Kenneth Surin, "Taking Suffering Seriously," in *Problem of Evil*, 347. John Wenham illustrates the danger of not taking human suffering seriously enough by appealing in an abstract way to a higher good and to divine sovereignty. He argues that while there is much terrible evil in the world, if we extract the evil caused by sin, then the world does look like something worthy of a good creator. But of course that is precisely the problem—God himself has not extracted the suffering and evil from the world. Wenham closes his argument by stating that "if God is both omnipotent and good, and God loves us, we have the answer to our question. Why do we suffer? We suffer (however strange and paradoxical it may sound) because God loves us" (*The Goodness of God* [Downers Grove, Ill.: InterVarsity, 1974], 48). Wenham's upbeat determinism rings very hollow in the presence of burning children.

23. For example, Sanders begins his monograph on divine providence by telling about his brother's tragic death, and shows great sensitivity to evil and suffering throughout the book (*God Who Risks*, 9–10, 253, 262–63).

24. See Louis Berkhof, *Systematic Theology* (Grand Rapids: Baker, 1942), 104–5. Berkhof argues, however, that with respect to sin the decree is "permissive," but this is not a passive permission that softens the certainty of the decree, but rather one which "renders the future sinful act absolutely certain." See also the Westminster Confession, 3.1: "God from all eternity did . . . ordain whatsoever comes to pass; yet so as thereby neither is God the author of sin, nor is violence offered to the will of the creatures"; cf. R. K. McGregor Wright, *No Place for Sovereignty: What's Wrong with Free Will Theism* (Downers Grove, Ill.: InterVarsity, 1996), 197–202. For a well-reasoned "semi-Augustinian" explanation of the decree that affirms God's sovereignty but denies that the decree of God is exhaustive of all events, see Gordon Olson, "Building Soteriology upon a Sound Foundation: An Inductive Study of the Sovereignty of God" (paper presented at the annual meeting of the Evangelical Theological Society, Orlando, Florida, 19–21 November 1998).

to declare "I wish very frankly and pointedly to assert that if a man gets drunk and shoots his family, it was the will of God that he do so."[25] This is based on Clark's Calvinistic understanding of the sovereign decree of God as the necessary explanation for all that transpires.[26] He writes "God is the cause of sin. God is the sole cause of everything. There is absolutely nothing independent of him. He alone is the eternal being. He alone is sovereign."[27]

This attribution of everything to the sovereign decree of God is, of course, a defining trait of Calvinism. Calvin himself in his discussion of election notes that God predestined the fall into sin for "God not only foresaw the fall of the first man, and in him the ruin of his descendents, but also meted it out in accordance with his own decision."[28]

Open view theologians on the other hand, correctly take great offense at the suggestion that a loving God would be responsible for evil. They rightfully assert that the triune God of Scripture is a loving God who continually works to bless his creation.[29] God created a perfect world. Sin and suffering come from Satan and human rebellion, not from God.[30] It is a horrible offense to charge God with being the author of evil. He cannot be tempted with evil, and he tempts no one (James 1:13). He is light, and in him there is no darkness (1 John 1:5). He is too pure to look on evil (Hab. 1:13). He hates evil and evil-

25. Gordon Clark, *Religion, Reason, and Revelation* (Grand Rapids: Baker, 1961), 221.

26. The later Augustine influentially developed the idea that everything must have a cause, and that the cause of everything in the universe is the will of God, and thus even sin is willed by God. David Griffin documents Augustine's development of these concepts (*God, Power, and Evil*, 55–71). Even John Calvin attributes to Augustine the concept that with respect to sin, there is no distinction between God's will and his permission, for "the will of God is the necessity of [all] things" (*Institutes*, 3.23.8). John Boykin correctly notes that if God's will determines all that comes to pass, then he is creating the very misery and evil that we Christians are called to alleviate (*The Gospel of Coincidence: Is God in Control?* [Grand Rapids: Zondervan, 1986], 52). On the complexity of understanding suffering to be the will of God, see John Edelman, "Suffering and the Will of God," *Faith and Philosophy* 10 (1993): 380–88.

27. Clark, *Religion, Reason, and Revelation*, 239.

28. *Institutes*, 3.23.7.

29. Clark Pinnock, *Flame of Love: A Theology of the Holy Spirit* (Downers Grove, Ill.: InterVarsity, 1996), 29–30, 49–77. Strong Calvinists who affirm limited atonement would certainly take issue with this statement, for they typically proclaim that God's love is limited to the elect. When one limits God's love to the elect and then emphasizes the wrath of God on sinners, the theodicy is no longer a problem. Hence the theodicy is solved by limiting or qualifying his goodness. For example, R. C. Sproul, in a discussion of God's goodness and suffering, states that "the difficult question is not how God could allow us to suffer but how he could allow us, who rebel against his majestic authority every day, who repay our Maker with incessant revolt, ever to experience pleasure. There is no logical problem of pain for sinners, only a problem of pleasure" (*Almighty over All: Understanding the Sovereignty of God* [Grand Rapids: Baker, 1999], 142). Based on this logic, the problem of suffering vanishes, for humans deserve all the suffering they ever get.

30. Boyd, *God at War*, 33–57; Sanders, *God Who Risks*, 253–55.

doers (Ps. 5:5–6; 45:7; Prov. 8:13). Thus when the unregenerate commit sin and evil they are, in fact, carrying out the will of Satan, not the will of God (2 Tim. 2:25–26). Even a staunch Calvinist such as Henri Blocher acknowledges that "Holy Scripture rejects as a satanic calumny and as blasphemy the least hint that God could be the accomplice of evil, that he should harbour its seed in his heart, or, which amounts to the same thing, that he should incorporate it in what comes forth from him. God is utterly, radically, absolutely good."[31]

Even though the fact that God is not responsible for evil might not seem to be an eschatological theme, it ultimately is. This is seen most poignantly when we note God's creative purpose. Cornelius Plantinga insightfully declares that God desires *shalom*—fullness, wholeness for creation. Sin is a vandalism of *shalom*, for it interferes with the way things are supposed to be.[32] Eschatology is the process of God reclaiming a fallen, broken creation and reestablishing *shalom* (cf. the picture of the new heavens and new earth in Isa. 65:17–25). Hence we distort eschatology when we make God responsible for evil. Open view theodicy correctly places blame for evil where it belongs—on divinely created beings who misuse their freedom.

The Final Eschatological Triumph of God over Evil and Suffering Is Affirmed

While open view theologians redefine God's present control of world events, they do affirm the triumph of God at the parousia of Christ. This is particularly true of Boyd, who in the final few paragraphs of his book states:

> In direct contrast to all this [unacceptable models of theodicy], the ultimate hope that the New Testament carries is eschatological. As sure as the Lord came the first time to defeat his cosmic enemy and our oppressor in principle, just as certainly he shall return again to defeat him in fact. . . . Paul has the inspired audacity to proclaim that, when the kingdom has finally fully come, the glory and joy that we shall know will render all the sufferings of this present world insignificant.[33]

While other open view theologians do not place as much emphasis on eschatology as Boyd does, they do rightfully affirm God's future victory over sin and evil.

---

31. Henri Blocher, *Evil and the Cross* (Downers Grove, Ill.: InterVarsity, 1990), 96; see also A. van de Beek, *Why? On Suffering, Guilt, and God* (Grand Rapids: Eerdmans, 1990), 121–99.

32. Cornelius Plantinga, *Not the Way It's Supposed to Be: A Breviary of Sin* (Grand Rapids: Eerdmans, 1995), 7–27.

33. Boyd, *God at War*, 293.

Problems with Open View Theodicy

In spite of the strengths of the open view theodicy, I propose that the model as a whole does not solve the problem of evil but exacerbates it. Given the manner in which the ontological nature of God is reformulated, it in fact undercuts the very basis for the ultimate triumph of God over evil and suffering. I will seek to demonstrate that the open view's flaws with respect to theodicy are largely eschatological in nature.

Gratuitous Evil and Eschatology

Much of the open view theodicy is built upon the necessity of gratuitous evil. Some say it liberates God from responsibility for evil.[34] William Hasker also argues that it is necessary to maintain morality, for if God intervenes to prevent evil, then morality is undermined.[35] Gratuitous evil is defined in open view theodicy as evil that is not necessary for some greater good; it is pointless evil.[36] The logic of this argument quickly unravels when one asks how something can be gratuitous if it is necessary. As Keith Chrzan notes, "After telling us that gratuitous evil is not necessary for the production of a great good, Hasker argues that it is necessary for preventing the undermining of morality. If an evil is justified because morality is undermined in its absence, it is odd to construe that evil as gratuitous: preventing the undermining of morality seems like a pretty great good."[37]

We can press this faulty logic further by noting that open view theologians differentiate their view from process theology by affirming that God is ontologically distinct from creation and that God can, and occasionally does, intervene in human history.[38] They emphasize, however, that he

---

34. Basinger argues that "we need not, for example, assume when someone dies that God 'took him home' for some reason, or that the horrors many experience in this world in some mysterious way fit into God's perfect plan" ("Practical Implications," in *Openness of God*, 170); also see Sanders, *God Who Risks*, 261–63.

35. William Hasker, "The Necessity of Gratuitous Evil," *Faith and Philosophy* 9 (1992): 29–30. Michael Peterson argues that God granting human free will necessitates the possibility of gratuitous evil (*Evil and the Christian God* [Grand Rapids: Baker, 1982], 103–5).

36. Basinger, "Practical Implications," 170; Sanders, *God Who Risks*, 262. One's specific definition of gratuitous evil is very important, for Griffin states that with clarification, process theologians deny the possibility of gratuitous evil (*Evil Revisited*, 227).

37. Keith Chrzan, "Necessary Gratuitous Evil: An Oxymoron Revisited," *Faith and Philosophy* 11 (1994): 135.

38. Clark Pinnock, "Systematic Theology" in *Openness of God*, 194 n. 49. Sanders has a similar understanding of God, but by stating that God cannot "habitually" prevent moral evil, he clearly implies that God occasionally prevents moral evil (*God Who Risks*, 258). Basinger similarly says that God cannot "consistently" use his power to intervene in human affairs and prohibit negative consequences (*Freewill Theism*, 34). He clearly states that God has the power to intervene, and implies that he occasionally does so. To remain evangelical one must acknowledge that God at least occasionally does intervene in human history to alleviate evil and suffering.

cannot intervene on a regular basis, or it would undermine the conditions of his creation project and would be incompatible with human freedom. But if it is incompatible with human freedom for God to intervene on a regular basis, then it is incompatible with human freedom for him to do so occasionally. Furthermore, if we accept the premise that God only intervenes in human history occasionally to alleviate suffering or evil, we must still ask why he would do so on these rare occasions. Why alleviate a little bit of suffering? At this point, the open view theodicy faces the same problem as does traditional theology, though with fewer resources.[39]

None of us can explain why God miraculously intervenes when he does, or why he does not intervene when he does not. The biblical record makes it quite clear, however, that God does intervene consistently to alleviate suffering and to eliminate evil. It is surprising that Pinnock, in particular, who identifies himself as a charismatic and says that Pentecostalism is the "most important event in modern Christianity," would so thoroughly undercut the basis for Spirit-generated miracles to alleviate human suffering.[40]

We need not be able to identify the reasons for God's intervention or failure to intervene in order to assert that such reasons do exist and that gratuitous evil is a wholly unbiblical concept. Why did God miraculously intervene to protect Mary, Joseph, Jesus, and the wise men (Matt. 2:12–14) but not the Hebrew children (Matt. 2:16–18)? Why was Herod able to kill James (Acts 12:2), while immediately afterward Peter was miraculously delivered from his grasp (Acts 12:3–11)? Why were Judean Christians ravaged and imprisoned by Saul (Acts 8:1–3), while Samaritan believers experienced miraculous healings and deliverance from evil spirits (Acts 8:4–8)? Why was Paul miraculously delivered from prison *after* being beaten in Philippi (Acts 16:25–27)? Why was Paul not delivered from prison at the end of his life (2 Tim. 4:6)?

The classic chapter on faith, Hebrews 11, highlights this mystery of God's broad, yet unpredictable intervention. The first portion (vv. 4–35a) lists person after person who trusted God and saw him intervene miraculously to alleviate suffering and overcome evil. Curiously, however, in the middle of verse 35, after mentioning women who received back their dead by resurrection, the author abruptly signals a shift in content by simply stating "and others." He then documents other men and women of equally commendable faith who were tortured, beaten, imprisoned, stoned, and even sawn in two. The language and concepts found in verses 35–36 are primarily drawn from the account of the gruesome torture and martyrdom of Eleazar and his sons re-

---

39. Edward Wierenga makes this criticism in his review of *Openness of God* in *Faith and Philosophy* 14 (1997): 251–52.
40. Pinnock, *Flame of Love*, 18.

corded in 2 Maccabees 7 and 4 Maccabees 5–6.[41] Second Maccabees 7:1–39 describes seven brothers being tortured on the rack, having their tongues cut out, scalped alive, having hands and feet cut off, and being fried in a pan over a fire because they refused to dishonor God by eating swine's flesh. Hebrews 11:35 accurately describes the brothers' behavior—they did not accept release (and avoidance of torture) in view of their resurrection by God (2 Macc. 7:11, 13, 29). While the Hebrews passage and the martyrdom accounts in Maccabees do not necessarily posit the same divine reasons for human suffering, both are predicated on the fact that reasons do exist; believers are to endure present suffering and evil in light of God's redemptive purposes that will be fully experienced in heaven. This point is made crystal clear in Hebrews 12:1–2. In light of the previous cloud of witnesses, we are to fix our eyes on Christ, who "for the joy set before him" endured the suffering and evil of the cross. Present suffering is the basis for future joy; therefore, suffering and evil are not gratuitous.[42]

Hebrews 11, like the rest of Scripture, is predicated on the fact that God can and often does intervene as he pleases to alleviate suffering and to repress evil.[43] While the author of Hebrews 11 certainly does not attempt to give a theodicy to explain those times God did not intervene, as we have already seen, we are at least given a category for understanding this mystery—eschatology. Hebrews 11:1 begins with an eschatological thesis statement about faith—it is "the assurance of things hoped for, the conviction of things not seen" (NASB).[44] The entire chapter revolves around this thesis, for the author demonstrates that whether one experiences miracles to alleviate suffering and evil or one does not, either way, the promises of God are at best only partially fulfilled in this life (both groups of people are said not to have received what was promised—vv. 13, 39). Thus the chapter ends with a powerful eschato-

---

41. F. F. Bruce, *The Epistle to the Hebrews* (Grand Rapids: Zondervan, 1964), 339–40. The word for "torture" in Heb. 11:35 refers to torture on the rack, which is described in 4 Macc. 5:32; 8:13; 9:12–22. The word for "mocking" is found in 2 Macc. 7:7, and a cognate in 2 Macc. 7:10. The term for "beating" and its verbal form are used through the martyrdom account in 2 and 4 Maccabees.

42. Marilyn McCord Adams notes that victims of torture can look to Christ, for "they see in the cross of Christ a revelation of God's righteous love and a paradigm of his redemptive use of suffering" ("Redemptive Suffering: A Christian Solution to the Problem of Evil," in *Rationality, Religious Belief and Moral Commitment*, ed. Robert Audi and William Wainwright [Ithaca, N.Y.: Cornell University Press, 1986], 267).

43. Note, for example, Jack Deere's refutation of the cessationist argument that biblical miracles are confined to three narrow periods of biblical history. Deere's table covering just the Old Testament demonstrates the broad range of miracles throughout the entire Old Testament (*Surprised by the Power of the Spirit* [Grand Rapids: Zondervan, 1993], 253–66).

44. William Lane says Heb. 1:1 reveals an "eschatological concept of faith," so that believers can move courageously into the unseen future supported only by the promises of God (*Hebrews 9–13* [Dallas: Word, 1991], 329–30).

logical promise—while we suffer and do not receive the promised blessings in this life (v. 39), God has provided something far better in the future (v. 40). This eschatological understanding of faith in the face of intractable human suffering is quite relevant to one argument for gratuitous evil. Michael Peterson claims it overrides the evidence of experience to deny the reality of gratuitous evil.[45] But this is precisely the point of Hebrews eleven—do not limit your view of God or of suffering to the horizontal plane of human history or it will seem pointless. God is working eschatologically to fulfill all of his promises, particularly the ones that appear threatened by human suffering and evil. This great faith chapter hardly supports the open view claim of purposeless suffering. Rather, gratuitous evil vitiates this biblical explanation of faith looking ahead to the future redeeming work of God.

What does it mean to say that in the face of our suffering we can find eschatological hope by looking ahead? This is not a disjunctive, escapist view of heaven as a time merely to forget about our earthly sorrows, but rather, we look ahead knowing that our present experiences of evil and suffering will be eschatologically redeemed.[46] In fact, given the inaugurated nature of New Testament eschatology, particularly in the Pauline Epistles, this eschatological overthrow and redemption of evil has already begun through the cross (1 Cor. 2:6–10; 2 Cor. 4:5–12; Col. 2:14–15).[47] God's redemption of evil is reflected in those passages that speak positively of the believer sharing in the sufferings of Christ (2 Cor. 1:5; Phil. 1:29; Col. 1:24).[48] Sanders apparently repudiates this view of eschatology, for he denies that present evil will necessarily result in higher good in the future. He concludes, "It is not at all clear that future goods justify the present evil."[49] The writers of Scripture, however, know nothing of this kind of eschatological pessimism. Paul, who endured great evil and physical suffering (2 Cor. 11:23–33) had the audacity to declare that "momentary, light affliction *is producing* for us an eternal weight of glory far beyond all comparison" (2 Cor. 4:17 NASB, italics added). Thus "the sufferings of this present time are not worthy to be compared to the glory that is to be revealed *to us*" (Rom. 8:18 NASB, italics added). The prospect of future eschato-

45. Peterson, *Evil and the Christian God*, 91–93.

46. J. Christiaan Beker notes that Paul's apocalyptic dualism was not the Gnostic dualism that deprecated this present world; rather, it was one that gave hope to a creation gone astray. He states, "Although the glory of God will break into our fallen world, it will not annihilate the world but only break off its present structure of death, because it aims to transform the cosmos rather than to confirm its ontological nothingness" (*Paul the Apostle: The Triumph of God in Life and Thought* [Philadelphia: Fortress, 1980], 149).

47. C. Marvin Pate, *The End of the Age Has Come: The Theology of Paul* (Grand Rapids: Zondervan, 1995), 43–70.

48. Beker argues that the "sufferings of Christ" are much like the Jewish messianic woes or tribulations that precede the glory to come, but they should not be simply endured (like the messianic tribulations in Judaism), for they signify the "redemptive meaning of the cross of Christ in the world" (*Paul the Apostle*, 302).

49. Sanders, *God Who Risks*, 253.

logical glory is what allows us to rejoice in present suffering (Rom. 5:2–4). Peter encouraged believers facing evil persecution that the current evil trials could be faced with joy, knowing that the evil could purify their faith and *result in* a much greater good (praise, glory and honor) at the parousia of Christ (1 Peter 1:6–7).[50]

Hence if we are to affirm the goodness of God, then we must conclude that God has his own good reasons for choosing not to intervene to alleviate suffering and evil, and these reasons are largely eschatological. This conclusion harmonizes perfectly with the repeated statements in Scripture that, while God is not the author of evil, he can and consistently does bring good out of it (Rom. 8:28; James 1:2–5; 1 Peter 1:6–7). While we will not seek to delineate the various ways eschatologically God brings a greater good out of evil, we will briefly note Marilyn McCord Adams's model. Adams responds to the issue of "horrendous evils"[51] by noting that eschatology is the only category to help us, for if those who experience horrendous evil are to have lives that are of good on the whole, it can only be that God is able to preserve them after death and put them in a nourishing environment where they can profit from his instruction and presence.[52] Furthermore, she draws from Simone Weil to demonstrate that in fact our earthly suffering is not just overcome in heaven, but rather may be used for a greater good by drawing us into the very life of God. In other words, suffering can draw us into more intimate union with God. This does not negate the horrendous aspect of this suffering. Rather, because "beatific intimacy with God is an incommensurate good for human persons, Divine identification with human participation in horrors confers a positive aspect on such experiences by integrating them into the participant's relationship with God."[53] This concept may be alluded to in Romans 8:31–39, where in the context of the love of God, we are told that no manner of suffering or evil can separate us from God; through them we "overwhelmingly conquer" (experience greater good).

---

50. In his article on the Pauline perspective on suffering, Scott Hafemann states that when Christians suffer, they are to have joy because they know the suffering is not senseless, but "becomes the divinely orchestrated means by which God strengthens their faithful endurance and hope by pouring out his own love and Spirit to sustain or deliver them in their distress (Rom. 5:3–5; 8:12–39; 2 Cor. 1:6)." Because of this sancifying work produced by suffering, "all believers will join Paul in experiencing not only the power of God made known in the cross of Christ as God sustains them in the midst of their adversities, but also the resurrection power of God as he uses their suffering as the pathway to sharing in Christ's glory (Rom. 8:35; 2 Cor. 4:14; 2 Thess. 1:7)" ("Suffering," *Dictionary of Paul and His Letters*, ed. G. Hawthorne et al. [Downers Grove, Ill.: InterVarsity, 1993], 920).

51. She defines "horrendous evils as evils which give prima facie evidence that those who experience them may not have had lives which were of great good on the whole" (Marilyn McCord Adams, *Horrendous Evils and the Goodness of God* [Ithaca, N.Y.: Cornell University Press, 1999], 26).

52. Ibid., 84.

53. Adams, *Horrendous Evils*, 166–67; see also Diogenes Allen, "Natural Evil and the Love of God," *RelS* 16 (1980): 439–56.

The open view theologians' assertion of "gratuitous evil," far from relieving God of responsibility for evil, horribly distorts his good character and makes suffering and evil truly unbearable. Gratuitous evil is inimical to the eschatological work of God in redeeming human suffering and evil.

A Limited God's Response to Suffering and Evil

An open view of God undermines the very basis for God's triumph over evil and suffering by positing a permanently limited God. It is one thing to say that God has chosen to give humans a significant measure of free will and that in so doing he temporarily chose to limit his response to alleviate evil and suffering (the freewill defense). It is quite another matter to say that God lacks the innate capacity to foresee or to fully control evil. As stated previously, open view theologians deny divine foreknowledge. They also deny traditional divine sovereignty, for God is said to be a risk-taking God who works with a world whose history he does not decide. God is vulnerable to his creation. His sovereignty is expressed much more in persuasion than in domination.[54] God is sovereign primarily in the sense that he "shoulders responsibility for creating this type of world."[55] While Pinnock concedes that God is free and could actualize a determined world, he adamantly insists that God did not do so with this world. Instead, in this creation "God rejected sovereignty in the form of domination and control." He chose to become "weak" by the decision to create a world he "would not control," which has a history whose outcome "is not predetermined," a world "that is able to resist."[56]

Again, these limitations of God's knowledge and sovereignty have great import for eschatology. If God cannot foresee future creaturely acts, then accurate predictive prophecy of Christ's first and second advents are impossible.[57]

---

54. Pinnock, "Systematic Theology," 115–16.

55. Sanders, *God Who Risks*, 216.

56. Clark Pinnock, "God's Sovereignty in Today's Word," *Theology Today* 53 (1996): 17–19. From a "warfare" perspective, Boyd also denies traditional divine sovereignty, and says we should view this world as one in which God is at war with evil, rather than one in which God controls evil. This cosmos is one which should be pictured as a vast society of free moral agents who have significant power to thwart God's will and inflict suffering. Satan is so powerful in fact, that at first even Jesus could not cast out some demons (*God at War*, 141–42, 192–93, 291).

57. Francis Beckwith, "Limited Omniscience and the Test for a Prophet: A Brief Philosophical Analysis," *JETS* 36 (1993): 357–62; D. A. Carson, "God, the Bible and Spiritual Warfare: A Review Article," *JETS* 42 (1999): 264–66; Bruce Ware, "On Opening What's Closed and Closing What's Open: Rethinking the Doctrine of God in the Light of the Openness Proposal" (paper presented at the annual meeting of the Evangelical Theological Society, Philadelphia, 16–18 November 1995). Sanders does acknowledge that a denial of divine foreknowledge makes consistently accurate predictive prophecy impossible, for he states that some prophecies in Scripture are simply erroneous because they do not come to pass at all, or at least not in the way God had predicted (*God Who Risks*, 75).

If God cannot fully control evil temporally, then there is no logical assurance that he can do so eschatologically.

The denial of divine omniscience has other serious ramifications. It means that God is so impoverished in his wisdom and knowledge that humans facing suffering or evil have to straighten him out. Sanders argues that when God called Moses and asked him to be his spokesperson to deliver the children of Israel from their suffering at the hands of the evil Egyptians, Moses had to inform God that he was not an effective public speaker. Moses supposedly also went on to refute God's assertion that people would listen to him. Sanders maintains that in both instances God changed his plans. After talking to Moses, he realized that Moses had a good point so he allowed Aaron to be the spokesman and gave signs to convince the people.[58] Sanders says this in spite of the fact that God responds to Moses' fear of public speaking by asserting that he is the one who makes the mouth dumb, and who makes the blind, the sighted and the deaf (Exod. 4:11). Furthermore, God's response to this dialogue with Moses is hardly one of warm concession upon being enlightened by Moses. Rather, the Lord's anger burned against Moses (4:14). God graciously makes concessions to Moses not due to his own epistemic weaknesses, but to Moses'.

Unlike the open view in which believers can correct God's strategy for alleviating suffering and evil, in Scripture we repeatedly find believers trusting in God's wisdom and power in the face of evil and suffering. This is typically framed eschatologically. Though these believers did not fully understand the suffering or evil they were experiencing, they trusted that in temporal human history and at the final judgment God was wisely in control and would deal in the best possible manner with evil. Examples of this perspective of God's wisdom and power abound. Job's enlightened response to his suffering was to declare, "I know that Thou canst do all things, and that no purpose of Thine can be thwarted . . . . I have declared that which I did not understand" (Job 42:2–3). When Jeremiah received a prophecy of the coming destruction of Jerusalem, he wept and grieved over coming suffering and destruction, including the starvation of children (Lam. 2:11–12; 4:4). While he declared that God is absolutely sovereign over these events (3:37; 5:19), he looked to the future with hope based on his confidence in God's goodness and wisdom (3:22–26, 33; 4:22). While Habakkuk agonized over wickedness in Judah (1:2–4), and then over God's use of the Chaldeans to execute judgment (1:5–2:1), he found resolution by praising God for his power over the nations (3:4–7) and for his wise purposes expressed in judgment (3:8–16). Habakkuk concludes by saying that though he trembled and quivered, he would wait quietly for judgment to fall and would rejoice in the sovereign God he trusted (3:16–19). In Revelation 6:9–11 the souls of martyred saints cry out for God to exact vengeance on their murderers.

---

58. Sanders, *God Who Risks*, 57–58.

Their cry is predicated on God's sovereignty, knowing that he will judge and avenge. They are told to trust patiently in God's wisdom, for God would judge their evil persecutors once the divinely prescribed number of believers had been martyred (v. 11). In the face of suffering and evil these believers were enjoined to trust in God's wisdom and sovereignty.

This point is extremely relevant to the theodicy. No one in this life will receive a satisfactory answer to the question of evil.[59] Righteous Job did not (Job 38:1–42:9) and neither will we. If, however, we refuse to trust in God's wisdom and sovereignty in the face of evil and suffering, assuming that we have a better way to solve evil than he does, we will not solve suffering and sin but will exacerbate it.

Ultimate Eschatological Victory over Suffering and Evil

Open view theologians generally affirm divine eschatological victory over sin and evil, but this conclusion is disjunctive from the rest of their theological model. If God is really a risk-taking God, and he cannot (either functionally or ontologically) control creation and determine the outcome of history, then there is absolutely no certainty of God's ultimate eschatological victory over suffering and evil. Open view assurances of divine victory in the end are hollow, for this theological model cannot give such assurance. How can a God who does not know the future and who does not fully control it guarantee a final triumph over evil? He cannot.[60]

From the first account of human sin to the last, Scripture repeatedly and emphatically declares the eschatological triumph of God over suffering and evil (Gen. 3:15; Rev. 20:7–15; 21:4–9). This declaration is made without the slightest equivocation or contingency. While in this present age evil continues to pose a real threat, the hope and certainty of biblical eschatology is that one day evil and suffering will be abolished (Ps. 2:1–12; Isa. 9:2–7; 25:6–8; Rom. 8:18–25; Rev. 21:4).[61] Paul was so confident of God's eschatological triumph

---

59. On the issue of God's hiddenness and evil, see R. McKim, "The Hiddenness of God," *RelS* 26 (1990): 141–61. McKim argues that the problem of evil is an aspect of God's hiddenness, and may result from human defectiveness, and from a divine desire to prompt humans to trust and not manipulate. Surin maintains that our attempts to formulate a theodicy are largely bound for failure due to historical, conceptual, and methodological factors. He suggests that in the final analysis, theodicy "has to be silence qualified by the stammering utterance of broken words" ("Theodicy?" 247).

60. Bruce Ware puts it well: "Openness proponents want it both ways. On the one hand, they want humans to have significant freedom, to stand against God's will or follow him, so that God's creation of humans is in a real sense a risky undertaking, but on the other hand, they assure us that God will win in the end. Is it a real risk or not?" ("On Opening What's Closed," 10).

61. Blocher, *Evil and the Cross*, 105–10, 119–27. Blocher gives a particularly clear explanation of the manner in which the coming of God's reign proclaimed during the earthly life of Christ involves the suppression of evil, whereas the future consummation of the kingdom involves the complete removal of evil.

that he speaks of it as already having occurred (Col. 1:20 ["having made peace"]; Col. 2:15 ["when He had disarmed the rulers and authorities, He made a public display of them" (NASB)]; cf. Rom. 8:30 ["whom he justified, these he also glorified" (NASB)]).

Confidence in God's complete eschatological triumph over suffering and evil is cardinal to New Testament theodicy.[62] It is the basis for believers having hope and endurance in the face of suffering and injustice. In Romans 12:19–20 Paul admonishes the Romans to be at peace with others and not to take revenge, but instead to leave room for the wrath of God, for vengeance is a divine prerogative. Their kindness to their enemies would heap coals of fire on their heads. The language used here is best understood eschatologically of God's future final judgment over evil.[63] Paul's message is that "the Christian's love of his enemy is grounded in his certainty that God will take vengeance on those who persist in the state of enmity toward God's people."[64] A very similar message of patience in the face of evil in view of God's certain eschatological judgment is given in 1 Peter 2:18–23 and 2 Thessalonians 1:4–12.[65] We are able to endure suffering produced by evildoers with boldness and grace, knowing that the evildoers who harm us cannot escape God's final judgment. This only works if we can have absolute confidence in God's sovereignty.

Unfortunately, bold confidence in God's complete eschatological triumph flies in the face of the open view eschatological vision. Sanders apparently perceives the eschatological implications of an open view's limited God and acknowledges that he has no assurance of a final divine victory. "Are there any guarantees that God will achieve the sort of future, in all details, that God desires? Here proponents of the risk model disagree. For Lucas the answer is yes." Sanders responds to Lucas's optimism regarding the eschatological triumph of God by declaring "in my opinion this betrays a rationalism that over-

---

62. For a clinical application of this principle to malevolent evil, including sexual abuse, see Dan Allender and Tremper Longman, *Bold Love* (Colorado Springs: NavPress, 1992), 185–200; and Steven Tracy, "Sexual Abuse and Forgiveness," *Journal of Psychology and Theology* 27 (1999): 222–23.

63. John Piper, *"Love Your Enemies": Jesus' Love Command in the Synoptic Gospel and the Early Christian Paraenesis* (Cambridge: Cambridge University Press, 1979), 114–19; Gordon Zerbe, "Paul's Ethic of Nonretaliation and Peace," in *The Love of Enemy and Nonretaliation in the New Testament*, ed. Willard M. Swartley (Louisville, Ky.: Westminster/John Knox, 1992), 188–200.

64. Piper, *"Love Your Enemies,"* 118.

65. John Pobee, *Persecution and Martyrdom in the Theology of Paul* (Sheffield: JSOT Press, 1985), 110–11. As Pobee notes, "The faithful endurance of persecution is rooted in the hope of the ultimate vindication by God of those who are faithful to him" (111). See also Gordon Zerbe, *Non-retaliation in Early Jewish and New Testament Texts* (Sheffield: Sheffield Academic Press, 1993).

looks the irrationality of sin."[66] On the contrary, Sanders betrays a skepticism that overlooks the power of God.

Absolute confidence in the future eschatological triumph of God over evil and suffering is central to New Testament theodicy. The open view model of God undermines the very basis for ultimate eschatological victory, making suffering and evil unendurable in this life and potentially unredeemable in the life to come.

Conclusion

The theodicy is a vexing theological problem that has generated many competing models. Open view theologians have sought to break this theological loggerhead by asserting that God is a risk-taking God who does not control creation. Thus evil and suffering are gratuitous byproducts of a world containing freedom. The open view theodicy has its strengths. It takes suffering and evil seriously, does not make God the author of evil, and affirms the eschatological triumph of God. Unfortunately, however, the open view reformulation of the nature of God undercuts the very basis for God's ultimate triumph over evil and suffering. Open view insistence on gratuitous evil is diametrically opposed to the biblical concept of God's eschatological work in redeeming evil and suffering. Furthermore, a God who cannot foresee or control evil in history cannot necessarily do so at the end of history. The writers of Scripture endured evil and suffering based on their firm conviction in the complete eschatological triumph of God, a conviction not tenable for open view theologians. Unfortunately, the open view theodicy, far from solving the dilemma of suffering and evil, makes it far more tragic and unbearable.

---

66. *God Who Risks*, 235.

Part 6

Eschatology in the Life of the Church

19

Messianic Intermezzo: Eschatology, Spirit, and Worship in the Church

David Nelson

Southeastern Baptist Theological Seminary

In his 1987 essay "Doxophany: A Trinitarian Eschatological Vision," Daniel Tappeiner articulated the need for a renewed "eschatological vision" in the church.[1] The purpose of this paper is to explore the possibilities of such an eschatological vision with reference to corporate Christian worship. Beginning with the reality of the church as the community of the Holy Spirit and the Spirit as "eschatological Spirit," and acknowledging the existence of an eschatological dimension in worship revealed in the New Testament, we will examine the influence such an eschatological vision may have on some current issues related to worship in the local church.[2]

The Church, Spirit, and Worship

The Community of the Spirit

"Do you not know that you are God's temple and that God's Spirit dwells in you?" (1 Cor. 3:16 RSV).[3] The apostle's question points to the crucial role of the Holy Spirit in the church. The church, one body fashioned from many

---

1. Daniel Tappeiner, "Doxophany: A Trinitarian Eschatological Vision," in *Church, Word, and Spirit: Historical and Theological Essays in Honor of Geoffrey Bromiley*, ed. James E. Bradley and Richard A. Muller (Grand Rapids: Eerdmans, 1987), 267.
2. I should note here that the focus in this paper on the role of the Spirit is not meant to in any way to diminish the essentially trinitarian nature of Christian worship.
3. Citations are from the NASB unless otherwise noted.

members, exists "by one Spirit" (1 Cor. 12:13). As well, the body of Christ is gifted for ministry by the Holy Spirit (1 Cor. 12), and the church enjoys "the fellowship of the Holy Spirit" (2 Cor. 13:13[14]). Further, Paul can speak of the Christian saints as those "in whom the whole building, being fitted together, is growing into a holy temple in the Lord, in whom you also are being built together into a dwelling of God in the Spirit." (Eph. 2:21–22). So, states Gordon Fee, "Created and formed *by* the Spirit, the early communities thus became a fellowship *of* the Spirit."[4]

Worship in the Community of the Spirit

Since the church exists as the community of the Spirit, it will be useful to briefly survey the role the Holy Spirit occupies in the corporate worship of the church.[5] To begin, the Spirit plays a role in the shift in emphasis from the location of worship (e.g., temple) in the Old Testament to the manner of worship in the New Testament. David Peterson notes this movement in the first chapters of the Gospel of John: "John moves from the idea of Jesus as the true tabernacle (1:14) and the true temple (2:19) to suggest that he fulfils the ideal of the holy mountain where God can be encountered (4:20–24)."[6] With the coming of Messiah the locus of worship moves away from the temple, designed and implemented by God, to the presence of a person, Jesus Christ. Those born again by Spirit will now worship "in Spirit and truth" (John 4:23): "'Spirit' and 'truth' are God's gifts through Jesus, by which he sustains us in genuine relationship with himself."[7] Paige notes, with reference to 1 Corinthians 3:16, "worship is not facilitated by a holy site, building or objects, but by the presence of God's Spirit."[8]

Ephesians 5:18–20 indicates that the Spirit is directly associated with both the didactic and doxological function of worship in the church. The instruction to be "speaking to one another in psalms and hymns and spiritual songs" in Ephesians 5:19 is given in the context of the command "be filled with the Spirit" in 5:18. Similar language is used in Colossians 3:16, where "teaching and admonishing" are in view. As well, the Spirit distributes the spiritual gifts,

---

4. Gordon Fee, *God's Empowering Presence*, (Peabody, Mass.: Hendrickson, 1994), 872, emphasis in original. Fee also states that Paul's "understanding of the Church is primarily as people of the Spirit" (115).

5. Ralph Martin speaks of "the pervasive influence of the Spirit in Christian worship in the New Testament." He lists eight central influences of the Spirit in worship (*Worship in the Early Church* [Grand Rapids: Eerdmans, 1964], 132). Cf. Ralph Martin, *The Worship of God: Some Theological, Pastoral, and Practical Reflections* (Grand Rapids: Eerdmans, 1982), 171–86.

6. David Peterson, *Engaging With God: A Biblical Theology of Worship* (Grand Rapids: Eerdmans, 1992), 97–98.

7. Ibid., 99.

8. Terence P. Paige, "Holy Spirit," in *Dictionary of Paul and His Letters*, ed. Gerald F. Hawthorne and Ralph P. Martin (Downers Grove, Ill.: InterVarsity, 1993), 411. See also Basil, *De Spiritu Sancto* 26.63.

including gifts like teaching and prophecy, which operate in the sphere of corporate worship (1 Cor. 12–14). The Spirit also assists believers in the ministry of prayer, inspiring "the confident 'Abba' prayer of the redeemed (Rom. 8:15–16; Gal. 4:6)" and directs "[the church] to pray properly (Rom. 8:26)."[9] So it is that Paul in Philippians 3:3 can speak of the "circumcision," those who "put no confidence in the flesh," as those "who worship in the Spirit of God and glory in Christ Jesus." Fee concludes that "for Paul the gathered church was first of all a worshipping community; and the key to their worship was the presence of the Holy Spirit."[10]

The Eschatological Spirit, the Church, and the Messianic Age

A notably eschatological dimension of the ministry of the Holy Spirit emerges in the New Testament. During his earthly ministry, Jesus linked the arrival of the kingdom of God with his exorcism of demons "by the Spirit of God" (Matt. 12:28). This association of the Spirit of God and the kingdom of God hints at the inauguration of the messianic age, an age marked not only by the arrival of Christ, but also by the outpouring of the Spirit.[11]

The apostle Paul uses three metaphors that illustrate the Spirit's role in God's eschatological plan. Two of these metaphors, "pledge" (ἀρραβών) and "sealing," (σφραγίζω), appear together in 2 Corinthians 1:22 and Ephesians 1:13–14. In Ephesians 1:13–14 Paul states that those who believe in Christ "were sealed in Him with the Holy Spirit of promise, who is given as a pledge of our inheritance." So, the "Holy Spirit of promise" is an "eschatological seal" for Christian believers.[12] In Ephesians 4:30 the Holy Spirit is designated as the one "by whom you were sealed for the day of redemption." Thus, the sealing is specifically associated with the promise of ultimate salvation for those in the believing community. In Ephesians 1:14 Paul states that the Spirit is the "pledge (ἀρραβών) of our inheritance." In this way the Spirit serves as security for the inheritance promised in Christ (cf. 2 Cor. 5:5). In addition to the idea of the Spirit as "seal" and "pledge," Paul associates the Holy Spirit with the "firstfruits" in Romans 8:23. Used in the Septuagint with relation to the temple cult, "here in Rom. 8 it is used with reference not to something offered

---

9. Ibid., 412.

10. Fee, *God's Empowering Presence*, 884. See also John Zizioulas, *Being as Communion* (Crestwood, N.Y.: St. Vladimir's, 1993), 131, for a similar view from an Eastern Orthodox perspective.

11. On Matt. 12:28 see Craig L. Blomberg, *Matthew*, New American Commentary 22 (Nashville: Broadman, 1992), 202–3; D. A. Carson, *Matthew: Chapters 1–12*, Expositor's Bible Commentary (Grand Rapids: Zondervan, 1995), 289.

12. Andrew Lincoln, *Ephesians*, WBC 42 (Dallas: Word, 1990), 39. See also M. Barth who, quoting Heinrich Schlier, associates the "sealing" of 1:13 with "eschatological preservation" (Markus Barth, *Ephesians*, AB 34 [New York: Doubleday, 1974], 143).

by man to God, but of something given by God to man, and the idea conveyed is that of the gift of a part as a pledge of the fuller gift yet to come."[13]

The Holy Spirit may be seen, then, as the eschatological Spirit in at least a few ways. He works in cooperation with Jesus Christ to inaugurate the messianic age foretold in the Old Testament. The Holy Spirit is also the Spirit of Christ by whom believers continually identify with Jesus as they await his return. As well, the Spirit is given by the Father as firstfruits, pledge, and seal of the promised salvation to come in the consummation of the kingdom. The church lives in the "already" of the kingdom in light of the "yet-to-come" guaranteed by the Spirit's ministry: "empowered by the Spirit, we now live the life of the future in the present age, the life that characterizes God himself."[14] The already/not yet tension of the church in the kingdom involves "a divine thrusting of the Spirit-empowered eschatological community into the world to fulfill its global mission,"[15] a mission that includes the worship of God by the saints in this messianic age.

Worship as Messianic Intermezzo

Worship may be viewed as messianic intermezzo[16] in that it occurs within the inaugurated but not yet complete messianic age and because it serves as a kind of doxological interlude, performed by the church, between two grand acts of God, the first and second advents. As such, it looks back to the first coming of Messiah and it looks forward to the second coming, the glorious return of Christ, and the final consummation of the kingdom of God. It is this latter, forward-looking aspect that is of interest here. Two lines of investigation into the biblical text will help develop this theme. First, the instruction in 1 Corinthians 11:26 to proclaim the death of the Lord "until he comes," given in the context of the Lord's Supper, suggests an eschatological motif. Second, an eschatological model of worship emerges upon examination of pertinent passages in the Apocalypse.

The citation of Jesus' words of institution in 1 Corinthians 11:26 is an indication of the eschatological dimension of the Lord's Supper: "For as often as you eat this bread and drink the cup, you proclaim the Lord's death until He comes." Fee comments: "By these final words Paul is reminding the Corin-

---

13. C. E. B. Cranfield, *Romans: A Shorter Commentary* (Grand Rapids: Eerdmans, 1985), 199.

14. Fee, *God's Empowering Presence*, 804.

15. Carl F. H. Henry, *God, Revelation and Authority*, vol. 6, *The God Who Stands and Stays*, part 2 (Waco: Word, 1983; reprint, Wheaton, Ill.: Crossway, 1999), 384.

16. The idea of Christian worship as "messianic intermezzo" comes from Jürgen Moltmann (*The Church in the Power of the Spirit: A Contribution to Messianic Ecclesiology* [Minneapolis: Fortress, 1993], 272–74 and passim). Moltmann takes the concept from A. A. van Ruler, *Droom en Gestalte: Een discussie over de theologische principes het vraagstuk van christendom en politiek* [Amsterdam: Uitgeversmaatschappij Holland, 1947]. An intermezzo is a relatively brief musical piece situated between two major portions of a composition.

thians of their essentially eschatological existence. . . . They have not arrived (4:8); at this meal they are to be reminded that there is yet a future for themselves, as well as for all the people of God."[17] The Table is commonly seen as a place of remembrance. Usually, it is the past event, the death of Christ on the cross, that is the focus of this ordinance.[18] Yet, the anamnetic function of the Supper applies not only to events past, but also to future events, a notion evident in the inclusion of the cup of Elijah in the Passover Seder.[19] Likewise, the Supper marks the church's dynamic remembrance of not only Christ's death on the cross, but also his promised return and the eternal kingdom. Robertson and Plummer comment on the phrase "until he comes": "The Eucharist looks backwards to the Crucifixion and forwards to the Return: *hoc mysterium duo tempora extrema conjungit* (Beng.) [This mystery joins together these two periods of time]."[20] In this way, the Supper plays a crucial role in the messianic intermezzo of the church. Not only does the celebration of the Supper itself have a valuable eschatological dimension, but it provides an eschatological principle for the entire worship life of the Christian community. Such a connection is drawn by Wolfhart Pannenberg between the anamnetic function of the Supper and the anamnetic role of preaching. Both, in his view, include remembrance of both past and future.[21] This anamnetic principle, including reference to the mighty works of God past, present, and future, may be applied to all the various elements of Christian worship. Further support for the development of the worship as messianic intermezzo is found in what may be called the eschatological model of worship foreshadowed in Isaiah 6 and more fully developed in Revelation.

17. Gordon Fee, *The First Epistle to the Corinthians*, NICNT (Grand Rapids: Eerdmans, 1987), 557.

18. This phenomena was part of the impetus behind Geoffrey Wainwright's *Eucharist and Eschatology*, where he speaks of the "comparative neglect of the eschatological perspective over many centuries in the West" (Geoffrey Wainwright, *Eucharist and Eschatology* [New York: Oxford University Press, 1981], 6).

19. On the eschatological dimension of the Seder see Leo Trepp, *Judaism: Development and Life* (Belmont, Calif.: Wadsworth, 1982), 309; Abraham Millgram, *Jewish Worship* (Philadelphia: Jewish Publication Society, 1971), 302–13. On the connection of the Passover to the Lord's Supper, including this future emphasis, see Ralph Martin, *Worship in the Early Church*, 126–27; Robert Saucy, *The Church in God's Program* (Chicago: Moody Press, 1972), 218. For discussion of the dynamic of ἀνάμνησις and the Hebrew זכר, see Joachim Jeremias, *The Eucharistic Words of Jesus* (New York: MacMillan, 1955), 159ff., and Douglas Jones, "ANAMNHSIS in the LXX and the Interpretation of 1 Cor. XI.25," *JTS* 4 (1955): 183–92, esp. 190–91.

20. Archibald Robertson and Alfred Plummer, *A Critical and Exegetical Commentary on the First Epistle of St Paul to the Corinthians*, ICC (New York: Scribners, 1911), 249–50. The quote is from J. A. Bengel, *Gnomon of the New Testament* (Tübingen, 1742).

21. For Pannenberg, the consummation which occurs in the final advent "forms the basis for recollection of the past event of salvation" since, for him, the certainty of the past event is conditioned by the fulfillment of the future promises (Wolfhart Pannenberg, *Systematic Theology*, vol. 3 [Grand Rapids: Eerdmans, 1998], 334).

The Revelation offers the church a glimpse of worship in heaven: "The Apocalypse of John is full of echoes of heavenly worship which sound the note of adoring praise to God as Creator (4:8–11) and Redeemer (5:9–14). The Church on earth shares in this exultant acknowledgement in the exercise of its priestly ministry (1:6)."[22] Donald Guthrie contends that "the worship scenes" of Revelation "are intentionally of a heavenly kind to provide a pattern and maybe a corrective for current patterns of earthly worship."[23] David Aune identifies "the presence of sixteen hymns or hymnlike compositions at various points in the narrative"[24] of Revelation. From these texts one sees various emphases that may inform the eschatological vision of worship. For example, the following themes are present: (1) a proclamation of the holiness of God (4:8) reminiscent of Isaiah 6; (2) God is recognized as Creator (4:11); (3) the eternal reign of God (5:13; 15:13); (4) the ceaseless praise of God (7:15—"they serve Him day and night"); (5) God's ultimate victory over evil opposition (11:17–18); (6) the judgment and reward of humankind (11:17–18); and (7) the justice of God (19:1). Though this worship will not be replicated in this age, the eschatological model should serve as a kind of plumb line for the church, offering to the church a unique vision for its liturgy.

The Application of Worship as Messianic Intermezzo

I would now like to suggest two possible applications of the idea of worship as messianic intermezzo. First, viewing worship from such an eschatological perspective offers a refreshing view of certain concepts and emphases in Christian worship that are sometimes obscured. Second, I want to explore in greater depth the possibility that sensitivity to the eschatological dimension of worship may lead to progress on the issue of the relationship between Christian worship and contemporary culture.

Concepts and Emphases

Max Warren, in his 1950 article "Eschatology and Worship," stated that he might, by examining the relationship of eschatology and worship, be able "to recapture that missing element in our worship which I would call a biblical expectancy."[25] There are several ways in which such an expectancy may apply.

First, attention to the eschatological should awaken the church to the reality of the kingdom of God. Schmemann argues that "the Liturgy is not to be treated as an aesthetic experience or a therapeutic exercise. Its unique function is to reveal to us the Kingdom of God."[26] The subject of the kingdom and the

---

22. Martin, *Worship in the Early Church*, 138.
23. Donald Guthrie, "Aspects of Worship in the Book of Revelation" in *Worship, Theology and Ministry in the Early Church: Essays in Honor of Ralph P. Martin*, ed. Michael J. Wilkins and Terence P. Paige (Sheffield: JSOT Press, 1992), 73.
24. David Aune, *Revelation 1–5*, WBC 52 (Dallas: Word, 1997), 315.
25. Max Warren, "Eschatology and Worship," *Theology Today* 4.4 (January 1950): 484.
26. Alexander Schmemann, "Liturgy and Eschatology," *Sobornost* 7.1 (1985): 13.

already inaugurated messianic age should issue in a renewed emphasis in worship upon the reign and lordship of God. To be sure, this kind of emphasis could lead to an untempered triumphalism in the church, but this need not be the case.

Second, the reality of hope should emerge from a renewed eschatological vision. In an age when depression and discouragement are prevalent even within the Christian community, an emphasis on the hope that "does not disappoint" (Rom. 5:5) would seem a welcome corrective (cf. Rom. 15:13).[27] Third, a view of worship as messianic intermezzo will demand a biblical emphasis on the reality of judgment and hell. This kind of emphasis is found in early liturgies like the *Apostolic Constitutions* and the *Liturgy of James* in the West and in the *Liturgy of Basil* and *Liturgy of Chrysostom* in the East.[28] An eschatological vision of worship should place the themes of hope and judgment/hell in proper perspective and will help foster a healthy interplay between the pastoral and prophetic in Christian liturgy.

Fourth, the issue of the corporate nature of the body of Christ and the biblical call to unity in the church may be advanced by an eschatological view of worship. The eschatological model of worship glimpsed in Revelation reminds the church of the telic nature of the messianic intermezzo. While the liturgy of the church is very much concerned with speaking the gospel and greatness of God with clarity to humankind, it must always remember that worship in this age constantly points the church toward the goal of eternal life in the age to come. In this way the worship of today should always have a movement toward the heavenly adoration of tomorrow, where worship is concerned exclusively with the glory of God and exaltation of Christ. Worship is telic in that it points toward this theocentric goal and away from any sort of anthropocentrism. Would ἀνάμνησις of this eschatological reality move the church away from divisions and factions and toward the unity of the Spirit? It is, after all, in the context of divisions (1 Cor. 11:18) and factions (1 Cor. 11:19), as the Corinthian church is called to unity around the Lord's Table, that Paul orders the celebration of the Supper as a commemoration of the Lord's death "until he comes." In a world filled with disunity and hostility, where the universal is so often destroyed by the particular, and where the individual crowds out the communal, the unifying vision of the eschaton may serve to bring harmony to the church that too often suffers from fractured fellowship.

Furthermore, this eschatological vision should lead to a renewed emphasis on purity in the church. The reality of the "marriage supper of the Lamb" (Rev. 19:9) and God's intent that the church be presented for this occasion as

27. Such an emphasis may enable the church the opportunity to offer a truly biblical "therapy" in our "therapeutic" age.
28. Wainwright, *Eucharist and Eschatology*, 62–64.

a holy bride (cf. Eph. 5:25–27) ought to remind the Christian community of the critical, and too often overlooked, relationship of worship and ethics, not only in the age to come, but in this present age.

Finally, I think that a view of worship as messianic intermezzo will assist the church in maintaining the centrality of the cross of Christ and the message of redemption. The concept of the Lamb who was slain in Revelation 5 should remind the church that the message of the death of Christ must not be diminished in congregational worship. In a day when it is tempting for the church to be distracted by many other messages, the eschatological vision reminds the church that the redemptive message of the cross must continually be spoken by the worshipping faithful.[29]

An Eschatological Perspective on Worship and Culture

The relationship between worship and culture is simply one aspect of the tension that exists between the church and culture. The issue of worship and culture is important to the contemporary church for at least two reasons. First, local churches often find themselves located today in a multicultural environment due to shifting populations and technological advancements that brings various cultures and subcultures to the doorsteps and into the living rooms of Christian homes. Simply put, there are a host of cultural options in the world today, and there are a host of cultural preferences that arise in such an environment. Inevitably, people of different cultural backgrounds and tastes find themselves worshipping in the same space. Tension, then, is bound to occur.

Second, the church exists in a hostile cultural environment such as the church perhaps has not seen since its early days. As a result, the theological and doxological work of the church must take on a more pronounced apologetic stance in contemporary culture. The church is faced with maintaining a biblical theology of worship while communicating to an increasingly multicultural and secularized congregation.

The tendency of the church has been either to succumb to the prevailing culture, letting the world set the liturgical agenda, or, conversely, to retreat from the world and its culture. When the former occurs, the church loses its prophetic voice; when the latter occurs, the church loses its voice altogether. As Alexander Schmemann asserts, "We cannot answer the world's problems by adopting toward them an attitude either of surrender or of escape."[30] I think that an eschatological vision of worship offers some insight into the resolution of the tension resident in the relationship of Christian worship and

29. This is, in my estimation, a good incentive for celebrating the Lord's Supper more often than once per quarter, as is the norm in a number of evangelical traditions. Since the death of Christ is central to the celebration of the Supper, the Table can serve as a constant reminder of the message of the cross.

30. Schmemann, "Liturgy and Eschatology," 13.

culture, and one that will avoid either extreme. Let me suggest a few ways in which this may occur.

First, I propose that a view of worship as messianic intermezzo will provide a sense of discontinuity with the present age that results in a proper counter to what we might call "culture-bound" worship. Culture-bound worship is that which is consumed with the here and now, and that which is controlled by the culture or subculture in which the local church exists. Wainwright observed, while living in his native England in 1976, that "instead of speaking divine judgment upon present sin and holding out to society a hope of what it might become, the new liturgies offer a cozy consecration of what is."[31] The same might be said of worship on the North American continent more than twenty years later.

The Spirit of God provokes discontinuity with the current culture as he points us beyond the here and now and reminds the church of the future hope that has been inaugurated in the messianic age. Since "we all, with unveiled face, beholding as in a mirror the glory of the Lord, are being transformed into the same image from glory to glory, just as from the Lord, the Spirit" (2 Cor. 3:18), we are, if we are sensitive to the Spirit of God, continually aware of the discontinuity that exists between life in the Spirit and the life of this world.[32] Awareness of this discontinuity should produce a healthy discontentment with culture-bound worship that, in turn, may lead the church toward engaging culture with a fully eschatological vision of the gospel in liturgy. As Paul suggests in 1 Corinthians 3:16, it is expected that God's temple, the body of Christ in which the Spirit dwells, is to be clearly distinct from the pagan temples of that day.[33] Likewise, in contemporary culture it is necessary for the church to regain its distinctive gospel voice: "It is perhaps not too strong to suggest that the recapturing of this vision of its [the church] being powerfully indwelt by the Spirit and serving as a genuine alternative (holy in the most holistic sense) to the world is the church's greatest need."[34]

Second, the idea of worship as messianic intermezzo points to the relationship of time and worship.[35] I would suggest that much thought about contemporary worship maintains a synchronic view of time. That is to say, contemporary worship is sometimes primarily concerned with the present, with less regard for either past or future. This is, to be sure, simply another facet of the problem of being culture-bound. If attention is given, however, to the eschatological dimension of worship, a more diachronic view of worship may

---

31. Geoffrey Wainwright, "Christian Worship and Western Culture," *Studia Liturgica* 12.1 (1977): 24.

32. Fee, *God's Empowering Presence*, 284.

33. Ibid., 116.

34. Ibid., 118.

35. For a discussion of the relationship of time and liturgy in the early church, see Don E. Saliers, *Worship as Theology: Foretaste of Glory Divine* (Nashville: Abingdon, 1994), 52–55.

emerge. A diachronic view of worship should cause the church to look through time, beyond the present, and to consider worship from a future perspective.[36] This includes, of course, the theological dimensions already discussed in relationship to the eschatological model of worship in Scripture. But, it is at this point that the eschatological vision may also have some bearing on the incessant discussion of musical styles in worship.

A synchronic approach to this issue will result in stylistic determinations that focus primarily on either the present time or a particular time in the past. As such, the church inevitably fashions its worship style after the cultural trends of that preferred time. This may appear at first blush to make the church "relevant" in a given culture. Yet, the actual result may be that (1) the church becomes indistinct in its culture and (2) the church faces the real difficulty of either constantly shifting with cultural tides or else becoming passé. A diachronic approach, on the other hand, offers the church the opportunity to retain its distinctive voice and to be driven not by culture, but by a vision that transcends culture. One could even hope that such a vision might lead the church to martial its creative forces to actually set trends rather than follow them.

Further, a diachronic view of worship should cause the church to give attention to the reality of salvation-history in the Scriptures and to take full account of the role of the church in the unfolding plan of God. Attention to the diachronic aspect of worship should also influence preaching and teaching in the corporate worship of the church. Such a diachronic view might encourage the leadership of a given church to expose a congregation, through the course of time, to the whole counsel of God, and to a well-conceived course of Christian doctrine.

Finally, it must be noted that worship cannot be entirely concerned with this eschatological vision. The idea of worship as messianic intermezzo is only one dimension of worship. To think otherwise would be to unduly minimize the temporal and physical realities of this world in which the church is called to live and serve. Also, the church must be careful not to diminish the rich heritage of its past. Instead, the future reality of the eschatological vision, the not-yet of the kingdom, must always remind the church of the works of God throughout history and in the messianic age, the already of the kingdom, both past and present. By keeping this in perspective, the worshipping community of the Spirit will effectively carry the gospel into this world as the modern church, joining in the liturgy of the early church, cries *maranatha,* and with the Apostle John prays, "Amen. Come, Lord Jesus!" (Rev. 22:20).

---

36. The church seems to do this quite naturally in one worship setting—the funeral rite.

The Significance of Eschatology for Christian Ethics

GUENTHER HAAS

Redeemer University College

It is clear from the testimony of Scripture that eschatology has a central place in Christian thought. The Bible attests to God's government of the world and his direction of human history so that his purposes will be fully accomplished at the second coming of Jesus Christ. In the glorious new age that the Messiah inaugurates, God will fully redeem his people, he will judge and punish his enemies, and he will inaugurate a kingdom characterized by righteousness, justice, peace, material blessings, the absence of sickness, pain and death, and the worldwide knowledge of the glory of the Lord.[1] All these depictions of the future consummation of God's kingdom constitute the hope of the Christian life.

In many forms of Christianity, especially in its popular expressions in North America, the eschatological expectations of believers has led them to direct their thoughts, not to the positive hope of the second coming of Christ, but to the anticipated rise of evil before his return. Many speakers and writers use biblical apocalyptic literature to try to identify the anti-Christ (Adolf Hitler, Josef Stalin, Saddam Hussein?) or to take some threatening escalation of evil (conflicts in the Middle East, the World Council of Churches, the actions of the United Nations?) as a sign that the end is near. Certainly, Scripture speaks of an increase of wickedness before the second coming (2 Tim. 3:1–5), of the rise of apostasy in

---

1. This portrait is found not only in many New Testament passages, such as Rev. 20–22, but also in numerous Old Testament passages, such as Isa. 11 and Ezek. 34.

the church (1 Tim. 4:1) and in society at large (2 Peter 3:3–4), and of a coalition of satanic forces against God and his kingdom (Rev. 17) before the victory of God over his enemies (Rev. 18–19). But the attempt to interpret the details of human history according to biblical apocalyptic symbolism is not a proper use of eschatology. Rather, as Edward Long notes, this is "a presumptuous employment of religious symbolism to manipulate history or at least to triumph over its vicissitudes."[2] Eschatology should not be employed to attempt to control history or to predict what is best left to the providential wisdom of God.[3] More importantly, the saddest feature of this approach to eschatology is its failure to appreciate the significance of the Christian hope for Christian living in the present era before Christ's return.[4]

The focus of this chapter is to present the positive significance of eschatology for Christian ethics. To gain this, we must first have a proper understanding of eschatology as redemption in Jesus Christ. This counters the misconception that eschatology has to do exclusively or primarily with the complex of events surrounding Jesus' second coming, or with the nature of new reality that his second coming brings into being. The first coming of Christ, culminating in his death and resurrection, has inaugurated the coming of the kingdom of God. In addition, as members of that kingdom, we must understand what it means to live according to that new order that Christ inaugurated. This order is one that participates in the new creation in Christ (2 Cor. 5:17), yet it is lived out in the old aeon of this world. This chapter gives some characteristics of this ethic that is lived out "between the times," characterized by the "already" of Christ's kingdom, but the "not yet" of its consummation. Finally, this paper examines the connection of the kingdom ethic to the creational ethic. The key issue here is the relation of redemption to the creational moral order. I argue that a creational ethic and a kingdom ethic must not be placed in opposition to each other, for the eschatological teaching of Scripture itself supports a continuity between the two.

Eschatology as the Coming of the Kingdom in Jesus Christ

The place to begin in our understanding of eschatology is to realize that it is rooted in Christology and is itself Christology. God's redemptive purposes for his fallen creation reach their fulfillment in the incarnation, death, and resurrection of Jesus Christ. Christ's coming and work inaugurates the new aeon, the eschatological time of salvation. Ridderbos notes that when Paul speaks of

2. Edward LeRoy Long Jr., *To Liberate and Redeem: Moral Reflections on the Biblical Narrative* (Cleveland: Pilgrim, 1997), 226.

3. Ibid., 227.

4. Noted by Peter Kuzmič, "History and Eschatology: Evangelical Views," in *Word and Deed: Evangelicals and Social Responsibility*, ed. Bruce Nicholls (Exeter, England: Paternoster, 1985), 137.

God's sending his Son in the "fullness of time" (NASB) in Galatians 4:4 (as well as in Eph. 1:10), he is referring not merely to the maturity of a matter in the framework of redemptive history, but to the fact that salvation has taken effect and been settled in principle. With the first coming of Christ, salvation is fulfilled in the eschatological sense.[5]

When Jesus begins his public ministry he announces the fulfilled time of the kingdom of God (Mark 1:15), and thus the end of the time of waiting. Beasley-Murray observes that in Jesus' words and work he proclaims "an *initiation* of the sovereign action of God that brings salvation."[6] This is evident in Jesus' exorcisms (Matt. 12:28), his binding of the strong man (Satan) (Luke 11:22), his healing miracles and proclamation of good news to the poor (Matt. 11:5–6), his forgiveness of sins (Mark 2:10), and his declarations that the great era of gathering into and growth of God's kingdom has begun (Matt. 13:47–50; Mark 4:1–9). Lohse observes that by his associating with sinners, eating with them, and speaking of God's grace to them, Jesus makes clear that "the coming of the kingdom of God means salvation for the suffering and freedom to those who are bound." Thereby, he indicates that the prophetic promises of the coming time of salvation are fulfilled.[7]

In Christ's death we see God's eschatological judgment upon sin. Christ has won the victory over death (1 Cor. 15:21–22), Satan (John 12:31), and all powers hostile to God (Col. 2:15). For those united to Christ through faith that judicial verdict has been discharged in Christ, and we can receive that eschatological judgment as a present reality.[8] The resurrection of Christ reveals the breakthrough of the new aeon. In him the new life of the re-creation has come to light and become a present reality for Christians. And that is ensured by his present reign over all things. So, although the kingdom of God is consummated in the future, "it has already achieved anticipatory reality in the present through the resurrection and reign of Christ."[9]

As the risen one, Jesus is referred to as the firstfruits (1 Cor. 15:20), not merely because he is the beginning of the eschatological harvest, but because in him the whole harvest becomes visible.[10] So, although believers' resurrection from the dead is a future reality, in Christ who is the resurrection and the

---

5. Herman Ridderbos, *Paul: An Outline of His Theology*, trans. John Richard De Witt (Grand Rapids: Eerdmans, 1975), 44–45. See also Anthony A. Hoekema, *The Bible and the Future* (Grand Rapids: Eerdmans, 1979), 13.

6. G. R. Beasley-Murray, *Jesus and the Kingdom of God* (Grand Rapids: Eerdmans, 1986), 74.

7. Eduard Lohse, *Theological Ethics of the New Testament*, trans. M. Eugene Boring (Minneapolis: Fortress, 1991), 41.

8. See Ridderbos, *Paul*, 163–67.

9. Karl Paul Donfried, "The Kingdom of God in Paul," in *The Kingdom of God in 20th Century Interpretation*, ed. Wendell Willis (Peabody, Mass.: Hendrickson, 1987), 187.

10. See ibid., 55–56.

life (John 11:25) it has reached back into the present age to be available to men and women.[11] Beasley-Murray notes that numerous texts in the Gospels indicate "that the emancipating power of God at work in Christ . . . destined to bring deliverance in the future is operative for that purpose in the present."[12]

Conversely, our present experience of salvation in Christ orientates us toward its future consummation.[13] Since Christ has won the victory over Satan and has fulfilled salvation in the past, the future eschatological events will simply complete what has already begun. "What will happen in the last days, in other words, will be but the culmination of what has been happening in these last days."[14] Berkouwer highlights this when he comments: "True eschatology, therefore, is always concerned with the expectation of the Christ who has already been revealed and who will 'appear a second time . . . to save those who are eagerly waiting for him' (Heb. 9:28)."[15] Herman Bavinck notes that Christ's second coming is the completion of the first, for it complements and crowns it.[16]

Since God has introduced a new aeon by the death and resurrection of Christ, everyone who is in Christ is included in, participates in, and belongs to this new creation (2 Cor. 5:17). Paul presents this in the figure of dying and rising with Christ in Romans 6:1–11. The old order of life has lost its control over those who are in Christ, for they have died to the aeon of sin, condemnation, and death. And they have risen with Christ to a new order of resurrection life and righteousness for him. Because of this definitive change, Paul exhorts believers to turn away from the sinful patterns of the old aeon, and to offer themselves to God as instruments of righteousness (Rom. 6:11–13). To become members of Christ's kingdom is to live a life consistent with the new aeon.[17] In that sense, the ethic of the kingdom is what Farmer calls "a response ethic, a response to the gracious salvific activity of God," which is experienced not only as a future hope, but also as a present reality.[18]

---

11. Noted by George Eldon Ladd, *A Theology of the New Testament* (Grand Rapids: Eerdmans, 1974), 305.

12. Beasley-Murray makes this specific comment on Matt. 12:28 and Luke 11:20 (*Jesus and the Kingdom*, 79).

13. David J. Bosch comments: "The resurrection of Christ necessarily points to the future glory and its completion" (*Transforming Mission: Paradigm Shifts in Theology of Mission*, American Society of Missiology Series, no. 16 [Maryknoll, N.Y.: Orbis, 1991], 143).

14. Hoekema, *Bible and the Future*, 77.

15. G. C. Berkouwer, *The Return of Christ*, trans. James van Oosterom, ed. Marlin J. Van Elderen (Grand Rapids: Eerdmans, 1972), 13.

16. Herman Bavinck, *The Last Things: Hope for This World and the Next*, ed. John Bolt, trans. John Vriend (Grand Rapids: Baker, 1996), 122.

17. See Hoekema, *Bible and the Future*, 30.

18. Ron Farmer, "The Kingdom of God in the Gospel of Matthew," in *The Kingdom of God in 20th Century Interpretation*, 127.

Life in the new aeon—eschatological existence—is life in the Spirit. The gift of the Spirit is the key indication that Christians are part of this new creation that Christ has inaugurated (Rom. 8:11; Gal. 4:6). Bosch observes that the Spirit's active presence in believers—the same Spirit who raised Jesus from the dead—"guarantees for Paul that the messianic age has dawned."[19] The redemptive workings of the Spirit now experienced by believers are the prelude to a richer and more complete redemption in the future.[20] Thus, the Spirit is the divine agent who enables them to live their lives in such a way that they manifest the realities of the new creation that has dawned in Jesus Christ (Rom. 8:15–16).

Living between the Times

Christians find themselves living in the era of the fulfillment of the kingdom with the first coming of Christ, but still anticipating the consummation of this kingdom with his second coming. We live with the tension between the "already" of the coming of the kingdom, but the "not yet" of its completion, or, to use Oscar Cullmann's famous analogy, we live between D-day (the decisive victory of Christ's kingdom) and V-day (the consolidation of that victory when Christ returns in full glory).[21]

Many popular forms of Christian eschatology place the emphasis on the discontinuity between this age and the age to come. The redemptive impact of the work of Christ is viewed in other-worldly terms. The purpose of Christ's work of salvation in his first coming is to gather a redeemed people into God's kingdom. But the manifestation of that kingdom is found only when Christ returns. He will come again to judge and annihilate this present evil world, and to create a totally new earth for a future age of glory. The present evil world is seen in pessimistic, almost fatalistic, terms as inevitably headed to destruction. There is no impetus for improving the institutions and structures of this age, since this world will be burned up in the fires of judgment. If the kingdom is entirely future, that is, not embodied in any significant way in the present world but realized only in the new creation inaugurated when Christ returns, then the focus for Christian living between the times is on evangelism—saving as many as possible in the lifeboat of the gospel—as this world, like the Titanic, moves toward its ultimate fate. All Christian hope is directed to the totally new earth that Christ will establish.[22]

---

19. Bosch, *Transforming Mission*, 44.

20. See Hoekema, *Bible and the Future*, 13.

21. Oscar Cullman, *Christ and Time*, trans. Floyd V. Filson (Philadelphia: Westminster, 1950), 87. See also Hoekema, *Bible and the Future*, 14, 34.

22. Kuzmič lists a number of these characteristics of the appropriation of eschatology by popular evangelicalism in "History and Eschatology," 150.

This other-worldly outlook fails to recognize the frequent biblical statements that the new creation of the eschaton has already appeared in human history with the first coming of Christ, and that those united to him participate in it. The proper response, then, is not to react to other-worldliness by placing the emphasis completely on the opposite pole, the "this-worldly" aspect of Christ's kingdom. In this opposite extreme, the tendency is to view eschatology as not merely fulfilled in this world, but also capable of being consummated through the activities of God's people before the return of Christ.[23] Rather than embracing either of these two approaches, the proper perspective is to reflect the biblical teaching on the continuity between this age and the age to come, while recognizing that there are elements of discontinuity as well.

The biblical teaching on redemption supports continuity between creation and the eschaton. In those New Testament passages that deal with the relation of this world with the one to come (Mark 13 par.; 1 Cor. 15:23–30; 2 Thess. 2), Berkhof observes that "it is entirely clear that the coming world will be the renewal and consummation of this one."[24] This is also evident in the biblical terminology used to refer to the redemptive work of Christ. As Wolters notes, the biblical words imply a return to an originally good state or situation. The numerous English words that begin with the prefix *re-* reflect this: re-demption, re-conciliation, re-newal, re-storation, re-generation. The sense of all these words is of a *restoration* of something good that was defaced or polluted.[25] This understanding of redemption is expressed in the statement: "Grace does not destroy nature but restores it."[26]

Christ's redemptive work deals with the cause of the corruption of God's creation, i.e., sin. Sin must never be viewed as a cosmic principle existing independently over against God, nor as that which can transform creation into irretrievable evil. Sin is a parasite on creation, that which distorts and perverts it. But while the effects of sin are pervasive, God is faithful in sustaining his creation. The helpful distinction that Wolters makes here is between the structure and direction of reality. *Structure* refers to "the order of creation, to the constant creational constitution of any thing, what makes it the thing or entity that it is." This is based upon God's faithfulness to his creation. *Direction* designates the degree to which these things and activities conform to, or fail to live up to, God's creational design for them. The corrupting effects of sin results in abnormal and distorted direction in creatures. But the redemp-

---

23. This tendency is often found in postmillenialism, and in some forms of liberation theology and the social gospel.

24. Hendrikus Berkhof, *Christian Faith: An Introduction to the Study of the Faith*, trans. Sierd Woudstra (Grand Rapids: Eerdmans, 1979), 520.

25. Albert Wolters, *Creation Regained: Biblical Basics for a Reformational Worldview* (Grand Rapids: Eerdmans, 1985), 57–58.

26. Quoted in Hoekema, *Bible and the Future*, 73.

tion purposes of God in Christ indicate the restorative direction that may be at work to direct these creatures to God's design.[27]

By removing, in principle, the source of corruption and distortion, redemption affirms the creational goodness, health, and life of this world. Christ's redemption affirms the enduring value of creation, which sin may have perverted but which it can never destroy. And his redemption also directs us to "the renewal of all things" (Matt. 19:28), when "the time comes for God to restore everything, as he promised long ago through his holy prophets" (Acts 3:21). Thus, we see that continuity between the work of Christ's first coming and that of his second coming is connected with the continuity between creation and the eschaton.

This is not to deny the discontinuity between this age and the age to come. The kingdom of God is present now only in a provisional and incomplete state. The struggle against sin continues throughout the present life. Along with the rest of creation, Christians groan as they await the final redemption at the return of Christ (Rom. 8:22–23). The words of Paul and Barnabas to strengthen and encourage the Galatian believers apply to the struggle with suffering that all Christians endure before Christ's return: "We must go through many hardships to enter the kingdom of God" (Acts 14:22).

Nevertheless, the quality and character of believers' lives are determined by the new reality established by Christ's kingdom. That is, the quality of the present lives of Christians must manifest its close connection with the quality of life in the age to come.[28] The discontinuity between the present age and the one to come must be seen from the perspective of the continuity between the two ages. As Berkhof observes, the discontinuity "is to serve and stands in the framework of the continuity."[29]

This continuity is reinforced by the biblical portrait of the supremacy of Christ in Colossians 1:15–20. He is the One by whom and for whom all things were created. He is the "firstborn over all creation" (1:15) because he has sovereignty and preeminence over it. Through Christ's death on the cross, all things have been reconciled to God. What was lost in Adam has been regained in a more glorious sense. His resurrection from the dead demonstrated this in history. The victory over Satan, sin, and evil, accomplished by Christ and his kingdom, will be fully manifested and realized when Christ comes again.[30]

Ethical Implications of the Coming of the Kingdom

The important biblical and theological truths of the coming of the kingdom in Jesus Christ, redemption as the restoration of the fallen creation, and the con-

---

27. Ibid., 49.
28. Noted by Hoekema, *Bible and the Future*, 71.
29. Berkhof, *Christian Faith*, 519.
30. See Ridderbos, *Paul*, 77; Bavinck, *Last Things*, 122.

tinuity between this age and the age to come, have a number of important implications for Christian ethics. First, as members of God's eschatological kingdom Christians are called to live the sanctified life in accord with that kingdom, and to avoid certain types of behavior that are contrary to the character of God's kingdom community.[31] As recipients of the Spirit of God, they must live a way of life consistent with the glorious presence of God in their midst.[32] This is accomplished by the work of the Spirit who changes their hearts and recreates them in the likeness of Christ for life in God's kingdom in obedience to him.[33]

Second, believers must live as a redeemed community—the church—where they celebrate their new life so as to be a sign of the dawning of a new age in the midst of the old age, thereby living as "the vanguard of God's new world."[34] The church functions by and under the power of love as the eschatological gift.[35] It is to be a place of mutual service, ministry, and care. Members of the church must not respond to evil with evil, but overcome evil with good (Rom. 12:21). Especially in a world of violence and revenge, the church must practice repentance and forgiveness to demonstrate that its members have been liberated from the cycles of revenge and violence by the eschatological event of the resurrection. They must live by hope in the new aeon, where God's truth and justice are fully manifested.[36]

Third, because Christ's salvation is the restoration of the fallen creation, Christians should seek to manifest the fruit of his kingdom in all areas of life here and now. The impact of his redemption is as broad as the impact of sin, that is, total and comprehensive. Christian ethics must not be confined to the Christian community, as expressed in the "house rules" of Ephesians 5:22–6:8 and Colossians 3:18–4:1. Ethics must be expressed in all spheres and callings of life. This means that the ethical impact of the kingdom must not confined to the private sphere of life or to the realm of personal individual repentance. It is a truncated eschatological hope that reduces the impact of Christ's kingdom to personal evangelism or personal piety. Bosch insists that the church must resist "a narrow individualistic piety and a view that restricts salvation to the church."[37] As important as personal piety and ecclesiastical life may be to

---

31. Paul lists the behavior that Christians must avoid in 1 Cor. 6:9–10.

32. Noted by Frank Thielman, *Paul and the Law: A Contextual Approach* (Downers Grove, Ill.: InterVarsity, 1994), 84.

33. Ibid., 111. See also L. Gregory Jones, *Embodying Forgiveness: A Theological Analysis* (Grand Rapids: Eerdmans, 1995), 67.

34. Bosch, *Transforming Mission*, 169.

35. Donfried, "Kingdom in Paul," 180.

36. The themes of forgiveness and repentance in the church as an eschatological community are explored in Jones, *Embodying Forgiveness*, especially 135–204; and Miraslov Volf, *Exclusion and Embrace: A Theological Exploration of Identity, Otherness, and Reconciliation* (Nashville: Abingdon, 1996), especially 275–306.

37. Bosch, *Transforming Mission*, 150.

the fulfillment of Christ's kingdom, by themselves they fail to acknowledge the lordship of Christ over all creation, which will be fully manifested when Christ returns.

The fourth implication of the eschatological nature of Christ's work is that we can work for social and cultural change in this aeon. If Christ's first coming (culminating in his resurrection) inaugurates the new creation, then we participate in that new reality by striving to change the present state of affairs so as to bring it into accord with God's redemptive will. Christians are not forced to a passive acceptance of existing structures and institutional procedures as they wait for Christ's return. Rather, the expectation of the eschaton creates the incentive toward change in the light of the age to come.[38] The inbreaking of God's kingdom in this age prompts Christians to work to transform things to bring them into line with the kingdom principles of justice and righteousness.[39]

Fifth, because the fulfillment of Christ's kingdom in this age is provisional, we cannot be taken captive to any utopian schemes for this age. Hoekema rightly insists that all of our historical judgments must be provisional, for we can never be certain whether particular events or movements are good, evil, or a bit of both.[40] The continuing presence of sin in this fallen world requires us to take account of the misuse of resources, relationships, institutions, and power. On the one hand, there cannot be a use of unbiblical coercion to force people to embrace and practice the new life of Christ's kingdom. But, on the other hand, there will always be the need for safeguards that prevent the misuse and abuse of resources, relationships, institutions, and power. Power must be dispersed; there must be accountability for the exercise of authority by individuals and institutions; and review and correction must function in many spheres of life to ensure justice and fairness. No social or cultural transformation will ever eradicate the need for these. At the same time, Christians are summoned to a distinctive way of life that is not merely appropriate to God's kingdom, but contributes to the movement toward its realization. That is, justice and righteousness are the pathways to that kingdom, over against the other options that our society may suggest to us.[41]

---

38. See Stephen C. Mott, "The Use of the New Testament for Social Ethics," *Journal of Religious Ethics* 15 (fall 1987): 242; and Bosch, *Transforming Mission*, 176.

39. Although I believe that Robin Scroggs wrongly sees great diversity and even contradiction in the New Testament ethic, I think he rightly notes the impetus toward ethical practice from those passages that stress that the "kingdom, bringing with it a transformed self, is already a force within the present order" ("The New Testament and Ethics: How Do We Get from There to Here?" in *Perspectives on the New Testament: Essays in Honor of Frank Stagg*, ed. Charles H. Talbert [Macon, Ga.: Mercer University Press, 1985], 91).

40. Hoekema, *Bible and the Future*, 37.

41. Noted by Bruce C. Birch, *Let Justice Roll Down: The Old Testament, Ethics and Christian Life* (Louisville: Westminster/John Knox, 1991), 273.

Sixth, the continuing presence of sin also requires Christians to embrace justice and obedience in the way of the cross, that is, with the understanding that it involves self-denial and the expectation of persecution and suffering for the sake of the kingdom. Schuurman rightly observes that "the form of the church's participation in the world should be one of the suffering servant, rather than triumphant ruler."[42] If evil people persecuted Christ, then they will also persecute his disciples. People benefit from the evil and unjust relationships and institutions that exist in a fallen world. They will resist those who attempt to change these to promote equality, justice, and peace. Christians must trust in the power of Christ at work in them to endure continuing evil as they follow the way of the cross in this broken world. We believe that God's power is made perfect in weakness (2 Cor. 12:9), and that our sufferings will be transformed with the glory that will be revealed in us (Rom. 8:18).

Seventh, the triumph of Christ's kingdom in the consummation encourages believers to persevere. The growth of evil, the resistance to justice, and the victories of the enemies of Christ's kingdom can tempt Christians to despair of effecting the morality of Christ's kingdom in their society. But eschatology affirms that divine morality is upheld by the redemptive intentions of God, and is consistent with his purposes for the history of the world. Christ's second coming assures Christians that his victory over evil on the cross will be universally realized when he returns. The continuance, and even increase, of evil is never cause for panic or discouragement. Christ reigns, and he will consummate his victory in his good time.[43] This does not depend upon human efforts alone, but upon the power of God. Thus, there is motivation for believers to endure faithfully and to face suffering and hardship for Christ's kingdom.[44]

The final implication of the eschatological nature of Christ's work is that the work that Christians do here endures in the eschaton. Continuity between the present age and the age to come strongly suggests that the positive results of our efforts in working toward a better world here and now will be preserved and perfected in the eschaton. Appealing to the description of the new heaven and the new earth in Revelation 21, Bavinck states: "All that is true, honorable, just, pure, pleasing, and commendable in the whole of creation, in heaven and on earth, is gathered up in the future city of God—renewed, re-

---

42. Douglas J. Schuurman, "Creation, Eschaton, and Social Ethics: A Response to Volf," *Calvin Theological Journal* 30 (April 1995): 158. Donfried notes that in the present age "the one in Christ lives under the sign of the cross, not the sign of glory" ("Kingdom in Paul," 178).

43. See Long, *To Liberate and Redeem*, 227–29. Christopher J. H. Wright remarks that the final judgment and destruction of evil, and the new creation of righteousness and peace in which God will dwell with his people, generates within a biblical social ethics "an irrepressible optimism . . . that God cannot fail to complete the redemptive work he has already begun" (*Walking in the Ways of the Lord: The Ethical Authority of the Old Testament* [Downers Grove, Ill.: InterVarsity, 1995], 20).

44. See Birch, *Let Justice*, 271; and Ridderbos, *Paul*, 224.

created, boosted to its highest glory."[45] If the new creation is a continuation of this creation, then it is reasonable to expect that those works done in the name and the power of Christ will be included in the new earth. Of course, these works need to be cleansed of the effects of sin and transformed into the future glory. But the biblical emphasis on continuity, and the specific passages that speak of the enduring works of believers (Rev. 21:24–26; 1 Cor. 3:10–15), support the continuance of our ethical labors.[46]

Creation Ethics and Kingdom Ethics

A discussion of Christian ethics in the light of eschatology would be incomplete without some comments on the nature and relation of creation ethics and kingdom ethics. These two are sometimes referred to as protological ethics and eschatological ethics, respectively. The key question that arises here is: Does the redemptive work of Christ inaugurate a new ethic—an ethic of the kingdom, or an eschatological ethic—that takes priority over and replaces the creational ethic?

It is generally acknowledged by those who accept the authority of the Bible for ethics that Scripture teaches an ethic that is grounded in creation. The norms and laws for human behavior are based upon God's ordering of his creation.[47] These norms are reflected in the Ten Commandments, are written on the hearts of all people (Rom. 2:14–15), and are, therefore, applicable to all, whether they know the true God and his written Word or not.

With the first coming of Christ and his fulfillment of redemption, the New Testament reveals a kingdom ethic. This ethic is addressed specifically to Christians, and it calls them to live in the eschatological reality of Christ's kingdom, which has broken into this present aeon. While the New Testament still affirms the ethics of creation, it gives priority to the ethics of the kingdom. Whereas the creational ethic is grounded in God, the Creator, and his creational norms for human life, the kingdom ethic is centred upon Christ the Redeemer, and the new age that he has established. While the creational ethic looks back to the origin of the world, the kingdom ethic looks ahead to the consummation of the kingdom in the new heaven and the new earth. What, then, is the relation of the two ethical perspectives for Christians living in the era of the gospel?

Some maintain that the ethic of the kingdom supersedes the ethic of creation. A good example of this view is found in the ethical writings of the New

---

45. Bavinck, *Last Things*, 160. Kuzmič appeals to this section in Bavinck to make the same argument ("History and Eschatology," 151).

46. This is also argued by Wolters, *Creation Regained*, 40–41; and Hoekema, *Bible and the Future*, 286–87.

47. See Michael Schluter and Roy Clements, "Jubilee Institutional Norms: A Middle Way between Creation Ethics and Kingdom Ethics as the Basis for Christian Political Action," *Evangelical Quarterly* 62 (January 1990): 38.

Testament scholar Richard Longenecker. He argues that in the New Testament, and especially in the Pauline Epistles, we find both ethical themes: life according to what God has done at creation, and life according to what God has done in the redemptive work of Christ. When applied to the pattern of social relationships, the ethics of creation stresses the hierarchical ordering of social structures, and the norms of subordination and submission, whereas the ethics of the kingdom highlights the norms of freedom, mutuality, and equality. One of the key passages that encapsulates the norms of the kingdom is Galatians 3:28: "There is neither Jew nor Greek, slave nor free, male nor female, for you are all one in Christ Jesus."[48] While the New Testament (and especially Paul) keeps both ethical themes united, the emphasis, and the priority, is given to the ethics of the kingdom.[49]

A number of other Christian ethicists agree with Longenecker's perspective on New Testament ethics, although they may disagree with him on some minor details. Consider two other ethicists. Stanley Grenz also acknowledges that the creation order is what constitutes a universal ethic. But the eschatological reality of the new creation, inaugurated by the work of Christ, is what Christians are to live out in this age. While present in embryonic form in creation, the eschatological reality is the transformation of this creation. Through the work of Christ, Christians can participate in the new creation now.[50] Miraslov Volf also claims that the New Testament presents the themes of creation and the eschaton. But he also approaches Christian ethics with the assumption that eschatology has the primacy.[51] The reason that he gives is that, because the eschaton indicates where creation is going, believers' lives must be shaped by eschatological ethics. He presumes that there is continuity between creation and the eschaton (for without this, we would have no categories to think about the eschaton at all).[52] Yet, even with this continuity, the eschaton must be understood as a transformation of the present creation. Of course, total transformation of creation in this aeon is not possible. Thus, it is the task of ethical reflection to struggle to determine to what extent the ultimate intention of God for creation can be realized in this present age.[53]

48. Richard N. Longenecker, *New Testament Social Ethics for Today* (Grand Rapids: Eerdmans, 1984), 84–88; Richard N. Longenecker, "Authority, Hierarchy and Leadership Patterns in the Bible," in *Women, Authority and the Bible*, ed. Alvera Mickelsen (Downers Grove, Ill.: InterVarsity, 1986), 81–82.

49. Longenecker, *Social Ethics*, 92; Longenecker, "Authority," 82.

50. Stanley J. Grenz, *The Moral Quest: Foundations of Christian Ethics* (Downers Grove, Ill.: InterVarsity, 1997), 223–27.

51. Miraslov Volf, "Eschaton, Creation, and Social Ethics," *Calvin Theological Journal* 30 (April 1995): 134–35.

52. Ibid., 134.

53. Ibid., 138.

The obvious question that arrises for this approach to Christian ethics is: How do we determine what a kingdom (eschatological) ethic calls us to? Grenz and Volf are much more tentative in describing what this means. But it seems to me that they suggest, or open the door to, what Longenecker presents in greater detail, namely, that there are indications, or signposts, in the New Testament for the way in which eschatological principles must shape a Christian ethic. I have already indicated that Longenecker argues for freedom, mutuality, and equality (appealing to Gal. 3:28) as central principles of kingdom ethics. In his book on New Testament social ethics, he argues that in the epistles we find a record of how the early church *began* to work out the implications of the ethics of the kingdom (notably in the areas of slavery, male-female relations, and ethnic relations). These implications were not always as full or adequate as later generations might prefer, but appropriate for their day and pointing the way to a fuller understanding and more adequate application in later times.[54] The obvious conclusion of this is that it is incumbent upon later generations of Christians to follow the pattern of the application of those kingdom principles by New Testament Christians, "seeking to carry out their work in fuller and more significant ways."[55] Notice that this approach views some New Testament applications of eschatological principles as deficient and incomplete. The reason that Longenecker gives is that the apostolic writers had inadequate understanding of how these principles applied to certain relations. For example, Longenecker maintains that Paul's application of these principles to Jewish-Gentile relations was much better than his application to male-female relations.[56]

For Longenecker, then, a kingdom ethic requires that we have a developmental hermeneutic in our appropriation of New Testament teachings. There are two facets to this: (1) recapturing the principles of the gospel that have ramifications for ethics, and (2) following the trajectory that New Testament writers marked out for the applications of those principles, by taking them further along the path they set out. Longenecker suggests the analogy of a growing plant and its original seed as the model for the relationship between the foundational core of ethics and the growth in understanding and application. Real growth consists in genuine innovations of structure, though the growth is controlled and judged by what is inherent in the seed.[57]

Longenecker maintains that the New Testament writers (especially Paul) kept the categories of creation and eschaton united, although the emphasis was on the eschaton.[58] I do not see how unity or continuity is maintained. How does one unify hierarchy (as a principle of creation) with freedom, mu-

---

54. Longenecker, *Social Ethics*, 27.
55. Ibid., 28.
56. Ibid., 93.
57. Ibid., 25.
58. Ibid., 92.

tuality, and equality (as principles of the eschaton)? In his presentation of the developmental ethic, the creational ethic is left behind, and, one would assume, annihilated when the eschaton arrives. This suggests a gnostic repudiation of the creational ethic for the superior good of the kingdom ethic. In addition, it implies that kingdom ethics is a higher level of existence—a *donum superadditum*—whereby we live in a mode of existence as people of God that supersedes the level of creation.[59] This clearly views life according to the kingdom as discontinuous with and transcendent of the creational ethic.

I think that many Christians are attracted to this view of an ethics of the kingdom that overrides an ethics of creation because they believe that the ethics of creation is static, a conservative acquiescence to the status quo. It appears simply to reaffirm the world-order as originally created, which people are called to obey. In contrast, kingdom ethics attempts to change given realities to conform them to the transformed pattern of the eschaton. It appears to recognize the need for transformation in social relationships and institutions to produce a greater degree of freedom and equality in human life.[60]

I have two responses to this. First, these characterizations of a creational ethic and a kingdom ethic are not empirically correct. There are advocates of a transformative ethic who defend the status quo. For example, a number of liberation theologians, whose advocacy of social change and transformation identifies their approach with the ethics of the kingdom, have been adamant in their defence of the Marxist regime in Cuba,[61] clearly a very repressive and reactionary regime when measured by the norms of religious freedom and justice under law. Alternatively, one also finds strong adherents to the ethics of creation who advocate change in the face of social and environmental problems. The Dutch economist, Bob Goudzwaard, who has been an advocate of the Kuyperian emphasis on a creational ethic, has called for the renewal of the international economic order to deal with the problems of poverty, pollution, and environmental degradation.[62]

My second response to the dichotomy posed between the ethics of the creation and the ethics of the kingdom is that it fails to acknowledge the continuity between creation and the eschaton that redemption proclaims. As O'Donovan has argued so well in his book *Resurrection and Moral Order*, redemption is the confirmation of the created order. "[T]he very act of God

59. Noted by Wolters, *Creation Regained*, 59. See also Oliver O'Donovan, *Resurrection and Moral Order: An Outline for Evangelical Ethics* (Grand Rapids: Eerdmans, 1986), 15, 55.

60. The following make comments along this line: Schluter and Clements, "Jubilee Institutional Norms," 37; Longenecker, *Social Ethics*, 87–88; and Volf, cited in Schuurman, "Eschaton," 150.

61. For example, see Gustavo Gutierrez, *A Theology of Liberation*, trans. and ed. Cridad Inda and John Eagelson (Maryknoll, N.Y.: Orbis, 1979), 88–92.

62. See Bob Goudzewaard and Harry de Lange, *Beyond Poverty and Affluence: Toward an Economy of Care*, trans. and ed. Mark R. Vander Vennen (Grand Rapids: Eerdmans/Geneva: WCC Publications, 1995).

which ushers in his kingdom is the resurrection of Christ from the dead, the reaffirmation of creation. . . . In the resurrection of Christ creation is restored and the kingdom of God dawns." Thus, in the resurrection God acts in the redemptive work of Jesus Christ to bring what he has made in creation to its fulfillment.[63] The opposition between the ethics of creation and the ethics of the kingdom fails to appreciate this.

At the same time, redemption does highlight the insufficiency of creation to overcome sin. As Schuurman notes, the discontinuity between creation and eschaton should be understood at the level of the capacity of creational realities to overcome sin. Though creation endures in a fallen world, and though it cannot be destroyed by sin, the creation order cannot defeat sin. A new and special act of God, accomplished in the death and resurrection of Christ, is necessary to purge creation of the corrupting effects of sin. This opens the way to a new experience of life in the kingdom, which will reach its consummation with the complete manifestation of God's love and our participation in it.[64] But this transformation of relationships (human-divine and human-human) in the eschaton so that they will be completely just and loving is based upon the creation order. God's power accomplishes it, but it remains an ethic of the creation order.[65]

Another aspect of discontinuity between creation and eschaton is a change in the manner in which we participate in the creation order as a result of Christ's redemptive work on earth. In Galatians 4 Paul speaks of believers participating in God's redemptive purposes, no longer as slaves (or underage heirs), but as adult children. O'Donovan observes that with the coming of Christ Christians are no longer subservient to the creation order, but they exercise dominion with a new status. As moral agents, Christians are "involved in deciding what a situation is and demands in the light of moral order." They are called "to interpret *new* situations, plumbing their meanings," to engage in "creative discernment."[66] Wolters echoes this viewpoint. Also appealing to Paul's letter to the Galatians, Wolters notes that, whereas God implemented his creational law for his people in the Old Testament era, in the New Testament he gives us the freedom in Christ to do our own implementing.[67] But what both O'Donovan and Wolters rightly emphasize is that the ethic that guides the people of God throughout history is based on the universal and constant principles of creation.

There is another important point that needs to be made to address the alleged dichotomy between creational and eschatological ethics. An ethic of cre-

---

63. O'Donovan, *Resurrection*, 15.
64. Schuurman, "Eschaton," 156–57.
65. See O'Donovan, *Resurrection*, 70.
66. Ibid., 24–25.
67. Wolters, *Creation Regained*, 34–35.

ation is often characterized as an ethic that attempts to restore the world to some pristine state, a return to the Garden of Eden. But a discerning creational ethic recognizes that this should not be done, and it really cannot be done. The reason is that God made creation to be historical in nature; it does not remain static. God placed human beings in the world so that they might develop creation by filling it through their fruitfulness and by forming it through their dominion (Gen. 1:28). (This is what is called the cultural or creational mandate.) Human cultural and societal developments unfold and open up the potential and possibilities in the natural and human realms of creation. These are guided by the laws and norms that God has established in his creation.[68] As human society progresses, there is development in understanding and application of creational laws and norms. While sin continues to be at work in the human and natural realms, the common grace of God through the general work of the Spirit produces positive advances in human culture.

What this means for Christian ethics is that redemption involves a restoration of the fruits of human cultural development at their current stage of development. Evil distortions are exposed and removed, and positive developments affirmed and reformed.[69] The calling of believers is to continue the historical development of creation in the service of the resurrected One who is now both the Lord of creation and the ultimate Goal of creation. In other words, Christians are called to engage in their cultural activities, and to function as moral agents, with the goal of bringing this order into perfect subjection to Christ.

It is via eschatology that we understand the end toward which all events are directed, and the goal toward which all creation strives. O'Donovan rightly notes that the eschatological transformation of the world is its fulfillment.[70] This understanding of development affirms the essential continuity between creation and eschaton. We must continue to respect the creational structures of this world; and we await the transformation that does not repudiate or annihilate present structures, but vindicates them and perfects them in a way that could not be done in a world of continuing sin. The key point here is that we must live with the eschatological end (*telos*) of creation in mind, not so that we might abandon the creation ethic by turning to a transcendent ethic of the kingdom, but so that we might have that eschatological *telos* to strive toward in our obedient lives in this age.[71] As Ridderbos states, the life and destiny of the disciples and the church must be again and again set in the eschatological light of the coming of the Son of Man.[72]

---

68. Ibid., 35–39.
69. Ibid., 63–64.
70. O'Donovan, *Resurrection*, 55.
71. Wright makes this point to support his claim that the two ethical themes of creation and kingdom "interpenetrate each other" (*Walking in the Ways*, 45).
72. Herman Ridderbos, *The Coming of the Kingdom*, ed. Raymond O. Zorn, trans. H. de Jongste (Philadelphia: Presbyterian & Reformed, 1969), 470.

In that light, discontinuity is relative. Of course, there is discontinuity between this age and the age to come. But the discontinuity has to do with the degree and intensity of our experience of participation in the new creation. Schuurman says it well: the "relative discontinuity" between creation and the eschaton is "for the most part one of degree rather than kind, of quantity rather than quality, of accident than essence. The Bible encourages us to see the eschaton as the *fulfillment* of creational potential, the *manifestation* of what is hidden and foggy, the *fullness* of what is partial, the *more* of the first fruits."[73] Bavinck insists that in the glory of the transformed creation, "*Substantially* nothing is lost."[74] While we do not fully understand what the new creation will be like, we can live lives of faithfulness to the creational norms of God, as members of the new creation that Christ has inaugurated, and as assured participants in the eschatological consummation that he will accomplish.

73. Schuurman, "Eschaton," 156.
74. Bavinck, *Last Things*, 160.

21

Till Every Foe Is Vanquished: Emerging Sociopolitical Implications of Progressive Dispensational Eschatology

RUSSELL D. MOORE

Southern Baptist Theological Seminary

Dispensationalists in the Public Square

Risking understatement, it may be said that history has rarely feared the establishment of a dispensational state church. From its very beginnings within J. N. Darby's Plymouth Brethren, dispensationalism has engendered a skeptical view of governmental and ecclesiastical power structures that historically has not lent itself to animated political participation. Lumping dispensational scholars Darby, C. I. Scofield, Lewis Sperry Chafer, Charles Ryrie, and John Walvoord with popular apocalypticists such as Hal Lindsey, evangelical historian Mark A. Noll faults traditional dispensationalism for an inherent anti-intellectualism and heightened supernaturalism through which it viewed its task as "rescuing unbelievers from sin and keeping themselves unspotted from the world."[1] The resulting cultural withdrawal stemming from eschatological pessimism, Noll argues, has had an acute impact upon the rest of evangelicalism.

---

1. Mark A. Noll, *The Scandal of the Evangelical Mind* (Grand Rapids: Eerdmans, 1994), 119. Noll does, however, seem to exempt emerging progressive dispensationalists from this indictment, viewing them instead within the more traditional categories of Protestant understanding of the covenants and the kingdom of Christ.

The rather noisy inception of the Reconstructionist/theonomy movement among some sectors of Calvinism has engendered yet another critique of the dispensationalist track record in the public square. Reconstructionists lay the blame not with cultural laziness or paranoia, but in an inherent defect within the premillennial eschatological system itself, namely, a self-consciously pessimistic "rapture fever" that short-circuits any concern for social and political righteousness.[2] Reconstructionists have charged premillennial eschatology with fostering a "pietist-humanist alliance" that abdicates responsibility for changing the structures of society.[3] Only "inconsistent dispensationalists" fail to see that their escapist pessimism precludes any meaningful social action, the Reconstructionists contend.[4]

If so, then the late twentieth century has seen several attempts at "inconsistent dispensationalism." While some traditional dispensationalist scholars have taken measured forays into the ethical arena,[5] most dispensational political activity has taken place on the popular level, particularly within the ranks of the new Christian right political movement. German theologian Jürgen Moltmann has expressed dismay that American dispensationalists who are engaged in an "apocalyptic flight from the world" have been "politicized through 'the moral majority' of Jerry Falwell and others, who since the time of Ronald Reagan have linked this apocalyptic fundamentalism with the political right in the USA, and with the preparation for a nuclear Armageddon."[6]

Sociologist Sara Diamond, a culturally liberal critic of the Christian political right, disagrees with the conventional wisdom that dispensational premillennialism has been averse to political activity. Even if millennial thinking is a distraction, she argues, "a good distraction can energize the faithful for the battles ahead."[7] She finds political overtones throughout the rhetoric of popular American dispensationalism, especially in the belief in a pretribulational rapture that she says rhetorically magnifies the chasm between the "saved" and the "unsaved," "us" and "them."[8] She argues that dispensationalism as a component of the larger American evangelical subculture shares evangelicalism's

---

2. Gary North, *Rapture Fever* (Tyler, Tex.: Institute for Christian Economics, 1993).

3. Gary North and Gary DeMar, *Christian Reconstruction: What It Is—What It Isn't* (Tyler, Tex.: Institute for Christian Economics, 1991), 70–71.

4. Ibid., 71.

5. For example, Norman Geisler, "A Premillennial View of Law and Government," *BSac* 142 (July-September 1985): 250–66; Robert L. Thomas, "Improving Evangelical Ethics: An Analysis of the Problem and a Proposed Solution," *JETS* 34 (March 1991): 3–20; and Ramesh Richard, "Hermeneutical Prolegomena to Premillennial Social Ethics" (Th.D. diss., Dallas Theological Seminary, 1982).

6. Jürgen Moltmann, *The Coming of God: Christian Eschatology*, trans. Margaret Kohl (Minneapolis: Fortress, 1996), 159.

7. Sara Diamond, *Not by Politics Alone: The Enduring Influence of the Christian Right* (New York: Guilford, 1998), 197.

8. Ibid., 202.

politically charged atmosphere, even if political activity is limited to keeping group members satisfied with the sociopolitical status quo.[9]

Dallas Theological Seminary theologian Robert Pyne concedes that dispensationalists "have a bad reputation when it comes to social issues."[10] He assigns much of the culpability for this sociopolitical inactivity to dispensationalism's separatist origins, pessimistic attitude toward social progress, relegation of the Old Testament law and Sermon on the Mount to other dispensations, conversion-oriented revivalism, background in southern culture, and reaction to the liberal Social Gospel movement. He asserts that while traditional dispensationalism has not necessitated cultural disengagement, it has "provided a theological loophole for those whose understanding of social ethics had been thrown out of balance by sin, controversy, and culture."[11] Even those dispensationalists and other evangelicals who have been politicized through the "culture wars" of recent years, Pyne laments, have charged ahead with political aims that are "usually indistinguishable from those of the non-Christian Republicans who share their neighborhoods."[12]

Recent years have seen large sectors of evangelical theological traditions coalesce around the concept of inaugurated eschatology, the idea that biblical eschatology includes both an "already" of initial fulfillment and a "not yet" of future consummation.[13] This "already/not yet" framework has proven to be a prevailing theme in some important streams of both amillennial and premillennial thought.[14] Interestingly, this inaugurated eschatology has also been adopted by a growing number of dispensational premillennialists dissatisfied with traditional dispensationalism. This new movement, dubbed "progressive dispensationalism," has upset classical eschatological categories by combining an inaugurated eschatology and a unitary understanding of the people of God with a vigorous defense of a premillennial hope for the restoration of national Israel.

---

9. Ibid., 10–11.

10. Robert Pyne, "The New Man in an Immoral Society: Expectations between the Times" (paper presented to the Dispensational Study Group at the annual meeting of the Evangelical Theological Society, Santa Clara, Calif., 20 November 1997), 1.

11. Ibid., 10.

12. Ibid., 15.

13. For a survey of these trends, see Bruce A. Ware, "New Dimensions in Eschatology," in *New Dimensions in Evangelical Thought: Essays in Honor of Millard J. Erickson*, ed. David S. Dockery (Downers Grove, Ill.: InterVarsity, 1998), 354–65.

14. The impact of inaugurated eschatology on covenantal amillennialism can be seen in Anthony Hoekema, *The Bible and the Future* (Grand Rapids: Eerdmans, 1979); Stanley Grenz, *Theology for the Community of God* (Nashville: Broadman and Holman, 1994), 793–806; and Raymond O. Zorn, *Christ Triumphant: Biblical Perspectives on Christ and His Kingdom* (Edinburgh: Banner of Truth, 1997). Inaugurated eschatology from a premillennial viewpoint is argued perhaps most cogently in George Eldon Ladd, *The Presence of the Future* (Grand Rapids: Eerdmans, 1997).

This emergence of progressive dispensationalism may foreshadow pivotal developments in the construction of an eschatologically-informed evangelical sociopolitical ethic. The cultural ramifications of progressive dispensationalist ideas are beginning to command attention from the evangelical world. Wheaton College professor Ashley Woodiwiss opines that the burgeoning social engagement of progressive dispensationalists signals "the grudging concession among pietistic individualists that the believer, sola, is not the starting point for Christian thought and practice."[15] Because no full-fledged treatment of sociopolitical concerns has been offered from the progressive dispensational camp, a full-orbed ethic of cultural transformation is yet to be developed.[16] Nonetheless, the theological issues raised by the progressive dispensationalists indict both triumphalistic dominion-taking and pietistic cultural withdrawal, while challenging evangelicals with what could lead to a new model for sociopolitical engagement.[17] The pivotal issues in constructing a progressive dispensational construct for cultural and political activism may lie within three broad areas of progressive dispensational theological distinctives, namely their understanding of the Davidic covenant as an inaugurated reality, their formulation of the church as an initial manifestation of the coming kingdom, and their conception of salvation as holistic and christological.[18]

Ironically, the lack of dispensational participation in political formulation may actually prove to be an advantage to progressive dispensationalists in constructing a theologically coherent social ethic. Having emerged from well over a decade of radically modifying some central theological tenets of their heritage, progressives may find themselves unfettered to pursue the political implications of their system without undergoing a process of discarding a recalcitrant dispensational political theory. As the debate within dispensationalism advances to the political front, the history of dispensational truancy from the public square may necessitate that the traditional/progressive debate on these issues will be primarily theological and only secondarily ethical in nature. Traditionalists and progressives within the dis-

---

15. Ashley Woodiwiss, "Revising Our Pledges of Allegiance: From 'Christian America' to the Gospel of the Resurrection," *Touchstone* 11 (September–October 1998): 31.

16. The most extensive treatments of sociopolitical issues from a progressive dispensational perspective thus far have been found in Pyne, "The New Man," along with Craig Blaising and Darrell Bock's concluding chapter on practical and ministerial issues in *Progressive Dispensationalism* (Wheaton, Ill.: Victor, 1993), 284–301.

17. Progressive dispensationalist Mark Saucy argues that evangelicalism's large-scale commitment to premillennialism can help to encourage "a healthy separation between the Kingdom's Already and its Not Yet which spares evangelical praxis from the snare" of such mainline ecumenical bodies as the World Council of Churches. See Mark Saucy, *The Kingdom of God in the Teaching of Jesus in Twentieth Century Theology* (Dallas: Word, 1997), 300.

18. This list is far from exhaustive. Exploration of progressive dispensational concepts on the inaugurated new covenant, the role of the Spirit, the precise nature of Ephesians' "New Man," and the understanding of the new heavens and new earth, among others, will be helpful in determining the ramifications the movement offers for sociopolitical righteousness. For the purposes of this discussion, the analysis will center on the central themes listed above.

pensational camp agree, however, that the theological conclusions of the newer group of dispensationalists are revolutionary enough to impact almost every facet of dispensational thought, including the motivation and method of sociopolitical engagement.

Initial Fulfillment of the Davidic Promise

Progressive dispensationalism's most noteworthy break from its traditional dispensational forebears may prove to be the idea of an "already/not yet" framework of fulfillment of the Old Testament Davidic covenant. The idea of an inaugurated Davidic covenant elicited debate from within the ranks of progressive dispensationalism while drawing fire from traditional dispensationalists.

Traditionally, most dispensationalists have seen the fulfillment of the Davidic promise as wholly future. Lewis Sperry Chafer outlined a careful understanding of the covenant in his systematic theology in which difficulty comes "only for those who are determined to metamorphose a literal, earthly throne and kingdom into some vague and wholly imaginary spiritual idealism."[19] Dispensationalist theologians have typically also asserted that the Davidic kingdom can in no sense be equated with the present session of Christ at the Father's right hand or with Christ's present rule over his church.[20] Early dispensationalists formulated a view of the kingdom in which Jesus offered to Israel an earthly, geopolitical Davidic kingdom which, when rejected, led to the formation of the spiritually-blessed church.[21]

Progressive dispensationalists join their more traditional forebears in affirming a future literal fulfillment of passages such as Isaiah 11, in which the nations rally around the Davidic ruler who mediates the promised blessings of the Abrahamic and Davidic covenants to the nations.[22] Even so, progressive dispensationalists, led by Craig Blaising and Darrell Bock, veered sharply from the older dispensationalist notion by asserting that the Old Testament Davidic hope sees initial fulfillment in the current messianic activity of the ascended Christ.

Thus far, Darrell Bock has shouldered much of the responsibility among progressives for defending the concept of an inaugurated Davidic covenant. Bock concludes that the New Testament, especially Luke-Acts, assumes a ful-

---

19. Lewis Sperry Chafer, *Systematic Theology* (Dallas: Dallas Seminary Press, 1948), 5:321.

20. J. Dwight Pentecost, *Thy Kingdom Come* (Wheaton, Ill.: Victor, 1990), 156.

21. For a discussion of theological development within dispensationalism, see Craig A. Blaising, "Development of Dispensationalism by Contemporary Dispensationalists," *BSac* 145 (July-September 1988): 254–80; and Timothy Weber, *Living in the Shadow of the Second Coming: American Premillennialism, 1875–1982* (Chicago: University of Chicago Press, 1983).

22. Craig A. Blaising, "Premillennialism," in *Three Views on the Millennium and Beyond*, ed. Darrell Bock (Grand Rapids: Zondervan, 1999), 157–227.

fillment of the Davidic covenant that does indeed include literal national and geopolitical aspects.[23] Like historic premillennialist George Eldon Ladd, however, Bock sees a sense of the onset of the kingdom in Jesus' healing and exorcism ministries.[24] Jesus does not completely initiate this reign, Bock qualifies, until the sending of the Spirit as a sign of the dawning eschaton with the inauguration of the new covenant in Acts 2.[25] Jesus asserts his regal authority as the seed of David by forgiving the sins of his people, Bock argues. "A king, indeed, shows his authority by ruling a kingdom," he observes. "Jesus rules by saving and calling a new community made from all nations."[26]

Bock identifies a clear explication of the "already" and "not yet" aspects of messianic fulfillment of the Davidic covenant in Acts 2.[27] He observes in Peter's Pentecost sermon a tying together of 2 Samuel 7, Psalm 16, and Psalm 110 into an apostolic assertion that situation "on David's throne is linked to being seated at God's right hand."[28] Because Psalm 110 is a regal Psalm that pictures the royal figure seated and reigning from God's right hand, Peter's contention for its fulfillment argues for "an initial yet uncertain fulfillment of the Davidic promise and is a presupposition to the right to bestow the Spirit in accordance with the new-covenant promise."[29]

Jesus' salvific activity is to be regarded, not as something severed from his role as fulfillment of the Davidic promise, as in traditional dispensationalism, but as an integral part of his identity as the anticipated Davidic ruler. Jesus pictured his exorcisms as part of his messianic role, Bock notes, and in the same way the forgiveness of sins necessitates rule and the subjugation of such enemies as Satan and fallen human nature.[30] Bock pointedly repudiates those who advance the argument that the early church never regarded Jesus as the already reigning Davidic king.[31]

23. Darrell L. Bock, "The Reign of the Lord Christ," in *Dispensationalism, Israel, and the Church: The Search for Definition*, ed. Craig A. Blaising and Darrell L. Bock (Grand Rapids: Zondervan, 1992), 38–39.

24. Ibid., 42. So also argues George Eldon Ladd, "The Kingdom of God and the Church," *Foundations* 4 (April 1972): 170–71.

25. Bock, "Reign of the Lord Christ," 42.

26. Ibid., 44.

27. "One should not fear 'already and not yet' terminology," Bock counsels. "Since all Bible students accept its presence in soteriology: 'I am saved (i.e. justified) already—but I am not yet saved (i.e. glorified)' is good theology" (ibid., 46).

28. Ibid., 46–47.

29. Ibid., 52.

30. Darrell L. Bock, "Current Messianic Activity and OT Davidic Promise: Dispensationalism, Hermeneutics, and NT Fulfillment," *Trinity Journal* 15 (1994): 64.

31. To the assertion that the catacomb drawings pictured Jesus in the roles of a philosopher, miracle worker, or good shepherd, Bock responds that the shepherd imagery of the Davidic son comes from Ezek. 34:23–24, which speaks of the shepherd as ruling over his flock (ibid., 65).

In his current salvific activity, as well as in his future coercive rule, Jesus exercises his authority as the "horn of salvation" from the house of David, Bock asserts. "Israel has a future hope of deliverance by the King who will rule over them (cf. Luke 1:31–35)," he observes. "But in his two volumes Luke's interest moved beyond Israel. People faced a battle with Satan and sin, a battle Jesus is winning as he brings people out of darkness and into light."[32] The use of Psalm 110:1 in Acts, Bock argues, vigorously presents Jesus' ruling function from God's side as the Davidic mediator of God's blessings. This ruling authority is exercised when his control over individual salvation is affirmed through religious rites such as baptism that are performed "in his name."[33]

To understand Jesus' current activity as Davidic ruler, progressives argue, one must look at the full-orbed Old Testament witness to the roles of the Davidic son, not to 2 Samuel 7 in isolation. Isaiah 9:2 speaks of the Davidic son as a light to the nations. The Davidic ruler is repeatedly characterized as demonstrating justice and righteousness. Isaiah 11:2 speaks of the Spirit of God resting on the Davidic ruler who brings wisdom and understanding to the people. Ezekiel 34–36 prophesies of the Davidic ruler not only as exercising authority over a flock, but also as mediating the cleansing work of the Spirit.[34] For progressive dispensationalists, the New Testament, even beyond Luke-Acts, contains a wealth of testimony to the initial christological fulfillment of the covenant. For example, Isaiah 11:2 and 1 Peter 4:14 correlate the Spirit that rests upon the Davidic heir with the Christians who share in his sufferings.[35] With such an argument for initial fulfillment, progressives conclude that the Old Testament Davidic covenant shares the same "already/not yet" elements in the New Testament as its counterparts in the Abrahamic and new covenants.[36]

Blaising and Bock argue that the Davidic covenant found fulfillment in the very center of Jesus' salvific activity, the events leading to his sacrifice at Golgotha. The warning from 2 Samuel 7:14 that God would correct the sins of his Davidic ruler by striking him with the rod, they contend, finds its fulfillment in the Gospel accounts of Jesus being beaten with rods prior to his crucifixion. The Davidic heir does indeed bear the rod of God's wrath, but not for his own personal sin. Blaising and Bock see unmistakable Old Testament imagery in Matthew's juxtaposition of Gentile soldiers beating the arrested Jesus with their mocking him as "King of the Jews" and "Son of God," both titles consistent with Davidic covenantal expectation.[37]

---

32. Darrell L. Bock, "The Son of David and the Saints' Task: The Hermeneutics of Initial Fulfillment," *BSac* 150 (October–December 1993): 448.

33. Ibid., 451.

34. Ibid., 452.

35. W. Edward Glenny, "Dispensational Hermeneutics: A Proposal" (paper presented to the Dispensational Study Group at the annual meeting of the Evangelical Theological Society, Orlando, Fla., 19 November 1998).

36. Bock, "Son of David and the Saints' Task," 454.

37. Blaising and Bock, *Progressive Dispensationalism*, 176.

This view of initial fulfillment of Davidic hope is not monolithic within the progressive dispensational movement, however. Robert L. Saucy, one of the early proponents of progressive dispensationalism, disagrees with Blaising and Bock's thesis, positing that Jesus' fulfillment of Psalm 110 refers to messianic authority, but not to his function as Davidic king.[38] The extension of salvation benefits exists, Saucy argues, in the extension of salvation benefits to the Gentiles because of Jesus' role as the Davidic Messiah of the entire earth, but does not express itself in a Davidic reign by Jesus over the church in the present age.[39] The present manifestation of the Davidic blessings is given, Saucy contends, not through the regal authority of the one ruling from David's throne, but through the persuasive power of Word and Spirit.[40] Likewise, his son, Mark Saucy, has articulated similar conclusions regarding the fulfillment of the Davidic covenant.[41] Despite the objections of the Saucys, Blaising and Bock's inaugurationist understanding of the initial fulfillment of the Davidic promise remains the majority report among progressive dispensationalists.

This embrace of inaugurated eschatology in relation to the Davidic covenant has motivated essentialist dispensationalists to charge progressives with deviation from their shared theological heritage. Traditionalist dispensationalists have indicted progressives with everything from a fundamental violation of dispensational hermeneutics to a simple misreading of the New Testament.[42] Stephen J. Nichols laments that the "already/not yet" view of the Davidic cove-

---

38. Robert L. Saucy, *The Case for Progressive Dispensationalism* (Grand Rapids: Zondervan, 1993), 70–76.

39. Ibid., 80.

40. Robert L. Saucy, "The Presence of the Kingdom and the Life of the Church," *BSac* 145 (January–March 1988): 44.

41. Mark Saucy, "Exaltation Christology in Hebrews: What Kind of Reign?" *Trinity Journal* 14 (1993): 41–62.

42. Robert L. Thomas contends that the progressive dispensational view of the inaugurated Davidic kingdom represents a decisive break from grammatical-historical hermeneutics. To equate the heavenly throne of Christ with the earthly Davidic throne is to grant the Old Testament texts more than one meaning in violation of dispensational hermeneutical principles, he argues. See Robert L. Thomas, "The Hermeneutics of Progressive Dispensationalism," *Master's Seminary Journal* 6 (spring 1995): 79–95; and "A Classical Dispensationalist View of Revelation," in *Four Views on the Book of Revelation*, ed. C. Marvin Pate (Grand Rapids: Zondervan, 1998), 183–85. Zane Hodges likewise charges progressives with illegitimately transforming the meaning of an earthly political throne into a present heavenly session. See Zane Hodges, "A Dispensational Understanding of Acts 2," in *Issues in Dispensationalism*, ed. Wesley R. Willis and John R. Master (Chicago: Moody, 1994): 174. Charles C. Ryrie, who has framed the distinction between Israel and the church as the sine qua non of dispensational theology, objects to the progressive view on the basis that it does not recognize the distinction between the New Testament identification of Jesus as the one who will reign one day as Davidic king and his present reign. The inauguration of the Davidic messianic reign at Jesus' ascension is impossible, Ryrie asserts, because Jesus' first act in this role would have been the sending of the Holy Spirit, which Ryrie concludes is not a provision of the Davidic covenant. See Charles C. Ryrie, *Dispensationalism* (Chicago: Moody, 1995), 167–70.

nant in progressive dispensationalism amounts to "already Ladd/not yet dispensationalism."[43] Although he concedes that the future consummation of the Davidic promise in progressive dispensationalism is more "Israelitish" than that of George Eldon Ladd's historic premillennialism, "the point still stands that, as far as the current, initial stage of fulfillment is concerned, Bock is following Ladd."[44] The progressives counter that their view of the Davidic kingdom does indeed share Ladd's understanding of initial fulfillment, but differs sharply from historic premillennialism in the "not yet" phase of fulfillment. A future geopolitical realization of the covenant in the context of a reconstituted Israel ensures that progressive dispensationalism remains distinct from covenantal premillennialism that absorbs the promises of Israel into the "New Israel" of the church.[45]

The "not yet" phase of the Davidic covenant as articulated by progressive dispensationalists retains the classical premillennial understanding of the coming kingdom as an everlasting messianic reign that "is not simply a higher order of spiritual reality which coexists with the present state of affairs, but is a complete replacement of present conditions on earth with a new worldwide and multinational world order."[46] Jesus did not argue that sociopolitical elements of the Davidic kingdom were mistaken, progressives argue, he merely affirmed that this nationalistic stage of the kingdom was not yet present (Acts 1:6).

The ramifications of this doctrinal modification for contemporary premillennialism are remarkable, since the very idea of a presently ruling messianic king is by its very definition political. Bock notes that Luke's references to Jesus as the Davidic son display theocratic royal expectations in which a "major burden of Luke's writings is to show how the Davidic ruler comes to have such comprehensive authority over all humans."[47] Throughout the Gospel accounts, from Herod at Jesus' birth to the Roman authorities at his execution, political leaders are pictured as threatened by the political implications of Jesus' role as Davidic Messiah. A progressive dispensational eschatology contends that these rulers' fears are well founded, if premature.

An understanding of the initial fulfillment of the Davidic covenant may well spur progressive dispensationalists to reexamine sociopolitical issues in light of the "already" phase of this prophetic hope. Jesus' present reign manifests itself in spiritual salvific terms in which his subjects receive the Spirit as evidence of his regal authority to dispense the blessings of the new covenant.

43. Stephen J. Nichols, "The Dispensational View of the Davidic Kingdom: A Response to Progressive Dispensationalism," *Master's Seminary Journal* 7 (fall 1996): 232.

44. Ibid.

45. Darrell L. Bock, "Why I Am a Dispensationalist with a Small 'd,'" *JETS* 41 (September 1998): 386–91.

46. Blaising, "Premillennialism," 41.

47. Darrell L. Bock, *Luke*, Baker Exegetical Commentary on the New Testament (Grand Rapids: Baker, 1994), 1:116–17.

Sinners recognize Jesus' messianic kingship by calling upon the name of the One who has authority to subjugate their enemies and rescue them from satanic domination and slavery to sin. The evangelistic task of the church is energized by the knowledge that the authority for Great Commission activity has been granted by the King to whom God has granted the right to crush his enemies with a rod of iron (Ps. 2:9).

Because the church is ruled in the present era by an already-exalted Davidic king, the church has the mandate to examine the features of their current political relationships in light of the characteristics of their now-ruling messianic king. Because the Davidic king rules with justice and wisdom (Ps. 72:1–2; Jer. 23:5), believers are given an authoritative standard by which they may condemn global tyranny. International human rights abuses may be resisted in light of the King who one day will exercise righteous diplomacy between the nations (Isa. 2:4). Believers cannot have the option of inaction against judicial abuses, since they are presently ruled by One the Scriptures describe as judging his subjects with fairness and equity (Isa. 11:3–4). Likewise, the political oppression of the poor cannot be ignored by a church that is governed even now by a Davidic king of whom it is said "with righteousness He will judge the poor" (Isa. 11:4 NASB).

When confronting the thorny ethical dilemmas of abortion and euthanasia, progressive dispensationalists can legitimately seek protection for the unborn and the elderly, not on the basis of natural law, the *imago dei*, or "two kingdoms" understandings alone, but from a distinctively coherent and all-encompassing theological, christological, and ecclesiological framework. Because the church is presently ruled by the Davidic heir who is described as an advocate "for the afflicted of the earth" (Isa. 11:4), progressive dispensationalists have the biblical impetus to plead for the life and liberty of the powerless.

Unlike classical dispensational formulations of the Davidic covenant in which Jesus' current messianic activity is compared to David's anointed and yet exiled status under Saul, progressives can legitimately call the church from cultural withdrawal since the throne of David is occupied and is active even now.[48] Because the Spirit is present within the community of faith, believers can confidently testify to the world of the Spirit-dispensing King who reigns over them in righteousness and in truth.

The "not yet" phase of the Davidic covenant likewise transforms the sociopolitical mandate of Christians. Progressive dispensationalists do not hesitate from joining with other dispensationalists in affirming an earthly millennial reign of Christ, centered on a reconstituted national Israel upon whom the

---

48. Robert Pyne, for example, called upon the Dispensational Study Group meeting at the 1997 annual meeting of the Evangelical Theological Society to pursue justice in American society and in seemingly intractable situations such as India, since such justice is "part of the King's agenda" according to Ps. 72:12–14 (Pyne, "New Man and Immoral Society," 15).

covenant God will lavish the geopolitical promises he pledged to them in the Old Testament. The very existence of a political rule of Christ over the nations repels dispensationalists from any notion that the gospel is unconcerned with politics. To the contrary, in the dispensational prophetic hope, history is moving toward a stunningly political climax. Progressive dispensationalist Craig Blaising has contrasted the political nature of millennial hope with the mystical "spiritual visionary hope" of Augustinian amillennialism that reduces Christian expectation to inward spiritual blessing rather than historical political resolution.[49]

A clear articulation of the "not yet" phase of the Davidic covenant is pivotal in a progressive dispensational critique of Reconstructionist postmillennialism, "Latter Rain" charismatic activism, and other triumphalistic religiopolitical movements on the right along with revolutionary liberation theologies on the left. Because the Son of David rules, political issues must matter to the church, but because he rules now invisibly and through the persuasive activity of his church, believers must eschew any delusions of subjugating society through brute force. "We do not bear a sword, but a cross," Bock warns. "The manifestation of dominion authority for saints is part of what is yet to come in the kingdom program."[50] Instead, Jesus' present messianic activity encompasses an invisible rule over his voluntary subjects, but does not yet include the political nationalistic elements that are still entirely future.[51] Progressive dispensationalists have been quick to assert that any attempt to legislate belief or to punish unbelief in the present era is a violation of the distinction between the two stages of covenant fulfillment.[52] On this point, progressive dispensationalists have allies in the public pronouncements of other inaugurationist premillennialists who also see the dominion-seekers' error in a failure to distinguish between the "already" and the "not yet."[53] The church does indeed

49. Blaising, "Premillennialism," 34.

50. Bock, "Current Messianic Activity," 85.

51. Bock, "Reign of the Lord Christ," 53–54. "Jesus rules in the present kingdom over the whole earth," Bock writes. "But it is not yet a full, direct rule over every person, nor does it reflect its future political, sociological character."

52. Blaising argues that a desire to coerce acceptance of the gospel has been the "error of some experiments of church and state in the past and it springs from a misunderstanding of the dispensation in which we live. There is to be no execution of law against unbelief until the coming of Christ Himself" (Blaising and Bock, *Progressive Dispensationalism*, 291).

53. For example, Brad Harper applies the inaugurated eschatology of George Eldon Ladd to the sociopolitical realm by noting that the rule of Christ "is present now by persuasion and must be received by faith; then, it will be present in power and all will be confronted with its irrefutable sovereignty. The current victories over evil are selective and occasional; then they will be comprehensive" (Brad Harper, "The Kingdom of God in George Eldon Ladd as a Theological Foundation for the Role of the Church in Society," in *God and Caesar: Selected Essays from the 1993 Evangelical Theological Society's Convention at Washington, DC*, ed. Michael Bauman and David Hall [Camp Hill, Pa.: Christian Publications, 1994], 198).

hold the regal authority of the Son of David, progressives argue, but in the present age they must proclaim his coming kingdom through cross-bearing humility, godly weakness, and persuasive love.[54]

Because progressive dispensationalists hold to the classical dispensationalist hope for the restoration of national Israel in the coming millennial reign, this too has implications for current sociopolitical activity. Spurred on by popular apocalypticism among the evangelical grassroots constituency, some dispensationalist leaders have translated their theological understanding into an almost unqualified support for the state of Israel. Believing that the nation's reestablishment in Palestine in 1948 was a fulfillment of Old Testament prophecies, many dispensational premillennialists within the new Christian right political movement have adopted the advancement of the Israeli state as a key component of their political worldview.[55] Not surprisingly, Israeli governmental officials have welcomed such overtures on the part of dispensational evangelicals and fundamentalists.[56] Progressive dispensationalists, however, have refused to grant such enthusiastic political support on the basis of biblical prophecy to the modern Israeli state. In fact, Blaising has suggested that dispensational zeal for the reestablishment of Israel has clouded recognition of the present activity of the Davidic heir as an agent of reconciliation and peace. Blaising marvels that contemporary dispensationalists could overlook Israeli human rights abuses against the Palestinians, since the Old Testament prophets explicitly condemned similar injustices.[57] Instead, progressive dispensationalists point to the restoration of Israel only when that nation embraces the Messiah, the Lord Jesus, at his return. In that sense, progressive dispensationalists may be said to have remained truer to the spirit of traditional dispensationalism than the traditionalists themselves.

A final sociopolitical implication drawn from the "not yet" aspect of the inaugurated Davidic covenant could be the confidence with which progressive dispensationalists may join with other Christians in combating contemporary secular apocalypticism.[58] Progressive dispensationalists can work for environmental protection because of the centrality of the earth in God's redemptive

---

54. Saucy, "Presence of the Kingdom," 44–46.

55. Daniel Wojcik gives the rather extreme example of premillennialist support for renegade Israeli groups bent on destroying the Dome of the Rock in Jerusalem in order that their prophetic expectations regarding a rebuilt Jewish temple might be expedited. Daniel Wojcik, *The End of the World As We Know It: Faith, Fatalism, and Apocalypse in America* (New York: New York University Press, 1997), 146.

56. For a discussion of this phenomenon, see Timothy Weber, "How Evangelicals Became Israel's Best Friend," *Christianity Today* (5 October 1998), 38–49, along with *Religion and the Culture Wars: Dispatches from the Front*, ed. John C. Green et al. (Lanham, Md.: Rowman and Littlefield, 1996): 330–55.

57. Blaising and Bock, *Progressive Dispensationalism*, 296–97.

58. For a discussion of "secular apocalypticism," see Richard Kyle, *The Last Days Are Here Again*, 165–84.

purposes, and they can labor toward peaceful reconciliation among the nuclear superpowers without succumbing to paralyzing scare tactics regarding an environmental Armageddon or nuclear holocaust. George Eldon Ladd has noted: "Man will not destroy himself from the face of the earth, nor will this planet become a cold lifeless star. The day is surely coming when the knowledge of God shall cover the earth as the waters cover the sea, when peace and righteousness shall prevail instead of war and evil."[59] Progressive dispensationalists who view the Spirit among them as a guarantee that the already-reigning Davidic king will consummate his promised kingdom have the added assurance that the moon that Psalm 89 mentions as a witness to the Davidic covenant will still indeed be shining at the cosmic unveiling of the Son of David.

The Church as the Initial Manifestation of the Kingdom

Closely linked to the progressive dispensational understanding of the inaugurated Davidic promise is their concept of the church as a "functional outpost" or "sneak preview" of the coming kingdom. Because the church has been knit together by the Messiah himself, and because they have received in inaugurated form the new covenant blessings he dispenses, the church is the focal point of the current regal activity of Christ. With such an understanding in mind, progressive dispensationalists have begun to suggest that the church is to be a "workshop of kingdom righteousness" in which the nature of the coming kingdom is revealed through its internal ministry, external pronouncements, and even by its very makeup as a multinational Spirit-created entity.[60]

Dispensational ecclesiology has always been somewhat problematic in relation to the construction of a meaningful sociopolitical ethic. Dispensationalist Michael Williams concedes that non-dispensationalists such as Millard Erickson accurately characterize a systemic flaw in dispensational theology when they claim that dispensationalism has historically diminished the role of the church.[61] Williams points to the inordinately "otherworldly strain" of C. I. Scofield and Lewis Sperry Chafer's conception of Christians as "heavenly citizens" who are merely passing through the created order on their way to eschatological bliss.[62] Citing Chafer's conception of the church as a "missionary· society" created to train witnesses for Christ, Williams sees the root of dispensationalism's weak ecclesiology in an eschatological grid that anticipates an apostate institutional church in the last days. As such, dispensationalists have had to locate the primary work of the Spirit within the individual.[63] Ironically,

---

59. George Eldon Ladd, *The Blessed Hope* (Grand Rapids: Eerdmans, 1956), 5–6.
60. Blaising and Bock, *Progressive Dispensationalism*, 285–88.
61. Michael D. Williams, "Where's the Church? The Church as the Unfinished Business of Dispensational Theology," *Grace Theological Journal* 10 (1989): 166–67.
62. Ibid., 167–70.
63. Ibid., 176–77.

Williams concludes that such individualism actually led to the encroaching secularism it was designed to protect against because the dispensational believer could isolate himself from social, political, and educational concerns while living life "as if the gospel did not even exist."[64] Progressive dispensationalists have attempted to answer such critiques by formulating a high view of the church as an eschatological community that provides an "illustration, an audiovisual, of the presence and outworking of God's love and compassion."[65]

Carl F. H. Henry's early manifesto for evangelical social engagement compared the two extremes of contemporary religiopolitical attitudes to the actions of the two thieves crucified with Jesus. The thief who mocked Jesus' kingship represents humanistic secularists who see no place for religion in public discourse, while the repentant thief who asked to be remembered "when You come into Your kingdom" represents those eschatologically-oriented fundamentalists who place all hope for sociopolitical renewal in the future consummation.[66] Progressive dispensationalism offers a forward-looking eschatology that sheds the cultural withdrawal of "the fundamentalist thief on the cross" without simultaneously plotting a theocratic takeover of the political power structures. Progressives can articulate such a social vision by avoiding both the classical dispensational understanding of the kingdom as wholly future as well as the self-styled kingdom optimism of the Social Gospel left and the Reconstructionist right. Progressive dispensationalist Robert Pyne sees the modified eschatology of the newer dispensationalists as igniting the possibility of a renaissance of premillennial sociopolitical activism by furnishing a theology that occupies "a middle ground between the 'kingdom now' view of liberalism and the 'kingdom then' view of earlier premillennialists."[67] This revision, he argues, has led progressive dispensationalism to become "a little more optimistic and socially relevant."[68]

Since progressive dispensationalists hold to a premillennial eschatology that understands the kingdom to be ushered in cataclysmically at the sovereign determination of God, they do not hold forth reformation of social or political structures as a method of hastening the progress of the kingdom. Thus, progressives view much of their cultural engagement as inherently evangelistic. Bock contends that Christian confrontation of injustice with God's standard of love and righteousness offers the occasion to prick the consciences of unregenerate sinners, "thus surfacing sin and the need for

64. Ibid., 180.

65. Bock, "Son of David and the Saints' Task," 456.

66. Carl F. H. Henry, *The Uneasy Conscience of Modern Fundamentalism* (Grand Rapids: Eerdmans, 1947), 60–66.

67. Pyne, "New Man and Immoral Society," 12.

68. Ibid.

Christ."[69] By opposing "sinful structures by which sinful men reflect hatred for others and inflict abuse on others," Bock argues that Christians can "create opportunities for some to seek refuge in Christ, as their ministry is motivated by his love for sinners, by a recognition of his current authority over sin, and by their desire to be the light of the world."[70] Blaising and Bock assert that progressive dispensationalists "would do well to explore the internal social holiness of the church as a form of witness to the external society."[71] With such an understanding of the church as a "sneak preview" of the coming kingdom, the church demonstrates to onlookers the love, peace, and righteousness that will be characteristic of the coming everlasting kingdom. As the outside governmental structures observe kingdom righteousness at work in alleviating poverty or resolving conflict within communities of believers, they find not only workable model solutions to social problems, but also a call to come under the authority of the messianic King who has brought the church together through the Spirit. In doing so, progressive dispensationalists not only testify to the need for personal conversion, but as the Messiah's new society, they are, in the words of one non-dispensational premillennialist, to "publish worldwide the criteria by which Christ at his return in power and glory will judge the human race and all the nations."[72]

Progressive dispensationalists have suggested that their surfacing eschatological impetus for church-based sociopolitical action may represent a novel development against the backdrop of a myriad of evangelical ethical options. Bock contends that a progressive dispensational model fits in none of H. Richard Niebuhr's five possible relationships between Christ and culture.[73] Instead, Bock locates the progressive dispensational understanding of the church as an inaugurated manifestation of the kingdom within terms of a new relationship: Christ as the transformer of his community as a model for other cultures.[74] Pyne sums up the emerging progressive dispensational consensus on this new paradigm by challenging his like-minded premillennialists to "get our own house in order by modeling reconciliation within the church."[75]

One crucial aspect of this prototype of reconciliation for the outside world includes the makeup of the church itself. Progressive dispensationalists carefully note that the church is not an ethnic group or a political entity, but a multinational, multiethnic, and transdispensational body that came into ex-

69. Bock, "Son of David and the Saints' Task," 457.
70. Ibid.
71. Blaising and Bock, *Progressive Dispensationalism*, 288.
72. Carl F. H. Henry, "Reflections on the Kingdom of God," *JETS* 35 (March 1992): 47.
73. Niebuhr's five categories are Christ against culture, Christ above culture, the Christ of culture, Christ and culture in paradox, and Christ the transformer of culture. See H. Richard Niebuhr, *Christ and Culture* (New York: Harper & Row, 1951).
74. Bock, "Son of David and the Saints' Task," 456.
75. Pyne, "New Man and Immoral Society," 15.

istence by the Spirit's action at Pentecost under the authority of the ruling Christ. The church, therefore, as an initial manifestation of a multinational messianic kingdom, must reflect reconciliation between diverse ethnic, economic, racial, and social groups.[76] Through such reconciliation, the church testifies to the global extent of the reign of the Son of David and demonstrates to a hostility-torn planet how personal peace and interracial harmony are possible through the vivifying work of the Spirit.

As with the progressive dispensational view of the inaugurated Davidic covenant, the understanding of the church as an inaugurated form of the kingdom serves to immunize the church from Social Gospel liberalism, revolutionary liberation theology, and theonomic Reconstructionism. In the "already," the church is the present form of the kingdom "existing among the other kingdoms of the earth," and only in the "not yet" will the kingdom "swallow up the other kingdoms and complete the promises made to Israel."[77] Progressive dispensationalists recognize that the fears of earlier dispensationalists regarding the confusion between the church and kingdom in the political arena may not have been justification for cultural withdrawal, but neither were they baseless. Pyne warns progressive dispensationalists that "many politically active Christians desire not just to be represented, but to take over."[78] He notes that he "would prefer to see the church as the prophet outside the wall than to see us as the emperor's mistress. When you're in bed with the emperor and the emperor is shot, you're in big trouble."[79] Recalling German liberalism that was "brought down in part by its Constantinian alignment with the war effort," Pyne counsels: "Today's conservatives dare not repeat the mistakes of yesterday's liberals."[80] Robert Saucy agrees by arguing that the task of the church according to Ephesians 6:10–13 is not the final subjugation of the powers that can only be achieved by the personal intervention of Christ, "but to be 'strong in the Lord and in his mighty power' and to equip itself with divine armor so that it can 'stand against the devil's schemes' and 'stand' against the onslaughts 'when the day of evil comes.'"[81]

For progressive dispensationalists, understanding that the church is the focus of current messianic activity also necessitates a reaffirmation of the traditional dispensational distinction between the church and the world. The church is not an ethnic rival of Israel or any other political body. Such a per-

---

76. Blaising is careful to note that the multicultural nature of the church does not mean that Christianity should embrace syncretism. Instead, he argues, it means "the conversion of multicultural paganism into multicultural Christianity" (Blaising and Bock, *Progressive Dispensationalism*, 291).

77. Bock, "Reign of the Lord Christ," 46–47.

78. Pyne, "New Man and Immoral Society," 15.

79. Ibid.

80. Ibid.

81. Saucy, *Case for Progressive Dispensationalism*, 166.

ception redefines political activity since "real answers for humanity are found in the community connected to Christ."[82] As such, political solutions are first implemented within the context of the local church. Even when political solutions are offered to the world outside the church, they must always be couched in language that recognizes the futility of cultural reform without personal regeneration. "We need to remember that without a transformation of the heart, a new Law risks being a dead letter," Bock counsels. "The lesson of Israel also applies here. She had great laws, but a dismal society due to a depraved heart. Just ask the prophets!"[83]

In an inaugurationist premillennialism such as progressive dispensationalism, every church building represents by its very existence a latent political challenge to the powers that be. Because progressive dispensationalists and other inaugurationist premillennialists see themselves as an initial form of a coming global monarchy, they proclaim with their presence on the landscape that the status quo will one day be shaken apart in one decisive act of sovereign authority. As such, the view that the church is a "sneak preview" of the kingdom reminds its members that although they are to submit to the governing authorities, their ultimate loyalty is to no transient political entity, but to the coming messianic kingdom they see even now breaking in around them through Spirit-propelled reconciliation, peace, and unity.

Salvation as Holistic and Christological

Since there have never been a multitude of amillennial television evangelists, it is not difficult to see some linkage between dispensationalism and popular American revivalism. Although the Second Great Awakening's foremost revivalist, Charles G. Finney, was an advocate of neither dispensationalism nor political disengagement,[84] later forms of Protestant revivalism often featured both. Convinced that the world was careening toward the jaws of hell, dispensationalist pastors, evangelists, and theologians exhorted their followers to mobilize not for social reform efforts, but for the desperate task of global evangelization.[85] Since Finney, many of the most prominent American reviv-

---

82. Bock, "Why I Am a Dispensationalist with a Small 'd,'" 11.

83. Ibid.

84. To the contrary, Finney mixed his conversionist revivalism with a type of nineteenth century postmillennial fervor and a passion for social justice causes such as abolitionism. He was not unique in this respect, but he is perhaps the most influential of the Second Great Awakening's revivalist evangelist/theologians. For a fuller treatment of his theology, see Charles G. Finney, *Systematic Theology* (reprint; Minneapolis: Bethany, 1976).

85. An excellent treatment of the relationship between dispensational eschatology and Protestant revivalism is included in Weber, *Living in the Shadow of the Second Coming*, 65–81. On page 71, Weber illuminates the premillennial cliché that believers are to man the lifeboats, not polish brass on a sinking ship, with the anecdote of C. I. Scofield using the metaphor at a 1912 Belfast memorial service for victims of the *Titanic* disaster.

alist preachers, D. L. Moody, Billy Sunday, Billy Graham, have to one degree
or another embraced a dispensational premillennial eschatological framework.
Likewise, dispensational theologians from Scofield to Ryrie and beyond have
emphasized the priority of personal individual regeneration as the message of
the church in this dispensation.

Progressive dispensationalists do not repudiate the conversionist message
of their dispensational forebears. They recognize personal regeneration as necessary for individuals to come under the saving refuge of the Messiah and
unite with the people of God.[86] Nevertheless, they have begun to call for evangelicals to broaden the message of salvation beyond merely an emphasis on the
rescuing of so many units of individual souls.

Blaising commends older dispensationalism for acknowledging that redemption in Christ encompasses earthly, national, political, spiritual, and social purposes, but he criticizes classical and revised dispensationalism for sev-
ering those aspects from the present ministry of the church.[87] He insists on a
view of redemption that sees God's spiritual and cultural-political purposes as
complementary, not independent of each other.[88] Aspects of redemption will
be emphasized to differing degrees in different dispensations, but all dispensations progressively build toward the final age in which all facets of God's redemption are manifested in a complementary fashion.

The key to understanding this holistic redemption for progressive dispensationalists is a Christology that takes into account the oneness of Christ's
human and divine natures.[89] As simultaneously the covenant God who
pledged to create a people for himself and the Davidic ruler of that people,
Christ offers a salvation that cannot be truncated into bare spiritual blessings
in one dispensation or mere political authority in another. Therefore, although the church does not yet wield political authority over the nations, it
must recognize that since the redemption it offers has a political element, sociopolitical matters cannot be disregarded as "unspiritual" or irrelevant to the
Christian task.

George Eldon Ladd recognizes to some degree the holistic nature of redemption when he argues from an historic premillennial viewpoint that Jesus'
earthly ministry refuted any idea that redemption in this age is exclusively
spiritual. He asserts that Jesus' healing miracles were not merely physical because they were connected with forgiveness of sin and the granting of spiritual

---

86. Darrell Bock credits dispensationalism's conversionist zeal with what he considers to
be a beneficial offshoot of the parachurch evangelistic movements, a healthy emphasis on all
believers as ministers (Bock, "Why I Am a Dispensationalist with a Small 'd,'" 11.

87. Blaising and Bock, *Progressive Dispensationalism*, 46–47.

88. Ibid., 48.

89. Blaising charges revised dispensationalism with being "strikingly anthropocentric" in
its reading of Scripture because it has placed human redemption rather than Christ at the center of biblical interpretation (Blaising and Bock, *Progressive Dispensationalism*, 298).

life. The healings were only "pledges of the life of the eschatological Kingdom that will finally mean immortality for the body."[90] Ladd concludes that the kingdom, and inferentially the church as a sign of that kingdom, "is concerned not only with people's souls but with the salvation of the whole person."[91]

Because progressive dispensationalists hold to such a holistic view of redemption, they cannot simply utilize social ministry or cultural engagement as an expedient vehicle for "truly spiritual matters" such as personal evangelism or church planting. Neither can they engage in reform efforts apart from a proclamation of the gospel. They maintain that the unity of the Messiah, the unity of the plan of redemption, and the unity of the people of God demand a unity of message.

Conclusion

The growing acceptance of inaugurated eschatology among evangelicals brings with it the opportunity for reflection and reconsideration on the sociopolitical role of the church in an increasingly post-Christian Western society. Any model of cultural engagement motivated by an "already/not yet" eschatology must shoulder the burden of refuting the contrary political paradigms offered by theonomists, "Christian America" conservative activists, socially active evangelical liberals, and pietistic cultural escapists.

Inaugurationist amillennialism counters the triumphalistic rhetoric of the Reconstructionists with weighty biblical evidence that the church is not to "take dominion" over the structures of government in this age. Nonetheless, amillennialists fail to answer the postmillennial challenge as to how their system is any less "pessimistic" than premillennialism in light of numerous biblical passages that seem to point to a Christ-ruled kingdom within the flow of this earth's history. Historic premillennialists have a ready answer for such questions with their vision of an earthly millennial kingdom, but their reinterpretation of Old Testament covenant promises to Israel as spiritualized blessings for an overwhelmingly Gentile church would seem to rob the redemptive plan of its central sociopolitical aspect. Traditional forms of dispensationalism affirm a governing authority for Christ as Davidic king over a geopolitically restored Israel, but they have employed what has often seemed to be torturous exegetical gymnastics to ensure that this messianic reign is restricted to the age to come.

Progressive dispensationalists have proposed a unique strain of inaugurated eschatological thought that may offer an innovative evangelical paradigm for sociopolitical engagement. Progressive dispensationalists salvage from tradi-

90. George Eldon Ladd, *A Theology of the New Testament* (Grand Rapids: Eerdmans, 1974), 74.
91. Ibid.

tional dispensationalism the political aspect of the future kingdom, while asserting that this reign is present in inaugurated form as a signpost to the coming kingdom. Christ has ruling political authority, but only invisibly over his church, not yet in coercive visible sovereignty over the world. National Israel as depicted in Scripture under the reign of an infinitely just, infinitely wise Davidic king serves as the object lesson for what true political righteousness actually means.

What would a theologically consistent, politically engaged progressive dispensational congregation look like? Such a body might speak prophetically on the basis of the Davidic king's concern for the exploited against a lucrative pornography industry that degrades women. Their leaders might testify before Congress regarding their efforts to guide an inner-city congregation through church-based welfare reform. A mission trip to war-torn Bosnia might include the attempt to establish a congregation of Croatian, Bosnian, and Serb Christians united in testifying of the reconciliation characteristic of the coming kingdom. The congregation's holistic ministry to their elderly might be pointed to against the backdrop of a state referendum to legalize euthanasia. They might respond to the burgeoning gay rights movement by simultaneously proclaiming the biblical warning that homosexuals will not inherit the kingdom of God (1 Cor. 6:9), while demonstrating the merciful nature of that kingdom by maintaining AIDS hospice care for those who come to Christ. While this eschatological framework will not provide instant political answers to the multitude of perplexing cultural questions faced by the church, it can offer a common theological starting-point for serious discussion of these issues.

The chief weakness of the progressive dispensational model remains its relative newness. Because the system has not yet filtered into large sectors of evangelical congregational life, the practical ramifications of the theology remain largely unseen. Additionally, comparatively little effort has been expended thus far in constructing a progressive dispensational social ethic. The years ahead, however, offer opportunities for exploration and perhaps implementation of a new theological model for social activity. After fifty years of conservative Christianity's uneasy conscience, it will prove ironic indeed if the evangelical Mother Teresa turns out to be a premillennialist.

22

Prophecy, Eschatology, and Apologetics

JOHN WARWICK MONTGOMERY

Trinity College and Theological Seminary (Indiana)

The early Christian church employed two major styles of apologetic: miracle and prophecy, the first directed especially to the Gentiles, the second particularly to the Jewish community.[1] A remarkable feature of the Christian apologetic was the inherent interconnection of the two approaches, owing to the fact that miracles central to the faith (such as the virgin birth of our Lord) had often been the object of specific Old Testament prophecies (Isa. 7:14).[2]

Today, three forms of prophetic attestation are offered to support the truth of Christian faith: *charismatic* (experiential) prophecy, *end-time* (futuristic) prophecy, and *fulfilled* (historical) prophecy. We shall look briefly at each, finding the first two varieties fundamentally deficient, and endeavoring to strengthen the third through probability considerations.

Charismatic Prophecy

It is frequently maintained in charismatic and Pentecostal circles that, in line with 1 Corinthians 14 and other related references in the New Testament, miraculous tongue-speaking occurs with fair regularity among believ-

---

1. John Warwick Montgomery, *Faith Founded on Fact* (Nashville: Thomas Nelson, 1978), 43ff., and the references there given. See also Mark Edwards et al., eds., *Apologetics in the Roman Empire: Pagans, Jews, and Christians* (Oxford: Oxford University Press, 1999).

2. The LXX translation, well before Christ's first advent, employs the word *parthenos*, which signifies "virgin," not merely "young woman." Contrast Islam, where alleged miracles, such as Mohammed's so-called Night Journey, are nowhere prophesied in the *Quran*. An interesting recent example is that of the "Holy Tomato" as reported in *The Independent* [London], 16 September 1999: a Muslim Pakistani woman living in Bradford found a tomato whose vein structure presented an Arabic inscription reading "There is no god but Allah."

ers today. Indeed, it is an article of faith with Pentecostals that a "Second Blessing" is properly to be sought by all Christians, and that with this empowering will normally come the miraculous gift of tongues. When the Christian speaks in tongues and another, possessing the gift of interpretation, makes known the meaning in an ordinary language, the miraculous truth of the faith is allegedly demonstrated.

What is the problem with this kind of "prophetic" apologetic? The difficulty will not be uncovered by higher critical dehistoricizing of the key New Testament texts, as practiced by radical theologians or misguided liberal evangelicals.[3] Nor will the difficulty go away by aprioristic attempts to relegate miraculous gifts to the age of the New Testament alone.[4] The central apologetic problems with miraculous tongues-speaking are (1) that which is spoken lacks the structural characteristics of a language, and (2) even if what were spoken *did* have genuine linguistic characteristics, the unbeliever has no way of knowing that the "interpretation" in fact represents the "prophecy."

William Samarin puts these points succinctly:

> We know more about language than the glossolalist does. We know enough to declare what is and what is not language. We know as much as a mathematician, who can tell the difference between a real formula and a pseudo-formula—one that *looks* like mathematical language but does not *say* anything. . . .
>
> A charismatist's religious experience can be real, revolutionary, reconstitutive. A glossolalist accepts this transformation as supernatural, that is, *caused* by God. If it is a dramatic change—taking place where one did not expect it or more quickly than one expected—it takes on all the more appearance of the supernatural. But none of this proves that glossolalia is supernatural. No number of "miraculous" transformations will make of glossolalia what it is not.[5]

At best, glossolalia can do no more than persuade the unbeliever on the basis of the drawing power of the believing assembly in which it is practiced, or by virtue of the sincerity and genuineness of the practitioners themselves. But this is no more than an experiential argument—indistinguishable from the experiential persuasiveness of non-Christian religions and of the plethora of sects vying for converts today. It is still true that inner faith per se "cannot validate God-talk."[6]

3. In the former camp, see Krister Stendahl, "Glossolalia and the Charismatic Movement," in *God's Christ and His People: Studies in Honor of Nils Alstrup Dahl*, ed. Jacob Jervell and Wayne A. Meeks (Oslo: Universitetsforlaget, 1977), 122–31.

4. Cf. B. B. Warfield's influential work, *Counterfeit Miracles* (New York: Scribner's, 1918).

5. William J. Samarin, *Tongues of Men and Angels: The Religious Language of Pentecostalism* (New York: Macmillan, 1972), 233–35. See also J. P. Kildahl, *The Psychology of Speaking in Tongues* (New York: Harper, 1972).

6. Kai Nielsen, "Can Faith Validate God-Talk?" in *New Theology No 1*, ed. Martin E. Marty and Dean G. Peerman (New York: Macmillan Paperbacks, 1964). Cf. J. W. Montgomery, *The Suicide of Christian Theology* (reprint, Newburgh, Ind.: Trinity, 1998), 99, 149, 260.

End-Time Prophecy

One can hardly avoid—even if one refuses to watch the televangelists—the vast number of current attempts to relate current events to the second coming and the end of the age. Not to be outdone by new editions of Nostradamus from the secular press, evangelical writers and publishers have been quick off the mark with their own millennial publications.[7]

Here is a very recent and sobering example from the lips of the Reverend Ian Paisley of Northern Ireland fame (notoriety?):

In his personal report from Strasbourg on the recent opening of Europe's fifth elected Parliament he described the new "crystal palace" which houses the MEPs as "space age" with a modern design of Star Trek crew seats. Of the 679 seats allocated to its members one seat remains empty at present; seat number 666. Dr. Paisley believes it will eventually be occupied in accordance with Revelation 13:18 which states: "Here is wisdom. Let him that hath understanding count the number of the beast: for it is the number of a man; and his number is Six hundred threescore and six." With conviction he stated, "Today that scripture is being fulfilled before our very eyes. The Antichrist's seat will be occupied. The world awaits his full and final development." As a Bible-believing Protestant he took pleasure in quoting the prophetic words of 2 Thess. 2:8: "And then shall that Wicked One be revealed, whom the Lord shall consume by the spirit of His mouth (the Word of God), and shall destroy with the brightness of His coming."

The leader of the Democratic Unionist Party is convinced that the "prophetic significance" of the European Union is steadily unfolding as it continues to develop. It has chosen as its symbol "the woman riding the beast" which features on its new currency, the Euro. He also disclosed that the "Tower of Babel" is being used on posters emanating from Europe and views this "as a truly suggestive prophetic sign."[8]

This reminds one of Hal Lindsey's earlier claim that the former European Economic Community (predecessor of the European Union) represented the ten toes of the great image in the Book of Daniel and thus was a vehicle of the antichristic end times.[9]

---

7. This author has nothing against responsible millennial scholarship; he himself contributed the article "Millennium" to *ISBE* 3:356–61, an article which appears in slightly different form in C. E. Armerding and W. W. Gasque's *Dreams, Visions and Oracles: A Layman's Guide to Biblical Prophecy* (Grand Rapids: Baker, 1977), revised and augmented as *A Guide to Biblical Prophecy* (Peabody, Mass.: Hendrickson, 1989).

8. News item, *Protestant Truth* [UK] (September–October 1999), 80.

9. Hal Lindsey, *The 1980s: Countdown to Armageddon* (New York: Bantam, 1982), 103–5. See J. W. Montgomery, *Human Rights and Human Dignity*, 2d ed. (Edmonton: Canadian Institute for Law, Theology and Public Policy, 1995), 43–44, 277–78.

One could, of course, point out the factual difficulties with these "prophecies": the EEC has never had precisely ten members, and the "Tower of Babel" posters in Strasbourg—which I saw this last summer—were actually advertisements for rock concerts, not publications of the European Union at all!

But the problem of futuristic prophecy as apologetic cuts much deeper. In essence, the intractable objection is that we simply do not have the perspective on our own time sufficient to be able to predict the future accurately or confidently relate biblical prophecy to what is happening at the moment.[10] A few illustrative examples may be helpful.

In 1866, the Reverend M. Baxter, "late missionary of the Episcopal Church," published his 355-page tome, with the lengthy and highly specific title: *Louis Napoleon the Destined Monarch of the World, and Personal Antichrist, foreshown in Prophecy to confirm a seven years' Covenant with the Jews about, or soon after 1864–5, and (after the Resurrection and the translation of the Wise Virgins has taken place two years and from four to six weeks after the Covenant,) subsequently to become completely supreme over England and most of America, and all Christendom, and fiercely to persecute Christians during the latter half of the seven years, until he finally perishes at the descent of Christ at the Battle of Armageddon, about or soon after 1872–3.*[11]

The end not having come as Baxter predicted, one S. D. Baldwin, A.M., President of Soule Female College, produced a second edition of his 480-page masterpiece, *Armageddon: or The Overthrow of Romanism and Monarchy; the Existence of the United States Foretold in the Bible, its future greatness; invasion by allied Europe; annihilation of monarchy; expansion into the millennial republic, and its dominion over the whole world.* The fortunate publisher of this work was the Southern Methodist Publishing House.[12]

Coming now to the twentieth century, we have People's Church, Toronto, pastor-evangelist Oswald J. Smith's *Is the Antichrist at Hand?—What of Mussolini*, which went through at least seven editions, accounting for some 22,000 copies.[13] Mussolini's candidature for Antichrist is supported by such obvious considerations as his self-styled attempt to revive accoutrements of the ancient Roman Empire and the unarguable fact that he was a "whore upon the seven hills" of Rome. (My copy of this paperback is quite rare, deriving from my ma-

---

10. This is, conceptually, exactly the same problem faced by secular philosophers of history, such as Hegel, Marx, Spengler, and Toynbee, when they endeavour to chart the future history of mankind; see Montgomery, *Where Is History Going?* (reprint, Minneapolis: Bethany, 1972). It is also the problem of the so-called theologians of hope such as Moltmann.

11. M. Baxter, *Louis Napoleon the Destined Monarch of the World . . .* (Philadelphia: James S. Claxton, 1866).

12. S. D. Baldwin, *Armageddon . . .* (Nashville: Southern Methodist Publishing House, 1878).

13. Oswald J. Smith, *Is the Antichrist at Hand?—What of Mussolini* (Toronto: Tabernacle Publishers, 1927).

ternal great-grandfather's book collection. I understand that after the fall of Mussolini, Smith himself tried to buy up all remaining copies of the book to destroy them.)

The point does not need to be belabored. We are not saying that such efforts at end-time prophecy reach the level of the false prophets condemned in the Old Testament: those who "speak a vision out of their own heart, and not out of the mouth of the Lord" (Jer. 23:16). But we *are* saying that end-time prophecy lacks the necessary factual grounding to make it an effective apologetic to the unbeliever—and that it can be and often is in reality *counterproductive*, lowering rather than raising the credibility of Christianity in the eyes of the outsider. The reason for this was well stated by Augustine in the fifth century; though he was speaking of cosmological theories propounded by Christians, his judgment applies, in a different context, to the evangelical purveyors of futuristic prophecy:

> Now it is an unseemly and mischievous thing, and greatly to be avoided, that a Christian man speaking on such matters, as if according to the authority of Christian Scripture, should talk so foolishly that the unbeliever on hearing him, and observing the extravagance of his error, should hardly be able to refrain from laughing. And the great mischief is, not so much that the man himself is laughed at for his errors, but that our authors are believed, by people without the Church, to have taught such things, and are so condemned as unlearned, and cast aside, to the great loss of those for whose salvation we are so much concerned.
>
> For when they find one belonging to the Christian body, falling into error on a subject with which they themselves are thoroughly conversant, and when they see him moreover enforcing his groundless opinion by the authority of our Sacred Books, how are they likely to put trust in these Books about the resurrection of the dead, and the hope of eternal life, and the kingdom of heaven, having already come to regard them as fallacious about those things they had themselves learned from observation, or from unquestionable evidence?[14]

Historically Fulfilled Prophecy

The third, and, in our judgment, the truly useful variety of prophecy for the apologetic task consists of an appeal to the prophecies of the Old Testament that have already been fulfilled—principally the prophecies of Christ's first coming. Though there are significant Old Testament prophecies of which secular history demonstrates the fulfillment (the destruction of Tyre and Sidon, etc.),[15] the most valuable for apologetic purposes are those con-

14. Augustine, *De Genesi ad litteram* 1.19.39.
15. See, for example, John Urquhart, *The Wonders of Prophecy* (Camp Hill, Pa.: Christian Publications, n.d.), and J. Barton Payne, *Encyclopedia of Biblical Prophecy* (New York: Harper & Row, 1973).

cerning the first advent of our Lord. This is because the center of the apologetic task is the demonstration of the truth of the gospel itself, its acceptance being the sine qua non for personal salvation. We of course want to bring the non-Christian to accept the revelational character of Scripture as a whole, but first must come his or her answer to the question, "What think ye of Christ?" And it is worth emphasizing that concentration on the New Testament fulfillments of Old Testament prophecies concerning our Lord will, in any case, add weight to our claim that the entire Bible is the product of divine revelation, since the fulfilled Old Testament prophecies come from a wide variety of Old Testament books, written at widely different times.

Fascinatingly enough, the value of such fulfilled prophecy can be specified mathematically. One can, by using the statistician's well-known "product rule," calculate the probabilities against mere chance accounting for a given number of such prophecies. The product rule states that the probability of the common occurrence of several mutually independent events is equal to the product of the probabilities that each of those given events will happen. Example: since the chances of coming up with a "2" when rolling one die is 1 in 6 or 1/6, the probability of rolling two "2s" is 1/6 x 1/6, or 1/36; the chances of rolling three "2s" is 1/6 x 1/6 x 1/6, or 1/216; etc. Generalizing, we have the formulation: *If the probability of one event's occurring is 1/x, the probability of a number of similar but mutually independent events will be $1/x^n$, where n = the number of events.*[16]

If one arbitrarily sets the probability of the occurrence of a single valid Old Testament prophecy of Christ at 50-50 (1/2), then the probabilities against twenty-five of them[17] happening by chance is $1/2^{25}$, or 1 in 33 million. But since the likelihood of any one of these prophecies succeeding is considerably less than 50-50 ("Behold a virgin shall conceive and bear a son," etc.),[18] we can legitimately lower the probability of one occurrence to 25 percent (1/4). The probability of 25 similar events transpiring would then be $1/4^{25}$, or 1 in a thousand trillion! After presenting this argument two generations ago, the then Chairman of Wheaton College's Department of Mathematics, Physics, and Astronomy wrote:

16. See any standard statistics text, e.g., Paul Gerhard Hoel, *Introduction to Mathematical Statistics*, 5th ed. (New York: John Wiley, 1984).

17. In point of fact, far more than twenty-five prophecies of Christ's first advent and earthly life occur in the Old Testament. For lists, see study editions of the Bible such as the *Thompson Chain-Reference Bible* and standard reference sources such as Halley's *Bible Handbook*.

18. Consider, for example, the highly specific numerical prophecy in Daniel concerning the first coming of Christ, as worked out by Sir Robert Anderson in his classic, *The Coming Prince*; the essence of his argument is presented in Irwin H. Linton's *A Lawyer Examines the Bible* (Boston: Wilde, 1943), 220–23, and in J. W. Montgomery, ed., *Jurisprudence: A Book of Readings*, 4th ed. (Strasbourg, France: International Scholarly Publishers, 1992), 494–97. See also J. W. Montgomery, *The Transcendent Holmes* (Ashcroft, B.C.: Calabash, 2000), 129–39.

Since there are many more than 25 prophecies of events surrounding the birth and life of Christ, and a compromise chance of success is undoubtedly less than 1 to 4, then the chance of success, if these predictions were all mere guesses, would be so infinitesimal that no one could maintain that these prophecies were mere guesses! The alternative must be true—these prophecies were all foreseen events, in which "*holy men of God spake as they were moved by the Holy Ghost.*" The prophecies were given by revelation—divinely inspired.[19]

What objections can be raised to this mathematical treatment of fulfilled biblical prophecy? Two counter-arguments require answers.

First, a statistical complaint. One may object that this is just a piece of statistical prestidigitation—the sort of thing treated in Darrell Huff's little gem, *How to Lie with Statistics.*[20] Or, more darkly, one might suggest that the argument parallels eighteenth-century Scottish mathematician and cleric John Craig's claim (a remarkable attempt at eschatological statistics) that by application of probability theory to the weakening of the force of testimony, one must conclude that the historical proofs of our Lord's ministry will decay entirely by the year 3150, such that Christianity would entirely disappear "unless the second coming of Christ prevent its extinction."[21]

More specifically, one might argue that our application of mathematical statistics to event-occurrences parallels that refuted by the California Supreme Court, the great Chief Justice Traynor concurring, in *The People v Malcolm Ricardo Collins.*[22] In that case, at trial court level, the prosecutor brought in as an expert witness a state college mathematics instructor to establish the probabilities against the defendants having committed the crime. The instructor arbitrarily set the probabilities for the individual elements of the crime, committed, as it was, by a Caucasian woman with a blond ponytail, accompanied by a Black man with a beard and mustache, the two driving a partly yellow automobile. On applying the "product rule," the instructor concluded that

19. Hawley O. Taylor, "Mathematics and Prophecy," in *Modern Science and Christian Faith*, ed. American Scientific Affiliation (Wheaton, Ill.: Van Kampen, 1948), 178. This essay is unfortunately not included in later editions of the book.

20. Darrell Huff, *How to Lie with Statistics* (New York: W. W. Norton, 1993).

21. John Craig (d. 1731), *Craig's Rules of Historical Evidence: From Joannis Craig Theologiae Christianae principia mathematica* ("History and Theory," Beiheft 4; The Hague, Netherlands: Mouton, 1964). Craig, to be sure, hopelessly misunderstood the application of statistics to historical testimony and was roundly refuted by, among others, Ditton, Houtteville, and his later editor Johann Daniel Titius. One Petersen upstaged Craig in 1701 by increasing the rate of the deterioration of testimony such that the events of the beginning of the Christian era would, according to him, become unbelievable by 1789—which turned out to be the very date of the French Revolution! See the brief biographical articles on Craig in Hoefer's *Nouvelle biographie générale*, the *Dictionary of National Biography*, and the *New Schaff-Herzog Encyclopedia of Religious Knowledge*.

22. 438 P2d 33 (1968).

there was but one chance in twelve million that anyone but the defendants could have committed the crime with which they had been charged.

The California Supreme Court, to put it mildly, reversed the lower court decision, pointing up "two basic and pervasive defects—an inadequate evidentiary foundation and an inadequate proof of statistical independence." The probabilities assigned by the instructor to the individual factors were in no way demonstrable (e.g., girl with ponytail: 1/10; interracial couple in car: 1/1000). And "to the extent that the traits or characteristics were not mutually independent (e.g., Negroes with beards and men with mustaches obviously represent overlapping categories), the 'product rule' would inevitably yield a wholly erroneous and exaggerated result even if all of the individual components had been determined with precision."

But our use of the "product rule" does not suffer from these defects. The prophecies of the Old Testament are indeed "mutually independent," in that they were set out by diverse authors at diverse times, and the fulfillments were recorded by more than one Gospel writer.[23] And though we do set arbitrary values for the probability of any one prophecy's occurrence, our values are exceedingly conservative: we are simply maintaining the a fortiori position that even if the likelihood of the success of a single prophecy were but 50 percent or 25 percent, the conclusion would be inescapable that the totality of fulfillments could hardly be attributed to chance.

A second objection to our argumentation involves a question of logic: even if we have shown the extreme improbability of chance fulfillments of Old Testament prophecies of Christ, we have (the objector argues) hardly established the nature of the non-chance explanatory factor. Probability reasoning does not automatically lead to conclusions as to specific causation! Logically, the "success" of these "predictions" could be due, not to divine inspiration, but simply to (1) Jesus having conformed his life to the prophecies, to "make" them come true, and/or (2) the New Testament writers having "fudged" the life of Christ to fit the Old Testament prophecies.

But neither of these alternative causal explanations will wash (if you can believe *them*, you should have no trouble believing in genuine fulfilled prophecy!). (1) Jesus might have been responsible personally for the fulfillment of a messianic prophecy when he said on the cross, "My God, my God, why hast thou forsaken me?" but he could hardly have set up the time, place, and manner of his own birth, the number of pieces of silver he would be sold for, etc. (2) Had the Gospel writers altered the facts of Jesus' life to fit the Old Testa-

---

23. A trait is "independent of a second trait when the occurrence or non-occurrence of one does not affect the probability of the occurrence of the other trait" ("Evidence: Admission of Mathematical Probabililty Statistics Held Erroneous for Want of a Demonstration of Validity," *Duke Law Journal* [1967]: 669–70; cf. David V. Huntsberger, *Elements of Statistical Inference* [London: Prentice-Hall, 1962], 77).

ment prophecies, they would never have gotten away with it. The preaching of the facts of Christ's life, death, and resurrection, as well as the circulation of the Gospel narratives of these events, took place while hostile witnesses of Jesus' career were still alive (the very Jewish religious leaders who had brought about his demise); it is unthinkable that they would not have easily refuted such claims to fulfilled prophecy when (a) they knew the Old Testament and (b) they knew the actual facts of Jesus' life.[24]

It follows that the "product rule" argument we have presented *is* sound, and, more important, so is the use of historically fulfilled prophecy in the defense of central Christian claims.[25] We encourage fellow believers to tie their prophetic wagon to this star rather than to the squibs of experientialism and futurism, which burn out almost before they are ignited.

24. I have developed these points of historical and legal apologetics at considerable length in several of my books. See, for example, *Where Is History Going?* and *Human Rights and Human Dignity.*

25. As exemplified, for example, by the old classics such as Alexander Keith, *Evidence of the Truth of the Christian Religion Derived from the Literal Fulfilment of Prophecy,* 16th ed. (Edinburgh: William Whyte, 1837) and E. A. Edghill, *An Enquiry into the Evidential Value of Prophecy* (London: Macmillan, 1906). For more recent material, see the essays by John A. Bloom and Robert C. Newman in *Evidence for Faith: Deciding the God Question,* ed. J. W. Montgomery (Dallas: Probe, 1991), 173–214.

Subject Index

Scripture Index